# Making Art History

*Making Art History* is a collection of essays by contemporary scholars on the practice and theory of art history as it responds to institutions as diverse as art galleries and museums, publishing houses and universities, school boards and professional organizations, political parties and multinational corporations.

The text is split into four thematic sections, each of which begins with a short introduction from the editor.

- Part I: "Border patrols" addresses the artistic canon and its relationship to nationalism, globalization and the ongoing "war on terror".
- Part II: "The subjects of art history" questions whether "art" and "history" are really what the discipline seeks to understand.
- Part III: "Instituting art history" concerns art history and its relation to the university and raises questions about the mission, habits, ethics, and limits of the university today.
- Part IV: "Old masters, new institutions" shows how art history and the museum respond to nationalism, corporate management models, and the "culture wars."

Contributors: Robert O. Bork, Christopher Bucklow, David Carrier, Anna C. Chave, Gregory T. Clark, Maureen Connor, Claire Farago, Finbarr Barry Flood, Marlite Halbertsma, Janet Kraynak, Christopher R. Marshall, Stephen Melville, Steven Nelson, Donald Preziosi, Eric Rosenberg.

**Elizabeth C. Mansfield** is Associate Professor of Art History at the University of the South. Her research focuses on art historiography and European art of the eighteenth and nineteenth centuries. She edited and contributed to *Art History and its Institutions* (2002).

# Making Art History

## A changing discipline and its institutions

Edited by
Elizabeth C. Mansfield

Routledge
Taylor & Francis Group
NEW YORK AND LONDON

First published 2007
by Routledge
270 Madison Ave, New York, NY 10016

Simultaneously published in the UK
by Routledge
2 Park Square, Milton Park, Abingdon, Oxon OX14 4RN

*Routledge is an imprint of the Taylor and Francis Group, an informa business*



Typeset in Perpetua and Gill Sans by
Florence Production Ltd, Stoodleigh, Devon
Printed and bound in Great Britain by
Antony Rowe Ltd, Chippenham, Wiltshire



*Library of Congress Cataloging in Publication Data*
Making art history: a changing discipline and its institutions/edited by
Elizabeth Mansfield.
p. cm.
1. Art—Historiography. 2. Art and society. I. Mansfield, Elizabeth C.
N7480.M35 2007
701′.18—dc22 2006037163

*British Library Cataloguing in Publication Data*
A catalogue record for this book is available from the British Library

ISBN10: 0–415–37234–8 (hbk)
ISBN10: 0–415–37235–6 (pbk)

ISBN13: 978–0–415–37234–3 (hbk)
ISBN13: 978–0–415–37235–0 (pbk)

# Contents

# Illustrations

# Contributors

**Robert O. Bork**'s research mostly concerns Gothic architecture. His publications include *Great Spires: Skyscrapers of the New Jerusalem* (2003), the edited volume *De Re Metallica: The Medieval Uses of Metals* (2005) and the forthcoming book *The Geometry of Creation: Architectural Drawing and the Dynamics of Gothic Design*.

**Christopher Bucklow**'s work can be seen in a number of public collections across the United States. Recent paintings and photographs will be found on the websites of his London and New York galleries: www.riflemaker.org and www.paulkasmingallery.com. Related writing is on the site www.chrisbucklow.com.

**David Carrier** is the Champney Family Professor, a post divided between Case Western Reserve University and the Cleveland Institute of Art. He has been a Getty Scholar, a Clark Fellow and a Senior Fellow at the National Humanities Center. His books include studies of Baudelaire's art criticism, Poussin's paintings and the art museum.

**Anna C. Chave** is Professor of Art History at Queens College and the Graduate Center, City University of New York. Since her 1989 monograph on Rothko, she has authored a book on Brancusi (1993) and numerous essays—on Minimimalism, Eva Hesse, Pollock and Krasner, and the *Demoiselles d'Avignon*, among other topics—concerned with how modernist art practices have been sexually and ideologically inscribed.

**Gregory T. Clark** is Professor of Art History at the University of the South. A scholar of manuscript illumination in northern France and the southern Netherlands, his books include *The Spitz Master: A Parisian Book of Hours* and *Made in Flanders: The Master of the Ghent Privileges and Manuscript Painting in the Southern Netherlands in the Time of Philip the Good*.

**Maureen Connor** teaches at Queens College, New York, and exhibits extensively with solo shows at the Queens Museum of Art, the Museum of Modern Art, New York, and the Museo de Arte Moderno, Buenos Aires. She has received fellowships from the National Endowment for the Arts and the Guggenheim Foundation.

**Claire Farago** teaches art and critical theory at the University of Colorado-Boulder. She has published extensively on Leonardo da Vinci, Renaissance art theory, museum studies, and historiography. Her most recent book is *Transforming Images: New Mexican Santos in-between Worlds* (2006).

**Finbarr Barry Flood** is Assistant Professor of Fine Arts at New York University. He is the author of *The Great Mosque of Damascus: Studies on the Makings of an Umayyad Visual Culture* (Brill, 2001) and *Objects of Translation: The Material Culture of Medieval 'Hindu-Muslim' Encounter* (Princeton University Press, forthcoming).

**Marlite Halbertsma** is a Professor of Cultural History at Erasmus University, Rotterdam, the Netherlands. She publishes on feminist art, the history of art history, and Rotterdam's art and culture. At the moment she is preparing a book on cultural heritage in an age of globalization.

**Janet Kraynak** is Assistant Professor of Contemporary Art at Parsons, the New School for Design/Eugene Lang College, New School University, New York. She received her PhD in the History, Theory and Criticism of Art from Massachusetts Institute of Technology in 2001. She edited *Please Pay Attention Please: Bruce Nauman's Words: Writings and Interviews* (2003).

**Elizabeth C. Mansfield** teaches at the University of the South. Her research focuses on art historiography and European visual culture of the eighteenth and nineteenth centuries. In addition to editing and contributing to *Art History and Its Institutions* (2002), she has authored the book *Too Beautiful to Picture: Zeuxis, Myth and Mimesis* (2007).

**Christopher R. Marshall** is a Senior Lecturer in Art History and Museum Studies at the University of Melbourne, Australia. His research interests range from contemporary museology and display to a parallel specialization in Neapolitan Baroque patronage, collecting, and the art market.

**Stephen Melville**, Professor of History of Art at Ohio State University, is the author of *Philosophy Beside Itself* (1986) and *Seams* (1996) as well as numerous articles on contemporary art and theory, and co-author, with Philip Armstrong and Laura Lisbon, of *As Painting* (2001).

**Steven Nelson** is Assistant Professor of African and African American Art History at the University of California, Los Angeles. He authored *From Cameroon to Paris: Mousgoum Architecture in and out of Africa* (2007), and is now working on his next book, entitled *Dakar: The Making of an African Metropolis*.

**Donald Preziosi** is a member of the History Faculty at Oxford University and the author of eleven books on critical and cultural theory, art history, and the historiography of cultural institutions, most recently *Brain of the Earth's Body* (2003) and *In the Aftermath of Art: Ethics, Aesthetics, Politics* (2006).

**Eric Rosenberg** is Associate Professor of Art History at Tufts University. With Lisa Saltzman, he co-edited *Trauma and Visuality in Modernity* (2006). He has written for journals such as *Artforum*, *The Art Bulletin* and *Art History* and has published on Thomas Eakins, Walker Evans, Friedl Dzubas, and The Beatles.

# Introduction

## Making art history a profession

Like most fields of scientific or humanistic inquiry, art history emerged from a diffuse collection of practices with similar, though by no means uniform, methods and goals. Art history coalesced as a distinct discipline during the nineteenth century, largely in response to competing institutional interests. Museums, universities, publishers, auction houses, galleries, and even mechanics' institutes were among the institutions to have a share in the nineteenth-century formation of the discipline. The essays collected in *Art History and Its Institutions* (Routledge, 2001) explored these institutional origins of art history. The present volume seeks to understand the discipline's more recent history in light of changing institutions and institutional practices.

An institution is essentially a deliberate and recognizable set of organizing principles. Typically, these organizing principles manifest themselves physically as well as discursively so that institutions occupy literal sites. Legislatures, churches, libraries, NGOs, and fast-food franchises are examples of institutions that promote their missions materially, in specific places.[1] Some institutions take a less tangible form. For instance, etiquette and language can be understood as institutions insofar as each is a deliberate and recognizable set of principles that organize thought and behavior. What is more, etiquette and language are every bit as able to promote particular habits, beliefs, and allegiances as Methodism or McDonald's. Thus any inquiry into the institutions with (or against) which art history now responds must take into consideration an array of institutional forms.

This anthology takes such a view. By bringing together essays that consider the practice of art history in relation to diverse institutions and institutional discourses, *Making Art History* aims to recalibrate our understanding of this discipline. Art history is not bound by any single institutional allegiance; its practice is not limited to the museum, gallery, auction house, or academy. Art history is better understood as a medium for the circulation of ideas—and ideology—throughout contemporary Western culture. The management of this circulation is the real work of a discipline and its institutions. None of art history's institutions has a stronger share in disciplinary management today than professionalization. In many ways, the history of art history's professionalization *is* the history of art history as it is practiced today.

Art history is now a profession. With its standardized training, specialized vocabulary, national and international associations and codes of ethics, art history shares much in common with longer-lived Western professions such as medicine or law.[2] Compared with these fields, art history's status as a profession is new, largely attained during the twentieth century. The processes that molded art history into a profession advanced through several steps beginning with the establishment of university curricula and advanced degree programs and culminating in the promulgation of global standards and practices. Prior to professionalization, art history comprised a set of disparate intellectual and commercial endeavors. Aesthetics, archaeology, connoisseurship, curation, valuation: these are just a few of the tributaries from which art history drew its methods and aims. Professionalization, however, re-routed the course of art history, moving it away from some of these early interests while drawing on others in an effort to delimit the discipline.

The circumscription of art history into a profession has had clear consequences. For one thing, professionalization has promoted the public stature of the field, helping to install it as a core component of higher education in many Western countries. In a similar vein, professionalization helped to democratize the field, casting the pursuit of art history as a career. Art history was accessible—and potentially gainful—to those able to attain the necessary credentials (typically an advanced degree at an accredited institution). Those seriously interested in the field prior to its professionalization required the means or patronage necessary to travel, collect, or study independently. Of course, this democratization of the discipline was limited, enfranchising some groups more readily than others. In the United States, for instance, those involved in the early stages of professionalization included white upper- and middle-class women and men, while African Americans and Latinos from all classes were largely excluded from participating in art history as professionals until the last quarter of the twentieth century.[3] This is just one of the ways in which professionalization can be seen to have limited the discipline.

Just as professionalization expanded access to art-historical careers to some groups and in some institutions, the process also codified and narrowed the discipline in such a way as to promote uniformity in training and practice. Standardization of the discourse of art history—which encompasses research methods, interpretive strategies and modes of dissemination—has inevitably foreclosed some avenues of inquiry. Given art history's motley intellectual and institutional origins, the process of refining the discipline has divorced it from its earlier willingness to borrow methods from such disparate sources as the natural and social sciences as well as philosophy and literary studies. While professionalization undoubtedly sharpened the discipline and reinforced its relevance as an independent mode of inquiry, it also discouraged the innovation that characterized the signal achievements of nineteenth-century art history. In recent decades, these divisions have begun to relax once again in the wake of sustained critiques of the ideological sources and consequences of disciplinary autonomy.[4] Interdisciplinary study has gained currency and with it art history has restored some of its former lines of communication with the social and natural sciences.

That art history functions today as a profession is indisputable. What is not immediately clear is the impetus for this transformation. Why did art history become a profession? Why did professionalization take place when it did? The answers are, of course, myriad, deriving from a complex of social, cultural, and individual impetuses. Some of the impulses behind professionalization left stronger marks than others, however. Two conditions underlying art history's professionalization in the West can be isolated as representative of this complex of forces: nationalism and social mobility. Both nationalism and the expansion of the middle class reached their zeniths during the first half of the twentieth century. Art history's professionalization in Europe, Australia, and North America can be seen largely as a response to these social circumstances.

Nationalism asserts itself materially and psychically. Materially, nationalism ties identity to a literal place. Physical landmarks, borders and frontiers, and natural resources are invested with overweening significance as manifest evidence of a nation's inevitability. The landscape is thus used to naturalize nationalism. For nationalism, a necessary fiction is that geography is destiny. Animating a nation's material body is its psyche. As the repository of memories, beliefs, values, desires, and fears, the psyche works to explain and justify the body's existence and actions. The psyche of a society is, of course, its culture. Nationalism requires a culture that will support its behavior and claims. This is where art history enters into the service of nationalism. Art history defines and interprets visual culture; art historians, then, help to shape a nation's sense of self. While the same may be said about authorities of all forms of culture, art historians are uniquely valuable when nationalism is a dominant social characteristic due to their purview over an especially valued class of material culture. The totemic character of artworks adds to their weight as indices of culture and history.[5] These objects confirm the robust health of a nation, for artworks by their very nature are marks of cultural abundance.[6] Art historians, like priests or shamans, manage these objects, eliciting from them confirmation of a society's righteousness.

Art history, therefore, steadily gained import in the West during nationalism's nineteenth-century crescendo, peaking in the first half of the twentieth century. To enhance art history's service to nationalism, it was necessary in this period to strengthen the discipline, to ensure that there were authorities available to delineate and justify cultural boundaries. Professionalization presented the surest means of securing arbiters of cultural meaning. If nothing else, professionalization defines authority. With its reliance on credentialing, membership in professional organizations and systems of peer review, professionalization designates publicly the bearers of authority in a given field. It is not surprising, then, that the first national professional associations for art historians appeared in the early twentieth century. This, perhaps more than any other single event, signaled the advent of art history's professionalization.

Nationalism was, of course, only one of many social forces leading to the professionalization of the field. The ascendance of the bourgeoisie in the West must also be reckoned among the impulses behind art history's claim to the status of a profession.[7] By "bourgeoisie," I mean to evoke the definition of the term presented by John Lukacs in his essay "The Bourgeois Interior." Noting that "bourgeoisie" and "middle class" are often used interchangeably, Lukacs argues that the term "middle class" simply designates a group that rests between the poor and the rich. All societies, he contends, have a middle class. On the other hand, "Not every society had, or has, a bourgeoisie . . . For bourgeois means something more than a social class: it means certain rights and privileges, certain aspirations, a certain way of thinking even more than of living."[8] Specifically, this way of thinking includes faith in social mobility, which the bourgeoisie "made a virtue." The bourgeoisie believe that:

> nobody should rest satisfied with his lot; he should always think of bettering it . . . The ambitious men and women and adolescents within the new middle classes emulate successful people within their own group. The aspiring bourgeois emulated the classes that still stood above them.[9]

It is from this group that art history's professionalization gained much of its strength. The unprecedented expansion of the bourgeoisie in the West during the late nineteenth and early twentieth centuries created one of the conditions necessary for art history's evolution into a profession.

As white-collar laborers, the growing middle class (not exclusively bourgeois) sought positions where special knowledge rather than physical effort could be exchanged for a salary. Art history is just one of the fields that grew to accommodate this expanding labor market. For those not pursuing the historic professions of medicine or law, new art-historical careers in education or cultural management developed alongside other nascent white-collar professions such as advertising or real estate.[10] Art history, what is more, possessed a uniquely powerful appeal for the bourgeoisie who, as Lukacs explains, hold social mobility as a virtue and who depend upon emulation of the aristocracy as a means of proving their social ascension.

Bourgeois access to careers in art history took flight in the early twentieth century as universities began to offer degree programs, especially graduate programs, in the field.[11] Of course, the middle class had already made a strong imprint on the discipline during the eighteenth and nineteenth centuries.[12] What changed in the twentieth century was not only accessibility for those able to attend college but also the imprimatur of a degree in the field. Such credentialing offered reassurance to students and their families, confirming that art history was a legitimate discipline, promising to bestow professional rank and status. Combined with such logistical and practical considerations was another lure that made art history especially attractive to the bourgeoisie. And this lure tripped an unconscious attraction to the field.

As Lukacs lays it out, one of the characteristics that set the bourgeoisie apart from the merely middle class is that the former "emulated the classes that still stood above them." Pierre Bourdieu accords with this view, but investigates further the role of culture as a sign of class difference. His book *Distinction: A Social Critique of the Judgement of Taste* records his effort to explain empirically precisely why and how this is the case. Bourdieu's sociological analysis confirms that "taste," or the ability to recognize and respond to aesthetic forms, is rooted in social location, with family and education most influential in the development of particular cultural predilections. "Tastes," he writes, "are the practical affirmation of an inevitable difference."[13] Emulation of another group's tastes is the habit of the bourgeoisie whereas the aristocracy controls the evolution of arbitrary preferences into "a system of aesthetic principles."[14] And this system highlights and helps to maintain class distinctions. The tendency of the bourgeoisie to emulate the aristocracy rendered art history a particularly appealing profession for the former because art history offers material confirmation of social advancement. In other words, social mobility has a goal: to reach the next step in the ladder. How is success confirmed? By adopting social habits and other visible signs of elevated status. Few proofs of high social rank supercede the possession of artworks.[15] Bourdieu's analysis leads him to the same conclusion: "Material or symbolic consumption of works of art constitutes one of the supreme manifestations of *ease*, in the sense both of objective leisure and subjective facility."[16]Although art historians may not literally possess the art, they do hold knowledge that endows them with authority over these objects. For this reason, a career in art history provided an expedient means for gaining psychic or emotional (and often physical) control over artworks, the very proof of social distinction.

This process is akin to one Bourdieu discerns in the circulation of culture among the classes. Culture, in this case specifically artworks, assumes the role of social currency:

> What is acquired in daily contact with ancient objects, by regular visits to antique-dealers and galleries, . . . is of course a certain 'taste', which is nothing other than a relation of immediate familiarity with things of taste. But it is also the sense of belonging to a more polished, more polite, better policed

> world, a world which is justified in existing by its perfection, its harmony and beauty, a world which has produced Beethoven and Mozart and continues to produce people capable of playing and appreciating them. And finally it is an immediate adherence, at the deepest level of habitus, to the tastes and distastes, sympathies and aversions, fantasies and phobias which, more than declared opinions, forge the unconscious unity of a class.[17]

Rarefied taste and the power to advance one particular cultural form over another was no longer the domain of the aristocracy. The bourgeoisie, through the profession of art history, could deploy these markers of social distinction. The means by which the bourgeoisie gained this power—education, credentialing, professional affiliation—made cultural authority into something that could be achieved or earned rather than simply something that one exercised with nonchalance.[18]

Some art historians working around the turn of the twentieth century, when art history was taking its first tentative steps toward professionalization, adopted the aristocratic model wholesale. The *sprezzatura,* exhibited by Bernard Berenson in making his seemingly intuitive judgments about the authenticity and value (aesthetic and commercial) of artworks, exemplifies this emulation.[19] But the need to ape the unstudied cultural authority of the aristocracy was erased as professionalization took root. The professional model exalted method, credentials, and peer review. The esoteric character of cultural authority gave way to the deliberate accretion of knowledge guided by university curricula. Acceding to positions as curators, dealers, scholars, and educators, middle-class art historians now wielded authority over material culture, much of which belonged formerly to aristocrats, whether secular or religious. In this way, the bourgeoisie fulfilled the fantasy it had been programmed to pursue, imagining itself risen to a social par with the aristocracy.

The ideological significance of artworks had another important effect on the relationship between the bourgeoisie and the field of art history. As already stated, this group invested artworks with symbolic meaning as markers of social prestige. Thus, now that they were largely in control of these artifacts, no one would be more invested in maintaining or even enhancing the significance of artworks than the bourgeoisie. Should the prestige of a certain group of artworks decline, the art historian who exercised authority over that collection (whether as a curator, a scholar, or connoisseur) would suffer a similar decline in the social imaginary of the bourgeoisie. In this way, the ideology of class mobility led the middle class to become ardent defenders of the cultural as well as commercial value of artworks. In other words, it's essential for art historians to invest in these objects tremendous cultural value. For without this value, then possession of authority over them would cease to provide any psychological or social reassurance.

Class mobility along with nationalism were but two of the many social and individual prods toward professionalization. This introduction, limited as it must be, cannot begin to provide an exhaustive account of art history's transformation into a profession. Instead, these remarks are offered in order to suggest the depth and complexity of art history's institutional history, of which professionalization is but one facet. As the following essays reveal, art history engages in diverse institutional conversations. Some of these conversations revolve around questions of canonicity, in defining precisely what *is* art history's purview. Canon formation is one means of designating the proper subject of art history, and the essays gathered in the first section of this volume share an interest in the causes and consequences of the discipline's preoccupation with the canon. The title of this section, "Border patrols: art history as identity," signals the canon's function as a means of establishing disciplinary, national, and personal identity. Here, the reader will find essays by Finbarr Barry Flood, Marlite Halbertsma, Gregory T. Clark, and Steven Nelson. In addition to arguments both for and against the necessity of canons, this section presents inquiries into the historical basis for the admission of some works into the canon and the refusal of others.

Part II, "The subjects of art history," negotiates a different set of questions. Instead of focusing on the objects of art-historical inquiry, the authors in this section propose that the discipline ultimately has no other aim than to provide a mechanism for the individual or cultural psyche to discharge unexpressed or unacknowledged fears and desires. In essays by Janet Kraynak, Eric Rosenberg, Donald Preziosi, and Christopher Bucklow, art history is cast fundamentally as a reflexive practice, as a means for exploring the self. The art historian, in the end, is the subject of art history according to these authors.

To trace the formation of the habits, assumptions, goals, and methods of today's art historian, the following section takes the reader to the academy. Titled "Instituting art history," this section considers art history in light of different modes of organizing knowledge. The university, of course, is a tangible manifestation of a particular way of conceiving knowledge as a product of distinct "disciplines" that order themselves along the lines demarcated as "curricula." The institutional habits of the university have become naturalized as a sign of modernity, essential for the continuing progress of Western technologies and economies. So seemingly obvious is the mission of the university to educate citizens and generate knowledge that few of its constituents question either the reasonableness of its stated aims or the validity of its structure. Contributors to this section interrogate the organization and behavior of the university as they examine its relationship to art history. Stephen Melville, Claire Farago, David Carrier, and Robert O. Bork demonstrate that art history is as much a product as producer of the academy. In each of their essays, an inquiry into the discipline's relationship to the academy necessarily raises larger questions about the mission, habits, ethics, and limits of the university as it exists today.

The final section turns to a consideration of one of art history's longest-lived institutional conversations: its dialog with the museum. Collected under the heading

"Old masters, new institutions: art history and the museum," essays by Anna C. Chave, Christopher R. Marshall, and Maureen Connor take up the issue of art history's long but not always comfortable relationship with its most visible institution. It is in the museum that art history reveals itself most directly to the public, and the popular understanding of the discipline comes largely through the mediation of this institution. This section looks at how art history and the museum are mutually responsive, and equally subject, to such diverse social pressures as nationalism, corporate management models, and the "culture wars."

Taken together, the essays presented in *Making Art History: A Changing Discipline and Its Institutions* give a sense of the diversity of institutions and institutional discourses with which the discipline remains engaged. By no means exhaustive, the account of art history's institutional commerce offered in these pages provides, nevertheless, some measure of the scope and complexity of disciplinary ties. To aid in navigating this network, each of the four sections described above begins with a short introduction to the general themes and specific arguments conveyed by the essays assembled there. This arrangement will, hopefully, permit the reader not only to follow the conversation among scholars anthologized here but also to discern threads of other arguments regarding art history and its institutions, arguments that will continue to develop as art history—as practiced as well as imagined—continues to change.

## Notes

1 Even as institutions such as libraries and churches assume electronic form, they can be said to inhabit a literal place, even if that place is a specific web server. In other words, the shift to electronic means of dissemination continues to depend on a physical center or locus of activity.

2 A useful discussion of the definition of profession forms the introductory chapter of Andrew Abbott's *The System of Professions: An Essay on the Division of Expert Labor* (Chicago: University of Chicago, IL, 1988) pp. 1–31.

3 This is not to say that there were no African American or Latino art critics, curators, and art historians earlier in the century. Rather, these voices were mostly kept apart from the professional discourse of art history. For recent discussions of race and ethnicity in relation to the practice of art history see, for instance, Jacqueline Francis, "Writing African American Art History: Commentary," *American Art* 17(1) (spring 2003): 2–10; Mary Ann Calo, "Recovery and Reclamation: A Continuing Project," *American Art* 17(1) (spring 2003): 10–14; and Catherine Soussloff, ed., *Jewish Identity in Modern Art History* (Berkeley, CA: University of California Press, 1999).

4 See, for instance, Donald Preziosi, *Rethinking Art History: Meditations on a Coy Science* (New Haven, CT: Yale University Press, 1989); David Carrier, *The Principles of Art History Writing* (University Park, PA: Pennsylvania State University Press, 1991); and Keith P. Moxey, *The Practice of Theory: Poststructuralism, Cultural Politics, and Art History* (Ithaca, NY: Cornell University Press, 1994); as well as the anthologies Mark A. Cheetham, Michael Ann Holly, and Keith Moxey, eds, *The Subjects of Art History:*

*Historical Objects in Contemporary Perspectives* (New York and Cambridge: Cambridge University Press, 1998) and Robert S. Nelson and Richard Shiff, eds, *Critical Terms for Art History*, 2nd edn (Chicago, IL and London: University of Chicago Press, 2003; orig. 1996).

5 On the totemic quality of artworks, see William Pietz, "Fetish," in ibid. *Critical Terms for Art History*, pp. 306–317.

6 Pierre Bourdieu, *Distinction: A Social Critique of the Judgement of Taste*, trans. Richard Nice (Cambridge, MA: Harvard University Press, 1984) p. 55.

7 John Lukacs, "The Bourgeois Interior," *The American Scholar* (1970): 616–630, esp. pp. 616, 619, and 628.

8 Ibid., pp. 616, 619.

9 Ibid., p. 628.

10 On the real estate profession as a marker of middle-class identity see Jeffrey M. Hornstein, *A Nation of Realtors* (Durham, NC: Duke University Press, 2005). A glimpse into advertising's accession to the status of profession is provided in Floyd Y. Keeler, *The Advertising Agency* (New York and London: Garland, 1985; orig. Harper and Bros, 1927) esp. pp. 1–6.

11 See David Van Zanten, "Formulating Art History at Princeton and the Humanistic 'Laboratory,'" in Craig Hugh Smyth and Peter M. Lukehart, eds, *The Early Years of Art History in the United States* (Princeton, NJ: Princeton University Department of Art and Archaeology, 1993) p. 175.

12 A number of influential early scholars came from the middle classes including J.J. Winckelmann, John Ruskin, J.A. Crowe, Giovanni Cavalcaselle, Gustav Waagen, and Emilia F.S. Dilke, to name a few.

13 Bourdieu, p. 56.

14 Ibid., p. 57.

15 See James Clifford, "On Collecting Art and Culture," in Simon During, ed., *The Cultural Studies Reader*, 2nd edn (London: Routledge, 1999, pp. 55–76); and Kathryn Maureen Liscomb, "Social Status and Art Collecting: The Collections of Shen Zhou and Wang Zhen," *Art Bulletin*, (March 1996) pp. 111–136.

16 Bourdieu, p. 55 *In Visible Touch: Modernism and Masculinity*, Terry Smith, ed. (Sydney: Power Publications, 1997).

17 Ibid., p. 77.

18 Bourdieu speaks of the aristocracy's assumption of a natural ease or *sprezzatura* as way of distinguishing their cultural and social position from the calculated attainments of the bourgeoisie. See Bourdieu, pp. 68–72, 252–256.

19 Berenson's negotiation of his own and others' class location is discussed by Meryle Secrest in *Being Bernard Berenson: A Biography* (New York: Holt, Rinehart and Winston, 1979).

# Part I

# Border patrols

## Art history as identity

### Introduction

Art history maintains a chicken-or-egg relationship with the canon. Was the discipline formed in response to an already existing hierarchy of cultural expression? Or does art history itself conjure these collections? The authors presented in this section proceed from different assumptions on this point, though all agree that the art-historical canon represents more than a mere corpus for intellectual or aesthetic contemplation: the canon shapes not only the identities of the cultures chosen for inclusion (and, thus, those excluded as well), it also positions the art historian culturally, socially, and economically. While none of the authors here advocates an abandonment of the canon—both Marlite Halbertsma and Steven Nelson argue that it remains an essential tool for art history—all insist that the discipline must respond to the canon with greater reflexivity. The canon, as the following essays reveal, offers the most reliable testimony about the aims and practices of art history today. Included in the recent disciplinary developments in which the canon played a role was the professionalization of art history in the west during the twentieth century.

Sociologist Andrew Abbott argues in *The System of Professions* that professionalization is essentially a process whereby authority or jurisdiction over a particular realm of knowledge is successfully asserted.[1] Thus, the most important step to be taken by a discipline seeking professional status is circumscription of its purview. For art history, its purview might be taken generally to be "art," but in concrete, quantifiable terms it is the canon that defines its jurisdiction. In this way, the canon can be seen as the central organizing principle of the discipline itself. This point was not lost on those aiming to professionalize the field in the early twentieth century. For instance, in the United States, the College Art Association promoted professionalization through dissemination of a canon to its members by publishing curricula as well as lists of essential study photographs, casts, books, and, later, slides.[2] The canon would be further reinforced with the promotion of a standardized qualifying examination recommended for all college students with questions supplied by the Association.[3] A clear purview—the art-historical canon—was understood to be essential to the discipline's professionalization.[4]

A profession experiences instability, according to Abbott, primarily when it registers threats to its jurisdiction. For the profession of art history, then, this would involve a critique of or challenge to the canon. The disciplinary "crisis" in which art history has been variously engaged since the 1970s can, therefore, be understood essentially as a reaction to renegotiations of the canon as it has been variously expanded, contracted, reasserted, and rejected outright in response to influences as diverse as Marxism, post-structuralism, feminism, and post-colonial studies as well as neoconservatism and globalization. Perhaps the most sharply felt recent critique of the art-historical canon—and, hence, of the discipline itself—has come from visual studies, a discipline claiming jurisdiction over all forms of visual culture, including those traditionally considered part of the art-historical canon. This incursion, which advanced during the late 1980s and 1990s, provoked a fair amount of wagon circling among those committed to the profession of art history.[5] While much of the discussion by art historians concerning the "legitimacy" of visual studies seemed to focus on questions of method, another source of anxiety consistently emerged: visual studies' threat to the integrity of the canon. By refusing to abide by a hierarchy of the visual arts, visual studies threatened to "level" culture, to lose sight of whatever distinctive character (aesthetic, political, material) made those works part of the art-historical canon. This would lead not only to the erasure of "art" as a distinctive class of material culture but also, some warned, to the loss of viewers' ability to discriminate among visual signs, to discern either the formal or ideological differences between images. By eliminating the canon, many art historians argued, visual studies would undermine rather than strengthen the aesthetic, political, and material autonomy of works of visual culture.

To what extent does preservation of the art-historical canon enable a clearer understanding of culture? This is one of the questions taken up by Marlite Halbertsma in her essay, "The call of the canon: why art history cannot do without." Arguing that the canon is essential to the study of art history, Halbertsma dismisses the idea of abandoning the canon "as ridiculous as studying theology without God." Instead of arguing about whether or not art history should have a canon, Halbertsma focuses her attention on the history of the concept of the canon itself. First tracing the idea back to antiquity, Halbertsma then follows the notion of the art-historical canon to the eighteenth century where she discerns the emergence of the modern canon, or canons—the Enlightenment, she explains, produced two forms of canon: a classical canon and a Romantic canon. The classical canon valorizes timeless aesthetic categories, admitting works without concern for cultural or historical specificity. This classical canon is elastic, Halbertsma argues, accommodating new works so long as they conform to the universal standards maintained by the canon.

The Romantic canon, on the other hand, rejects universal aesthetic principles in favor of local specificity: artworks are embraced precisely for their success in conveying the essence of a particular culture or period. The Romantic canon, according to Halbertsma, demands authenticity without regard for quality. It is this Romantic offshoot, she contends, that gave rise to the rigid, exclusionary, and oppressive canon that has been under fire since the 1970s.

Steven Nelson likewise offers a defense of the art-historical canon, though his conception of the canon and its utility differ sharply from that of Halbertsma. In "Turning green into black, or how I learned to live with the canon," Nelson begins with an account of the history of the canon of African American art. Developed in the early twentieth century as a means to assert cultural parity in a society where institutionalized racism had for so long denied the possibility of legitimate artistic expression among people of color, the African American canon evolved into a standard of difference as much as equality. The political expedience of a canon that valorizes blackness above other criteria has run its course. To be part of the late-twentieth-century African American canon, Nelson explains, an artist or artwork needed somehow to express essential blackness. This restrictive approach, he argues, has resulted in the exclusion of important African American artists because their work does not conform to narrow standards about what it means to be or to represent blackness. Rather than eliminate the canon, Nelson proposes "to stretch it, not only in terms of the artists it includes but also with respect to the theoretical tools in its arsenal." Toward this end, he proposes a new canon of African American art that sees race not as something monolithic or essential but as a set of identities and practices that involve contradiction and ambivalence as well.

Finbarr Barry Flood does not offer an apology for the canon, though he shares Nelson's and Halbertsma's concerns about the canon's overweening emphasis on authenticity and originality. In the field of Islamic art, the canon reflects Western cultural and political assumptions regarding "non-Western" artworks. As Flood explains in "From the Prophet to postmodernism? New World Orders and the end of Islamic art," only those works that exhibit sufficient "authenticity" are admitted into the canon of Islamic art. To be authentic, the work must have been produced prior to contact with colonizing Europeans. This means that most accounts of Islamic art break off in the eighteenth century, leaving two centuries worth of cultural production unacknowledged. Works that display traces of modern Western influence are rejected as contaminated and not sufficiently authentic. The canon of Islamic art is, therefore, better understood as a kind of cultural quarantine, ostensibly intended to protect Islamic forms from Western contamination, though Flood finds evidence that the infection from Islam may be the real concern. He outlines the irony of contemporary, politically motivated (though generally well-intentioned) appeals for the visual arts to be used to facilitate greater cross-culture understanding between predominantly Muslim regions and the West. Because the canon of Islamic art contains only objects produced before the nineteenth century, it serves mainly to reinforce assumptions about Islam as a culture of the past, immune to progress, resistant to change. Thus, the canon of Islamic art only confirms what seem insurmountable differences.

Attempts at policing cultural "purity" are not only a concern for those working with non-Western cultural artifacts. Even a field as seemingly divorced from contemporary political exigencies as fifteenth-century European manuscript illumination finds its canon subject to cultural gerrymandering. Gregory T. Clark provides an account of the consequences of the changing linguistic, political, and cultural character of modern Belgium for contemporary art historians. Of central concern to scholars and citizens of Belgium are references to "Flanders." For those living outside northern Europe, the region of Flanders and the descriptive term "Flemish" carry little other than generally geographic or stylistic meaning. Students in the United States, for instance, will find in most survey textbooks a unit on "Flemish" art that treats the adjective as much as a stylistic designation as a geographical or political one. But for modern Belgians and their neighbors, Flanders stands for much more than a northern school of early modern art. While Halbertsma's observation that "art history hardly pays any attention to national divisions" may be true, Clark reveals that art historians pay a great deal of attention to these boundaries. What is more, contemporary political disputes and assumptions can influence not only an art historian's access to artworks but also the aesthetic and cultural status of the works themselves.

Taken together, these essays show that the canon ultimately has little to do with purely formal, aesthetic, or even commercial concerns. Instead, the canon serves as a means to demark cultural and social boundaries. The canon establishes not only *what* is in or is out, but, more importantly, *who* is in or out. A realization of a culture's self-conception, the canon asserts an idealized cultural identity by embracing what a culture wishes to be as it rejects what it doesn't wish to be (or refuses to believe it is). The art-historical canon, perhaps more than any other canon, allows a society to visualize itself in the form it imagines itself to hold. Unlike a literary or historical canon, a canon of artworks gives material form to a society's fantasy of collective identity.

## Notes

1 Andrew Abbott, *The System of Professions: An Essay on the Division of Expert Labor* (Chicago, IL: University of Chicago Press, 1988) pp. 2, 250.

2 A report on the list of books appeared in *Art Bulletin* (1917); the list itself appeared in *Art Bulletin* in 1920.

3 In 1926, the Committee on Standards was asked by the board to develop a comprehensive examination/contest for students of painting and drawing. *Art Bulletin* IX 3: 281.

4 See Holmes Smith, "Problems of the College Art Association," *The Bulletin of the College Art Association,* I(1) (1913): 6–10.

5 See, for instance, the responses to the "Visual Culture Questionnaire," sent by the editors of *October* magazine to several scholars in *October* 77 (Summer 1996): 25–70; and Eloy J. Hernandez, "Art History's Anxiety Attack," in *Afterimage* 2 (May/June 1997): 6–7.

Chapter 1

# The call of the canon

## Why art history cannot do without

*Marlite Halbertsma*

"Canon," like "classic" or "culture," is a word that is often used loosely. When attempting to define it more precisely or account for its content, it becomes apparent that various disciplines in the arts use "canon" in different ways. In literature the canon consists mainly of the basic texts that are taught to students at university level whereas in history it comprises the historical facts that pupils at primary and secondary school learn. In recent years newspapers and magazines in the Netherlands have featured numerous articles about the way history is taught, arguing that it should be more national and international in order to accommodate multicultural classes in Dutch schools. Education should relate more to the international backgrounds of the different sections of society while, at the same time, providing more information about Dutch history to encourage integration.

The discussion surrounding the literary canon has been revived with equal vigor, focusing on questions such as which texts deserve to be treated in textbooks, anthologies, and lectures; who should make the selection; whether the selection of a limited number of compulsory texts ensures that different social groups enjoy at least some share of their literary heritage; and with which texts should every American, British, or Dutch person be familiar.[1] At the heart of this debate, which some have dubbed the "canon wars," lies a crisis in the humanities. Since the 1960s, humanists have wrestled with the notion of relativism and other similar ideologies that have in many ways undermined the very existence of their disciplines.[2]

In art history, comparatively little has been written about the canon in recent years.[3] How the art-historical canon emerged as a collection of the world's best art, and how it is maintained and studied is not really the subject of debate.[4] Why is this? As a discipline, art history hardly pays any attention to national divisions, and unlike literature and history, its ties with the world of compulsory education are minimal. As a result, art history is rarely discussed in a general public forum. Most people outside the art world care little if at all which artists art historians prefer to research, or which artists are shown in museum galleries and which are consigned to the depots.

The close ties that connect museums, the art trade, and art history have also contributed to the absence of a major debate about the art-historical canon. History and literature are not tied to powerful institutions such as museums, art dealers, and tourism, which involve significant financial interests. For institutions and companies that earn their income in a free market there can be no room for a hierarchy not based on quality, however attractive the idea that works by lesser names might one day appear on a gallery wall or in lavishly illustrated auction catalogs rather than languish in the basement. Today, several leading museums such as Tate Modern in London, the Museum of Modern Art (MoMA) in New York and soon the Rijksmuseum in Amsterdam are experimenting with innovative presentations. But despite this penchant for new ideas, the canon remains untouched. There is little chance that the Picassos in New York and the Rembrandts in Amsterdam will be exchanged for a Henri Le Fauconnier or a Gesina Ter Borch.

Canon and politics act in collusion when it comes to the definition and preservation of cultural heritage. While it is the canon of architectural history that determines which monuments are proposed for UNESCO's World Heritage List, what eventually gets included is, above all, the result of political negotiations. The distribution of sites on the World Heritage List reflects the cultural and political power of various countries and regions.[5]

Not that debates about the canon are unknown in the art-historical world. In the 1960s and 1970s the discussion focused on including more women in the canon.[6] Twenty years later it was the Western perspective in art history that came in for criticism, which resulted in a new form of art history, World Art History, leading recently to the publication of a novel reference work, the *Atlas of World Art*.[7] Exhibition catalogs and surveys questioned the traditional categorization of historical styles and the division into artistic disciplines, such as *ModernStarts: People, Places, Things* at the MoMA in New York and *Art Since 1900*.[8]

These recent surveys, which break away from the traditional pattern, might be expected to call the art-historical canon into question, but that is not the case. Indeed they tend to confirm the canonical status of the art-historical masterpieces. New interpretations are spun around the traditional canon of masterpieces, and new great masters, women, and "world artists" have nestled in the folds. Today's art history is as canonical as it ever was, perhaps even more so. The Grand Narratives may have been surpassed, but the Great Masters remain.

Amid all the debate about the canon it is sometimes forgotten that the term and the idea are rooted in art history. Art history was more or less invented around the time that the notion of the canon was introduced into Western thought. For that reason I shall start by discussing the canon and art history in the ancient world. Following this I shall examine the origins of two modern approaches to culture and their concomitant canons. Finally, I shall look at art history, art, and the canon in the twentieth century, concluding with a number of questions about the relationship between art history and the canon.

## Canon and art history in the ancient world

In the chapters relating to minerals and metals of his encyclopedic *Naturalis Historia* ("Natural History"), written in AD 77, Pliny the Elder provides a history of the visual arts. For ancient authors it would have been inconceivable to write history without identifying protagonists by name. Pliny therefore supplies us with lists of ancient painters, architects and sculptors whose innovations contributed to the development of the arts.[9] This he based on Greek sources which have since been lost.

In the section on metallurgy (chapter 34: 55–56), Pliny discusses the sculptor Polykleitos of Sikyon, a student of Hegelades, who lived at the time of the 90th Olympiad, around 426 BC.[10] Polykleitos, Pliny informs the reader, made the *Diadumenos*, a boy tying on a headband, and the *Doryphoros*, a figure of a spear bearer. He also made a sculpture that the artists called "canon," because they based the basic rules of art on that work. Polykleitos was the only artist, Pliny relates, who, by creating a work of art, created art as such. Pliny mentions a series of statues by Polykleitos: an athlete scraping his body, a naked man pulling someone's leg and two boys playing with jacks (*Astragalizontes*), a *Mercury*, a *Hercules*, a general picking up his armor and an *Artemon*, known as the "man in the sedan chair." Pliny also notes that Polykleitos was the first sculptor to depict a subject resting on one leg.[11] Pliny concludes by citing the Roman scholar Marcus Terentius Varro, who described Polykleitos' works as "quadratus," "well-proportioned," and claimed they were all made after the same model.

When writing his copious *Natural History* Pliny made ample use of other authors and it is questionable to what degree his assertions are based on his own findings. In the nineteenth century the *Spear Bearer*, known from numerous copies, was identified with Pliny's description of Polykleitos' *Doryphoros*, and by extension to the canon,[12] although in Pliny's discussion the link between the *Spear Bearer* and the canon is not explicit. The passage in which the canon is mentioned does indeed follow his reference to the *Doryphoros*, but it is a new sentence, which starts "Fecit et quam canona artifices vocant." I would translate this as "There is also one [statue] which the artists call the canon." It is generally assumed that a written version of Polykleitos' canon existed, representing the first theory of art in writing. The statue is the application of this theory, its tangible proof.

Whether or not the canon, Polykleitos' *Doryphoros* and the various copies of the famous *Spear Bearer* are one and the same, Polykleitos' contribution to art was obvious to Pliny. In his sculpture, Polykleitos had demonstrated the basic rules of art, thus defining what art was. The canon represents the rule and the work, the standard and the example. Here we see in concise terms how the canon functions as art, art theory, and example.

Pliny provides the basic ingredients of art history. He incorporates the notion of development, viewed here as a series of innovations connected to various famous artists. We find chronology, here the 90th Olympiad, and beside their dates, the geographical origins of artists (e.g. Sikyon). We know who trained Polykleitos (it was Hegelades) and which statues he produced. These are given titles to identify them and are described in relative detail. Pliny also indicates where some of the works are located: the *Astragalizontes* stands in Emperor Titus' atrium, while the *Mercury* once stood in Lysimachea and the *Hercules* now stands in Rome. Canon and art history are inseparable for Pliny, since it is the creation of major, innovative works of art that earns an artist a place in the art-historical overview. If art fails to innovate, art history would stop, "cessavit deinde ars," "from then on art vanished."[13]

Besides the similarities with today's art history there are also differences. Pliny describes the history of art primarily as the achievement of increasing perfection in the depiction of visual reality based on insight into nature.[14] The ideal of perfection can be found in Polykleitos' theory of proportion, which probably relates to Pythagoras' concept of the divine harmony of the correlation of numbers.[15] Varro called his statues "quadratus," "well-proportioned." This may also be translated as "thickset."[16] Indeed, *quadratus* can also be taken literally as "square," or as "built with squares." Polykleitos' canon was probably, in my opinion, an illustrative theory about the proportions of the human body.

Reading Pliny further, there is a passage that supports this view in a section on the work of the later sculptor Lysippos (34: 65), whose figures are more elegant and taller. Lysippos, states Pliny, adhered closely to "symmetria." This is a Greek word, Pliny writes, for which Latin has no equivalent. Lysippos adopted a new, unprecedented method and broke with the "quadrate" figures of the old sculptors ("quadratas veterum staturas"). It is possible to read "quadratas staturas" as "thickset figures," in contrast to Lysippos' tall figures. But to judge from Pliny's next sentence it clearly implies something else: "He [Lysippos] often said that his predecessors depicted people as they were, but he as they appeared to him." "Quadratus" probably means that artists used a system of measurements developed on the basis of a study of the human body, "as they were," while Lysippos depicted people from a visual perspective, "as they appeared to him."

The word *symmetria* refers to the notion that the rules of art should not be applied rigidly, but interpreted individually according to the location of the work.[17] The difference between Polykleitos and Lysippos is that Polykleitos applied the theory of proportion strictly and mechanically in every statue ("all figures are made from the same model," Pliny cites Varro), while Lysippos varied his approach and realized that the appearance of an object is not necessarily the same as its physical shape.[18] Lysippos lived later than Polykleitos, and Pliny notes (34: 61) that he was no one's pupil, and that he had taken the artist Eupompos' admonition to heart that artists should follow nature, not artists. So Polykleitos' canon did not apply for all time: it could be changed and adapted to suit new views and insights. Yet that does not detract from the importance of Polykleitos in the development of Greek sculpture.

The Greek word *kanoon* is related to the Hebrew word for reed, and in Greek it can also mean the strip of wood used in weaving. "Standard" is the literal translation of canon. If a permanent standard exists for art, with the achievement of perfection as the highest goal, then the next stage is to rate all works of art according to their degree of perfection. This was done in literature in the Hellenistic period, with the best works listed by rank per genre. The authors of these best works were called *enkrithentes*, translated by the Romans as *classici*, in analogy to the Roman citizens in the highest tax bracket.[19] In this way the canon, meaning standard, is transformed to mean the "classic works," the examples for future generations. Later, the word canon was linked to the choice of texts included in the Bible.[20] These texts and the rules they contained, along with the statements of councils, also known as *canones*, acquired an absolute, canonical status, beyond question. In this way, aesthetic values made way for moral categories.

From Pliny's text it is clear that canonical works served as examples for artists. They were not admired for their aesthetic value alone, but as models for artists to follow, and as teaching material. Just as ancient texts survived in the Middle Ages because they formed part of the curriculum, canonical art served a function in the training of artists.[21] Originals were generally unavailable to most artists until the advent of museums in the eighteenth century. But the major works of antiquity, and later of the Renaissance and Baroque, were obtainable as copies or as plaster models, and there were prints of many statues. This was the standard teaching material for burgeoning artists. By following and learning the standard repertoire of forms and techniques, an artist established a place in the art world.[22] Of course artists were not required to just slavishly reproduce these examples. The principal examples, known to artists and their public alike, were subject to endless variations and occasionally even surpassed. People appreciated the individual adaptations and variations that artists produced within the parameters defined by canonical works.

## Two canons

During the Enlightenment in the eighteenth century, a concept of culture emerged based on ancient and Renaissance ideas, which I call the "classical concept of culture." The history of culture was perceived as the advance of civilization. Testimony to this could be found in mankind's progress since antiquity in the arts and sciences and in the organization of society through legislation, administration, and education. The concept of civilization implied the notion of refinement, the improvement of what was rough and unformed. Later, in the nineteenth century, the classical concept of culture of the Enlightenment split into civilization (based on the progress of science, technology, and society) and culture (involving artistic activity and its products).[23]

In the classical concept of culture, culture is a collective process geared toward ever greater perfection, in which the contributions of artists, scientists, and statesmen form part of a larger entity that collectively benefits mankind. Culture is the sum of all the great works of mankind; the canon of artistic masterpieces demonstrates what human ingenuity can achieve. This canon of "high art" is a source of inspiration and a model for artists of all periods, as well as a source of enjoyment and knowledge for all people, whenever and wherever they may live.

Although each contribution to this collection of masterpieces is necessarily the product of its geographical and historical background, in essence, the classical canon is not bound by either time or place. The Egyptian pyramids, the Acropolis, the Taj Mahal, Hokusai's woodcuts and Vincent van Gogh's paintings have lost none of their eloquence over the centuries and remain relevant to people across the world. The classical canon forms the basis for the UNESCO Convention of 1972, which led to the formation of the UNESCO World Heritage List.

As the examples discussed above show, the classical canon consists of more than just ancient works or works from periods in which artists found inspiration in ancient art. In the early eighteenth century, with the so-called "Querelle des Anciens et des Modernes," the literary clash between the classical and contemporary modern age, the question at issue was whether the level achieved in the arts in the ancient world was superior in every respect to contemporary art.[24] The conclusion was that the modern age had surpassed the ancient world significantly on a number of terrains. In modern times, people supposed in 1700, it was possible to attain a higher degree of perfection than in ancient times. The greatest achievements in art were not fixed for all time: in theory they could be superseded by even greater perfection.

Vasari had already concluded 150 years earlier in his introduction to part III of his *Lives*, that Raphael had probably surpassed the perfection of Apelles and Zeuxis. For Vasari it was obvious that Michelangelo outshone every artist that had preceded him, even those of antiquity: "He surpasses not only all those who have, as it were, surpassed Nature, but the famous ancients also, who surpassed her." His sculptures "are in every respect much finer than the ancient ones," Vasari wrote, noting further that "if by chance there were any works of the most renowned Greeks and Romans which might be brought forward for comparison, his sculptures would only gain in value and renown as their manifest superiority to those of the ancients became more apparent," concluding with the complaint that this progress toward perfection might continue even further, if only artists were better paid: "It is believed that if there were just rewards in our age we should become undoubtedly greater and better than the ancients."[25]

Thus the classical canon is not carved in stone forever, but can certainly admit new works, depending on the advent of new major artists. And so the canon grows in time and space. In the twentieth century the canon expanded to include masterpieces of photography, film, and art from non-European cultures. Works produced in formerly less respected artistic disciplines, such as decorative art and design, were gradually co-opted into the canon. In the classical concept of culture the canon as a comprehensive list of all the major works of art continues to function as it has over the centuries, even though the last 100 years saw the canon expand into a broader and more pluralist platform.

The classical canon is based on the premise that quality can be objectively determined and can in theory be recognized by everyone, even by those yet to be born and from elsewhere. The classical canon can be described as selective, because it consists of high art. But the classical canon is also expansive and dynamic because it is not confined by spatial or temporal bounds that limit the kind of art it contains. In that sense the classical canon is autonomous because the artistic value of a masterpiece is ultimately separate from the context in which it was made. The classical canon is open because no one, artist or audience, is excluded. The core concept of the classical concept of culture and its accompanying classical canon is quality.

In the early nineteenth century an alternative concept of culture developed. The idea of culture, which I call "Romantic," began as a critique of the Western-oriented classical concept of culture based on Greco-Roman civilization. Peoples in other parts of the world, whose art, technology, and science had flourished at other times, also possessed interesting cultures. There is not just one culture whose progress reflects the general cultural history of mankind (the premise of the classical concept of culture), but several cultures that reflect the development of different peoples. The values and norms of these peoples are found in everything they do, in their customs and traditions, in their religious rituals, and in their artistic expressions. At first sight, according to philosophers such as Johann Gottfried Herder, the cultural development of many non-European communities beyond the European periphery appears to lag behind ours, but that does not make it worth less. In fact Herder and later Romantics considered the lack of development a positive advantage since these so-called primitive societies held certain values, which had disappeared in other more evolved cultures. These Romantics also believed that the earliest cultural activities and products were the more original and therefore better, since they were closest to the character of the society before it had come into contact with other cultures. In the Romantic concept of culture a society's identity is embodied by that which remains unchanged, in contrast to the notion of permanent change as improvement, which characterizes the classical concept of culture.

To learn to appreciate the ostensibly strange and imperfect artistic products of particular cultures they need to be viewed from the perspective of the unique characteristics of the society concerned. A society's cultural and artistic products should not be judged by the level of artistic perfection attempted, but by the degree to which these represent the identity of the people or group.

Identity, not quality, forms the core of the Romantic concept of culture. This identity can become attached to anything, even to cultural activities and products that the makers never intended as works of art. The Romantic canon based on the Romantic concept of culture is therefore heteronomous, since the value of a particular object does not depend on the object itself but relates to values extraneous to that object. In the classical canon artistic expression cannot be of value without works of art: the quality of Michelangelo's sculpture can only be appreciated by viewing his works and those of other artists. But in the Romantic canon the object is first and foremost a material reflection of the characteristics of a people or society. The objects may, though not necessarily, be works of art. The characteristics of that society would exist without these artworks and may be reflected in other kinds of objects. The objects are essentially interchangeable. The Romantic canon is therefore much broader than its classical counterpart and lies much closer to the concept of culture that prevails in anthropology: culture as the collection of activities of a society, each activity being imbued with the norms and customs of that society.

This concept of culture forms the basis for the new UNESCO Convention for the Safeguarding of the Intangible Cultural Heritage, which was adopted in 2003. The reason why this Intangible Heritage list was compiled in addition to the existing World Heritage List was to correct the Eurocentric imbalance of the former list: many societies have cultural heritage, but it may not always be in the tangible form of temples, cathedrals, and palaces.

The UNESCO definition of intangible cultural heritage encompasses all the characteristics of the Romantic concept of culture. It comprises all society's cultural and social activities and rather than identifying humanity as the owner of cultural heritage it refers to societies, groups, and individuals for whom this establishes and maintains their identity. Intangible heritage may comprise "oral traditions and expressions, including language as a vehicle of intangible cultural heritage; performing arts; social practices, rituals, and festive events; knowledge and practices concerning nature and the universe; traditional craftsmanship."[26]

A society's identity and the degree to which people identify and establish themselves within it is generally expressed on a scale of association or alienation. Only members of a group are able to understand and value the finesses of the practices and products of their culture; for outsiders this is impossible. That is a major difference with the classical concept of culture, in which artistic products, at least those of major artistic quality, can be considered outside their original cultural context as the property of all mankind. Culture binds people together, rather than dividing them.

The Romantic canon is relatively static, since it is based on the culture that particular societies and groups have acquired over long periods of time; it is regressive in that it places higher value on the earliest and most traditional products; it is relative since it recognizes no general standards; it is indiscriminate because it can comprise anything that expresses a society's identity; and it is closed because outsiders can never comprehend the finesses of a national or group culture. Whereas the classical concept of culture only has one canon, the Romantic can have many: each society, each group, even each individual has their own canon.

In this way, two canons emerged in the course of the nineteenth and twentieth centuries : a "classical" and a "Romantic." I have discussed these two canons here as ideals, as if each existed in a separate universe. In reality, however, they interconnect, although their basic principles remain recognizable. The classical canon came first. In the eighteenth and nineteenth centuries the first museums were filled with works that conformed to the classical canon. Museums were the cultural ambassadors of their countries, and the status of their most valued masterpieces reflected on the museum as institution and on their owner, the state. Apart from the objects, the "museum" soon became a label that imbued status in its own right to all the objects it housed. If it was in a museum, it had to be valuable. Collectors of objects who adhered to the criteria of the Romantic canon soon demanded museums for their collections. In the course of the nineteenth century numerous ethnographic, folk art, and open-air museums were established explicitly focusing on objects relating to pre-industrial society.

Later in the nineteenth century smaller geographical units, such as cities and provinces, also established their own museums, as did the states that achieved independence in the late nineteenth century or after the Second World War. Since this often implied that these institutions were too late to acquire major masterpieces, many of them only contain objects that conform to the Romantic canon. In the closing decades of the twentieth century social groups which had achieved emancipation (women, gays and lesbians, ethnic groups) also established museums: founding a museum became a step in the ladder of social acceptance.

For the preservation of Romantic heritage, forms of presentation and conservation are employed that are identical to those associated with art in the classical canon, even though these objects are often more properly associated with the term "low culture." Despite its antagonistic stance toward the classical concept of culture, the Romantic canon nevertheless yearns for the status that the classical canon bestows on works of art. The Romantic canon may well have changed the content of our museums and the criteria by which objects are selected; it has yet to develop entirely new forms of presentation and conservation. The Romantic canon will therefore never be able to divorce itself entirely from its classical counterpart. It is thus impossible to dispense with the classical canon, for we would otherwise pull the rug from under the Romantic canon. The status of the Romantic canon is determined by the status of the classical canon, just as the world's intangible heritage is linked since the UNESCO convention of 2003 to the status of objects on the World Heritage List of 1972.

## Art historians, art, and the canon

Art historians have concerned themselves with both canons. In the early nineteenth century archaeology and art history went their separate ways. Art historians concentrated on drawing up inventories and analyzing the art treasures of European countries. In the nineteenth century a European classical canon emerged of non-ancient European art of masterpieces from Italy, France, and the Netherlands from the Middle Ages to the nineteenth century.

Around 1900 the European canon came under fire from several directions. First from German art historians, subjects of the newly forged German Empire (1871).[27] They demanded an equal place in the European canon for German art. Since German art diverged in certain ways—particularly in its expressive character—from the criteria established for French, Dutch, and Italian art, German art historians developed new criteria, which linked the characteristics of German art to the characteristics of the German nation. They presented the emotional and spiritual qualities of German art as augmenting what they saw as the rational, ideal, and material focus of French, Italian, and Dutch art. In this way German art was absorbed into the wider palette of European art styles while retaining its individual qualities. This form of national art historiography bridged the gap between the classical and Romantic canon.

Around the same time, the Austrian Alois Riegl went a step further. Given the large number of peoples encompassed by the Austro-Hungarian Empire, it was not possible to link Austrian national characteristics to a recognizable Austrian art. The empire was too large and too culturally diverse. Riegl broke the bounds of the art-historical canon in a different way. According to Riegl there could be no absolute, general artistic qualities, or progress to ever-greater perfection. Each period should be viewed in its own context: differences in form, technique, and subject matter were the result of an autonomous *Kunstwollen* which dictates the art forms of each age. No artist is ever able to escape this.

With this Riegl introduced a variation on the Romantic concept of art. Instead of forming a teleology toward ever-greater perfection, the history of art shows a development from what he termed the objective (plastic, realistic) to the subjective (optical and abstract) which characterized art in his day. Riegl linked the period and the national character, since the *Kunstwollen* of a particular age may suit one national character more than another.[28] National characters did not change. These were static. The art historian's task is to study the *Kunstwollen* of each age, the geographical variations of the *Kunstwollen* within each age, and the long-term transformation of the *Kunstwollen*.

In another publication Riegl again undermined the reliance on established criteria for inclusion of art works in the canon. In his article "Der moderne Denkmalkultus. Sein Wesen und seine Entstehung" (1903), he wondered what made a structure a monument.[29] A monument might be important for its "historischer Wert" (historical value), with which Riegl meant that the building in question might represent a key moment in architectural history. But contemporary criteria could also establish a building as a monument. Buildings may be judged according to a variety of contemporary criteria, such as "Gebrauchswert" (use) and "Neuheitswert" (newness), since the public—certainly in Riegl's day—set greater store by a new, useful building than by an old, unusable structure. Another contemporary criterion established by Riegl is also relevant to the debate about the canon, namely that of "relativer Kunstwert" (relative artistic value). With this Riegl meant that buildings whose appearance reflects the contemporary *Kunstwollen* are appreciated more than those which do not.

Appreciation of old art is always linked to developments in modern art. Since the nineteenth-century artists have played a key role in the "recycling" of older, non-Western art, folk art, or low-art, and have led the way as trendsetters in new appreciation of forms which until then were not considered to have artistic merit, from Lucas Cranach to Japanese woodcuts to comic strips.[30] Once artists have embraced objects as interesting they eventually find their way into the classical canon. Some (especially non-Western) objects have found their way into both the classical and the Romantic canon, which is why ethnographic and art museums are finding increasingly common ground, with ethnographic museums taking on some of the attributes of art museums and vice versa. It is hardly surprising that German art should be absorbed into the European canon at a time when expressionism was at its height in contemporary German art, just as the art-historical study of African art began when artists such as Picasso started to adapt its formal qualities in their own art.[31] The canon is influenced by the taste, art, and fashion of the day—yet it is also under attack because if something can be said to be "in," something can also be said to be "out." Art-historical research is likewise directed by current vogues.[32]

Modern art also began to establish a canon in the early twentieth century. The modernist avant-garde may have had no more than a passing interest in the European canon and tended to eschew the work of their predecessors, but the first propagandists of modern art—museum directors, critics, and art historians—had to justify their interest and their budgets. They presented modern art not as a collection of random styles, as diverse as the plurality of styles of the nineteenth century, but as the logical consequence of an inevitable historical process. In the first books on modern art, such as those that appeared in the 1920s, the development of modern art was explained by attributing a pedigree. This need to explain and clarify historical connections led to schematic overviews like the famous diagram by the director of the MoMA in New York, Alfred Barr, on the cover of the *Cubism and Abstract Art* exhibition catalog of 1936 (Figure 1.1).

It explained the development of modern art as a hop-skip-and-jump from the late nineteenth century to 1936. Diagrams tend to simplify and the result was a structure comprising a handful of movements and artists. This was the course that

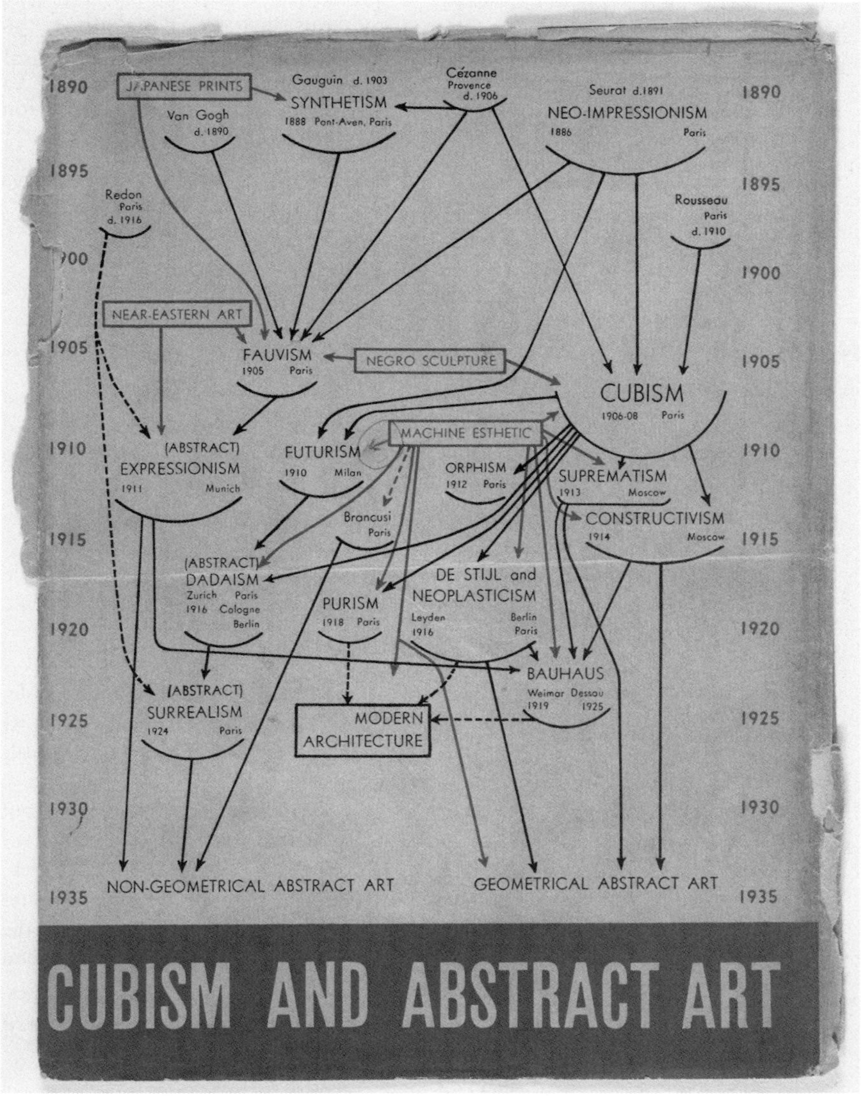


*Figure 1.1* Alfred Barr, cover of *Cubism and Abstract Art*, 1936. Courtesy of Art Resource. Digital Image © 2004 MoMA, New York.

museums of modern art followed after the Second World War as they built up their collections, with each movement represented by one or more now canonical artists.[33] As we have seen, today's reference works and museum presentations are different, but the canon of major artists still takes pride of place.

## Conclusion

Even though art historians may use different methods, just as in Pliny's time, the canonical artists and their works still form the building blocks of art-historical dialog. Art history would be impossible without a canon. In my view it would be as ridiculous as studying theology without God for art historians to study art history without a canon. A more sensible approach would be to investigate which cultural and social processes play a role in canonization.[34] At the same time it is important to establish which canons exist, how they differ, and how they influence each other.

## Notes

1 E.D. Hirsch, *Cultural Literacy: What Every American Needs to Know* (Boston, MA: Houghton Mifflin, 1987); Alan Bloom, *The Closing of the American Mind* (New York: Simon and Schuster, 1987); Jan Gorak, *The Making of the Modern Canon: Genesis and Crisis of a Literary Idea* (London: Athlone, 1991); Paul Lauter, *Canons and Contexts* (New York and Oxford: Oxford University Press, 1991); Harold Bloom, *The Western Canon: The Books and School of the Ages* (New York: Harcourt Brace, 1994); Jan Gorak, ed., *Canon vs. Culture: Reflections on the Current Debate* (New York: Garland, 2001); Tony Bennett, Lawrence Grossberg, Meaghan Morris, *New Keywords. A Revised Vocabulary of Culture and Society* (London: Blackwell, 2005) pp. 20–22.

2 Gorak, 1991, p. x.

3 Editor's note: a notable contribution to the discussion is Gill Perry and Colin Cunningham, *Academies, Museums, and Canons of Art* (New Haven, CT: Yale University Press in Association with the Open University, 1999). The book, however, only deals with the seventeenth to nineteenth centuries.

4 *Art Bulletin* 78(2) (1996) was presented as a theme issue, "Rethinking the Canon," but consists of a rather loose collection of articles not explicitly about the canon. The survey by Donald Preziosi, *The Art of Art History: A Critical Anthology* (Oxford and New York, 1998), contains only one article (written in 1991) about the art-historical canon, Nanette Salomon, "The Art Historical Canon: Sins of Omission," pp. 344–355, in which the formation of the art-historical canon is explained from the perspective of "repression of homosexual desire."

5 Bart J.M. van der Aa, *Preserving the Heritage of Humanity? Obtaining World Heritage Status and the Impacts of Listing*, PhD Dissertation, Rijksuniversiteit Groningen, 2005 (Groningen: University Library Groningen, 2005).

6 Roszika Parker and Griselda Pollock, *Old Mistresses: Women, Art and Ideology* (New York: Pantheon, 1981).

7 John Onians (ed.), *Atlas of World Art* (London: Laurence King, 2004).

8 John Elderfield *et al.* ed., *ModernStarts: People, Places, Things* (New York: Museum of Modern Art, 1999); Hal Foster, Rosalind Krauss, Yve-Alain Bois, Benjamin H. Buchloh, *Art Since 1900: Modernism, Antimodernism, Postmodernism* (New York: Thames and Hudson, 2004).

9 On Pliny see J. Isager, *Pliny on Art and Society: The Elder Pliny's Chapters on the History of Art* (London: Routledge, 1991); Sorcha Carey, *Pliny's Catalogue of Culture: Art and Empire in the "Natural History"* (Oxford: Oxford University Press, 2003). The text used here is: Roderich König and Karl Bayer, eds, *C. Plinius Secundus d.Ä. Naturkunde* (Munich and Zurich: Heimeran, 1989) XXXIV, pp. 46–47.

10 Pliny sees Polykleitos as a person who lived at the time after Phidias, but today we place Polykleitos before Phidias, in the mid-fifth century.

11 In other words, that the body's weight is supported by one leg, while the other rests ("Stand- und Spielbein"). This makes the statue more lively than the previous custom of showing the figure standing at attention.

12 Warren G. Moon, ed., *Polykleitos, the Doryphoros, and Tradition* (Madison, WI: University of Wisconsin Press, 1995).

13 *Naturalis Historia*, 34: 51.

14 Isager, p. 105.

15 John Onians, *Art and Thought in the Hellenistic Age: The Greek Worldview 350–50 BC* (London: Thames and Hudson, 1979) p. 59.

16 König, p. 47.

17 On the relationship between Polykleitos' canon and symmetria see J.J. Pollitt, "The Canon of Polykleitos and Other Canons," in Moon 1995, pp. 19–24; and Erwin Panofsky, "The History of the Theory of Human Proportions as a Reflection of the History of Styles," in *Meaning in the Visual Arts* (Harmondsworth: Penguin, 1970) pp. 82–132. Panofsky assumes that the canon is principally a theory about proportions of the human body. He does not believe that the result was a combination of squares (p. 93). Neither does he discuss the meaning of "quadratus" in Pliny or Varro's negative opinion.

18 Onians, 1979, p. 42.

19 Onians, 1979, 61, George A. Kennedy, "The Origin of the Concept of a Canon and Its Application to the Greek and Latin Canon," in Gorak 2001, pp. 105–116, 106–109.

20 Marc-Aeilko Aris, "Kanon und Entscheidung," *Kunsttexte.de*, 2(1) (2005): 1–4; Gert Ueding, ed., *Historisches Wörterbuch der Rhetorik*, IV (Tübingen: M. Niemeyer, 1998) section 869–882.

21 Kennedy, p. 109.

22 William Weber, "Canon and the Tradition of Musical Culture," in Gorak, 2001, pp. 135–152.

23 Terry Eagleton, *The Idea of Culture* (Oxford: Blackwell, 2000).

24 Anne-Marie Lecoq, Marc Fumaroli, and Jean Robert Armogathe, *La Querelle des Anciens et des Modernes* (Paris: Gallimard, 2001).

25 Giorgio Vasari, *The Lives of the Painters, Sculptors and Architects*, trans. A.B. Hinds (London: Dent, 1963; orig. 1550 and 1568) II, 154–155.

26 http://portal.UNESCO.org/culture. "The 'intangible cultural heritage' means the practices, representations, expressions, knowledge, skills—as well as the instruments, objects, artefacts and cultural spaces associated therewith—that communities, groups, and, in some cases, individuals recognize as part of their cultural heritage. This intangible cultural heritage (. . .) is constantly recreated by communities and groups in response to their environment, their interaction with nature, and their history, and provides them

with a sense of identity and continuity, thus promoting respect for cultural diversity and human creativity."

27 Marlite Halbertsma, *Wilhelm Pinder und die Deutsche Kunstgeschichte* (Worms: Wernersche Verlagsgesellschaft, 1992).

28 Alois Riegl, *Das holländische Gruppenporträt* (Vienna: Österreichische Staatsdruckerei, 1931). On Riegl see also Margaret Iversen, *Alois Riegl: Art History and Theory* (Cambridge, MA and London: The MIT Press, 1993); Andrea Reichenberger, *Riegl's "Kunstwollen": Versuch einer Neubetrachtung* (Sankt Augustin: Academia Verlag, 2003).

29 Alois Riegl, "Der moderne Denkmalkultus. Sein Wesen und seine Entstehung," in *Gesammelte Aufsätze* (Augsburg und Vienna: Dr. B. Filser, 1928) pp. 144–193; trans. and summarized as "The Modern Cult of Monuments: Its Essence and Its Development" in Nicholas Stanley Price, M. Kirby Talley Jr., Alessandra Melucco Vaccaro, *Historical and Philosophical Issues in the Conservation of Cultural Heritage* (Los Angeles, CA: Getty Conservation Institute, 1996) pp. 69–83.

30 Kirk Varnedoe and Adam Gopnik, *High and Low. Modern Art and Popular Culture* (New York: Museum of Modern Art, 1990); Thomas Crow, "Modernism and Mass Culture in the Visual Arts," *Modern Art and the Common Culture* (New Haven, CT and London: Yale University Press, 1996) pp. 3–39.

31 Donald E. Gordon, "German Expressionism," in William S. Ruben, ed., *'Primitivism' in 20th Century Art. Affinity of the Tribal and the Modern* (New York: Museum of Modern Art, 1984) II, pp. 368–403, 373 and 393.

32 Frank Kermode, *Forms of Attention* (Chicago, IL and London: University of Chicago Press, 1985) pp. 5, 30, 72–75.

33 Fieke Konijn, "Engagement en distantie. Canonvorming in overzichtsboeken van moderne kunst," *Jong Holland*, 18(2) (2002): 50–57.

34 John Guillory, *Cultural Capital: The Problem of Literary Canon Formation* (Chicago, IL: University of Chicago Press, 1993).

Chapter 2

# From the Prophet to postmodernism?

## New world orders and the end of Islamic art

*Finbarr Barry Flood*

> When I read of Islam in the papers these days, I often feel I am reading of museumized peoples. I feel I am reading of people who are said not to make culture, except at the beginning of creation, as some extraordinary, prophetic, act.
>
> Mahmood Mamdani, "Good Muslim, Bad Muslim—an African Perspective"

> The breach between two kinds of art history, which treat either historical or modern art, and do this under different paradigms, no longer makes sense. We are just as poorly served by a rigid hermeneutic framework perpetuating a dogmatic strategy of interpretation. It is perhaps more appropriate to regard the interrogation of the medium of art, of historical man and his images of the world, as a permanent experiment.
>
> Hans Belting, *The End of the History of Art?*

Ever since its inception as a sub-field of art history, no one has been quite sure of where to locate Islamic art and architecture within its master narratives. In Sir Banister Fletcher's *History of Architecture* (first published in 1896) "Saracenic" architecture belongs with the non-historical styles, branching (along with Byzantium) from the trunk of a decidedly Eurocentric family tree somewhere between Rome and Romanesque.[1] While (generally speaking) the century since Fletcher's tree was drafted has seen Islamic art admitted into the exclusive club of historical styles, the problem of where to house it is no less current, a point reflected in its treatment within universal surveys of art. In the eleventh edition of *Gardner's Art Through the Ages* (2001), for example, the chapter on Islamic art is located between Byzantium and Ancient America, whereas the subject is entirely absent from the sixth edition of H.W. Janson's magisterial *History of Art* published in the same year.[2] The enquiring reader who, seeking even a trace of Islamic culture in Janson's narrative, turns to the index will find only two entries there under the heading *Islam*: "art of" and "threat to Europe from."[3] The juxtaposition has a disquietingly contemporary resonance, although the Europe in question turns out to be that of the ninth-century Carolingians. Nevertheless, the clear distinction between Europe/not Europe within which this single reference to Islam occurs reflects the frisson of alterity upon which the reception and accommodation of Islamic art has been predicated historically.

The problem of where to locate Islamic art stems, at least in part, from the peculiarities of the term itself, an invented rubric that must accommodate a vast array of artistic production stemming almost 1,400 years and spanning every continent.[4] If artistic appreciation fulfills some of the cultural functions of religious adulation, then the position of Islamic art is particularly fraught, with the qualifying adjective caught between a religious identity and cultural identification. The resulting ambivalence is reflected not only in the lengthy apologias that accompany its use, but also in the tendency to oscillate between media-based and dynastic taxonomies, and in the appearance of ethnically or regionally based surveys.[5]

Many of these qualities were manifest in a myriad of new survey books on Islamic art and architecture published in the United States and Europe in the decade between 1991 and 2001.[6] In addition to offering a chronological overview of Islamic art to the general reader, these texts were intended for use in undergraduate courses. The artifacts, manuscripts, and monuments represented within them show a remarkable coherence in terms of their chronological and geographic range, a coherence manifest in the repetitious appearance of both specific works and the object types that they represent. Through such consistencies in their inclusions and exclusions, the new surveys may be seen as constituting and consolidating a canon, an 'imagined community' of select artifacts and monuments that define the appropriate objects of this relatively new sub-field of art history.

To this extent, they provide a representative impression of the field as currently constituted, over a century after its emergence at the intersection of text-based Oriental studies, archaeology, connoisseurship, and museology.[7] There is for example a relative balance among architecture, painting, and the 'minor' arts, an emphasis on elite artistic production rather than material culture, and on the central Islamic lands at the expense of the Maghrib, East Asia, and sub-Saharan Africa. Objects in London, Paris, and New York (and other US cities) are well represented, with occasional inclusions from Istanbul, St Petersburg, and the new collections of Islamic art in the Gulf States. Conversely, objects in Tehran, Cairo, Delhi, or the Central Asian Republics may be referred to in passing but are generally not illustrated. In other words, the works illustrated are those most readily accessible to European and American scholars, reminding us of Michael Camille's observation that the selection of valorized objects is less important to the formation of a canon than the possibilities of their reproduction.[8]

Each of these facets of the canon and their implications merits consideration, but my concern here is with what is arguably the most striking commonality among these surveys: their unanimity in excluding any art produced in the Islamic world after about 1800.

With some minor variations, most of the expository narratives in the survey texts follow a linear trajectory, tracing the history of Islamic art from the birth of Islam in the seventh century, through the rise of the first Islamic dynasties with their capitals in Damascus and Baghdad, to the breakdown of centralized authority and the emergence of regional artistic centers in the tenth. After a brief digression entailing Shiʿi-Sunni rivalry and the Crusades in the eleventh and twelfth centuries, the advent of the Mongols and their sack of Baghdad in 1258 marks a watershed in the narrative of Islamic art: most survey courses (and some texts) break at this point. After the narrative resumes in the wake of the Mongol devastations, the focus shifts to the emergence of regional and trans-regional polities in Iran and Central Asia. From around 1500 (give or take a few decades), three regionally based polities—the Ottomans of Turkey, the Safavids of Iran and the Mughals of India—dominate. Then things get rather vague.

Although the Mughal state endured until 1857, when its last emperor was exiled to Burma in the wake of the Sepoy Revolt, and the Ottoman sultanate until 1922, when it was dissolved in the wake of the First World War, the later history of Mughal and Ottoman artistic production is ignored. Indeed, the narrative of Islamic art generally ends much earlier—usually in the seventeenth century, occasionally in the eighteenth. As Nasser Rabbat has observed, Islamic art history relates the development of a more or less insular tradition of art-making "that began with the building of the Mosque of the Prophet in Medina around AD 620, and inexplicably fizzled out with the dawn of the colonial age in the late eighteenth century."[9]

Frequently commented upon by my undergraduate students (the very audience for whom such texts were presumably intended), the phenomenon of art history *interruptus* is either completely ignored or only obliquely addressed by the authors of these surveys. Although there have been a number of important recent studies on nineteenth-century artistic production in the Islamic lands and the collecting practices through which the objects of Islamic art came to rest in European and American collections, these have yet to exert a major impact on the canon.[10] The impact of Islamic art on nineteenth-century Europe or the persistence of calligraphy in the Islamic world might be briefly mentioned in concluding, but most authors seem to take it for granted that no art worthy of comment was produced in the Islamic world after 1800. This bias for the historical is reflected in the absence of contemporary artifacts and monuments from the (predominantly American and European) collections, exhibitions and texts that shaped the nascent field of Islamic art history.[11] More than two decades ago, Oleg Grabar noted that the peculiarity "suggests that Islamic creativity may have meaning for Westerners only if it dates from before 1700."[12]

The location of Islamic art in a valorized past from which "living tradition" is excluded, amounts to a denial of coevalness with the art of European modernity. The point was underlined by a 2001 exhibition at the Fondation Beyler in Basel, which juxtaposed modern European art with examples of "non-Western" art, including pre-modern (rather than contemporary) art from the Islamic world in order to demonstrate common aesthetic values of abstraction. The endeavor was curiously reminiscent of the MoMA's much criticized 1984–1985 exhibit *'Primitivism' in 20th Century Art: Affinity of the Tribal and the Modern*, although the parallels seem to have gone unremarked.[13]

The precedent for exclusion was set by nineteenth-century European scholars and travelers, who consistently heralded the death of Islamic art from Morocco to India. The sentiment is typified by Maxime du Camp's observation, made in 1854: "Egyptian art is not even in decadence, it simply no longer exists."[14] Among the more ironic consequences of such attitudes, one might cite the reception of the work of Muhammad Racim (1896–1975). Racim was an Algerian artist whose "revival" of a Persianate miniature idiom previously unknown in Algeria and inflected by experiments with linear perspective was rapturously received by French critics, including Georges Marçais, the pre-eminent scholar of Islamic art and architecture in the region. Coining a striking metaphor, the critic Edmond Gojon avowed that Racim's work gave the lie to assertions that art died in Muslim lands "just as the blackened rose loses its leaves in the deadly hands of the leprous."[15]

It should be emphasized that these obsequies for Islamic art were coterminous with the inception of its disciplinary study. One consequence is that unlike surveys of European art, which proceed in linear (and more or less teleological) fashion from cave painting to minimalism and beyond, in surveys of Islamic art it is axiomatic that the advent of modernity heralds the end of art. Marking a tension between aesthetic, ethnographic, and historical value that has inflected the disciplinary study of Islamic art since its inception, this privileging of the pre- or early modern is something more than a reflection of the fact that historically, most Islamicists have been trained as medievalists.[16] It is directly related to the rise of European colonialism and the new "global" patterns of circulation and consumption that it engendered.[17]

The vagaries of "Iranian" art in the recently published *Dictionary of Art* are a case in point. While artistic production between 1000 BC and AD 651 in the region broadly coterminous with the modern state of Iran is accommodated in volume 15 within various subheadings under the rubric of "Iran, ancient," with the advent of Islam in AD 651 the arts of "Iran" suddenly achieve trans-regional status, and are consequently to be found under the relevant subsections of the extensive entry "Islamic art" in volume 16. Once again, however, the period around 1800 marks a taxonomic watershed, and readers keen to inform themselves about art and its institutions in nineteenth- and twentieth-century Iran need to revert to a further entry entitled "Iran, Islamic Republic of" in volume 15.[18]

In trying to understand the logic underlying these divisions, the reception of the art produced under the Qajar dynasty that ruled Iran from the late eighteenth century until 1925 is instructive. Caught between the threat of British and Russian colonialism, the strictures of traditionalism, and the exigencies of modernity, the Qajars initiated a process of cultural and social reform whose ramifications arguably extend until the present day. In contrast to the pre-eminence afforded Persian art from earlier periods, however, it is only in the past two decades that tentative attempts have been made to include Qajar works in the narrative of Islamic art. Largely the result of two groundbreaking exhibitions in New York and London and the catalogs that accompanied them, this development is manifest in the inclusion of Qajar art as an epilogue in at least one of the survey texts referred to above, thereby postponing the demise of Islamic art for several decades.[19]

The art of the Qajar period is characterized both by an engagement with the artistic legacies of the distant Iranian past and the artistic practices of contemporary Europe. Diverging from earlier painting traditions in the Islamic world, many of the works produced by Qajar artists were large-scale paintings executed in oil paints on a canvas ground. In addition, Qajar artists (some of whom studied in Europe) were quite capable of mining European royal portraiture for inspiration, adapting details, poses, and iconographic conventions. After the advent of photography in the 1840s, the new technology was enthusiastically taken up, not only as a medium in its own right, but also as a technical aid to the production of painted images.[20]

This receptivity to European art was nothing new. On the contrary, the artistic production of Iran has been historically marked by the reception, appropriation, and adaptation of non-indigenous iconographies, media, and techniques, especially when conditions were favorable to the circulation of artists and materials. In the fourteenth century, for example, the *Pax Mongolica* established by the trans-regional hegemony of various Mongol khanates fostered the rapid emergence of an Iranian aesthetic characterized by the adoption of Chinese stalwarts such as peonies and lotus motifs for ceramics, textiles, book painting, and architectural decoration. These developments have been consistently hailed by Islamicists as evidence for the emergence of a new visual language shaped by contemporary "global" circulations and characterized by innovation and vibrancy.[21]

If the hybridity of the art produced in Iran under Mongol rule has been traditionally seen as a breakthrough for Iranian artists, the reception of Qajar art has been less enthusiastic, as the entry on Qajar painting in the *Cambridge History of Iran* makes plain:

> Just as in the Mongol period of the fourteenth century Persian artists were busy absorbing Chinese ideas and conventions, so in our period they were

> struggling to accommodate themselves to the artistic canons of Europe. We cannot blame them, however deplorable the tendency may seem; increasing contact made such a development inevitable.[22]

While engagement with a non-indigenous Asian tradition is a sign of artistic inventiveness, the faltering reception of European artistic conventions is a sign of aesthetic decadence characterized by a loss of artistic autonomy.

The location of artistic greatness in a pre-colonial past is deeply rooted in a nostalgia that is elsewhere manifest in Orientalist painting, whose relationship to nineteenth-century colonial scholarship merits more attention than it has received. The emphasis on artistic autonomy and authenticity as anterior to contact with European culture is common to the reception of other forms of "non-Western" art (a category that is necessarily exclusionary); the phenomenon has been especially well explored in relation to the disciplinary study of African art, whose exclusions and occlusions are in many ways familiar.[23] Equally relevant is the location of cultural and market value in singularity, a quality guaranteed not only by geographic distance but also by temporal remoteness; as Steiner notes, canonicity is dependent on the (literal) death of the author/artist.[24]

The negative evaluations of Qajar art contrasts with the generally more positive assessments of art produced under the Ottomans of Turkey, the Mughals of India, or the Safavids of Iran during the fifteenth through seventeenth centuries that also drew upon European artistic conventions and forms.[25] While earlier Iranian artists might mine Chinese painting or even European prints and drawings with impunity (even adulation), the closer one gets to the time of the European narrator, the more negative the aesthetic evaluation of "hybrid" art-making traditions. This curious distinction between the distant past and recent memory reflects the status afforded the contemporary (as opposed to earlier) European images mined in Qajar art as not only anterior in a temporal sense, but culturally prior.

The phenomenon is by no means specific to histories of nineteenth-century Iran, on the contrary it is a generalized characteristic of Islamic (and other fields of "non-Western") art history. During the same period, for example, the aesthetic tastes of the Nawabs, the Muslim rulers of the nominally independent state of Avadh in northern India, were excoriated by European travelers and colonial officials, their striking combination of European neoclassicalism and indigenous forms read as vulgar signs not only of cultural but also of moral and political decadence. Writing in the last quarter of the nineteenth century, the British architectural historian James Fergusson described the "pseudo-Italian" palaces of Lucknow as resembling Napoleon III's remodeled Palais du Louvre and Tuileries Gardens in Paris, "but instead of the beautiful stone of Paris, all was brick and plaster; and instead of the appropriate details of that palace, the buildings surrounding the great court at Lucknow are generally two storeys in height and singularly various in design." In his description of the Begum Kothi, one of the component pavilions of the Lucknow palaces, Fergusson developed the theme:

> Like all the other specimens of Oriental Italian Architecture, it offends painfully, though less than most others, from the misapplication of the details of the Classical Orders. Of course no native of India can well understand either the origin or motive of the various parts of our Orders . . . It is, in fact, like a man trying to copy an inscription in a language he does not understand, and of which he does not know the alphabet . . . fashion supplies the Indian with those incentives to copying which we derive from association and education; and in the vain attempt to imitate his superiors, he has abandoned his own beautiful art to produce the strange jumble of vulgarity and bad taste we find at Lucknow and elsewhere.[26]

The sense of physical revulsion conveyed by this passage is reminiscent of an assessment of Qajar painting made by the Comte de Rochechouart in the 1860s: "as for the paintings that the Persians themselves produce, they make one gnash one's teeth."[27] The count locates the production of this sensation in the hybrid style of the *farangi* (i.e. Europeanizing) paintings then popular in Iran, which he sees as incompetent copies of second-rate European prints and engravings such as might adorn the shopfronts of provincial wig-makers:

> Having no idea of design, ignorant of the most simple laws of perspective, not understanding art in the way that we do and, consequently, lacking any critical faculty with which to focus their judgment and illuminate their taste, they copy the most flat and absurd compositions with minute care, and exert themselves to extinguish the brightness of their colors in order to approximate as closely as possible the gloomy and false color of polychromatic lithographs.[28]

For the count, as for other nineteenth-century commentators, a perceived absence of linear perspective, chiaroscuro, and verisimilitude in Qajar art obviated its classification as fine art, its interest lying primarily in a documentary value for the ethnographer.[29]

Caught between tradition and modernity (categories that are interdependent but generally assumed to be incommensurate), nineteenth-century Indian and Middle Eastern artists were condemned to perform derivative and reiterative parodies of European norms that they could only aspire to.[30] Consequently, both the absence and presence of forms, idioms, media, and techniques seen to have their origins in Europe constituted an aesthetic affront that simultaneously reaffirmed while undermining the privileged status afforded contemporary European artistic production. To borrow Homi Bhabha's term, as they oscillated between alterity and mimesis, the "inappropriate" objects of Qajar or Avadhi art manifested their perceived mimicry as both resemblance and menace.[31]

The attribution of the death of Islamic art (and the cultures that it represents metonymically) to the inappropriate or incompetent reception of European "influence" follows a trajectory from the narratives of nineteenth-century colonial historians down to their present-day successors. With the rise of neoconservative discourses emphasizing the failure of Muslims to make the transition to Euro-American modernity, this paradigm has once again gained currency. It appears for example in *What Went Wrong? Western Impact and Middle Eastern Response*, a recent work by the Princeton Islamicist and White House advisor Bernard Lewis, which purports to explain why Middle Eastern civilizations lag behind the West. Discussing the Nuruosmaniye Mosque in Istanbul, built in 1755, Lewis notes its "Italian Baroque" exterior decoration, concluding in familiar vein: "When a foreign influence appears in something as central to a culture as an imperial foundation and a cathedral-mosque, there is clearly some faltering of cultural self-confidence."[32]

The reductive absurdity of this analysis is apparent when one considers that just six decades later, on the eve of his rule over a burgeoning mercantile empire, the Prince Regent and future British monarch George IV commissioned the Royal Pavilion at Brighton (1815–1823), a palace that manifests an eclectic blend of Indian and Islamic forms.[33] However, the *Western* of Lewis's title emphasizes a uni-directional flow of "influence" rather than an active engagement with its objects, the passive reception of superficial signs of a modernity located elsewhere. Consequently, the resulting "hybrid" works constitute signs of a cultural bankruptcy that merits censure and, ultimately, amelioration.

Lewis's work highlights the utility of cultural history (including art history) in the ideological struggles that have gained in ferocity and pace since the atrocities of September 11, 2001. In the past five years, historians of Islamic art have come under increasing pressure to provide a cogent perspective on these struggles. In particular, the idea that Islamic art and art history can "bridge the cultural divide" between the Islamic world and "the West" has been mooted with increasing frequency.[34] Although it is upon the museum in particular that this burden has fallen, it is no less relevant to the classroom. Indeed a renewed interest in Islamic cultures after 2001 has been manifest in the funding of several new academic positions and in burgeoning student enrollment in survey classes on Islamic art, a phenomenon that has come under attack from neoconservative activists bemoaning the demise of the Western canon.[35]

Although utopian, the idea that Islamic art holds the potential to answer the many questions raised by the horrors witnessed nightly on our laptops and television screens is entirely understandable, especially given the paucity of critical analysis and reliable information in the media. However, the sundering of the pre-modern from the modern (and even postmodern) that is such a hallmark of the canon as currently constructed means that historians of Islamic Art are peculiarly ill-situated to address contemporary issues. Where we have attempted to do so, we have inevitably fallen back on the kind of reactionary nostalgia that is so marked in the reception of Qajar art. The problem is illustrated by an oddly equivocal statement attributed to Oliver Watson, then chief curator of the new Museum of Islamic Art in Doha: "People say that at this moment it is more important to recognize that the Middle East and the Islamic world was in its day as advanced culturally, as well as economically and militarily, as any country or empire in the world."[36] Like some recent international exhibitions of Islamic art, the qualification "in its day" begs a question that it cannot answer, but that provides an opening for the increasingly vocal purveyors of the "what went wrong" paradigm of Islamic history. To this extent, the peculiar end of Islamic art facilitates and reinforces narratives of fallen greatness that are central to the recuperative projects of contemporary neo-imperialism.

The ideological implications of the production of Islamic art as a closed system, a finished story, were highlighted by Donald Preziosi even before the events of 2001:

> Art-historical objects have thus always been object-lessons of documentary import insofar as they might be deployed or staged as cogent 'evidence' of the past's causal relationship to the present, enabling us to thereby articulate certain kinds of desirable (and undesirable) relations between ourselves and others. No longer overtly discussed in art-historical discourse in this regard is the (silent) contrast between European 'progress' in the arts in contradistinction to the coincident 'decline' of Europe's principal Other in early modern times, the (comparably multinational and multiethnic) world of Islam.[37]

As noted above, in art-historical narratives from the nineteenth century onwards, the decline of the arts in the Islamic world has been directly correlated to the rise of Europe and its "influence." The notion of a pre-lapsarian "golden age" corrupted through the inappropriate reception of European cultural forms is of course common to the ideologies of both Islamists and their neoconservative opponents, as is a tendency to mine the past for models of appropriate behavior that can be deployed in the present. In the terminal paragraph of *What Went Wrong?*, Bernard Lewis warns of the likelihood that the Middle East will be subject to "alien domination" should its peoples continue on their present path of a "grievance and victimhood," a prescient threat counterposed to the possibility that the inhabitants of the region "can once again make the Middle East, in modern times as it was in antiquity and in the Middle Ages, a major center of civilization."[38]

The threat and promise conveyed by this passage are predicated upon an implicit suggestion that the answers to the problems posed by "current events" can be found by careful contemplation of the past. Occluding the awkward verities that have helped shape the development of living Islamic cultures—colonialism and its legacy, modernity, postmodernity, and globalization—this displacement permits the espousal of a paradoxical "back-to-the-future" model of Islamic modernity. As Neil MacGregor, the director of the British Museum, put it recently:

> The new interim government in Iraq will have to consider how it defines Iraq's identity. And it will be surprising if it does not turn, as every other government in the Middle East has turned, to historical precedents to define the wished-for future. There is nowhere better to survey those precedents than the British Museum.[39]

Even in a world where museum directors are under constant pressure to demonstrate the relevance of their collections, this is a remarkable claim. Championing the utility of the instantiated past as a resource to be deployed in the present, it recalls Preziosi's suggestion that the utility of art history since its emergence as a discipline has lain in its production of a past:

> *that could be effectively placed under systematic observation for use in staging and politically transforming—that is, performing—the present.* A past that could be imagined as bearing a causative relation to the present, yet at the same time a pre-modernity that could be imagined to be a detached object, 'independent' of the analytic gaze of the present.[40]

James Clifford has noted that the museum often possesses the qualities of a contact zone between cultures, a quality manifest in "an ongoing historical, political, moral, *relationship*—a power-charged set of exchanges, of push and pull."[41] This push and pull engages the unstable social identities of material culture, a dialectic of reification and consumption that produces "truths of seduction rather than presence."[42] Over the past five years, these phenomena have been increasingly manifest in the economic and institutional entanglements of Islamic art history with contemporary global politics, and in the instrumental deployment of museological archives to bolster specific representations of Islam and Islamic cultures.

The former point is illustrated by *Palace and Mosque*, an exhibition held at the National Gallery of Art in Washington, DC between 2004 and 2005.[43] This was a traveling exhibition of select objects from the collections of the Victoria and Albert Museum in London, one of the most significant European collections of Islamic art, whose galleries were undergoing a $9.7 million renovation funded by the president of a Saudi Arabian automobile conglomerate. The chronological range of the exhibition conformed to the canon, although accompanying publicity material put the end of Islamic art as 1918, in the wake of the First World War and the subsequent emergence of secular regimes in Iran and Turkey. The cost of the exhibition was underwritten by Prince Bandar bin Sultan, Saudi ambassador to Washington (and now Secretary General of the National Security Council of Saudi Arabia). The prince is a controversial figure whose relationship with the Bush family reflects the historical entanglements of American oil corporations and conservative Islamic movements.[44] At a time when the Saudi star had fallen to an all-time low in the United States (with the notable exception of the White House), Prince Bandar's sponsorship of the exhibition was part of an extended public relations exercise designed to improve his own standing and that of the regime that he represented. To that end, it manifested an eclectic and ecumenical vision of historical Islam rather than the considerably more circumscribed contemporary variant promulgated in the Saudi kingdom.

The exigencies of contemporary global politics also framed the conception and reception of *Turks: A Journey of a Thousand Years, 600–1600*, a major exhibition held at the Royal Academy of Arts in London in 2005. The objects comprising *Turks* illustrated the migrations of Turkic peoples from Central Asia with a range of objects dating from the seventh to the seventeenth century. Despite the pre-modern focus in the choice of artifacts, this was a trajectory that led inexorably westwards, toward the project of European modernity. As the British Prime Minister Tony Blair wrote in a foreword to the catalog:

> the long and complex journey [of the Turkic peoples] through Central Asia, the Middle East and, of course, Europe is something we should understand and reflect upon. It demonstrates that the interaction of different cultures in our world is crucial if we are to survive.

Writing alongside the British premier, the prime minister of Turkey Recep Tayyip Erdoğan was less coy:

> Cultural diversity is a source of richness for all nations. This exhibition comes at a most propitious time, as Turkey's aspirations toward membership of the European family of nations in the European Union are centre stage. I am confident that this fascinating exhibition will further enhance mutual understanding, tolerance and peace.[45]

Such projects do not always obscure the ideological crucible of their own making. Announcing the elevation of the Islamic art section of the Louvre into a new department of Islamic art in 2002, the French Minister of Culture and Communications Jean-Jacques Aillagon explained:

> Obviously, this has a political dimension . . . It's a way of saying we believe in the equality of civilizations . . . Many immigrant youths do not fully adhere

> to our culture, nor do they know their own culture of origin. It's good to show that the republic respects, displays and studies this culture.[46]

Three years later, his successor Renaud Donnedieu de Vabres elaborated:

> In a world where violence expresses itself individually and collectively . . . where hate erupts and imposes its expression of terror, you dare to affirm the conviction that is yours—that is ours—that the dialog of peoples and cultures, the richness of patrimonies, the values of sharing are the responses of intelligence to the bitter experience of conflicts.[47]

A common trope in these attempts to press the objects of Islamic art into the service of the state or super-regional ideological projects is an emphasis (manifest or latent) on the ability of medieval artifacts to bolster or construct a "true" notion of Islamic faith and culture. In the recent heated controversy over caricatures of the Prophet Muhammad published in Danish (and later other European) newspapers, museum holdings from Washington to Edinburgh, London to Istanbul functioned as an archive which could be deployed to confront protesting Muslims with the fact that pre-modern Muslims had in fact created images of the Prophet. The contemporary geopolitical context against which the global controversy unfolded and which was central to its meaning was largely displaced by a retrospective emphasis on a past age when images were apparently less contentious.[48] According to a statement issued by the Freer Gallery of Art and the Arthur M. Sackler Gallery in Washington, DC and widely quoted in the media:

> Contrary to widespread assumptions today, the traditional arts of Islam, whether Sunni or Shiite, often did reverently depict the prophet, as abundantly attested by manuscript illuminations ranging in time from the thirteenth to the eighteenth century, and in space from Turkey to Bengal. Pictorial representations of the prophet remain accepted by many Shiites today, although they have been generally frowned upon by most Sunnis since about the eighteenth century.[49]

Although not specified, this *terminus post quem* coincides with the rise of European colonialism and the culturally conservative strain of Sunni Islam favored in Saudi Arabia and elsewhere, events that are not unrelated. The point was not lost on at least one commentator, who connected this angst about figuration to a decline in cultural confidence and a concomitant recourse to more retrogressive modes of Islamic belief: "What their paintings show is this: Once upon a time—in the era of the caliphs and the sultans and the shahs, when the faithful felt triumphant, and courtly learning blossomed—the prophet *did* appear in great Islamic art."[50]

The implicit contrast between "modern" (intolerant) interpretations and manifestations of Islam and their more tolerant (and better informed) predecessors figures the objects of Islamic art as valorized repositories of an originary Islam corrupted through time, accepting the premise of "fundamentalist" Muslims, but inverting its meaning. Critiques of the latter often reiterate European criticisms of nineteenth- and twentieth-century art-making practices in the Islamic lands for their lack of authenticity in blending "tradition" and "modernity," two states of being usually spatialized as the local and the (Euro-American) global, or temporalized as past and present. In a recent critique of this position, the anthropologist Talal Asad observed:

> This kind of description paints Islamic movements as being somehow inauthentically traditional on the assumption that 'real tradition' is unchanging, repetitive, and non-rational. In this way, these movements cannot be understood on their own terms as being at once modern and traditional, both authentic and creative at the same time.[51]

The cartoon controversy highlights the potential utility of Islamic art in attempts to locate prescriptive models for the ideal Muslim citizen. In keeping with the retrospective tendencies discussed above, these models are found in a valorized past rather than a turbulent present marked by new patterns of engagement with both tradition and modernity. Donating $20 million for the construction of the new Islamic art gallery at the Louvre in July 2005, the Saudi prince Walid bin Talal predicted that the gallery would "assist in the true meaning of Islam, a religion of humanity, forgiveness and acceptance of other cultures."[52] The prince's words mirror those of President George W. Bush in the wake of the September 11th attacks: "The face of terror is not the true faith of Islam. That's not what Islam is all about. Islam is peace. These terrorists don't represent peace. They represent evil and war."[53] As the author of the passage cited above put it: "though museums often seem distant from the news, this isn't always so."[54]

The engagement of the field with wealthy patrons seeking political capital from the association has a long history—a particularly influential exhibition of Persian Art held in London in 1931 was, for example, co-sponsored by the British monarch George V and Reza Shah Pahlavi of Iran, an ambitious army officer who had deposed the last of the Qajar rulers six years previously.[55] What is new and particularly disturbing is the way in which the objects of Islamic art are increasingly co-opted into an emergent (if embryonic) exhibitionary regime that not only aims to project a model of peaceful coexistence but to locate and provide an appropriate model of Islam itself. The increasing pressures on secular institutions to bolster and promote the right kind of Islam (as defined by such neutral observers as President Bush and Prime Minister Blair) are comparable to and stem from the same sources as contemporary pressures on Muslim communities to produce the right kind of Muslim, or universities in the United States to produce the right sort of Islamicist.[56]

The deployment of Islamic art and its (primarily Euro-American) histories to this end engages a performative quality that Donald Preziosi has noted as a general characteristic of art history, whose objects are "legible as object-lessons; as 'illustrating' (or 'representing') desirable and undesirable social relations in the (perpetually) modernizing nation."[57] The slippage between categories of religious identity and cultural identification referred to at the outset is directly relevant to the utility of Islamic art in the high-stakes public relations game that is integral to the war on a constantly shifting kaleidoscope of abstractions (evil, fundamentalism, terror, etc.). Equally relevant is a canonical (and often awkward) emphasis on Islamic art as a predominantly "secular" art produced for and patronized by temporal rulers whose piety was nominal and (with rare exceptions) confined to appropriate domains.[58]

We are confronted here with a series of major paradoxes: a sub-field of art history marked by the eschewal of any engagement with the problems of modernity and their political ramifications is increasingly situated within contemporary Euro-American debates about the nature of Islam; with the collaboration of avowedly secularist governments and Saudi princes, the museum—an institution founded on the secularization of religious fetishes—assumes a pedagogical role in providing models not only of cultural understanding, but also of authentic religious belief; in a global conflict in which the opponents of the New World Order are often said to be characterized by a medieval mindset, the antique objects of the museum point the way toward a brighter future in which the right kind of Islam will prevail, modernized, and rejuvenated under the aegis of Euro-American tutelage.

For those of us uncomfortable with these developments, there is a pressing need to imbue the narrative of Islamic art with a degree of reflexivity that is currently lacking. Challenging "the fictitious creed of immaculate classification" that facilitates the co-option of the materialized past in service of a "New World Order," we need to adumbrate synchronic histories of intention and origin with diachronic accounts of circulation, consumption, and reception.[59] Instead of occluding the entangled histories of colonialism, capitalism, and the canon, it is essential to explore the ways in which these imbrications are manifest in the practices of collecting and re-presentation through which the field was constituted, and the contentions that currently shape it.

The most obvious way of doing this is to broaden the canon, including artists and works that problematize the history and reception of Islamic art since the nineteenth century. The nostalgia that is central to the latter might, for example, be explored through the work of Osman Hamdi (d. 1910) who trained as an Orientalist painter in Paris, practiced in the late Ottoman state, founded the Academy of Fine Arts in Istanbul in 1883, and helped shape a nascent Ottoman museological practice that he also drew upon in his work.[60] Hamdi's variant of Orientalist nostalgia is ambiguous in its engagements with modernity: claimed as a site of resistance to the more outré conventions of the genre within which it operated, it might equally be read as a form of self-Orientalization. In a similar vein, the complex intersection between Orientalist scholarship on Islamic art and medieval revivalism in Islamic architecture might productively be investigated.[61]

Among the very many *contemporary* artists whose work engages the binary disjunctions between the historical and the contemporary, the local and the global is Shadafarin Ghadirian, a young Tehran-based photographer. Ghadirian stages photographic tableaux based on Qajar-era studio photographs of women but marked by the intrusive signs of a global modernity (Coke cans, for example, or mountain bikes) that draw attention to their status as meta-images of a contemporary cosmopolitanism.[62] This deployment of strategic anachronism offers a paradigm that opens the potential for academics, curators, and scholars to treat the objects of "Islamic" art not as teleological markers in a master narrative that occludes the circumstances of its own production (and ongoing reproduction), but as contested objects within a disjunctive and tendentious discourse.

Paradoxically perhaps for an institution deeply implicated in the history of European colonial adventures, the British Museum offers another model for rethinking the traditional canon. One of the very few institutions whose Islamic collections include both pre-modern and modern art from the Islamic world, since the 1980s the museum has been acquiring contemporary works on paper. Some of these were seen in the recent exhibition *Word into Art: Artists of the Modern Middle East*. Reflecting a widespread focus on calligraphy (generally seen as the most "Islamic" of arts) as a medium for negotiating "tradition" and "modernity," the exhibition problematized the term Islamic, using the ambiguities and ambivalences associated with it to explore the way in which contemporary global and local politics have inflected artistic production in the Middle East over the past three or four decades.[63]

In its frank engagements with contemporary politics, the London exhibition stood in marked contrast to *Without Boundaries: Seventeen Ways of Looking*, an exhibition held at MoMA in New York earlier in 2006. The exhibition was a curiously apolitical attempt to explore contemporary artistic engagements with "Islamic" tradition. Despite director Glenn Lowry's rather oblique reference to "the tension between old and new," any reference to contemporary politics or the ongoing wars on Afghanistan and Iraq (a potential source of controversy and thus financial sanction) were fastidiously avoided in both exhibition and catalog.[64] Originally subtitled *Fifteen Ways of Looking*, the exhibition focused on questions of identity, tradition, and modernity. It included work by fifteen artists of varied Middle Eastern backgrounds and two American artists whose heritage was not Middle Eastern and who were not influenced by artists from the Islamic world, but were said to "share interests, references, and strategies with them."[65] Among the latter were Bill Viola and Mike

Kelley, whose contribution consisted of *Untitled* (1996–1997), a silk rug handwoven to the artist's specifications in the Iranian city of Ghom. The accompanying wall label informed the viewer the green background and the central shamrock was an allusion to his Irish heritage, and that although "this is the one object in the exhibition that most closely follows an Islamic prototype," in its "impurity" it subverted binary notions of identity. In common with their colonialist predecessors, such evaluations emphasize questions of hybridity, but invert its meaning: formerly excoriated as decadent, the blending of "traditional" and "modern" forms, iconographies and idioms is now valorized as subversive. Aware of the dangers of privileging the claims of global modernity, in her accompanying essay Fereshteh Daftari emphasized not only the disjunctive relations to works produced in the pre-modern Islamic world, but the fact that many of these "traditional" works were themselves "hybrid," a term that would bear more interrogation than it generally receives.[66]

As these attempts to grapple with questions of identity, modernity, and the nature of "Islamic" art suggest, the problems discussed above can be addressed neither *merely* by expanding the chronological range of the canon nor by introducing more material and qualifying adjectives. Although the term "modern Islamic art" has entered circulation, it is if anything more fraught than its generally accepted predecessor.[67]

If the expansion or reconfiguration of the canon promises an amelioration rather than a solution, fantasies about abolishing, exploding, or transcending it are not only utopian but have the potential to lead us back to where we started.[68] I am not, for example, in agreement with James Elkins when he suggests that the aporias of the canon might be addressed by a "decisive break" with the "western" institutions and paradigms that have historically structured the discipline of art history, and that now have a global reach.[69] Indeed, Elkins's critiques of post-colonial theorists for their embrace of "western" epistemologies and academic institutions and their concomitant failure to recuperate some authentically nativist model of art criticism is not only curiously immune to questions of knowledge/power but comes perilously close to the essentialist demands for authenticity critiqued above.[70]

A more productive approach is suggested by James D. Herbert in an essay that notes the impossibility of situating an art-historical practice within the elusive "post" of post-colonial:

> We can instead abandon this fantasy of escape. What if, rather than collapsing hopelessly back into colonialism at the end of our argument, we concede from the start that scholarly discourse necessarily and productively operates from a base within the colonial? The ironic turn of postcolonialism then occurs inside the ideological space of the colonial. It thereby opens up the complexities and ambiguities of that ideology; it recognizes a multivocality that allows for the possibility of resistance and disruption from within—both in the past and in the present.[71]

Herbert's suggestion resonates with the post-colonial project of "provincializing Europe," a rethinking of modernity and its epistemologies through local histories of "translation" and transformation, and the fresh perspectives that they offer on modernity from what is usually thought of as its fringes.[72] The undertaking holds the potential to undermine the identity of temporal anteriority and cultural priority that is central to reductive histories of reception.

A similar scenario has been envisaged by Ikem Okoye, who imagines the "possibility of framing art history simultaneously from a multiplicity of positions and locations" rather than privileging a single Euro-American perspective.[73] Oleg Grabar has noted the potential utility of Islamic art history for understanding pre-modern European art, and its particular abilities to contribute to contemporary theoretical concerns within the discipline.[74] Following Okoye's lead, there is no reason that such contributions should be restricted to additive inclusion rather than occasioning a more radical reorientation, one that might see a history or historical critique of Italian Renaissance art from the perspective of an Ottomanist, for example, or a course on modernism (including its American European variants) offered from the perspective of a specialist in Iranian modernism.[75]

Any response to the challenges posed by the pressures exerted on the field of Islamic art history by contemporary geopolitics will inevitably require the development of new skill sets. It may even lead to the fragmentation of the field as it is currently constituted. This is an eventuality that many would find unappealing within an academy subjugated to market forces and fierce competition for an intra-disciplinary division of spoils.[76] However, what has been aptly dubbed the "unwieldy" sub-field of Islamic art history is in many ways a fractal of the "unruly" discipline as a whole.[77] Its ultimate fate may be therefore inseparable from that of the universal narratives in which it is currently imbedded, narratives whose imminent demise has been repeatedly predicted over the past decades, however prematurely.[78]

## Notes

1 Sir Banister Fletcher, *A History of Architecture on the Comparative Method*, 16th edn (London, B.T. Batsford Ltd., 1954) pp. iii, 934–964. For similar points made in relation to the study of Byzantine Art see Robert Nelson: "Living on the Byzantine Borders of Western Art," *Gesta* 35(1), (1996): 3–11. See also Oleg Grabar, "Islamic Art and Archaeology," in Leonard Binder, ed., *The Study of the Middle East, Research and Scholarship in the Humanities and the Social Sciences* (New York: John Wiley and Sons, 1976) p. 242.

2 Fred S. Kleiner, Christian J. Mamiya, and Richard J. Tansey, *Gardner's Art Through the Ages* (Orlando: Harcourt College Publishers, 2001) pp. 359–384. H.W. Janson and Anthony F. Janson, *History of Art* (New York: Prentice Hall Inc., 2001).

3 Janson, *History of Art*, p. 982.

4 For a range of perspectives on this problem see Mehmet Aga-Oglu, "Remarks on the Character of Islamic Art," *The Art Bulletin* 36(3) (1954): 175–202; Oleg Grabar, "Islamic Art 1.1: Definitions," *The Dictionary of Art*, vol. 16 (New York: Grove's Dictionaries,

1996) pp. 99–101; Oliver Leaman, *Islamic Aesthetics: An Introduction* (Edinburgh: Edinburgh University Press, 2004); Coco Ferguson, "Islamic Arts at a Crossroads," *Bidoun: Arts and Culture from the Middle East* (Fall, 2004): 52; Judith Ernst, "The Problem of Islamic Art," in Miriam Cooke and Bruce B. Lawrence, eds, *Muslim Networks from Hajj to HipHop* (Chapel Hill, NC: University of North Carolina Press, 2005) pp. 107–131.

5 See, for example, Oktay Aslanapa, *Turkish Art and Architecture* (New York: Praeger Publishers, 1971); Wijdan Ali, *The Arab Contribution to Islamic Art from the Seventh to the Fourteenth Century* (Cairo: American University Press, 1999). For a discussion of these issues see J.M. Rogers, *The Uses of Anachronism: on Cultural and Methodological Diversity in Islamic Art* (London: School of Oriental and African Studies, University of London, 1994) pp. 8–9; Sheila S. Blair and Jonathan M. Bloom, "The Mirage of Islamic Art: Reflections on the Study of an Unwieldy Field," *The Art Bulletin* 85(1) (2003): 152–184.

6 Barbara Brend, *Islamic Art* (Cambridge, MA: Harvard University Press, 1991); Robert Hillenbrand, *Islamic Architecture: Form, Function and Meaning* (Edinburgh: Edinburgh University Press, 1994); Sheila S. Blair and Jonathan M. Bloom, *The Art and Architecture of Islam 1250–1800* (New Haven, CT: Yale University Press, 1996); Jonathan Bloom and Sheila Blair, *Islamic Arts* (London: Phaidon Press, 1997); Robert Irwin, *Islamic Art in Context: Art, Architecture, and the Literary World* (New York: H.N. Abrams, 1997); Robert Hillenbrand, *Islamic Art and Architecture* (New York: Thames and Hudson, 1999); Richard Ettinghausen, Oleg Grabar, and Marilyn Jenkins-Madina, *Islamic Art and Architecture 650–1250* (New Haven, CT: Yale University Press, 2001). Arabic survey books on Islamic art appeared as early as the 1930s; see, for example, Zaki Muhammad Hasan, *Funūn al-Islām* (Cairo: Matba'at al-Nahdah al-Misrīyah, 1948).

7 Stephen Vernoit, "Islamic Art and Architecture: An Overview of Scholarship and Collecting, *c.*1850–*c.*1950," in Vernoit, ed., *Discovering Islamic Art: Scholars, Collectors and Collections, 1850–1950* (London, I.B. Tauris, 2000) pp. 1–61.

8 Michael Camille, "Prophets, Canons and Promising Monsters," *The Art Bulletin* 78(2) (1996): 200.

9 Nasser Rabbat, "Islamic Architecture as a Field of Historical Enquiry," *Architectural Design* 74(6) (2004): 19.

10 Vernoit, *Discovering Islamic Art*; Stephen Vernoit, *Occidentalism: Islamic Art in the 19th Century* (New York: Nour Foundation, 1997); Stephen Vernoit and Doris Behrens-Abouseif, eds, *Islamic Art in the Nineteenth Century: Tradition, Innovation and Eclecticism* (Leiden: Brill, 2006).

11 Vernoit, *Occidentalism*, pp. 13–14.

12 Oleg Grabar, "Reflections on the Study of Islamic Art," *Muqarnas* 1 (1983): 5.

13 Markus Brüderlin, ed., *Ornament and Abstraction: the Dialogue between Non-Western, Modern and Contemporary Art* (New Haven, CT: Yale University Press, 2002); James Clifford, *The Predicament of Culture: Twentieth Century Ethnography, Literature, and Art* (Cambridge, MA: Harvard University Press, 1988): 189–214.

14 Cited in Blair and Bloom, *Art and Architecture of Islam*, p. 311.

15 "Une oeuvre . . . qui . . . fera mentir avec éclat ceux qui prétendent que l'art se meurt au pays musulman, comme la rose desséchée noircit et s'effeuille aux mains fatales des lépreux:" Mustapha Orif, "De l'art indigène' à l'art algérien," *Actes de la recherche en science sociales* 75 (1988): 37; Roger Benjamin, "Colonial Tutelage to Nationalist Affirmation: Mammeri and Racim Painters of the Maghrib," in Jill Beaulieu and Mary Roberts, eds, *Orientalism's Interlocutors: Painting, Architecture, Photography* (Durham, NC: Duke University Press, 2002) pp. 45, 60–68.

16 Vernoit, *Occidentalism*, p. 12.
17 In colonial Algiers of the 1930s, for example, the decline of Islamic art was attributed to 'foreign' imports and their corrupting influence on the purity of 'local' forms: Zeynep Çelik, "'Islamic' Art and Architecture in French Colonial Discourse: Algeria, 1930," in Irene A. Bierman, ed., *The Experience of Islamic Art on the Margins of Islam* (Reading: Ithaca, 2005) p. 106.
18 *The Dictionary of Art* (New York: Grove Dictionaries, 1996), Vol. 15, pp. 896–923; Vol. 16, pp. 94–561. For a discussion of this arrangement see Oleg Grabar, "On the Study of Islamic Art," *Journal of the David Collection* 1 (2003): 21.
19 Layla S. Diba with Maryam Ekhtiar, *Royal Persian Paintings: The Qajar Epoch 1785–1925* (London: I.B. Tauris, 1998); Julian Raby, *Qajar Portraits* (London: Azimuth Editions, 1999); Bloom and Blair, *Islamic Arts*, pp. 417–419.
20 This subject was explored by David Roxburgh in a paper entitled "Intersections between painting and photography in Qajar Iran" in the panel *Islamic Art: Between 'Western' and 'Non-Western,'* College Art Association annual meeting, New York, February 22, 2003.
21 Linda Komaroff and Stefano Carboni, eds, *The Legacy of Genghis Khan: Courtly Art and Culture in Western Asia, 1256–1353* (New Haven, CT: Yale University Press, 2002) pp. 168–225.
22 Basil Robinson, "Persian Painting under the Zand and Qājār Dynasties," in *The Cambridge History of Iran*, Vol. 7: *From Nadir Shah to the Islamic Republic* (Cambridge, MA: Cambridge University Press, 1991) p. 870. See also Oliver Watson, "Almost Hilariously Bad: Iranian Pottery in the Nineteenth Century," in Behrens-Abouseif and Vernoit, *Islamic Art in the Nineteenth Century*, pp. 333–362, especially p. 339.
23 Ruth B. Phillips and Christopher B. Steiner, "Art, Authenticity, and the Baggage of Cultural Enounter," in Phillips and Steiner, eds, *Unpacking Culture: Art and Commodity in Colonial and Postcolonial Worlds* (Berkeley, CA: University of California Press, 1999) pp. 9–10; Christopher B. Steiner, "The Taste of Angels in the Art of Darkness: Fashioning the Canon of African Art," in Elizabeth Mansfield, ed., *Art History and its Institutions: Foundations of a Discipline* (London: Routledge, 2002) p. 134.
24 Christopher B. Steiner, "Can the Canon Burst," *The Art Bulletin* 78(2) (1996): 215. See also Ruth B. Phillips, "Why not Tourist Art? Significant Silences in Native American Museum Representations," in Gyan Prakash, ed., *After Colonialism: Imperial Histories and Postcolonial Displacements* (Princeton, NJ: Princeton University Press, 1995) p. 115; Fred R. Myers, "Introduction: The Empire of Things," in Myers, ed., *The Empire of Things: Regimes of Value and Material Culture* (Santa Fe: School of American Research Press, 2001) p. 10.
25 Milo C. Beach, "The Gulshan Album and its European Sources," *Bulletin Museum of Fine Arts, Boston*, 63) (1965): 63–89; Ebba Koch, "The Influence of the Jesuit Missions on Symbolic Representation of the Mughal Emperors," in *The Akbar Mission and Miscellaneous Studies*, C. W. Troll, ed., *Islam in India: Studies and Commentaries*, 1 (New Delhi, 1982) pp. 14–29; Gauvin Bailey, *The Jesuits and the Grand Mogul: Renaissance Art at the Imperial Court of India, 1580–1630* (Washington, DC: Smithsonian Institution, 1998); Julian Raby, "Pride and Prejudice: Mehmed the Conqueror and the Portrait Medal," in J.G. Pollard, ed., *Italian Medals* (Washington, DC: National Gallery of Art, 1987) pp. 171–194; Sheila Canby, "Farangi Saz: the Impact of Europe on Safavid Painting," *Silk and Stone: The Art of Asia*, Jill Tilden, ed. (London: HALI Publications, 1996) pp. 46–59.
26 James Fergusson, *A History of Indian and Eastern Architecture* (London: John Murray, 1910) Vol. 2, pp. 326–328; Rosie Llewellyn-Jones, *A Fatal Friendship: the Nawabs, the British and the City of Lucknow* (New Delhi: Oxford University Press, 1999) pp. 235–240.

27 "Quant aux peintures que les Persans produisent eux-mêmes, c'est à faire grincer les dents:" Julien M. de Rochechouart, *Souvenir d'un voyage en Perse* (Paris, Challamel Ainé, 1867) p. 261.

28 "N'ayant aucune notion de dessin, ignorant les lois les plus simples de la perspective et ne comprenant pas l'art à notre manière, et par conséquent, n'ayant aucune critique pour fixer leur jugement et éclairer leur goût, ils copient avec un soin minutieux les compositions les plus plates et les plus absurdes, et s'efforcent d'éteindre l'éclat de leur coloris afin de se rapprocher le plus possible de la couleur morne et fausse des lithographies coloriées:" Rochechouart, *Souvenir*, pp. 264–265.

29 Vernoit, *Occidentalism*, p. 12.

30 Shiva Balaghi, "Iranian Visual Arts in 'The Century of Machinery, Speed, and the Atom': Rethinking Modernity," in Shiva Balaghi and Lynn Gumpert, eds, *Picturing Iran: Art, Society and Revolution* (New York: I.B. Tauris, 2002) pp. 23–24. On the interrelationships between modernity and tradition see Nicholas B. Dirks, "History as a Sign of the Modern," *Public Culture* 2(2) (1980): 27.

31 Homi K. Bhabha, *The Location of Culture* (New York: Routledge, 1994) p. 86.

32 Bernard Lewis, *What Went Wrong? Western Impact and Middle Eastern Response* (Oxford: Oxford University Press, 2002) pp. 137, 148–149. See also Edward Said's response: "Impossible Histories: Why the Many Islams Cannot Be Simplified," *Harper's Magazine*, July 1, 2002.

33 Stefan Koppelkamm, *Der imaginäre Orient: Exotische Bauten des achtzehnten und neunzehnten Jahrhunderts in Europa* (Berlin: Willhelm Ernst and Sohn, 1987) pp. 40–57.

34 Alan Riding, "An Essay: Islamic Art as Mediator for Cultures in Confrontation," *The New York Times*, April 6, 2004.

35 "Ironically, instead of ensuring that students understand the unique contributions of American and Western civilizations—the civilization under attack—universities are rushing to add courses on Islamic and Asian cultures," Jerry L. Martin and Anne D. Neal, eds, *Defending Civilization: How our Universities are Failing America and What Can Be Done about It?* (Washington, DC: Defense of Civilization Fund, November 2001) p. 7.

36 Riding, "Islamic Art as a Mediator."

37 Donald Preziosi, "Performing Modernity: The Art of Art History," in Amelia Jones and Andrew Stephenson, eds, *Performing the Body/Performing the Text* (New York: Routledge, 1999) p. 37.

38 Lewis, *What Went Wrong?*, pp. 159–160.

39 Neil MacGregor, "In the Shadow of Babylon," *The Guardian*, June 14, 2004, p. 12.

40 Ibid., p. 31, emphasis original. As if to underline this insistence upon a critical distance that is not merely geographic and temporal but also cultural, a recent survey of Islamic art history by two leading scholars in the field notes the declining role of "white non-Muslims," warning that "The interests and opinions of those seeking to understand their own heritage can be very different from those who are seeking to understand and explain something they consider distant in time and place:" Blair and Bloom, "The Mirage of Islamic Art," p. 176.

41 James Clifford, *Routes: Travel and Translation in the Late Twentieth Century* (Cambridge, MA: Harvard University Press, 1997) p. 192.

42 Nicholas Thomas, *Entangled Objects: Exchange, Material Culture, and Colonialism in the Pacific* (Cambridge, MA: Harvard University Press, 1991) p. 176.

43 Tim Stanley, *Palace and Mosque: Islamic Art from the Middle East* (London: Victoria and Albert Museum, 2004).

44 Timothy Mitchell, "McJihad: Islam in the U.S. Global Order," *Social Text* 20(4) (2002): 1–3.

45 David J. Roxburgh, ed., *Turks: A Journey of a Thousand Years, 600–1600* (London: Royal Academy of Arts, 2005) p. 9. A similar theme informed an exhibition held at the Linden-Museum in Stuttgart in 2003–2004, which traced the 'long way of the Turks' from their status as warriors of the Central Asian steppe to that of *gastarbeiters* in modern Germany: Johannes Kalter, *Der lange Weg der Türken: 1500 Jahre türkische Kultur* (Stuttgart: Irene Schönberger, 2003).

46 Riding, "Islamic Art as a Mediator."

47 John Tagliabue, "Louvre Gets $20 Million for New Islamic Wing," *The New York Times*, July 28, 2005.

48 Tariq Ramadan, "Cartoon Conflicts," *The Guardian*, Monday February 6, 2006. For an exception noting the difference between representation and caricature see Holland Cotter, "What Does Islam Look Like?," *The New York Times*, February 26, 2006.

49 Paul Richard, "In Art Museums, Portraits Illuminate a Religious Taboo," *The Washington Post*, Tuesday, February 14, 2006. See also Stephen Bates, "An Internalized Image," *The Guardian*, February 2, 2006.

50 Richard, "In Art Museums."

51 Talal Asad, "Modern Power and the Reconfiguration of Religious Traditions," *Stanford Electronic Humanities Review*, special issue, *Contested Polities: Religious Disciplines and Structures of Modernity* 5(1) (1996): http://www.stanford.edu/group/SHR/5–1/text/asad.html (consulted August 6, 2006).

52 Tagliabue, "Louvre Gets $20 Million." On the ambiguities associated with the co-option of Islamic art in this way see Holland Cotter, "Beauty in the Shadow of Violence," *The New York Times*, October 17, 2001.

53 Remarks by the President at Islamic Center of Washington, DC, September 17, 2001: http://www.whitehouse.gov/infocus/ramadan/islam.html (consulted August 6, 2006).

54 Richard, "In Art Museums."

55 Blair and Bloom, "The Mirage of Islamic Art," p. 155.

56 Mahmood Mamdani, *Good Muslim, Bad Muslim: America, the Cold War, and the Roots of Terror* (New York: Pantheon Books, 2004).

57 Preziosi, "Performing Modernity," p. 32.

58 Richard Ettinghausen, "Interaction and Integration in Islamic art," in Gustave E. von Grunebaum, ed., *Unity and Variety in Muslim Civilization* (Chicago, IL: University of Chicago Press, 1955) p. 109.

59 Steiner, "Can the Canon Burst?," p. 217. See also Zainab Bahrani, *The Graven Image: Representation in Babylonia and Assyria* (Philadelphia, PA: University of Pennsylvania Press, 2003) pp. 40–49.

60 Zeynep Çelik, "Speaking Back to Orientalist Discourse," in Jill Beaulieu and Mary Roberts, eds, *Orientalism's Interlocutors: Painting, Architecture, Photography* (Durham, NC: Duke University Press, 2002) pp. 19–42; Wendy M.K. Shaw, *Possessors and Possessed: Museums, Archaeology and the Visualization of History in the Late Ottoman Empire* (Berkeley, CA: University of California Press, 2003).

61 Robert Ilbert and Mercedes Volait, "Neo-Arabic Renaissance in Egypt, 1870–1930," *Mimar* 13 (1984): 26–34; Donald Malcolm Reid, "Cultural Imperialism and Nationalism: the Struggle to Define and Control the Heritage of Arab Art in Egypt," *International Journal of Middle East Studies* 24 (1992): 57–76; Nasser Rabbat, "The Formation of the

Neo-Mamluk Style in Modern Egypt," in Martha Pollock, ed., *The Education of the Architect: Historiography, Urbanism, and the Growth of Architectural Knowledge* (Cambridge, MA: The MIT Press, 1997) pp. 363–386.

62 Rose Issa, Ruyin Pakbaz, and Daryush Shayegan, eds, *Iranian Contemporary Art* (London: Barbican Art, Booth-Clibborn, 2001) pp. 106–109, 130.

63 Venetia Porter, *Word into Art: Artists of the Modern Middle East* (London: British Museum Press, 2006). See also, Silvia Naef, "Reexploring Islamic Art: Modern and Contemporary Creation in the Arab World and its Relation to the Artistic Past," *Res* 43 (2003): 163–174.

64 Glenn D. Lowry, "Gained in Translation," *ARTNews*, March (2006): 122. This led to public criticisms by Shirin Neshat and Emily Jacir, two of the artists whose work appeared in the exhibition, that any political content had been "whitewashed": Tyler Green, "MoMA Keeps the Walls Clean; Islamic Show Sans Politics," *New York Observer*, April 3, 2006.

65 Fereshteh Daftari, "Islamic or Not," in *Without Boundary: Seventeen Ways of Looking* (New York: MoMA, 2006) p. 10. See also Daftari, "Beyond Islamic Roots—Beyond Modernism," *Res* 43 (2003): 175–186.

66 Daftari, "Islamic or Not?," pp. 14, 18. See also Homi Bhabha's essay "Another Country" in the *Without Boundary* catalog, pp. 30–35. For some of the problems associated with the term see Robert J.C. Young, *Colonial Desire: Hybridity in Theory, Culture, and Race* (New York: Routledge, 1995) and Tony K. Stewart and Carl W. Ernst, "Syncretism," in Peter J. Claus and Margaret Mills, eds, *South Asian Folklore: An Encyclopedia* (New York: Routledge, 2003) pp. 586–588.

67 Wijdan Ali, "The Status of Islamic Art in the Twentieth Century," *Muqarnas* 9 (1992): 186–188; Ali, *Modern Islamic Art: Development and Continuity* (Gainesville: University Press of Florida, 1997).

68 For differing perspectives on the question of enlarging canons of 'non-Western' art see Zeynep Çelik, "Colonialism, Orientalism, and the Canon," *The Art Bulletin* 78(2) (1996): 202–205 and Steiner, "Can the Canon Burst." At least two eminent scholars of Islamic art have stated their opposition to any such expansion: Blair and Bloom, "The Mirage of Islamic Art," p. 175.

69 James Elkins, "Why It Is Not Possible to Write Art Histories of Non-Western Cultures," in *The Past in the Present: Contemporary Art and Art History's Myths* (Bratislava: Nadácia—Centrum Sučasného Umenia, 2002) p. 255; Elkins, *Stories of Art* (New York: Routledge, 2002).

70 James Elkins, *Visual Studies: A Skeptical Introduction* (New York: Routledge, 2003), 115–118; Elkins, review of David Summers, *Real Spaces: World Art History and the Rise of Western Modernism* in *The Art Bulletin* 86(2) (2004): 378.

71 James D. Herbert, "Passing between Art History and Postcolonial Theory," in Mark A. Cheetham, Michael Ann Holly, and Keith Moxey, eds, *The Subjects of Art History: Historical Objects in Contemporary Perspective* (Cambridge: Cambridge University Press, 1998) p. 219.

72 Dipesh Chakrabarty, *Provincializing Europe: Postcolonial Thought and Historical Difference* (Princeton, NJ: Princeton University Press, 2000); Dilip Parameshwar Gaonkar, ed., *Alternative Modernities* (Durham, NC: Duke University Press, 2001).

73 Ikem Stanley Okoye, "Tribe and Art History," *The Art Bulletin* 78(4) (1996): 613. See also Robert S. Nelson, "The Map of Art History," *Art Bulletin* 79(1) (1997): 40.

74 Grabar, "Islamic Art and Archaeology," p. 255.

75 See, for example, Talinn Grigor, "Of Metamorphosis: Meaning on Iranian Terms," *Third Text* 17(3) (2003): 207–225.

76 On possible futures for the field see Oleg Grabar in *The Dictionary of Art*, vol. 16, p. 101; Grabar, "What Should One Know About Islamic Art," *Res* 43 (2003): 9. See also Rogers, *Uses of Anachronism*, pp. 6–7, and Souren Melikian's plea for a disaggregation of the field into regionally based art histories: "Toward a Clearer Vision of 'Islamic' Art," *International Herald Tribune*, April 24, 2004.

77 Gill Perry and Colin Cunningham, *Academies, Museums and Canons of Art* (New Haven, CT: Yale University Press, 1999) pp. 7–8; Blair and Bloom, "Mirage of Islamic Art."

78 Hans Belting, *The End of the History of Art?*, translated by Christopher S. Wood (Chicago, IL: University of Chicago Press, 1987) p. 57. See also James Elkins's review of *Real Spaces,* pp. 377–378.

Chapter 3

# Turning green into black, or how I learned to live with the canon

*Steven Nelson*

In 1922 James Weldon Johnson wrote in his preface to *The Book of American Negro Poetry*:

> A people may become great through many means, but there is only one measure by which its greatness is recognized and acknowledged. The final measure of the greatness of all peoples is the amount and standard of the literature and art they have produced. The world does not know that a people is great until that people produces great literature and art. No people that has produced great literature and art has ever been looked upon by the world as distinctly inferior.[1]

Johnson's anthology, along with Alain Locke's 1925 *The New Negro* and V.F. Calverton's 1929 *An Anthology of American Negro Literature,* were serious attempts to create a canon of black literary achievement that would serve as weapons in black struggles for a recognition that would, once and for all, show that white arguments of the fundamental inferiority of African Americans had no basis in reality. Moreover, such texts were also aimed at convincing black people to shed their coats of internalized racism. Along such lines, this new canon would give legitimacy and weight to the achievements of black literary production, particularly in the face of a racist society. The formation of a canon of African American art fueled by Alain Locke's *The New Negro,* his 1941 *The Negro in Art,* as well as James Porter's groundbreaking *Modern Negro Art* in 1943, followed similar lines.

In 2004, I was invited to give a paper on a panel called "Constructing the Canon" at Harvard University's "Bridging the Gaps: African American Art Conference, 2004." Thinking that there was indeed a canon of African American art in place, one that over the past sixty-plus years had been remarkably stable with respect to both the artists included and the methodological apparatuses used to analyze the work, I questioned the efficacy of such a model to encompass work that did not fall neatly in what I perceive to be articulations of what Cornel West has called "black authenticity." West's criteria could not accommodate some of the artists who are "in" as well as the scholars and critics who write about them.[2] To my amazement, there were calls from the audience, as well as from Henry Louis Gates, Jr. himself, about the need for a "Norton Anthology of African American Art."

There is no way to practice a canon-free art history. Moreover, with the 2006 publication of Michael Lewis's *American Art and Architecture,* a text that makes no mention of the Harlem Renaissance and ignores important artists such as Henry Ossawa Tanner, Jacob Lawrence, Faith Ringgold, and Adrian Piper, to name only a few, the formation of a canon of African American art is still necessary, and, in light of the sterile and neatly packaged, and alarmingly conservative history that Lewis proffers, a canon of African American art is critical. That said, it is also imperative, and, I think, productive, to question the canon, to try to stretch it, not only in terms of the artists it includes but also with respect to the theoretical tools in its arsenal.

African American artists have always brought together concerns and ways of working from near and far in their disparate practices. Renée Green, for example, combines personal memory with critical theory, Black Nationalism, her interest in Robert Smithson, and her obsession with the 1970s in *Partially Buried in Three Parts,* which she produced between 1996 and 2000 (Figure 3.1). The work of Robert Ryman, Fluxus, conceptual art, psychoanalysis and his personal experiences with poverty inform William Pope.L's practices (Figure 3.2). That said, scholars and critics of African American art habitually do not take such connections seriously,

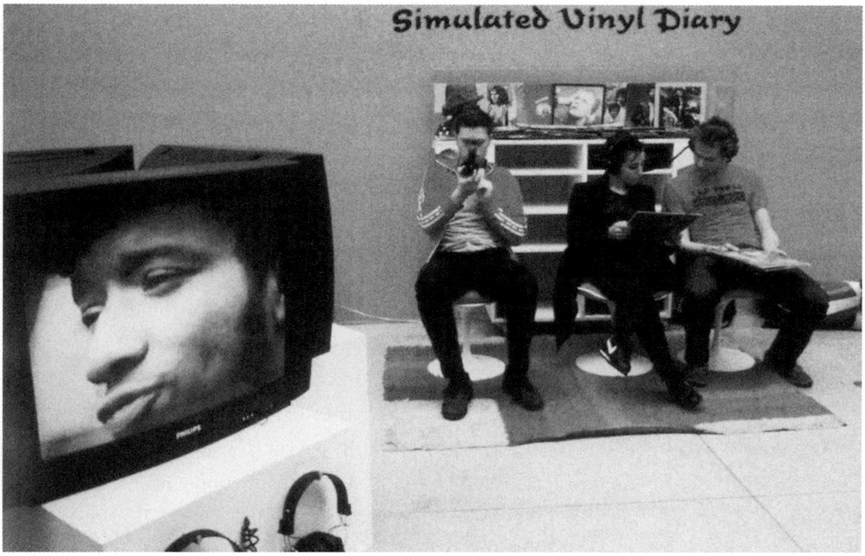


*Figure 3.1* Renée Green, "Partially Buried" from *Partially Buried in Three Parts,* 1996. Installation view at the Pat Hearn Gallery, 1996. Courtesy of the artist.

*Figure 3.2* William Pope.L, *Estimate*, 1997. Photograph by Paul Fortin. Courtesy of the artist.

instead preferring to insist upon the intimate, symbiotic relationship between African American art and African American subjectivity. The result is a focus on how the work of black artists articulates an (often) essentialized "blackness." While such a goal is important, particularly in a field that came to being in the face of racist and racialized discourses, to limit inquiry to such issues flattens out the complexity of black visual practices. Moreover, such a limit suggests an exploration of African American art that takes place in a vacuum.

Given its genesis in a racist society, much of the work about African American artists, exemplified by Samella Lewis's 1978 survey *African American Art and Artists* and Harry Henderson and Romare Bearden's 1993 survey *A History of African-*

*American Artists from 1792 to the Present*, revels in the biographical celebration of the black artist who has struggled against all odds to achieve "greatness" as an artist. In such a paradigm all of the work becomes a site for talking about the means through which African American artists beat a racist system. Such victories were vitally important, not just to the artists themselves, but also to the communities that supported them, particularly given the almost wholesale exclusion before the 1980s of black artists from mainstream texts and exhibitions (and their almost wholesale exclusion from Michael Lewis's just-published text). However, such celebrations in text tended to obscure the complexity of artistic practices. While a reader can understand and appreciate Lois Mailou Jones's education at the School of the Museum of Fine Arts in Boston, an extremely rare accomplishment for a black woman in 1927, these details take precedence over a discussion of her work, which in the 1930s was in a direct conversation with primitivism, Cézanne, and other French modernists.

Following American art history, African American art history has relied heavily on social history. In the drive to show how African American art articulates "the black experience" or "the black community," we understand quite well how, for example, Romare Bearden's 1960s projections portray black life, but we learn little about his relationship with the larger New York art world, particularly to the Pop artists. Concerning both biography and social history, African American art all too often becomes a social document; one that celebrates the mastery of the artist while it proposes a one-to-one relationship between art object and social reality. Absent for the most part in this body of work is any consideration of the art object or its internal logic, outside of its role in illustrating an essentialized notion of blackness (a notion often belied by the work itself).

Unlike American art, the social history of African American art generally lacks any kind of critical engagement with social class. Moreover, this absence is one of a number of issues that results in the silencing of ambivalence and profound angst in the work of many African American artists. The pages of black periodicals such as *The Crisis* or *The Messenger* from the 1920s are filled with anxiety over the representation of black people in literature and the arts; moreover, the very foundations of the canons of black literature and black art were bourgeois endeavors. In the periodicals, writers prescribed and proscribed what kinds of black people to represent; others, most notably Langston Hughes, asserted their right to depict any aspect of black life they saw fit.[3] More to the point, between March and November 1926 *The Crisis* published, "The Negro In Art: How Shall He Be Portrayed?" Conceived by W.E.B. DuBois as a symposium conducted in print, many writers, publishers, and artists were asked to respond to seven questions regarding the types of African Americans art should represent. While all of the questions revolved around class issues, questions four and five most dramatically raise middle-class anxieties surrounding black representation:

4. What are Negroes to do when they are continually painted at their worst and judged by the public as they are painted?
5. Does the situation of the educated Negro in America with its pathos, humiliation, and tragedy call for treatment at least as sincere as "Porgy" received?[4]

Within the milieu of the New Negro and its connection to DuBois's conception of the "Talented Tenth," a select group of refined and educated blacks who would lead the masses to equality, these questions, in effect, created a binary between middle-class African Americans and their proletarian counterparts. Seeing a trend toward the increased representation of the black underworld of Harlem, which was well on its way to becoming one of the worst slums in New York City, these questions articulate the New Negroes' belief that the increased representation of the black middle class would serve as a far more effective strategy in changing white views concerning blacks. While the proponents of the Harlem Renaissance fostered an idealized perception of black unity rooted in the successes of its middle class, this unity was, in fact, a myth. While the necessity for the perception of unity was politically urgent in the black struggle for equality at the time, it was not embraced by all.

Such demurral registers in the work of Palmer Hayden, whose 1930s canvas *The Janitor Who Paints* beautifully explores the artist's own ambivalence around his career as an artist (Figure 3.3). Commentators on the painting, choosing not to engage with the painter's ambivalence, have instead chosen to attempt to explain away (unconvincingly) the artist's satirical use of stereotypical caricature (a formal strategy that predates by decades the work of contemporary African American artists such as Robert Colescott, Michael Ray Charles, and Kara Walker) or to represent such use in the best possible light.[5] The only dissenting voice in the bunch was Porter, who, in the case of this painting, took off his kid gloves. In his words, Hayden:

> tried to paint satirical pictures of Negro life in Harlem, and in these, including the one entitled *The Janitor Who Paints,* we see a talent gone far astray. Not only are the forms in these works confused, but the application of the humor is ill-advised if not altogether tasteless.[6]

What Porter could not abide was Hayden's caricatured, almost stereotypical working-class figures that, for many, flew in the face of what most African Americans, particularly those proponents of the representation of the pathos of the middle class, would have considered to be a positive representation of the race.

This positive/negative binary was one that was at the crux of anxiety surrounding the representation of African Americans in the 1920s, and it is an anxiety that simply will not go away. Most of the debate around the representation of African Americans

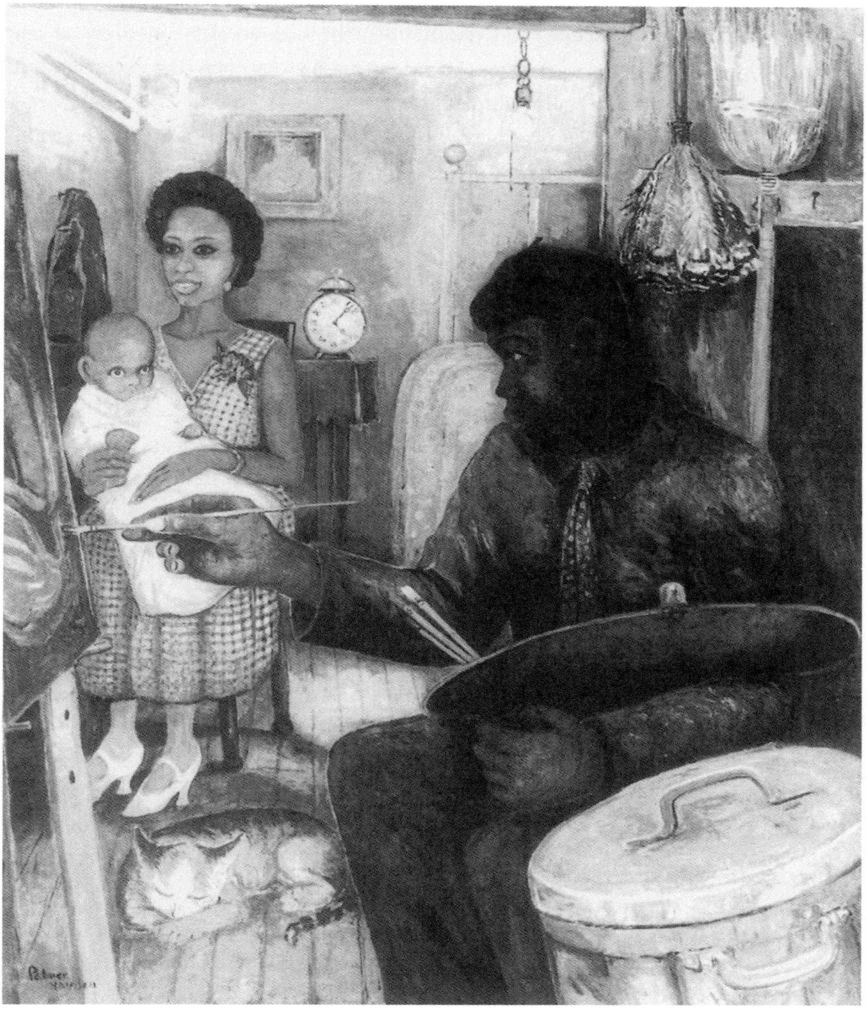

*Figure 3.3* Palmer Hayden, *The Janitor Who Paints*, oil on canvas, 1930s. Smithsonian American Art Museum. Gift of the Harmon Foundation.

engages such a binary, and it is a binary that still fuels a large part of the scholarship in African American art history. One only needs to note the reactions and attention paid to Kara Walker's infamous silhouettes of the 1990s to see the power that this binary still holds. In Hayden's case, satire and the caricature were not only ways to articulate his own views of life in Harlem in the 1930s, but also a means to explore the very definitions of positive racial images. Hayden's practice, undervalued even today, has been sorely misread and misunderstood under a rubric that foreclosed any conversation other than the positive or negative attributes of the blacks on his canvases. His genre scenes did not fit into the conservative ideological and methodological paradigms of African American art history. Hayden is certainly in the canon, but at best as a marginal player.

Today, contemporary African American artists fare somewhat better at the hands of scholars and critics. Indeed, a new generation of African Americanists is beginning to utilize other theoretical models to understand African American visual production. Even here, however, there is still a genealogy of African American art that, at times, serves as the axis around which some of this new scholarship revolves. That is to say, if the canon of African American art history is methodological, it is also genealogical: there is still a tendency to tie all black art somehow to Alain Locke and the Harlem Renaissance.[7] In doing so, African Americanists attempt to reinforce the idea that, as in black literature, there is something in black visual art that can be called a tradition, one discernable from its Euro-American counterpart. Moreover, such ties exemplify the unfailing attempt in the field to lay claim to something approximating a black aesthetic, which can be understood as African American art history's counterpart to moves in culture-at-large to fortify and articulate a unitary black voice.

But what do such moves say about blackness? Is there an essential blackness that all people of African descent share? Can we think of blackness as something not biological or authentic but rather as something contingent, as something ever-changing? Is blackness something we can *use*? If one thinks through the complex ways that blackness works and applies it to African American art, what would become highlighted is a vast array of complicated, and, at times, contradictory concerns. In that sense, I would like to think of blackness in African American art as not just an end in itself, but as something that organizes visual practices, as something that is a tool, and something that is sometimes a mode of reception. Both Renée Green and William Pope.L, though not commonly addressed in African Americanist texts (each has a wider following in the mainstream art world than they have in African American circles), have visual and performative practices that exemplify the slippery, impossible-to-pin-down notions of blackness that pit it as something other than primordial essence.

Green's *Partially Buried in Three Parts* consists of multi-screen video, installation, photographs, books, album covers, and 1970s paraphernalia all of which are set in environments decked out in 1970s colors—oranges, rusts, harvest golds—and furnishings. Coming out of an exploration of 1970, when Green herself was a child living in Ohio, *Partially Buried*, which takes its name from Robert Smithson's 1970 *Partially Buried Woodshed*, focuses on memory, time, as well as national belonging, and is structured along genealogical lines. Part one, entitled "Partially Buried," centers on Smithson's site-specific work, exploring his interest in entropy in a way that brings in the history of his piece, his canonization in the art world and Green's own memories of Kent State University into conversation with one another. Part two, titled "Übertragen/Transfer" (not addressed in this essay), interrogates how the United States was imagined from abroad as well as how the years around 1970 in this country were imagined by people of German descent who now live here. Part three, "Partially Buried Continued," concentrates, like part one, on the intersection of past and present, questioning the connection between self and other by means of a juxtaposition of Green's father's experiences in Korea during the Korean War and her own as an itinerant artist in Kwangju.

Part one of *Partially Buried* exists in the intersection of time and individual experiences of Kent State University in 1970, including Green's own. Smithson's *Partially Buried Woodshed* takes center stage not only as art object to be recovered but also as an object that allows for an examination into the events of 1970 as well as Green's relation to Smithson in particular and conceptual art more generally. On May 4, 1970, a mere four months after Smithson executed his piece, members of the National Guard massacred four students who were protesting against the Vietnam War on the Kent State campus. At that time, someone painted the date on *Partially Buried Woodshed.* Smithson responded by putting an anti-war poster on the structure. Art had become monument, and its meaning had changed. May 4 takes on much importance in Green's piece, becoming the site of massacre, and source of recollection. Interviewing herself, Green notes that her mother was at a workshop on campus during the massacre, and that Green herself heard the news while listening to the Jackson 5 and Sly Stone. Images of Kent State in 1996 are juxtaposed with archival footage of assistants making Smithson's piece. Also, textual passages and voiceovers in both German and English highlight Smithson's importance in contemporary art after his death at the age of 35 in a 1973 plane crash. Moreover, images of Black Panthers in Ohio, album covers of everything from Cher to Roberta Flack to the Carpenters are included in the array of images and installation objects, and piles of books about the Kent State massacre are placed upon cement blocks, the only things left of the shed. Alongside these pieces, or more appropriately fragments, texts about her parents appear as well.

It is in these meetings that Smithson meets Sly, conceptual art meets popular culture both black and white, art takes on meanings personal, political, and historical, while Green also surveys her family history, memories of her childhood, and the multiple locations—Ohio, New York, and Germany—that make up her lived experience. As part of the scenario, Green highlights black agency both in the events of Kent State in 1970 and more broadly in equality struggles played out in the United States. This black agency is one of the predominate "returns of the repressed" explored in Green's practice.

While *Partially Buried* is centered in Ohio, "Partially Buried Continued" further complicates the genealogical. Here, Korea is the site where Green explores connections both familial and artistic. Juxtaposing her father's 1952 pictures from his tour of duty during the Korean War with her own, taken on a trip to Kwangju in 1997, "Partially Buried Continued" blurs the boundaries between bloodlines and artistic connections. With respect to her family, Korea ties Green to her father, if only tenuously. We hear:

> Visiting this place, she imagines, she links herself in some possibly obscure way to her father. But she can't see what he saw, yet she can walk in Seoul and see how it doesn't match those still clear images, which she can see with her eyes closed or opened, before having arrived.

In terms of the artistic Green looks at the work of Theresa Hak Kyung Cha, a Korean conceptual artist, who, like Smithson, died violently in her 30s. *Dictée*, Cha's autobiography, is much like Green's work in its combination of family history and poetry as well as images, and the volume explores alienation, language, and displacement. As Cha is introduced, on the screen appears a diagram, one that shows the overlays and differences between Cha and Smithson. We hear another voiceover: "She invokes two dead artists and ponders the traces of their lives in the continued wake of their deaths. Indices. Quotes. Birth parents, blood relations, artistic forbearers. The usual artist's roster tugs at her."

However, overlaid with her personal journey through space, time, and art is an exploration of the massacre that took place in the wake of the May 18 Kwangju Uprising of 1980. Memories of the events collide and merge with Green's personal and artistic journey, the Kwangju Uprising merges with the Korean War, time moves backwards and forwards, ceasing to be linear. What this addresses is the present, and the ways in which memory—in all of its sublimation and desublimation—has the power to create, the power to distort, and the power to destroy. Here, as is the case with Green's desublimation of African American history at Kent State, this history of the Kwangju Uprising constitutes the return of the repressed. In that sense, blackness, while not overtly present, is an underlying principle that allows Green to disrupt given notions of history; blackness here allows Green to think about the terms of history and whom it serves. Green goes on to ask three questions, which are inflected by her displacement, blurry experiences, and the montage of fragments:

> "Who owns History?"
> "Who can represent its complexity?"
> "Who cares?"

The juxtapositions of genealogy, legacies of race, politics, popular culture, art, and theory in *Partially Buried* are entropic. That is to say they create irreversible changes in our understanding of place (or non-place), time, and language. Moreover, Green's attention to entropy comes straight out of the writings of Smithson, who thought of entropy as an irreversible process of change that moved toward equilibrium and, at times, erosion. To illustrate this, Smithson used a simple example:

> Picture in your mind's eye the sand box divided in half with black sand on one side and white sand on the other. We take a child and have him run hundreds of times clockwise in the box until the sand gets mixed and starts to turn grey; after that we have him run anti-clockwise, but the result will not be a restoration of the original division but a greater degree of greyness and an increase of entropy.[8]

Entropy, moreover, was an attribute that was at the center of Smithson's earth-works, and *Partially Buried Woodshed* was no exception. Green well understood this fact, and it has inflected her understanding of his work. Alongside Super 8 images of backhoes digging earth and the sounds of Sun Ra drumming, we hear Smithson's words:

> One's mind and the earth are in a constant state of erosion, mental rivers wear away abstract banks, brain waves undermine cliffs of thought, ideals decompose into stones of unknowing, and conceptual crystallizations break apart into deposits of gritty reason. Vast moving faculties occur in this geological miasma, and they move in the most physical way. This moment seems motionless, yet it crushes the landscape of logic under glacial reveries. The slow flowage makes one conscious of the turbidity of thinking. Slump, debris slides, avalanches all take place within the cracking limits of the brain.[9]

But in this slow, entropic, irreversible dissolution of mind and matter, Smithson, Sun Ra, Cha, and Kwangju, Green opens up an in-between space, one that Homi Bhabha suggests, in the context of Green's earlier work, is "at once a vision and a construction—that takes you 'beyond' yourself in order to return, in a spirit of revision and reconstruction, to the political *conditions* of the present" (author's italics).[10]

In work that has inflections similar to those of Green, William Pope.L, who calls himself "the friendliest black artist in America," satirically and ironically uses blackness in its intersection with power, masculinity, and class. While his practices are informed by abstract art, Fluxus, and the Happenings of the 1960s, he changes all of these things by implicating them in a rubric that highlights the ways in which blackness functions in social, cultural, economic, and political matrices. Perhaps the opposite of what the proponents of the New Negro would have envisioned for themselves, blackness, for Pope.L is a lack, a lack worth having. It is the place of disenfranchisement in which is embedded the possibility of active opposition. In his own words, "blackness is a negotiation, not a necessity," and such a statement resonates with the lived experiences of many African Americans. In Pope.L's hands, blackness is not merely articulated; it is the knife that cuts both ways. Through his body of work Pope.L points not to discrete constructions of black subjectivity but rather to the effects of racism, politicizing the racialized characterizations of African Americans, particularly males, in the social landscape.

Pope.L's 1997 painting, entitled *Estimate*, takes on histories of abstract art while it takes aim at African American sacred cows and myths of the sexual prowess of black men. At the bottom of the work reads, "MLK PENIS AS SEEN FROM PLUTO," and with this text, the painting, directly descended from Ryman's white paintings of the 1960s and 1970s, undercuts through hyperbole notions of black men as walking phalluses while it also attempts to rewrite the legacy of Martin Luther King, Jr. In this sense, for Pope.L, such a painting effects a movement of the legacy of the slain civil rights leader from what he calls, "the catacombs of celebration and presence [to] the lived moment of contraries where we all have to deal."[11] While humorous (at least to me), the painting through its confrontation with Ryman's white canvases, which Pope.L first saw in the early 1970s, also consciously, as Mark Bessire has suggested, exposes the presumed invisibility of whiteness and the purity of abstract painting.[12] As Pope.L himself insists:

> As the son of Robert Ryman, it is my job to walk in his footsteps to the front door of the family mansion and burn it to the ground; then claim that the conflagration is not so much a rejection or celebration but a negotiation-worth-having, which must be lived consciously in the space between contradictions. In this sense, there is no such thing as contradiction, only the fire that burns amidst the networks made up of them.[13]

In that sense, *Estimate* consciously seeks, in an Oedipal fashion, to kill the father. Furthermore in this murder, Pope.L, recognizing, as Kristine Stiles has noted, the patriarchical nature of Ryman's work, rescripts whiteness, in a Foucauldian move, as contingent upon and relative to blackness. That relativism—and the power such relativism engenders in terms of the very attributes we associate with white and black in the United States—is fundamental to Pope.L's body of work.[14]

Pope.L is perhaps best known for his crawls. Since the late 1970s the artist has performed crawls in cities in the United States, Europe, and Asia, and their reception changes depending on the venue of the performance. In *The Great White Way: 22 miles, 5 years, 1 street*, performed during the 2002 Whitney Biennial, Pope.L, ironically clad in a Superman outfit, uses his body and the city to interrogate the intersection of race, class, masculinity, and power. Crawling up Broadway, Pope.L's black, horizontal body registers as lack: lack of power, lack of enfranchisement, and lack of wealth. It comments on the ways in which blackness has been aligned and stereotyped as the visible sign of homelessness, which Americans consistently code as black. Reception plays a huge role in Pope.L's crawls. For example, C. Carr notes the reaction of an African American spectator to Pope.L's 1991 *Tompkins Square Crawl*, when the performance "evolved quickly from racial metaphor to racial tension as the black spectator challenged the white cameraman [hired by the artist to document the piece]."[15] Such a scene directly not only shows how people of all colors make assumptions based on race and how they are tied to perceptions of power (the crawling Pope.L is powerless; the white cameraman is in charge of the scene). It also points to the burden of representation placed on artists of color, particularly when the spectator exclaims, "You're running around the street like this in a goddamn suit . . . I wear a suit like that to work!"[16]

While race and class converge in Pope.L's crawls, they do so just as strongly in his 1997 *ATM Piece*. Attached to a Manhattan ATM by a chain of sausages, Pope.L, decked in a skirt of dollar bills, had intended to give money to passers-by. Although the performance was stopped almost immediately by the New York City police, Pope.L attempted to explore the ways in which homelessness and panhandling are conflated with racial stereotypes, and in the push and pull of public space, the passer-by, like in the crawls, becomes implicated not only in the performance, but admonished to think through his/her views about race and class.

Race is not only a badge we wear or a thing we choose. In Pope.L's practice race it is also a commodity that literally can be consumed. In his 2001 performance *Eating the Wall Street Journal*, Pope.L, sitting on a toilet atop a ten-foot tall tower, ate pieces of the newspaper. But race is not the only thing consumed here. Power, and by extension whiteness, embodied by the *Wall Street Journal,* is eaten as well. In this act of consumption, food, the body, race, power, and the abject all come together as a means to interrogate the commodity as fetish.

Renée Green and William Pope.L are only two of many artists who provide provocative ways to think through the complexities inherent in the intersection of blackness and visual practices. For both artists, blackness is a discursive tool that is disruptive, constructive, and deconstructive. Their work involves race, yet it is about the ways in which race—and specifically blackness—works in a range of different frameworks. As such, blackness in their hands is slippery, it is contradictory, it is ambivalent, and it is part of the construction of their work. What would happen if we looked at other African American artists, both contemporary and historical, in a more discursive and dialectical fashion? What would happen if we paid more attention to ambivalence in African American visual practices? How might such investigations change our field? I suspect they would open up the canon to include a broader range of methodological frameworks and allow for provocative and oppositional work in new and effective ways.

## Notes

1 James Weldon Johnson, *The Book of American Negro Poetry* (New York: Harcourt, Brace and Company, 1922) p. 9.
2 Cornel West, *Race Matters* (New York: Vintage Books, 1994) p. 42.
3 See Langston Hughes, "The Negro Artist and the Racial Mountain," *The Nation,* 122 (3181) (June 23, 1926): 692–694.
4 See "The Negro in Art: How Shall He Be Portrayed," *The Crisis* 31(5) (March 1926): 219–220; 31(6) (April 1926): 278–280; 32(1) (May 1926): 35–36; 32(2) (June 1926): 71–73; 32(4) (August 1926): 193–194; 32(5) (September 1926): 238–239; 33(1) (November 1926): 28–29.
5 See for example Harry Henderson and Romare Bearden, *A History of African-American Artists from 1792 to the Present* (New York: Parthenon Books, 1993) p. 159; Alain Locke, "Advance on the Art Front," *Opportunity: A Journal of Negro Life,* XVII(5) (May 1939): 136; Regenia A. Perry, *Free Within Ourselves: African-American Art in the Collection of the National Museum of American Art* (Washington, DC: Smithsonian Institution, 1992) p. 89 and David Driskell, "The Flowering of the Harlem Renaissance: The Art of Aaron Douglas, Meta Warrick Fuller, Palmer Hayden, and William H. Johnson," in *Harlem Renaissance: Art of Black America* (New York: Studio Museum in Harlem, 1987), p. 132.
6 James A. Porter, *Modern Negro Art* (New York: Dryden Press, 1943) p. 110.
7 See for example Gwendolyn DuBois Shaw, *Speaking the Unspeakable: The Art of Kara Walker* (Durham: Duke University Press, 2004).
8 Robert Smithson, "A Tour of the Monuments of Passaic, New Jersey (1967)," in Jack Flam, ed. *Robert Smithson: The Collected Writings* (Berkeley: University of California Press, 1996) p. 74.
9 Robert Smithson quoted in Renée Green, *Shadows and Signals* (Barcelona: Fundaciò Antoni Tàpies, 2000) p. 85.
10 Homi Bhabha, *The Location of Culture* (New York: Routledge, 1994) p. 3.
11 Lowery Stokes Sims, "Interview with William Pope.L," in Mark H.C. Bessire, ed., *William Pope.L: The Friendliest Black Artist in America©* (Cambridge, MA: The MIT Press, 2002) p. 63.
12 Mark H.C. Bessire, "The Friendliest Black Artist in America," in Bessire, p. 25.
13 William Pope.L quoted in Kristine Stiles, "Thunderbird Immolation: Burning Racism," in Bessire, p. 39.
14 Kristine Stiles, "Thunderbird Immolation: Burning Racism," in Bessire, p. 39.
15 C. Carr, "In the Discomfort Zone," in Bessire, p. 48.
16 Bessire, p. 175.

Chapter 4

# What's in a name?

## "Flanders," language, and the historiography of late medieval art in Belgium since federalization

*Gregory T. Clark*

For Belgium, my favorite enigma

In 2000, I published a study entitled *Made In Flanders: The Master of the Ghent Privileges and Manuscript Painting in the Southern Netherlands in the Time of Philip the Good* with Brepols of Turnhout, Belgium. Its principal subject, an anonymous mid-fifteenth-century illuminator known as the Ghent Privileges Master, takes his name from his greatest achievement, the luxuriously decorated copy of the privileges and statutes of Ghent and Flanders owned by Philip the Good, duke of Burgundy (Vienna, Öst. Nationalbibl., Cod. 2583).

Of all the reviews of my book, the most perspicacious was written by my colleague and friend Dominique Vanwijnsberghe, Project Leader at the Royal Institute for Cultural Heritage, a Belgian federal agency in Brussels. His review appeared in 2001 in the *Belgian Journal for Archeology and Art History*.[1] While most of Vanwijnsberghe's reservations about *Made In Flanders* made perfect sense to me, his concern about the appearance of the term "Flanders" in its title left me puzzled.[2]

The Ghent Privileges Master and his collaborators made manuscripts in or for the southern Netherlandish cities of Ghent, Tournai, and Mons between about 1440 and 1460. In the strictest sense, however, only Ghent was located in the fifteenth-century county of Flanders. That geographical entity was bounded by the duchy of Brabant to the east, the southern estuary of the Scheldt river to the north, the North Sea to the west, and the counties of the Artois and the Hainaut to the south (see Figure 4.1). While the northernmost sliver of late medieval Flanders is now part of the province of Zeeland in the Netherlands and the French *département* of Nord corresponds to most of *la Flandre française*, the better part of fifteenth-century Flanders is now divided between the modern Belgian provinces of East and West Flanders.

Mons, in contrast, was and is in the Hainaut, while late medieval Tournai and the surrounding region, the Tournaisis, was a French island engirded by the counties

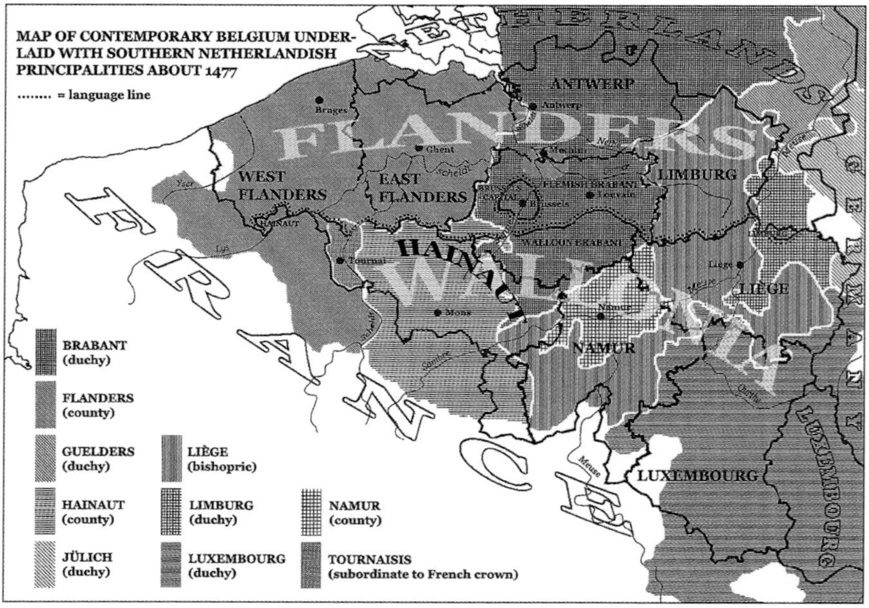


*Figure 4.1* Map of contemporary Belgium underlaid with southern Netherlandish principalities about 1477. Author image.

of Flanders and the Hainaut in much the same way that West Berlin was surrounded by the former German Democratic Republic. Vanwijnsberghe was concerned that "Flanders" was too reductive and could confuse readers without a full grasp of the complexity of the geographical situation of the late medieval southern Netherlands. While recognizing that it was not as "eye-catching" (*accrocheur*) or as evocative as "Flanders," Vanwijnsberghe wondered whether a phrase such as the Scheldt river valley (*la région scaldienne*) would have been preferable.

As he noted in his review, Vanwijnsberghe had voiced these concerns to me even before I published *Made In Flanders*. One of my counter-arguments at that time had been that the inclusion of the term "southern Netherlands" in the second half of the book's title would have made it clear that the geographical region under study was larger than just the county of Flanders.[3] I also pointed out that while both Tournai and Ghent do indeed lie in the Scheldt river valley, Mons does not. Naming the book *Made in the Scheldt River Valley and the Hainaut* would, I feared, have glazed over both my eyes and those of many other potential readers even before they opened the volume. Finally, I observed that the late Maurits Smeyers, our mutual colleague at the Catholic University of Louvain, had just published a study entitled *Flemish Miniatures from the 8th to the Mid-16th Century: The Medieval World on Parchment*.[4] Although Smeyers's painted subjects were made as far to the east as the bishopric of Liège and as far to the south as Picardy, no qualifying term such as "southern Netherlandish" appeared in his book's title.

That Vanwijnsberghe nonetheless remained uncomfortable with the name of my book deeply troubled me; was there something I was missing? To answer that question, I embarked on the research that underpins this essay. Before I began, I thought that I knew Belgium and its people reasonably well. After all, I can muddle through in both French and Dutch, I lived in Brussels from August of 1982 to August of 1983, and I have regularly returned to Belgium to do research and see both French- and Dutch-speaking friends and colleagues ever since.

What I soon came to realize, however, was that Vanwijnsberghe was not the only critic to question overly inclusive definitions of the term "Flanders." The reason why, I have concluded, is that the word has become a hot-button term—if not an outright F-word—for many as Belgium has increasingly polarized along linguistic lines since federalization.[5] While negotiating the minefield of language is second nature for natives, most non-Belgians are entirely unaware of the powerful forces at work just beneath the country's deceptively placid surface. As a consequence, the present essay is primarily intended as a window onto Belgian linguistic identity politics for foreign art historians. At the same time, I hope that readers will recognize that the essay is also a heartfelt billet-doux from me to Belgium in her entirety.

Before we consider some of the consequences of the politicization of the term "Flanders," a capsule history of language in Belgium is in order. When the independent kingdom of Belgium was wrested from the Netherlands in 1830, the newly formed nation had two principal linguistic groups. The netherlandophones lived north of the language line that bisects the country from east to west (see Figure 4.1). While the francophone heartland lies south of the line, French was also the language of the educated classes north of it.[6] Given both the size and the power of Belgium's francophone neighbor to the south and the role of French as a lingua franca in the nineteenth-century west, this facility with French within Belgium's educated classes was hardly surprising. Further giving French the edge in the newly established kingdom was the fact that the nation's industrial wealth was founded in large part on the coal and iron ore that occurred south of the language line.

The unfortunate consequence of these facts both on and in the ground was that French became the official language of the entirety of the newly minted Belgium.[7] This decision relegated the kingdom's netherlandophones to the status of second-class citizens, even though they were demographically in the majority. As French was the language of government, business, and higher education, ambitious netherlandophone Belgians flocked to francophone high schools (*lycées*) to assure their mastery of the dominant tongue. In contrast, most francophone Belgians made little or no effort to learn Dutch.[8]

Already in the late nineteenth century, however, netherlandophones began to fight for official recognition of their language and culture.[9] In 1898, the Equality

Law finally put francophones and netherlandophones on the same legal footing. In 1921, Dutch became the official administrative language of netherlandophone Belgium. (Various netherlandophone dialects were and are still spoken in northern Belgium, but Dutch is the official language of the region.[10]) In 1930, three unilingual regions were recognized in Belgium.[11] French was and is the official language south of the language line, Dutch the official language north of the line, and German the official language of the tiny region south of the line on the German border known as the Eastern Cantons. In contrast, both Dutch and French are recognized as official languages in the capital of Brussels. It was also in 1930 that the University of Ghent became the first in Belgium to offer all courses of instruction in Dutch.

In spite of these concessions, tensions between Belgium's two linguistic regions increased in the third quarter of the twentieth century. As francophone Belgium's traditional mining, metallurgical, and manufacturing industries waned, the taxpayers of Dutch-speaking Belgium, where a more modern industrial mix attracted greater investment, found themselves footing more and more of the bill for the subsidies that kept the south afloat. Many netherlandophones also resented the privileged position that French continued to enjoy among many educated Belgians north of the language line. One result was the partition in 1968 of the previously bilingual Catholic University of Louvain. The parent campus, in the Dutch-speaking portion of the province of Brabant, became an entirely netherlandophone institution and a brand-new francophone campus was established just south of the language line at Louvain-la-Neuve.

The waxing desire of French- and Dutch-speaking Belgians for completely separate institutions led to a series of constitutional reforms in 1970, 1980, 1988, and 1993 that transformed Belgium into a federal state. Today francophone Belgium is the region of Wallonia; netherlandophone Belgium is Flanders; and bilingual Brussels is the region of Brussels-Capital. Francophone Belgians are members of the French Community of Belgium (Communauté Française de Belgique); the German speakers of the Eastern Cantons are a protected community within the French Community; and netherlandophone Belgians are members of the Flemish Community of Belgium (Vlaamse Gemeenschap van België).

Each Community has its own banner and its own national holiday. These are the rampant lion and the commemoration on July 11 of the Battle of the Golden Spurs for the Flemish Community and the fighting cock and the celebration on September 27 of the Commemoration of the Days of September for the French Community. Each national holiday celebrates a defeat for speakers of the other Community's language. The former commemorates the crushing of French forces near Courtrai at the hands of the count of Flanders and communal militias in 1302; the latter celebrates the expulsion of the forces of King William I of the Netherlands from Brussels by "Belgian" partisans in 1830. (Because the Belgian national anthem, "La

Brabançonne," refers to bilingual Lady Brussels, it has thus far managed to survive the nation's federalization unscathed.)

Over the course of the past two decades, the French and Flemish Communities have increasingly grown apart, so much so that early twenty-first-century extremists on both sides now threaten to secede from Belgium entirely. The extent of the nation's transformation since federalization is reflected in the changing subtitles of Brussels author Geert van Istendael's highly popular essay *The Belgian Labyrinth.*[12] When it was first published in 1989, the book's subtitle was *The Beauty of Deformity*. The subtitle in the fully revised Dutch edition that appeared at the end of 2005 was *Waking Up In Another Country*.

Perhaps needless to say, most members of the French Community are not French citizens and many members of the Flemish Community do not reside in the provinces of East and West Flanders. Their Community also includes all of the inhabitants of the provinces of Antwerp, Limburg, and Flemish Brabant and many residents of the agglomeration of Brussels as well. The adjective "Flemish" and its parent noun have been further weighted by the rise of the ultranationalist Dutch-speaking political party known as the Flemish Interest (Vlaams Belang).[13] Established in the late 1970s as the Flemish Bloc (Vlaams Blok), the party had quickly to rename itself in November of 2004, when it was condemned by Belgium's High Court for championing discrimination and racism.

Because of all of this, "Flanders" became a highly charged term in many quarters at the end of the twentieth century, a rallying point for some and a red flag for others. What consequences has this had for the study of the history of art? I will try to answer this question by considering three recent instances in which the term has played a prominent role.

In 1949, the Royal Academy of Sciences, Letters, and Fine Arts of Belgium established the National Center for the Study of the Flemish Primitives (Centre national de recherches "Primitifs flamands"). The initial impetus was the need to examine and restore Jan van Eyck's great *Ghent Altarpiece*, which had just been returned to Belgium from salt mines near Salzburg; Paul Coremans's *L'agneau mystique au laboratoire* (1953) was the book-length fruit of that undertaking. Since its founding the center, located in Brussels, has continued to document panel paintings produced in the fifteenth-century southern Netherlands in three series of publications: the Corpus, the Repertory, and the Contributions.

When the center was founded, most Belgians did not object to the phrase "Flemish Primitives." After all, the term had long been favored by both French and Dutch speakers to describe panel painters working on both sides of the language line in the fifteenth-century southern Netherlands; one thinks, for example, of the highly influential 1902 Bruges exhibition *Les Primitifs flamands et l'Art ancien*.[14] The phrase was clearly not acceptable, however, to Jules Destrée, a francophone Socialist politician from Charleroi who in 1912 published an open letter to king Albert I of Belgium on the subject of the separation of Wallonia from Flanders.[15] Although usually remembered today for his declaration there that "there are Walloons and Flemings in Belgium, but no Belgians," Destrée also claimed in his letter that:

> They [the Flemings] have taken our [Walloon] artists from us. The deeply moving master of Tournai, Roger de la Pasture, one of the greatest artists of the fifteenth century, is counted among the Flemings under the name of Van der Weyden. Flemish art shines with a radiant brilliance; Walloon art is unknown.[16]

Eighty years later, in 1992, the apparently like-minded Jean-Maurice Dehousse, a Socialist politician from Liège, the French-speaking stronghold on the river Meuse, became the national Minister of Scientific Policy. In that year or early in 1993, Dehousse informed the Center for the Study of the Flemish Primitives that he would "not pay for 'Flemish primitives'."[17] The minister was apparently unmoved by the fact that the full title of the institute's most important series of publications was Corpus of Painting in the Southern Netherlands in the Fifteenth Century (*Corpus de la peinture des anciens Pays-Bas méridionaux au quinzième siècle*). As the Center relied on federal funding, delicate negotiations were immediately undertaken to come up with an acceptable appellation. The rather cumbersome result, made official in 1993, was the International Center for the Study of Medieval Painting in the Scheldt and Meuse River Basins (Centre international d'étude de la peinture médiévale des bassins de l'Escaut et de la Meuse).

While the inclusion of "Meuse River Basin" must have been deeply gratifying to Monsieur Dehousse, the institute's new name described only a small part of the territory documented by the Center. In 2003 the institute adopted the more inclusive name by which it goes today, the Center for the Study of Fifteenth-Century Painting in the Southern Netherlands and the Principality of Liège (Centre d'étude de la peinture du quinzième siècle dans les Pays-Bas méridionaux et la Principauté de Liège).

Jean-Maurice Dehousse's efforts to slay the dragon—or perhaps more accurately the lion—of Flanders did not end in 1993, however. In 1995 he resigned the post of national Minister of Scientific Policy to become mayor of Liège, a position he held until 1999. In his first year as mayor, Dehousse rescinded the agreement made the year before by the Museum of Walloon Art in Liège to lend paintings by Lambert Lombard of Liège to a major exhibition mounted in Brussels and Rome in 1995.[18] The reason was the name of the show: *Flemish Artists in Rome, 1508–1608* (*I Fiamminghi a Roma*, 1508–1608).

Monsieur Dehousse was not in a position to banish the word "Flemish" from the title or the text of Maurits Smeyers's *Flemish Miniatures*, the monumental survey published in Dutch and French in 1998 and in English in 1999. As was mentioned at the beginning of this essay, Smeyers's subject codices were made well beyond the county of Flanders and even the southern Netherlands.

In the introduction to his volume, Smeyers describes how various counts of Flanders held dominion over Picardy, the Artois, the Hainaut, Brabant, and the bishopric of Liège at one time or another over the long course of the Middle Ages.[19] Although he never says so directly, Smeyers implies that Flanders's intermittent dominion of neighboring counties, duchies, and bishoprics justifies the use of the term "Flanders" for the entire region. What is certain is that he treats "the southern Netherlands" and "Flanders" as interchangeable terms throughout his introduction.

Smeyers's conception of "Flanders" was commented upon in a number of reviews, three of which I would like to consider here. The first, by French scholar François Avril, appeared anonymously in 1999 in the *Bulletin critique du livre en français*.[20] There Avril expressed discomfort with the book's title because Smeyers's subject matter was not medieval Flemish illumination, but rather book painting of the Middle Ages in the southern Netherlands and northern France. Avril was also unimpressed by the author's justifications for the use of the term "Flanders" in the introduction, especially as the Carolingian and Romanesque manuscripts with which Smeyers begins predate the rise of the county of Flanders as a major regional power. To sum up, Avril described *Flemish Miniatures* as "a useful book for its rich documentation, but to be plumbed with caution on account of its underlying politico-cultural suppositions."[21]

The second review of *Flemish Miniatures* that I would like to cite was published in 2000 in the Polish journal *Modus*; its authors were Katarzyna Plonka-Balus and Joanna Zietkiewicz-Kotz.[22] Like Avril, Plonka-Balus and Zietkiewicz-Kotz were troubled by the mismatch between the title of the book and its subject matter. Noting that French scholars found Smeyers's point of view difficult to accept, the authors wondered if they could entertain it from the "removed and neutral" (*éloignée et neutre*) safe house of their native Poland. Plonka-Balus and Zietkiewicz-Kotz could not help but be disturbed, however, by the similarities between Smeyers's "historico-ethnic" vantage point and those of unnamed but presumably German-nationalist art historians writing about Polish art in medieval Silesia and the former territories of the Teutonic Knights. As a consequence, the authors concluded that Smeyers's use of the term "Flanders" could only have been justified had he identified a "Flemishness" (*flandrinité*) common to all of the illumination covered in his book.

While the reviews both of Avril and of Plonka-Balus and Zietkiewicz-Kotz are quite straightforward, this is not entirely the case for the third and last review I would like to consider here. Written by Belgian scholar Alain Arnould, it appeared in 2000 in *Scriptorium*.[23] Like the three other reviewers, Arnould was troubled by the fact that "the title *Flemish Miniatures* does not do justice to the contents of the book." Arnould's concern seems rather surprising, however, when one remembers that he and his co-curator Jean-Michel Massing gave their 1993 Cambridge catalog and exhibition on late medieval art in the southern Netherlands and well beyond the title of *Splendours of Flanders*.[24]

That title may perhaps at least partly be explained by the fact that Arnould's and Massing's catalog and exhibition were granted a subvention by the Flemish Community of Belgium. The introduction to the catalog is by Luc Van den Brande, then the Minister-President of the Government of Flanders.[25] There Van den Brande notes that *Splendours of Flanders* "serves as a showcase of late medieval Flemish art" and that "the [Flemish] Minister of Culture, Hugo Weckx, and I have decided to appoint this exhibition a Cultural Ambassador of Flanders."

The research center that Smeyers founded at the Catholic University of Louvain in 1983 and directed up until his untimely death in 1999 was also named a Cultural Ambassador of Flanders in 1993. For the first ten years of its existence, the institute was called the Center for the Study of the Illuminated Manuscript in the Netherlands (Centrum voor de Studie van het Verluchte Handschrift in de Nederlanden). In 1993 the Center was rechristened the Center for the Study of Flemish Illuminators (Studiecentrum Vlaamse Miniaturisten). It retained this appellation until 2004, when it was more inclusively renamed To Illuminate: Study Center for the Art of Miniature Painting (Illuminare: Studiecentrum voor Miniatuurkunst). These name changes cannot help but bring to mind those in 1993 and 2003 of the research center in Brussels for the study of fifteenth-century panel painting in the southern Netherlands.

It was also in 1993 that the Center helped mount the Louvain exhibition *Medieval Magic: Flemish Miniatures before Van Eyck* (*Tover van de middeleeuwen: Vlaamse miniaturen voor Van Eyck*). An international conference, *Flanders in a European Perspective*, was timed to overlap with the opening of *Medieval Magic* on September 8 of that year.[26] As I gave a paper in the colloquium, I had the opportunity to hear Minister-President Van den Brande give one of the opening speeches at the conference. Although the official language of the colloquium was English, the Minister-President spoke in Dutch. Bleary from jet lag though I was, I remember clearly that Van den Brande used the words "Flemish" and "Flanders" so many times that I feared (or perhaps wished) that I was hallucinating. At the reception that followed, an especially beloved Belgian colleague came up to every foreigner who she thought might have been able to follow the Minister-President's speech to apologize for its divisive tone.

Both that cherished colleague's embarrassed regrets and the renamings of the research centers in Louvain and Brussels in 2004 and 2003, respectively, demonstrate that many Belgians on both sides of the language line determinedly see themselves as Belgians first and members of the French or Flemish Communities second. It is my sincere hope that all Belgians choose to recognize and affirm in the twenty-first century that they share a history and cultural patrimony that should not be sundered. Like the baby whom King Solomon of Israel proposed to cut in half for the two mothers who both claimed him, Belgium is much greater than the sum of its parts.

## Acknowledgement

A stay at the Getty Center in January of 2005 enabled me to complete much of the secondary research for this essay. I would like to thank Thomas Kren, Curator of Manuscripts, and Brandi Franzman, Senior Staff Assistant in the Department of Manuscripts, for making that stay possible. My thanks also go out to all of the Belgian colleagues and friends, both French-speaking and Dutch-speaking, who have helped me to understand the vexing issues of language and identity in contemporary Belgium. Several of those scholars and American colleagues Margaret Goehring, Elizabeth Moodey, and Anne van Buren were also kind enough to read and critique my text. At Sewanee, David Syler in the Academic Technology Services Department enabled me to create the map that accompanies this essay. All translations from French and Dutch into English are my own.

## Notes

1 Dominique Vanwijnsberghe, "Le Maître des Privilèges de Gand et de Flandre," *Revue belge d'archéologie et d'histoire de l'art*, 70 (2001): 183–190.
2 Ibid., p. 189.
3 The use of the term "Flanders" as a *pars pro toto* appellation for the entire southern Netherlands—and even the Low Countries as a whole—can be traced back to the early modern period. See in this regard P.J. van Kessel, *Van Fiandra naar Olanda: Veranderende visie in het vroegmoderne Italië op de Nederlandse identiteit* (Mededelingen der Koninklijke Nederlandse Akademie van Wetenschappen, Afdeling Letterkunde, Nieuwe Reeks, Deel 56, No. 5), Amsterdam: Koninklijke Nederlandse Akademie van Wetenschappen, 1993, pp. 7–8; Paul Janssen, Harry De Kok, Edward De Maesschalck, and Hugo De Schepper, "De wereld van de Lage Landen: Het verhaal van een naam," in *De Gouden Delta der Lage Landen: Twintig eeuwen beschaving tussen Seine en Rijn* (Antwerp: Mercatorfonds, 1996) pp. 9–15; and Reginald de Schryver, "Geschiedenis van Vlaanderen," in *Nieuwe Encyclopedie van de Vlaamse Beweging I: A–F* (Tielt: Lannoo, 1998) p. 19.
4 Smeyers's *Flemish Miniatures* was published in 1999 by Brepols of Turnhout, Belgium. The original Dutch-language version (*Vlaamse miniaturen van de 8ste tot het midden van de 16de eeuw: De middeleeuwse wereld op perkament*) had been brought out by Davidsfonds of Louvain in 1998. In the same year a third publishing house, La Renaissance du Livre of Tournai, put out a French-language translation (*L'art de la miniature flamande du VIIIe au XVIe siècle*).
5 For an exemplary English-language overview of the history of the Low Countries, see J.A. Kossmann-Putto and E.H. Kossmann, *The Low Countries: History of the Northern and Southern Netherlands*, 8th edn (Rekkem: Flemish-Netherlands Foundation (Stichting Ons Erfdeel), 2004).

Among native popular chroniclers of contemporary Belgium, three especially stand out. The first is the French speaker Patrick Roegiers. His richly illustrated vest-pocket volume *La Belgique: Le roman d'un pays* (Paris: Gallimard, 2005) is an excellent introduction to the history of the kingdom. Roegiers's *Le mal du pays: Autobiographie de la Belgique* (Paris: Seuil, 2003), named after a painting by Belgian artist René Magritte, takes the form of a mordantly witty and ironic dictionary.

Of the many popular books on Belgium written in Dutch, two are especially favorites. The first, a history of Flanders both as a concept and as a reality, is Marc Reynebeau's *De droom van Vlaanderen, of het toeval van de geschiedenis* (Antwerp: Manteau, 2002; also published in French translation as *Le rêve de la Flandre, ou les aléas de l'histoire*, Tournai: La Renaissance du Livre, 2004). The second, by Geert van Istendael, is *Het Belgisch labyrint, of De schoonheid der wanstaltigheid* (Amsterdam: Arbeiderspers, 1989). In 2004 Istendael revised this critical but even-handed and very successful history of Belgium (there have been no fewer than twelve Dutch-language printings) for translation into French as *Le labyrinthe belge* (Bordeux: Le Castor Astrale); it is this revised text that I cite in this study. A fully updated (*geheel herziene*) Dutch-language revision appeared in December of 2005 under the revealing title of *Het Belgisch labyrint, of Wakker worden in een ander land* (Amsterdam: Arbeiderspers).

Two thoughtful and very personal examinations of modern Belgium by American authors also deserve mention. The first, by the sociologist Renée C. Fox, is *In the Belgian Château: The Spirit and Culture of a European Society in An Age of Change* (Chicago: Ivan R. Dee, 1994). The second, *The Factory of Facts* (New York: Pantheon, 1998), is the wry autobiography of the novelist Luc Santé, a Belgian-American born in French-speaking Verviers but largely raised in New Jersey.

Finally, two Europeans living in Belgium have written books that offer valuable insights into their adoptive homeland. First, Richard Hill, a francophone Briton who has resided in Brussels for thirty years, writes perceptively and affectionately about Belgium in *The Art of Being Belgian: Brussels, Belgium, and Beyond* (Brussels: Europublications, 2005). Second, Derk-Jan Eppink, a Dutch lawyer and journalist, describes his seduction by Belgium in *Belgian Adventures: A European Discovers Belgium* (Tielt: Lannoo, 2004). It must be stressed, however, that the title of the English translation of Eppink's book is quite misleading; in the original Dutch version, his essay is entitled *Adventures Of A Netherbelgian: A Dutchman Discovers Belgium* (*Avonturen Van Een Nederbelg: Een Nederlander Ontdekt België*). The Dutch-language title is much closer to the mark, for Eppink's book reveals as much about the Protestant Netherlands as it does about Catholic Belgium.

6 So pervasive was francophonism among Belgium's educated classes that in 1904 Henri Bouchot, Keeper of the Print Room at the Bibliothèque nationale de France, could claim in the catalog for the groundbreaking Paris exhibition *Les primitifs français* that "as the inhabitants of Bruges spoke French, their painters could (at least until the middle of the fifteenth century) be included in the French school" (quoted from Francis Haskell, *History and Its Images: Art and the Interpretation of the Past*, New Haven: Yale University Press, 1993, p. 466).

7 See in this regard Van Istendael 2004 (note 5) pp. 25–26, and Roegiers 2005 (note 5) p. 76.

8 This is still the case today; see Van Istendael 2004 (note 5) pp. 97–98.

9 Van Istendael 2004 (note 5) pp. 26–31.

10 To judge from recent articles in two American periodicals, this fact has escaped notice in some quarters. In a report entitled "15-Nation Study Finds Cheap Tuition Does Not

Always Increase Access" (*Chronicle of Higher Education*, April 22, 2005), author Sara Lipka provides two rankings for Belgium in her "Affordability and Accessibility" table. While French speakers come in at number 6, "Flemish speakers" find themselves ranked number 4. Likewise, Manohla Dargis's review in *The New York Times* (August 26, 2005) of Belgian director Erik Van Looy's "The Memory Of A Killer" states that the film is in "Flemish and French, with English subtitles." Six weeks before, on July 8, 2005, Dana Stevens had written in the same newspaper that Felix van Groeningen's movie "Steve + Sky" was "in Flemish Dutch, with English subtitles."

11 Van Istendael 2004 (note 5) pp. 119–120.

12 For a partial description of the publishing history of Van Istendael's *Belgian Labyrinth*, see note 5 above.

13 Van Istendael 2004 (note 5) pp. 264–268, and Roegiers 2005 (note 5) p. 127.

14 With respect to the term "Flemish Primitives," see Haskell 1993 (note 6) pp. 445–468; Janssen, De Kok, De Maesschalck, and De Schepper 1996 (note 3) p. 11; Lisa Deam, "Flemish versus Netherlandish: A Discourse of Nationalism," *Renaissance Quarterly* 51 (1998): 1–33, and especially 12–13; and Keith Moxey, *The Practice of Persuasion: Paradox and Power in Art History* (Ithaca: Cornell University Press, 2001) pp. 21–26. None of the four authors, it should be noted, questions the *pars pro toto* use of the term "Flanders" for the southern Netherlands.

For the use of the term "Flemish" to characterize the art made in the southern Netherlands in the early modern period, see Hans Vlieghe, "Vlaamse Kunst en Vlaamse identiteit: Voorstellingen uit het interbellum," in Bert Cardon, Jan Van der Stock, and Dominique Vanwijnsberghe, eds, *'Als ich can': Liber Amicorum in Memory of Professor Dr. Maurits Smeyers* (Louvain: Peeters, 2002) pp. 1597–1604, with a full raft of references to earlier literature on the subject on pp. 1603–1604.

15 Entitled "Lettre au Roi sur la séparation de la Wallonie et de la Flandre," the essay first appeared in the *Revue de Belgique* on August 15, 1912. The entire letter is reprinted, with annotations, in Jules Destrée, *La lettre au Roi, suivie d'extraits de 'L'introduction à la vie socialiste'* (Gembloux: Wallonie Libre, 1968). One finds on page 16 of that reprinting the famous statement "Il y a en Belgique, des Wallons et des Flamands; il n'y a pas de Belges."

16 Ibid., p. 22: "Ils nous ont pris nos artistes. Le maître pathétique de Tournai, Roger de la Pasture, l'un des plus grands artistes du XVe siècle, est incorporé parmi les Flamands sous le nom de Vander Weyden. L'art flamand brille d'un éclat radieux. L'art wallon est ignoré." Destrée went on to write a monograph on the painter entitled *Roger de la Pasture—Van der Weyden* (Brussels: Van Oest, 1930).

17 The *affaire Dehousse* of 1993 is outlined by Hans Vlieghe in "Flemish Art: Does It Really Exist?," *Simiolus* 26 (1998): 192.

Interestingly, some contemporary French scholars do not share Monsieur Dehousse's allergy to the F-word. In 2005, for example, the Center for the Study of Fifteenth-Century Painting in the Southern Netherlands and the Principality of Liège published a two-volume catalog entitled *Collections du Nord-Pas-de-Calais: La peinture de Flandre et de France du Nord au XVe et au début du XVIe siècle* as volume 5 of its Repertory series. Orchestrated by French scholar Christian Heck of the University of Lille, the catalog includes paintings by Antwerp artists such as Jan Sanders van Hemessen (cat. no. 28) and even a follower of the northern Brabantine painter Hieronymus Bosch (cat. no. 12) under the umbrella of "Flanders."

Likewise, the Museum of Fine Arts in Lille mounted an exhibition in 2005 (May 13–September 9) entitled *The Master of the Embroidered Foliage: Secrets of Flemish Workshops of the Late 15th Century*. The accompanying colloquium (June 23–24, 2005) was called "Master of the Embroidered Foliage. Secrets of the Workshops: Artists' Procedures and Methods of Attribution to an Anonymous Flemish Primitive." The subject of the show, however, cannot be localized to East or West Flanders. In fact, the Embroidered Foliage Master is usually thought to have worked in Brussels.

Finally, French scholar Hélène Loyau described Tournai as "la ville flamande" in her and Carla Bozzolo's presentation on the "Cour amoureuse dite de Charles VI" at *Campin In Context*, the international colloquium held in Tournai from March 30 to April 1, 2006.

18 This *affaire* is cited in Vlieghe 1998 (note 17) pp. 192–193.

19 Smeyers 1999 (note 4) pp. 17–19. Interestingly, Smeyers subtitled his introduction (pp. 9–20) "The Great Labyrinth." Is this an indirect reference to Geert Van Istendael's book *The Belgian Labyrinth* (see note 5)?

20 Anonymous, review of Maurits Smeyers, *L'art de la miniature flamande du VIIIe au XVI siècle*, Tournai, 1998, in *Bulletin critique du livre en français* 608 (May 1999): 1081, no. 179303. I identify François Avril as the review's author in this essay with his express permission.

21 "Un livre utile donc pour sa riche documentation, mais à utiliser avec précaution en raison des présupposés politico-culturels qui le sous-tendent."

22 Katarzyna Plonka-Balus and Joanna Zietkiewicz-Kotz, review of Maurits Smeyers, *L'art de la miniature flamande du VIIIe au XVI siècle*, Tournai, 1998, in *Modus: Prace z historii Sztuki*, 1, 2000, pp. 93–99, and especially p. 94.

23 Alain Arnould, review of Maurits Smeyers, *Vlaamse miniaturen van de 8ste tot het midden van de 16de eeuw: De middeleeuwse wereld op perkament* (Louvain, 1998) in *Scriptorium*, 54(2) (2000): 121–122*, no. 315.

24 Alain Arnould and Jean-Michel Massing, *Splendours of Flanders: Late Medieval Art in Cambridge Collections* (Cambridge: University Press, 1993).

25 Ibid., p. ix.

26 The conference papers were published by Maurits Smeyers and Bert Cardon, eds, *Flanders in a European Perspective: Manuscript Illumination around 1400 in Flanders and Abroad. Proceedings of the International Colloquium, Leuven, 7–10 September 1993* (Louvain: Peeters, 1995).

# Part II

# The subjects of art history

## Introduction

The proper subject of art-historical enquiry has for some decades been a source of dispute. Disagreements generally revolve around the question of whether "visual culture" more accurately describes the discipline's purview. Contesting the inherently hierarchical and Eurocentric preoccupation with "art" that the discipline has conventionally evinced, advocates of visual studies instead urge consideration of a broader class of objects while also demanding a sustained critique of the habits, assumptions, and methods of art history.[1] To the dialog between partisans of visual studies and art history is owed the recent and robust genre of art historiography. Despite this disciplinary self-critique, the subject of art history may yet go unrecognized. Indeed, the discipline's preoccupation with designating its *objects* may have helped to keep hidden its real *subjects*. The authors gathered in this section do not consider the subject of art history simply to be artworks or examples of visual culture. Instead, the following essays characterize art history as an inherently reflexive discipline, preoccupied either with negotiating its discursive and institutional boundaries or with providing a means for art historians to manage their own social and psychic identities.

Janet Kraynak observes in "Art History's Present Tense" that art criticism and art history have, since the nineteenth century, been understood to be distinct endeavors. With its interest in judging the relative aesthetic success or failure of contemporary works, art criticism accepts the subjectivity of its mission. Art history, according to Kraynak, has long defined itself in opposition to art criticism's overt subjectivity. That is, until the mid twentieth century. During the 1960s Kraynak discovers that the barricade art history erected between itself and art criticism fell to ruins. What lay siege to art history's disciplinary defenses? Kraynak argues that the advance of structuralism and post-structuralism into the field called into question long-held notions of history, without which the discipline could not maintain its integrity. Now the present posed as much of a problem for art history as the past had. The present needed as much, if not more, critical attention as history. This concern for the present lent to art criticism a new legitimacy:

> The challenges posed by alternative models of history were extensive, begetting for art history a particularly fraught relationship to time. If history is not composed of a series of logical stages . . . then the present becomes an autonomous subject in its own right: one that has been the purview of criticism and largely ignored by art history.

The recognition of history as inescapably contingent and subjective, Kraynak argues, led art history, as practiced and theorized in the last decades of the twentieth century, to become likewise contingent and subjective, in other words to become like art criticism.

Eric Rosenberg, too, finds the boundaries between art history and art criticism to be unstable. And, like Kraynak, he turns to the mid twentieth century for evidence of a breach. In Rosenberg's "The Totality of Form: S.J. Freedberg's Criticism and Clement Greenberg's History," the art historian and critic named in the essay's title are enjoined into conversation with one another, revealing a great deal of accord in their approaches and conclusions. In Freedberg's *Painting of the High Renaissance in Rome and Florence*, Rosenberg discovers a formalist approach that bears a marked kinship to the art criticism of Greenberg. This formalism, Rosenberg explains, is not simply a way of analyzing visual phenomena but also a means of conceptualizing time and, hence, history. For these formalist thinkers, time is "an accumulation of simultaneous instances." Instead of constructing history through the rearview mirror as a linear sequence of events distinct from the present, the formalist conception of time holds that the "present is only present to the extent that it *is* also past." Paintings produced in the sixteenth century can, therefore, be analyzed "alongside"—and in the same terms—as painting of the twentieth century.

Rosenberg's analysis of Freedberg's art history supports Kraynak's contention that "To overcome the limitations of the present has been art history's unstated, but habitual objective." Whereas most art historians, Kraynak indicates, have attempted to pursue ostensibly "objective" modes of inquiry by rooting out any trace of personal, subjective opinion from their writing, Rosenberg brings to light a rather different strategy. In the case of Freedberg, we find an art historian who avoids the thorny problem of temporal distance and subjective response by reconfiguring time itself. Thus, for Freedberg, his analyses of sixteenth-century artworks are as immediate and personal as his encounters with works by his contemporaries. In this way, Freedberg's art history might be seen as proof of what Kraynak describes as the "profound transformation of art history's relation to time and, by association, to criticism itself."

Situated historically, Kraynak and Rosenberg's arguments fix the erosion of borders between art history and art criticism in a particular moment: the mid twentieth century in the United States. Donald Preziosi and Christopher Bucklow approach the integrity of disciplinary boundaries using a different tack. Specifically, both Preziosi and Bucklow argue that such disciplinary frontiers are themselves inherently fictive. Products of the unconscious, the bounds between art history and art criticism—or even between art history and art making—exist only as a means of disguising unacknowledged personal or cultural fears or desires. To attempt to historicize the discipline, to assert and manage not only its relevance but also its very existence, is to avoid confronting the unconscious motivations propelling the participation of individuals and institutions in the endeavor labeled "art history." The real question, for Preziosi as it is for Bucklow, is not *how* art history operates, but *why*. Both assert that it is a largely unconscious response to personal needs. For Preziosi, this remains a historical problem: it is "the modern practice of the self" that requires investment in the discipline, profession, and institutions of art history. Art history, for Preziosi, is a product of the Enlightenment. Bucklow, too, points to a contingent notion of self, finding in the era of Romanticism a renegotiation of ideas of personal will and authority that gives rise to disciplinarity.

But neither Preziosi nor Bucklow focuses here on the historical circumstances that gave rise to the discipline. Instead, both pursue in very different ways a question posed by Preziosi: "What is it about practicing 'art history' that allows practitioners to come into contact with their deepest fears and desires without their entering their consciousness?" Preziosi indicates that secularism—driven by the economic and social demands of the modern nation-state—endowed artworks with a new, more powerful role in the social as well as individual psyche. Art history—for any society where it is practiced—is necessary for the management of essential cultural and personal fetishes, that is artworks. Bucklow takes a different approach in his exploration of the unconscious attraction of art history. His is a personal narrative: "I was using the study and the practice of [art history] writing to search for answers to a set of questions that I did not know I was asking."

Formerly a professional art historian, Bucklow abandoned the profession in order to make art instead. He had never received artistic training nor had he previously engaged in art making. With a good position and a career that would, by most measures, be deemed successful, he quit to make art. Looking back now at his work as an art historian, Bucklow believes that the topics he took up and exhibitions he mounted spoke to his unconscious need to understand and, also, to create. "My choice of subjects had an existential dimension that was intensely personal . . . [and] those choices were made unconsciously." By pursuing art history, as opposed to another field of humanistic inquiry or social science, Bucklow put himself into a kind of psychic dialog with artworks: the pre-eminent symbols of self. What is more, Bucklow contends, his situation was not unique. Far from it. "The artist and the artwork and all its paradigms then become signs of the writer or curator's self." The real subject of art history, then, may not be the objects we claim to study, but our practice as art historians and, ultimately, ourselves.

## Note

1 For a useful summary of the relationship between visual culture and art history, see James D. Herbert, "Visual Culture/Visual Studies," pp. 452–464, in Robert S. Nelson and Richard Shiff, eds, *Critical Terms for Art History*, 2nd edn (Chicago and London: University of Chicago Press, 2003).

Chapter 5

# Art history's present tense

*Janet Kraynak*

Historically, art criticism and art history have been perceived as close, yet still separate fields, enjoying a relative autonomy that has persisted. Most studies that address the history of criticism or of art history, while referring to their inevitable overlap, nonetheless tend to focus on one or the other, with less attention devoted to their contentious, yet symbiotic relationship, as well as the shifting nature of this relationship since their emergence as modern disciplines.[1] An absence of such an examination now feels particularly acute, given that, since the 1960s, the boundaries of criticism and art history have continuously eroded, to the point that the line where one ends and the other begins has become increasingly hard to define. Discursively, rhetorically, and methodologically, the fields have never been so closely aligned. Contemporary art—traditionally the purview of criticism—has now been absorbed into the canon of art history: a development that is as productive as it is fraught. All of these factors raise important and timely questions regarding criticism and art history's institutional identities and allegiances, as well as their fluctuating relationship.

At the same time, such an investigation may seem somewhat belated or even irrelevant, given that both disciplines—albeit for somewhat different reasons—are currently experiencing a crisis. With the expansion and globalization of the art world, the increased professionalization of the artist, and the rise of the curator as a more prominent arbiter of contemporary art, the authority of the critic has seriously eroded. Correspondingly, in the aftermath of alternative theories of knowledge and history that reshaped the humanities starting in the mid-to-late 1960s, art history has been unmoored from its conceptual and methodological foundations, leaving the art historian to mine perilous territory. Here, an astonishing range of ideas and methods from widely diverse fields must be partially "mastered," lest she be left tethered to presumptions and operative principles that have been thoroughly questioned, and even delegitimated.

Given these developments, however, there is an acute demand to evaluate what I am describing as the *present tense* of art history. On the one hand, this refers to the current state or conditions of the discipline, in light of these aforementioned changes. On the other hand, the present tense refers to art history's relation to *the present*—that is contemporary reality and the art of the contemporary. The central conceit of this essay is that while the present tense has traditionally represented art history's blind spot—or the thought it cannot entertain within its institutional identity—recent developments, which have revealed the limitations of the discipline's traditional historical methods, have altered this view. The result is a sea change, in which the present tense is now central to art history's being, as well as its ongoing vitality as a method of cultural analysis.

* * *

The disciplinary distinctions that have shaped criticism and art history stem from the fields' respective historical origins, the contexts in which each developed, and the ideological missions that impacted their critical biases: all of which remained largely unaffected for decades, even centuries. A brief accounting of some of the salient features of this history is warranted.[2]

As is well known, the growth of the modern practice of art criticism was inextricably tied to the development of the Salon system in France from the seventeenth through the nineteenth centuries. During this period, the Salon provided not simply a critical and commercial staging ground for artists seeking exposure and acclaim, but also a form of popular entertainment. Criticism—whether brief descriptive passages featured in pamphlets or more ambitious literary writing appearing in journals—functioned as an integral component of the Salon, and as a mouthpiece for the official dictates of the Academy. After the French Revolution, the exhibition's restrictions were loosened, so that artists who were not members of the Academy could submit work to the jury for inclusion; in the aftermath of this institutional change, criticism came to serve the needs of the expanding publics for art.[3] According to Dario Gamboni, during this post-revolutionary period, criticism was professionalized.[4] Freed from merely reinforcing or countering doctrinaire principles determined by the Academy, the critic now provided lively, accessible, and often opinionated commentary on the display of new art, thereby greatly influencing not just popular opinion, but also the career of living artists and the sales potential of their work.

As the century progressed, the critic's function within a market system of objects and letters became a crucial aspect of the practice, leading to an assumed and inextricable association of the critic and the socio-economic *habitus*, to use Pierre Bourdieu's term, of the "art world": itself an entity born of modern capitalism. The art world—a system of production and exchange with its own distinct rules and principles—was a product of the demise of the Academy as the sole arbiter of taste and artistic success. Referring to Charles Harrison and Cynthia White's argument, Gamboni remarks "during the second half of the nineteenth century, a new system of diffusion and consecration of art (called the 'dealer-critic' system), based on a free market of economic and symbolic values progressively replaced the traditional Academy- and State-ruled system."[5] Similarly, Richard Wrigley writes: "In the modern world, the art critic has come to be treated as a decidedly ambiguous stereotype." He continues:

> either a seer dealing in aesthetic revelation whose texts anchor whole art movements, or a cynical broker in reputations, infamously influential thriving on a mixed diet of venality and animadversion. However much steeped in partiality, the critic is nevertheless acknowledged as an essential inhabitant of the art world. As Raymonde Moulin has demonstrated for the modern period, art critics act out certain pragmatic roles in relation to artists, dealers, and the media.[6]

As a result of this proximity to the art world, a taint has traditionally marred the fortunes of the critic, who is perceived to be beholden to a set of economic interests and relations that unduly, if even unconsciously, influence critical opinion. But whether the critic was seen to operate as a voice of opposition during the days of the Academic Salon,[7] or a fixture in the more recent "dealer-critic system," the actual forms of critical writing have remained relatively consistent. In either case, rhetorical strategies that operate most effectively as tools of persuasion have predominated.

Criticism is thus viewed as possessing a subjective voice, in which the writing reveals not just insight about its object of analysis, but also the writer's individuality. With the importance of this embodied critical voice, the critic rose as a persona on par with that of the artist. In part shaped by modern concepts of subjectivity, this reputation is reinforced by the perceived goal of the critic, who is charged with illuminating the meaning—and ultimately "truth"—buried within the work of art.[8] As a result, the critic's taste and ego are reflected in prose, a situation that has been both a blessing and curse. As art critic Max Kozloff, writing in the 1960s, notes: ". . . much of past art writing has seemed precisely to be affirmation of the self. Surely this has been the classic objection to the practice—one hesitates to call it the discipline—of art criticism."[9]

While art criticism was most significantly shaped in the French context, which to some extent accounts for its literary preoccupations, modern art history's German roots in metaphysical philosophy have similarly influenced its character and principles.[10] Unlike criticism, where emphasis was placed on the object as an embodiment of aesthetic truth, and the critical voice as the conduit in revealing this truth, art history's philosophical origins placed the question of the nature of art—and by association, a notion of art—at the center of its disciplinary self-consciousness. While one could easily argue that such questions are themselves interpretive, from Heinrich Wölfflin to Erwin Panofsky and beyond, they have been addressed through an appeal to supposedly impersonal historical systems. A formal or symbolic structure is seen to guide the choices and conclusions of the historian, who remains removed from his/her object of analysis, rather than directly invested in it. In addition, as a field traditionally preoccupied with achievements of the past, an attendance to history and interest in historical progress or development, have also been central.[11]

During the nineteenth century, when art history's modern identity emerged, the two most significant philosophical influences were Immanuel Kant and Friedrich Hegel, who both wrote aesthetic philosophy. For Kant, aesthetics occupied a special domain, distinct from normal experience. Kant was particularly interested in the nature and validity of aesthetic claims or judgments, which, he maintains, are necessarily *subjective*, but not *personal*: a distinction that is important in relation to criticism's own voice. According to his theory, claims regarding the nature of the beautiful or of creative genius express not simply a personal predilection, but represent a higher truth that is universal and constant. As Michael Podro explains:

> aesthetic judgment is held to be valid for anyone; it is not held to be dependent upon something which varied from one individual to another . . . We believe that in judging something to be beautiful we are expressing more than a personal preference; we are expressing a sense of rightness which we believe valid for all men because it is based on the nature of the mind itself.[12]

Like Kant, Hegel reserved a special place and function for art, but unlike his counterpart, Hegel was invested in the progress of art and its ultimate finitude: an unfolding of History as the progress of Spirit, in which Art assumes a position at the apex. In his teleological schema, Hegel was concerned with the continued vitality or possibilities of past art to the present, and also with the specific value of art as "an exercise of the mind's freedom, its role in the life of the Spirit," to borrow Podro's words. To these ends, Hegel devised an evolutionary system, in which art passed through a series of progressive stages on its way to its fulfillment as Spirit or Mind, thereby overcoming matter. For Hegel, Art was essentially a domain isolated from the material world, finding its fullest expression as a purely mental activity, or moment of self-consciousness.[13]

The philosophical imperatives of Kant and Hegel shaped art history's emerging identity, both informing and coinciding with central tenets of modernism—in particular, the ideal of aesthetic autonomy.[14] The notion of art as a self-contained field echoed both Kant's and Hegel's theories, in that, according to them, the definitive activity of the mind is self-reflection. This self-reflexivity of mind is analogous to the self-reflexivity of medium at the heart of modernist theory. The notion of autonomy, however, is not just a legacy of idealist philosophy; rather, it also has to do with the discipline's institutionalization. In seeking its own legitimation, art history found it necessary to sanction off its field of activity—and as such, its object scrutiny—from any other. What ensued was the formation of a set of objective criteria from which putatively truth-bound conclusions could be drawn: ones based not upon the contingencies of taste or the vicissitudes of critical faculty, but upon historical and even quasi-scientific evidence. To these ends, art history equally embraced positivism and empiricism. In contrast to an abstract concept of aesthetic experience found in metaphysical philosophy, an empirical approach allowed for the verification of phenomena through direct experience. Giovanni Morelli's theories of authentication and attribution (which Eric Fernie aptly describes as "scientific connoisseurship") are exemplary of the empirical method.[15] In this way, art history occupies an oddly contradictory place, unifying the two dominant philosophical tendencies of the eighteenth and nineteenth centuries—idealism and empiricism—within one discipline.

* * *

One might summarize that both criticism and art history are products of modernism, but slightly differing aspects of this phenomenon. Generally speaking, criticism is intimately connected to the expanding marketplace and publics for art. Shaped by modern notions of subjectivity, the critic has operated as an agent or conduit whose judgment in the presence of an art object is paramount. The historian, on the other hand, informed by idealist aesthetics and methods of empirical deduction, has pursued objectivity. While an intimate proximity to his object of study also prevails, it is nonetheless undertaken under the guise of critical distance: one that is seen to legitimize interpretation as an impersonal rather than subjective outcome, and to place it within the broader processes of history rather than punctual judgment.

Criticism, one could assert, engages with the *presence* of the artwork, while art history is concerned with its *passage* and progress. Here Stephen Bann's distinction serves as a useful template: criticism, he writes, "provides an extratemporal evaluation of the object," while art history "follows the fortunes of an object in time."[16] The critic beholds his/her object of analysis in order to generate a response. In the introduction to his anthology on art criticism in nineteenth-century France, Michael Orwicz explains: "As art criticism was given a place, the established tradition was to presume that the critics' interpretations were themselves formulated in their *direct engagement* with the work of art, and functioned simply as a reflection of the art that the discipline so unyieldingly held at center stage."[17] Exacerbating criticism's relation to presence is its subject, which as a rule is the art *of* the present.

Alternately, art history not only has typically engaged with the art of the past, but the past itself is seen to possess a specific function and value. Here its Hegelian roots are significant in that Hegel's philosophy of art is one and the same as his philosophy of history: progressively overcoming alienation toward a purer future of dialectical reconciliation.[18] Art history's teleological perspective, where the present represents a fulfillment of the past, is indebted to this model. Also relevant is its mission of historical retrieval or recreation: the attempt to determine the conditions of art's original creation and reception. What this entails essentially is an *elimination* of the perspective of the present, which is viewed as necessarily and problematically subjective. To overcome the limitations of the present has been art history's unstated, but habitual objective: one that is diametrically opposed to criticism's aims.

The distinction described above might be summarized in terms of *synchrony* versus *diachrony*: *in time* versus *through time*. Put another way, criticism and art history engage in and proffer different modalities of time. As such, temporality—or a relation to time and concepts thereof—is a recurring, underlying theme, working itself sometimes invisibly, but persistently, into the very fabric of disciplinary and institutional identity. But under the pressure of several key developments in the 1960s—a period of intellectual, political, and social upheaval—this temporal model begins to erode. The result is a profound transformation of art history's relation to time and, by association, to criticism itself.

* * *

To speak of the recent transformation of art history necessarily entails a broader revisiting of key events in post-war intellectual history, in which longstanding tenets and methods of scholarship were revisited. Fueled by the social and political crises of the period marked by the First World War and the Vietnam War, this reassessment included two intertwining themes: a loss of faith in metaphysical philosophy and the principles it espoused regarding historical meaning and progress, and the rise of theory.

As Michael Roth, in a study of post-war French Hegelianism, contends, for the generation of thinkers following Alexandre Kojève, Jean Hyppolite and Jean-Paul Sartre, Hegelian historicism was a prime target of critique. The notion that history was a source of truth, and that it purposefully moved forward toward a more fulfilling and harmonious future, was increasingly met with skepticism if not outright disbelief. "Hegelian historicizing declined with the loss of faith in the meaningfulness of history," Roth remarks, "Contemporary events seemed to undermine even the thought of heroic or radical political change, and the development of sophisticated methodologies of the synchronic in linguistics, anthropology, and cybernetics legitimated a retreat from the historical."[19]

For certain post-Hegelian philosophers—Michel Foucault and Gilles Deleuze chiefly among them—Roth contends that Nietzsche replaced Hegel as "the locus of philosophic authority in France in the 1960s."[20] This shift in philosophical loyalties aimed to counter Hegel's notion of history, which is synonymous with progress. Within this schema, the dialectic—the movement of thesis, antithesis, synthesis—represents the motor driving this future possibility. Both Foucault and Deleuze, however, rejected Hegel's dialectic "in favor of the construction of a genealogical history of the present," on the part of Foucault, and of a radical anti-humanism for Deleuze. "Nietzsche was the thinker who provided Deleuze with a vehicle both for abandoning anthropologism," Roth writes, "a code word for the Hegelian idea of creative change through negation—and from thinking instead the primacy of difference and the free play of affirmative possibilities."[21]

In Nietzsche, Foucault and Deleuze found a radical critique of the notion of history as progress, and the concept of origins or, metaphorically, of *depth* itself—equated now with the miscalculations of Hegelian historicism. Foucault's method of genealogy demonstrates this perspective: history contains not essences, but interpretations; and not continuities but discontinuities.[22] There is no larger, meta-narrative or meaning that coheres the past and the present, but only a radically disjunctive field of hermeneutic play and rupture.

Similarly, for Deleuze, Nietzsche was a thinker who displaced unities and logical continuities with a fragmentary model. "The history of a thing, in general, is the succession of forces which take possession of it and the co-existence of forces which struggle for possession. The same object, the same phenomenon changes meaning according to the force which appropriates it."[23] Deleuze's reference to *force* relates to his notion of the *event*: a non-spatialized model of time that is not made up of distinct and logically progressing moments, but fits and starts, of flashback and recurrence. Contemporary reality, for Deleuze, is formed by and can only be understood through an event-structure.

Foucault and Deleuze's transformation of history via Nietzsche represents an important transitional moment in intellectual history, when prevailing principles in the humanistic disciplines came under scrutiny. For Frederic Jameson, this epistemological revolution is part of a general "mutation in culture," which marks the period of the 1960s.[24] In Jameson's essay—titled "Periodizing the Sixties"—however, the idea of a "period" is approached not as a false historical unity, but rather as a series of "structurally homologous breaks" between various "levels" of culture—including philosophy, revolutionary politics, and economics, to name a few. Both in its subject and its method of analysis, Jameson's study proposes an alternative form of historicizing: working synchronically and intertextually—or across and through cohabitating fields and themes—he moves swiftly from a discussion of the Fanonian model of struggle to contested notions of subjectivity to the emergence of media culture: all of which, he remarks, are equally capable of revealing historical trends.[25]

Among the significant trends addressed is the advent of what Jameson terms the "slogan" theory. Here he defines theory in a negative way—as a "withering away of philosophy," in which philosophy, "as a discipline and institution," is thoroughly challenged.[26] Philosophy is treated both as an isolated subject and as a trope, embodying the traditionally institutionalized and codified discipline that possesses its own unique traditions, characteristics, and principles. In contrast to philosophy's discreteness, theory proposes a radical breakdown of categories, to the point where disciplinary integrity—or the presupposition that each field maintains its own unique subject and intellectual purview—is displaced by a more fluid "intertextual" mode of working. "Henceforth, the new 'philosophical' text will no longer draw its significance from an insertion into the issues and debates of the philosophical tradition," Jameson writes:

> which means that its basic 'intertextual' references become random, an *ad hoc* constellation which forms and dissolves on the occasion of each new text. The new text must necessarily be a commentary on other texts . . . yet those texts, drawn from the most wildly distant disciplines (anthropology, psychiatry, literature, history of science), will be selected in a seemingly arbitrary fashion . . . The vocation of what was formerly 'philosophy' is thereby restructured and displaced: since there is no longer a tradition of philosophical problems in terms of which new positions and new statements can meaningfully be proposed, such works tend toward what can be called *metaphilosophy* . . . [27]

During the post-war period, history itself becomes a contested subject, and philosophy a contested method of working. These conditions both motivated and were a byproduct of the theoretical turn in knowledge, constituting a central "paradigm shift" in history. As we will see, the stakes of this situation prove to be crucial for art history's negotiation of the problem of time.

* * *

While the effects of this theoretical turn on art history were not immediate, they slowly penetrated, with the pace of change quickening in the mid 1970s upon several important occurrences. First was the publication of T.J. Clark's now famous 1974 article, "The Conditions of Artistic Creation."[28] In this article, Clark calls for the renunciation of art history as it has been known and practiced, arguing for the singular viability of an approach based in socio-historical analysis, with an emphasis on the Marxian concept of ideology. Shortly afterwards, in 1975, Rosalind Krauss and Annette Michelson, two former contributing editors of *Artforum* during the magazine's period of critical ascendance (an overlap whose significance will be emphasized below), along with several other colleagues, founded the journal *October*.

In an explicit challenge to modernist (read traditional) art history, *October*'s stated ambition was to disseminate the then novel theoretical approaches emerging mostly from France. Although bound by a different set of theoretical allegiances than Clark—namely structuralism and post-structuralism—the editors of *October* similarly argued for a renunciation of conventional art history, foregrounding the question of method as a central subject of art-historical enquiry.[29]

Despite their differences, Clark and Krauss's approaches equally demonstrate the influx of theory into art history—Marxist cultural criticism and structural linguistics respectively.[30] The result of this importation of ideas culled from a broad and complex disciplinary field was what came to be known (by its defenders as well as detractors) as "new art history."[31] Although the often contentious debates concerning new art history did not materialize until the 1980s, the effects of this transformation were particularly acute.[32] Given its philosophical foundations in idealism and empiricism, art history's intellectual foundations were now thoroughly shaken. Materialist analysis forced an examination of the economic and institutional (in the Althusserian sense of the term) conditions of art, a subject previously dismissed as relevant exclusively to criticism. Alternative theories of subjectivity, which foreground a multiplicity of subject-positions, rendered the authoritative voice of the historian, with its pretense of distance, objectivity, and neutrality (not to mention lack of cultural, racial, or sexual specificity) unstable. With structuralism's pursuit of the sign and its polyvalence, notions of truth and meaning were displaced by the endless play of signification, a dynamic captured by Jacques Derrida's influential notion of *différance*, or the continual deferral of meaning. The emergence of postmodern notions of representation, indebted to structuralist and post-structuralist theory, further complicated the art-historical perspective. Now representation did not exclusively mean the picturing of the world, but connoted a semiotic system linked to other semiotic systems, in which the conditions of signification—or how meaning is actively *made*—were at issue.

These developments, among others, pressured the field of art history, forcing a deferred response to the intellectual schism with Hegelian historicism that had motivated intellectuals in the 1950s and 1960s. Long resistant to change, an emergent methodological self-consciousness was now made imperative by this theoretical turn. What it revealed was the extent of art history's internalization of a particular conception of history, one underlying even the most divergent of the conventional interpretive methods of the discipline.[33] Formalist or contextualist, empirical or idealist, the notion of art as progressively marching toward a more complete stage of development was the predominant dynamic: from the Hegelian progress of Spirit to the Marxian progress of society, where art equally plays a transformative role.

Within this structure, relations of present to past and future were relatively stable: the past constituting the logical origin of the present, and the present meaningful only in relation to future possibility. A return to Hegel's conception of history—or more specifically, of time—is relevant here.

As Roth writes, Hegel "develop[ed] a concept of time which gives primacy to the future." He continues:

> The meaning of a now is contained in its future and in the relation of that future to the past of the now. Hegel gives us, first and foremost, a conception of *human* time, because we humans are beings who determine our present by our orientation—hope, expectation, work—toward the future and by the connection we see between that future and our past.[34]

This view of the present not only subordinates it to other moments in time, but these moments are themselves defined in spatial terms, forming an unbroken continuum: a plane of chronological time that Deleuze's event-structure contradicts. Equally, the notion of "human time" is itself notable, as the pretense that historical and political processes are effectuated by human action or controlled by its will, is a central critique of structuralism, which externalizes history and the subject, rendering them *effects* of "institutions" (broadly defined, including discourse) rather than in control of them.[35] Art history, however, always tarried in this human conception of time and history, driven by a sequence of names (artists, art historians) that comprise a coherent story of art.

On a concrete level, historicism saturated the most fundamental and durable "tools" of the field: from the canon formation of movements and individual artistic genius to seemingly immutable concepts as style and quality. Indeed paradigmatic is the very foundation of introductory art history, the survey text. As Mitchell Schwarzer writes:

> the survey text embodies the nineteenth century vision of history *to unify the art of the past into a coherent and relevant story for the present* . . . Their surveys tell us about the construction of history according to ideas of progress and linearity, and the division of world culture through rankings of artistic quality.[36]

The challenges posed by alternative models of history were extensive, begetting for art history a particularly fraught relationship to time. If history is not composed of a series of logical stages, if the present is not merely a fulfillment of the past and an emblem of future potentiality, and if the present cannot be cast off as an unnecessarily subjective burden, then the present becomes an autonomous subject in its own right: one that has been the purview of criticism and largely ignored by art history.

* * *

As the fortunes of art history were waning, those of criticism were increasing. In the United States, a significant factor was the prominence of Clement Greenberg and the example his work set for an entire generation of intellectuals. Although he began writing for the *Nation* in the 1940s and was long established as an important critic, the influence of Greenberg on post-war intellectual life was not fully felt until the 1960s. With Greenberg, a powerful model was offered: a form of critical writing that was persuasive, polemical, and serious, rather than journalistic, personal, or literary in the *belle lettriste* sense of the term. Along with other prominent critics, Greenberg helped set the stage for the emergence of art criticism as a meaningful pursuit. As Hal Foster notes in reference to the circle of writers associated with *Artforum* in the 1960s (including Barbara Rose, Michael Fried, Rosalind Krauss, and others), and their indebtedness to key critical mentors:

> Greenberg was not the only star in the art critical sky; in fact it was only after *Art and Culture*, his collection of essays, appeared in 1962 that his thought worked its way deep into this generation . . . Several witnesses also attest to the formative influence of the contextual teachings of Meyer Schapiro, the art historian at Columbia University, whose writings ranged from Romanesque architecture to Rothko abstractions. The triangulation of father figures was completed by Harold Rosenberg, later art critic at *The New Yorker* and professor at the University of Chicago, who moved methodologically between the other two patriarchs, and who served as a role model for an additional subset of *Artforum* writers, Max Kozloff chief among them. [37]

During the 1960s, *Artforum* became the single most influential source for information about new and often progressive artistic practices, and also for new forms of critical writing.[38] To some extent, the changing fortunes of art criticism were in response to the nature of contemporary art itself, which self-consciously sought to question art's conceptual and ontological foundations—in a manner parallel to the self-critical approach that accompanied the rise of theory in academia. In the introduction to his anthology, *The New Art*, Gregory Battcock refers to the central role criticism came to play during this era of artistic change:

> Today's critic is beginning to seem almost as essential to the development—indeed the identification—of art as the artist himself . . . [I]n keeping with the new role of the critic as interpreter, the pieces included in this anthology do more than simply describe, or even define their subject; their authors are actively and consciously engaged in the preparation of a new aesthetic, so much so that it is on occasion difficult to dissociate their work from the art it purports to evaluate.[39]

Out of this convergence of rigorous writing and difficult art, a new model arose—the *scholar–critic*, who has one foot in the academy, with all its attendant scholarly precision, and the other in the art world, with its network of dealers, artists, and collectors.[40] If in the nineteenth century, as Gamboni argues, criticism was professionalized, in the late twentieth century, it was *academicized*.[41] Critic Sidney Tillim, in a symposium on criticism in the 1960s (which took place in 1966) says as much:

> there is not so much new in criticism as a new tone in criticism, a certain aggressiveness sponsored by the new social-critical awareness . . . There is also a new kind of critic: the art historian who has deserted the academy to identify with the present as future rather than the past, and who has brought to bear on the problems of modernist style both the psychology and methodology of the historian, thus lending a characteristic inflection to what is essentially a literature of conversion. For the critic–historian is at once pedantic and hortatory—half-teacher, half-preacher.[42]

The scholar–critic represents a blurring of institutional and discursive boundaries: the academy and the art market, the scholarly journal and the art magazine, the object and the text. But on a more abstract level, it also erodes the boundaries of time. In Tillim's quote cited above is a subtle recognition of this fact, in the observation that the critic–historian now "identif[ies] with the present as future rather than the past," suggesting a shift in temporal loyalties. Available evidence certainly furthers the case, as scholars trained in eighteenth- and nineteenth-century art no longer feel beholden to a specific historical period, moving outside their narrow fields of specialization to write criticism on contemporary art.[43] Following their mentors' example, many graduate students (even if their departments are not supportive) pursue an involvement in contemporary criticism as a natural extension of their scholarly activity.

While these are merely anecdotal observations, they do reveal the degree to which a central question of *historical* investigation has become *methodological*. In other words, given the turn toward theory and the emergence of the scholar–critic, specialization has become less defined primarily by historical period than interpretive or methodological approach, one that can be employed effectively outside a narrow historical range. In short, the art historian has been freed from the constraints of time.

For art history, the impact has been profound, resulting in the admittance into its purview of something conventionally beyond its disciplinary confines: namely, *the present tense* which, as a result of intersecting imperatives of criticism and new art history, must now be confronted.

* * *

A key question materializes: what does it mean to produce a *history* of the present? Put another way, one could query, what does it mean to think about or theorize the present? This is a subject that preoccupied Foucault in his reassessment of the function and meaning of history. Surprisingly, however, Foucault's main theoretical inspiration came not from the writings of Nietzsche, but from a previously little-known text by Kant.

In an essay first published as an English translation in 1984, "What is Enlightenment?" (the title of which is taken from Kant's text of the same name), Foucault writes that Kant was the first philosopher to raise "the philosophical question of the present day."[44] While past thinkers have also engaged with this question, Foucault explains, it was usually from one of a limited number of perspectives. To paraphrase Foucault: the present is represented as belonging to a certain era of the world, distinct from others through innate characteristics; the present bears signs of, or foretells, a pending event; or the present is approached as a transitional moment on the road to the dawning of a new world.[45] Kant, however, introduces the question of the Enlightenment—that is *his* present—in a radically novel way, emphasizing *difference* over and above continuity. "It is neither a world era to which one belongs," Foucault writes:

> nor an event whose signs are perceived, nor the dawning of an accomplishment. Kant defines *Aufklärung* in an almost entirely negative way, as an *Ausgang*, an 'exit,' a 'way out.' In his other texts on history, Kant occasionally raises questions of origin or defines the internal teleology of a historical process. In the text on *Aufklärung*, he deals with the question of contemporary reality alone. He is not seeking to understand the present on the basis of a totality or of a future achievement. He is looking for a difference. *What difference does today introduce with respect to yesterday?*[46]

For Foucault, the very "modernity" of Kant's thought is located in this subtle, yet significant, shift. By defining the present through difference, Kant adapts a critical mode in which modernity is characterized not as a period, with fixed attributes (reason, rationality, etc.), but as an *attitude* that breaks with the past in a meaningful way.[47] "The hypothesis I should like to propose," Foucault writes, "is that this little text is located in a sense at the crossroads of critical reflection and reflection on history." He continues:

> It is a reflection by Kant on the contemporary status of his own enterprise . . . it is the first time that a philosopher has connected in this way, closely and from the inside, the significance of his work with respect to knowledge, a reflection on history and a particular analysis of the specific moment at which he is writing and because of which he is writing. It is in the reflection on 'today'

> as difference in history and as motive for a particular philosophical task that the novelty of this text appears to me to lie.
>
> And by looking at it this way, it seems to me we may recognize a point of departure: the outline of what one might call the attitude of modernity.[48]

This adjustment of modernity as an "attitude" leads to an alternate understanding of the Enlightenment and its legacy. Rather than a fixed set of principles (that is, rationality) or philosophical allegiances (that is, humanism), the Enlightenment, for Foucault via Kant, represents a "certain manner of philosophizing" that he identifies as "modern." And modernity is characterized by a central dynamic: a struggle with a persistent *counter*-modernity, one that maintains a disdain for the present—or a resistance to confronting the nature of contemporary reality. Kant's form of interrogation, in contrast, seeks to "problematize man's relation to the present." As a result, Foucault insists, "the thread that may connect us to the Enlightenment is not faithfulness to doctrinal elements, but rather the permanent reactivation of an attitude—that is, of a philosophical ethos that could be described as *a permanent critique of our historical era*."[49]

The premise of a "reflective relation to the present," central to Foucault's under-standing of Kant's modernity, represents a powerful rejoinder to Hegel's historical model. Here, the present is not a spatially fixed moment, but a process predicated upon difference. In Kant's rumination on the subject of the Enlightenment is a significant move, where two putatively distinct enterprises—critical reflection and reflection on history—are unified into one form of critique. Importantly, this very same division has separated the practices of art criticism and art history, granting them partial autonomy. Owing to a number of forces discussed in this essay, however, this semi-autonomy has been breached. One result is that art history also must entertain critical reflection—confronting the *difference* of contemporary reality.

* * *

Above, it was noted that for art history, a consideration of change over time—a commitment to history—distinguished the field from criticism. This distinction, I want to suggest, still constitutes an area of ongoing tension. While the subjects and rhetorical modes of argument of the two fields may now be almost indistinguishable, the *question* of the present poses a critical problematic for art history in a way that it does not for criticism—the latter which still largely accepts it not as a problem to investigate, but as a given, or a reality to which it has always been tied. The crucial change is that for art history, the present now constitutes a *historical* question—that, importantly, must be addressed outside the bounds of historicism. Following Roth, questions of use or function have replaced those of significance or meaning. "In the retreat from Hegelian history," he notes, "is a shift from 'What does history mean?' or 'How can we make sense of our past?' to 'How does history work?' or 'How is the past put together?' "[50] To this, I would add, "How does the present work?" or "How does the present *change* the past?"

In terms of art history, contemporary reality is not available as a means to *recover* the past, but in order to *transform* it. Assumed now is a historical view of the present as a "permanent critique of contemporary reality." The perspective of and on the present is now utterly indispensable, a way of transforming the past so that history becomes a porous and mutable object, constantly being rewritten and challenged rather than received.

If, as Jameson contends, the "situation" of the 1960s can be organized (rather than unified) around a series of structurally homologous breaks, it follows that this is another one. Art history's ultimate schism with historicism—which has transformed its mission to be equal parts critical reflection *and* reflection on history—amounts to an embrace of the present tense: the thought that was absent from its past, but which now defines its present.

## Notes

My thanks to Rachel Haidu for her feedback and insightful comments during the preparation of this essay, to Stuart Laxton for helpful bibliographic suggestions, and to Elizabeth Mansfield for the editorial guidance her book provided in conceiving the essay's arguments.

1 Which is not to say that the subject has not been addressed: The Getty Center recently held a symposium on art history and criticism, but, unfortunately, no extant documents are available. In a roundtable on criticism hosted by the journal *October*, a number of the participants also touch on the topic ("The Present Conditions of Art Criticism," *October* 100 (Spring, 2002): 200–228. In addition, in the literature cited below (see note 2), several of the authors allude to the relationship of the fields.

2 Among the excellent sources on the history of criticism, see Elizabeth Gilmore Holt, ed., *The Triumph of Art for the Public 1758–1848: The Emerging Role of Exhibitions and Critics* (Princeton: Princeton University Press, 1979); Michael R. Orwicz, ed., *Art Criticism and Its Institutions in Nineteenth Century France* (Manchester: Manchester University Press, 1994); Richard Wrigley, *The Origins of French Art Criticism from the Ancien Regime to the Restoration* (Oxford: Clarendon Press, 1993); Anita Brookner, *Genius of the Future: Essays in French Art Criticism: Diderot, Stendhal, Baudelaire, Zola, the Brothers Goncourt, Huysmans* (London: Phaidon, 1971). On the history of art history, again among the many good sources, see: Michael Podro, *The Critical Historians of Art* (New Haven: Yale University Press, 1982); Vernon Hyde Minor, *Art History's History* (Englewood Cliffs, NJ: Prentice-Hall, 1994); Eric Fernie, *Art History and Its Methods* (London: Phaidon Press, 1995); Michael Ann Holly, *Panofsky and the Foundations of Art History* (Ithaca: Cornell University Press, 1984).

3 On the Salon's shifting relationship to the public and public sphere, see Thomas Crow's important study, *Painters and Public Life in 18th Century Paris* (New Haven: Yale University Press, 1985).

4 He writes, ". . . during the nineteenth century, and particularly in its latter half, as a result of the expansion of the press and a transformation in the system of diffusion and consecration of art, art criticism in France went through a process of professionalisation. It is at this point that the journalistic pole gained dominance, the scientific pole became specialised as 'art history' dealing, in principle, with art of the past, and the literary pole was marginalised into a form of 'pure literature.'" Dario Gamboni, "The Relative Autonomy of Criticism," in Orwicz, p. 183.

5 Ibid., p. 188. Elsewhere Gamboni adds: "In 1903, [critic Camille] Mauclair described (negatively) 'the critic' at the commercial and institutional heart of the art world. 'He is connected with the dealers, indirectly negotiates purchases and sales. He intrigues for official charges, the Fine Arts inspectorate, the insignia, the participation in State commissions.'" Ibid., p. 185.

6 Wrigley, p. 9.

7 Wrigley notes, "Salon criticism's great attraction for aspiring critics was that, from the mid-eighteenth century, it was understood to be a thorn in the side of the Académie and the establishment. For its authors, this function probably took precedence over any practical didactic role." Ibid., p. 164.

8 As Michael Orwicz explains, "Since the overriding objective of art criticism here has been to illuminate works of art or artists, its authority, legitimacy and indeed its very 'truth' have ultimately been seen to be embedded in the work itself." Orwicz, p. 2.

9 Kozloff's comment is from a symposium held at Brandeis University in 1966, the papers for which were subsequently published in the booklet, *Art Criticism in the 60s: A Symposium of the Poses Institute of Fine Arts*, edited by William C. Seitz (New York: October House, 1967): np. Reference to this publication appears in Amy Newman's introduction to her book, *Challenging Art* (see note 38).

10 Although there are other non-German traditions that are significant to the development of the modern discipline, the German tradition is particularly influential and has, more than any other, shaped the discourse in the United States and Europe. As Michael Podro emphasizes, these traditions, moreover, intersect: "[The] German tradition is not altogether isolated; it is not without relation to the writing of Ruskin, Pater and Fry in England, or to Viollet-le-Duc, Taine and later Focillon and Francastel in France, or to that of Croce, Leonello Venturi and others in Italy . . ." Podro, p. xxi.

11 Michael Podro makes the important point, however, that one can't divide questions of historical fact from those of a notion of art. See Podro, p. xvi.

12 Ibid., p. 10.

13 Hegel's disengagement of art and aesthetics from the material world is a key point of critique for subsequent philosophers and historians. As Podro makes clear, "The difference was between a conception of art as part of contemplative and part of active life—as tied primarily to thought or primarily to social relations." (Ibid., p. xxiii). Marx's own rewriting of Hegel's concept of history, moving from historical idealism to historical materialism, would significantly inform an alternative conception of art that locates the latter within the realm of human wordly activity, as opposed to mental or "spiritual" processes.

14 As Hal Foster notes, ". . . the development of art history as an academic discipline at the end of the nineteenth century coincided with the development of modernist art as an autonomous activity during the same period." Foster, "Antinomies in Art History," *Design and Crime and Other Diatribes* (London: Verso, 2002) p. 84.

15 Fernie, p. 13. In this context, Fernie also discusses the writings of Gottfried Semper.

16 Bann's remark is cited by editors Salim Kemal and Ivan Gaskell in their introduction to *The Language of Art History* (New York: Cambridge University Press, 1991) p. 1. The editors also emphasize the centrality of the theme of "presence" in consideration of the proximity of criticism and art history. "Some academic art historians may prefer to play down the fact of this inter-relation," they write, "for art history's concern with historical retrieval—not with criticism—primarily sanctions it as an academic activity . . . The inextricability of criticism from art history is clear from the very first chapters of [this] collection. These examine the 'presence' of art works. This issue also demonstrates the propinquity of art-historical and philosophical interests," pp. 1–2.
17 Orwicz, p. ix (emphasis added).
18 On Hegel's conception of history, see Michael S. Roth, *Knowing and History: Appropriations of Hegel in Twentieth Century France* (Ithaca: Cornell University Press, 1988). Roth's text is discussed in more detail below.
19 Ibid., p. ix.
20 Ibid., p. xii; 190.
21 Ibid., p. 194.
22 See Michel Foucault, "Nietzsche, Genealogy, History" in Paul Rabinow, ed. *The Foucault Reader* (New York: Pantheon Books, 1984): 76–100. For a discussion of this text, see also Roth, pp. 204–206.
23 Gilles Deleuze, *Nietzsche and Philosophy*, trans. Hugh Tomlinson (New York: Columbia University Press, 1995), cited by Roth, p. 195.
24 Frederic Jameson, "Periodizing the Sixties," in Sohnya Sayres *et al.*, eds, *The Sixties Without Apology* (Minneapolis: University of Minnesota Press in cooperation with *Social Text*, 1984).
25 Ibid., p. 179.
26 Ibid., pp. 192–193.
27 Ibid. p. 193 (emphasis added).
28 T.J. Clark, "The Conditions of Artistic Creation" *Times Literary Supplement* (May 24, 1974): 561–562.
29 Many of Krauss's important essays of the 1970s and early 1980s, which originally appeared in *October*, were later anthologized in her *Originality of Avant-Garde and Other Modernist Myths* (Cambridge: The MIT Press, 1985). In her introdution to the book, Krauss explicitly emphasizes questions of method over and above meaning or significance: a structuralist move that weaves through her essays as well.
30 Ironically, while the two represent a more recent methodological split, they restage the contextualist versus irreducibility arguments that fueled earlier philosophical debates, but now recast in terms of post-war theory.
31 In the introduction to *The New Art History* (London: Camden Press, 1986), editors A.L. Rees and Frances Borzello write of the instability "new art history" generated. Speaking from the British context, their remarks are equally valid for an American one: "By [the mid 1980s] new art history was represented among the modules and credits of the Open University, and was beginning to enter the gates of the enclosed kind, too. In November 1985, the journal *History Today* asked six art historians 'What is the History of Art?'. Nowhere were the words 'new art history' mentioned, but the admissions of doubt and dissatisfaction which mingled with their explanations and defence of their subject revealed a discipline asking itself a number of awkward questions," p. 3
32 As Rees and Borzello note, the first use of the term "new art history" they were able to identify was in 1982 (Ibid., p. 3). They also remark: "The academics grumbled about

jargon, but by 1980 the prestigious Association of Art Historians [based in Great Britain] had opened its conference and journal *Art History* to the new trends, adding to its traditional papers on attributions and influences, new sections on methodology, feminism and social art history," p. 3.

33 For an analysis of the ramifications of art history's dependence on Hegelian historicism, see Keith Moxey, *The Practice of Persuasion: Paradox and Power in Art History* (Ithaca: Cornell University Press, 2001); in particular, Chapter 1, "Art History's Hegelian Unconscious: Naturalism as Nationalism in the Study of Early Netherlandish Painting," pp. 8–41.

34 Author's emphasis. Roth takes the notion of human time from Alexandre Koyré's reading of Hegel. See Roth, pp. 7–8.

35 On this point, see Jameson, 190. He writes, "This lesson might well be described as the discovery, within a hitherto antagonistic and 'transparent' political praxis, of the opacity of the Institution itself as the radically transindividual, with its own inner dynamic and laws, which are not those of individual human action or intention, something which Sartre theorized in the Critique as the 'practico-inert,' and which will take the definitive form, in competing 'structuralism,' of 'structure' or 'synchronic system,' a realm of impersonal logic in terms of which human consciousness is itself little more than an 'effect of structure.'"

36 Mitchell Schwarzer, "Origins of the Art History Survey Text," *Art Journal*, special issue *Rethinking the Introductory Art History Survey*, 54(3) (Fall, 1995): 24 (emphasis added).

37 Foster, "Art Critics in Extremis," *Design and Crime*, 107–108.

38 On the history of *Artforum*'s emergence and lasting influence, as well as a fascinating account of the figures who comprised the journal's critical voice and the internecine struggles that characterized it, see Amy Newman, *Challenging Art: Artforum 1962–1974* (New York: SoHo, 2000).

39 My attention was drawn to Battcock's introduction by Francis V. O'Connor in his article, "Notes on patronage: the 1960s," (*Artforum*, September 1972: 53). The quote cited above appears in the revised version of Battcock's text, but O'Connor cites the original volume's introduction, which contains a similar sentiment, but with a slightly different emphasis. "Art is not merely a question of understanding, but of acceptance and response. Since people have so much to lose by facing up to the challenge of art, they will not—cannot—do so. Insecurity, intolerance, and reaction are all incompatible with art appreciation . . . The critic has, as it were, to paint the painting anew and make it more acceptable, less of the threat that it often is. It is scarcely an exaggeration to say that the art of our time simply could not exist without the efforts of the critic."

40 The emergence of the scholar–critic appeared at the same time as the rise of another figure: the artist–critic. Challenging the theory/practice dichotomy, numerous artists, starting in the mid-to-late 1960s, also became noted critics in their own right. Among the many important writings that resulted are Donald Judd's "Specific Objects" (1965); Sol LeWitt's "Paragraphs on Conceptual Art" (1967); Robert Smithson's "Entropy and the New Monuments" (1966); Robert Morris's "Notes on Sculpture" and "Anti-Form" essays (1966–1968); and Mel Bochner's "The Serial Attitude" (1967). It is notable that all of these essays were originally published in *Artforum*.

41 Hal Foster makes a similar observation. "On the one hand, there is a decline in the old model of the critic based on the New York intellectual, liberal in culture and politics, with one foot in the Old Left and 'one foot in the loft' (as artist–author Brian O'Doherty puts it here). On the other, there is a rise in a new sort of critic bound up with a different kind of avant-garde, one involved in critical theory and inspired by feminist politics,

more subversive in the short run but perhaps more academic in the long term." Foster, "Art Critics in Extremis", p. 117.

42 Tillim in Seitz, *Art Criticism in the 60s: A Symposium of the Poses Institute of Fine Arts*, np.

43 Key examples of this phenomenon include: Thomas Crow, a scholar trained in eighteenth-century art, who has published numerous writings on modern and contemporary art, including *Rise of the Sixties: European and American Art in the Era of Dissent, 1955–69* (London: George Weidenfeld and Nicolson, 1996), and *Modern Art in the Common Culture* (New Haven: Yale University Press, 1996), among others; also notable is Molly Nesbitt—an expert on nineteenth- and early twentieth-century art, but who writes extensively on contemporary art—a contributing editor to *Artforum*, and who has also been involved curatorially with contemporary art (most notably, the exhibition *Utopia Station*, co-curated with artist Rirkrit Tiravanija and curator Hans Ulrich-Obrist, which originally opened at the Venice Biennale in 2003, and which continues to appear in different manifestations around the world); and Norman Bryson, a nineteenth-century historian, who has written on contemporary artists Yasumasa Morimura, Cindy Sherman, Mark Dion, and others.

44 Michel Foucault, "What is Enlightenment?" in *The Foucault Reader*, p. 34. Foucault's original French text was unpublished.

45 Ibid., p. 34.

46 Ibid., p. 34 (emphasis added).

47 A reading that aroused controversy, particularly from the philosopher Jürgen Habermas, who considered himself to be the true inheritor of Kantian Enlightenment thought. In fact Foucault's interest, and stated indebtedness, to Kant's philosophy played an important role in his "debate" with Habermas (the two actually never debated, but Habermas wrote a number of scathing theoretical attacks on Foucault). Habermas maintained that Foucault's entire critical and philosophical project represented abdication of key Enlightenment principles, chief among them Reason, and thus he could never legitimately claim to be an intellectual heir of Kant, but rather a cynical progenitor of postmodern nihilism. See Jürgen Habermas, *Philosophical Discourse on Modernity: Twelve Lectures*, trans. Frederick D. Lawrence (Cambridge, MA: The MIT Press, 1987); and Michael Kelly, ed., *Critique and Power: Recasting the Foucault/Habermas Debate* (Cambridge: The MIT Press, 1994).

48 Foucault, p. 38.

49 Ibid., p. 42 (emphasis added).

50 Roth, p. 190.

Chapter 6

# The totality of form

## S.J. Freedberg's criticism and Clement Greenberg's history

*Eric Rosenberg*

No discursive institution regulated more persistently the practice of art history in the twentieth century than a certain formalist language, in its commercial, journalistic and academic guises. As a result, and though modified convincingly and forcefully by the "New Art History" of the last quarter of the century, it is easy, except in certain highly visible instances, to gloss over what of substance, especially as *history*, might obtain for this body of writing. Still, to recover something of the historicist nature of classic art-historical formalism is to try and rehearse something of a long, tenacious engagement with the material appearances of art in Western society since at least the Renaissance.

Of course, much of the formal history of art produced in the twentieth century can seem to hide its historicism in a language of descriptive fluency wed to the moment of the work's objectivity and some sense of that objectivity's similarity to other instances of such *over time*. It does little good then to test such discursive examples for historical resonances perpendicular to a by now familiar history of forms hermetic and solipsistic in its formation. In order to find the material of a philosophized history in the formalism of twentieth-century art history it is necessary to look at an example that more outwardly pushes the boundaries of language in order to get at something not so readily expected from the model itself. In one particular instance a fortuitous concatenation of interests conspires to offer a glimpse of such in the period between the publication of S.J. Freedberg's *Painting of the High Renaissance in Rome and Florence* in 1961 and Clement Greenberg's celebration of the same in 1964.

* * *

The force of vanguard painting's criticism, *the force of vanguard painting*, was such in the late 1950s and early 1960s, that the lines between critical and historical discourse, to and for those practitioners following with the utmost rigor how painting's historical trajectory unfolded from the Renaissance to the present, could seem blurred. Certain connections made possible by the work of Freedberg and Greenberg make obvious such a claim, but it is in the work itself, particularly the writing of Freedberg and subsequently its appeal for Greenberg as manifested in his criticism, that it can seem at times as if what characterizes contemporary painting and what stands for the achievement of High Renaissance painters is one and the same thing; that to understand one, was to learn simultaneously how to write about the other, or perhaps vice versa.

In no way, however, is such an assertion meant to indicate a failure or lack of rigor in either the critical writing or the historical arguments of the moment, or those specifically of either named practitioner. If in the end I seem to argue here for a teleological relationship between the origins of painting under the Western perspectival system and their apogee in the work of painters such as the Abstract Expressionists, it is in fact to try and identify a historical thread that "ravels" over a longer rather than a shorter period of time. The assertion of such is intended to secure the notion that pregnant in Freedberg's work, as a result perhaps of his own experience as a critic of contemporary painting,[1] is the belief that what culminates in his own time vis-à-vis painting's possibilities, is already manifested to some extent in the work he examines historically. This is the result of a profound engagement with the materialism of painting as a formal practice that occurs *in* history, but it also speaks to the necessity of fluid boundaries between practices such as history and criticism in a moment wherein it may seem that in fact the distances between such were being that much further reified due to the increasing establishment in the United States of art history as an academic discipline. As we will see a bit later in this paper, Greenberg makes something precisely of this issue, arguing for the distance between Freedberg's work and that of the normal run of academic art historians, meanwhile asserting Freedberg's utter professionalism as a scholar, precisely because he practices art history *as* criticism.

The purpose of this chapter then is to take a long view of history as it describes a practice such as painting, to acknowledge that certain of the problems obtaining for paintings in 1958 are still precisely those confronting a Pontormo or a Raphael. Where then does this leave us in regard to the problem of context? The skeptic might well ask whether I am seeking to read such a condition of interpretation out of the practice of art history. Context must, however, be a variegated creature of historical construct, and its necessarily multivalent personality can't always announce itself vis-à-vis the utter strictures of what we most closely assume consciously to be a historical moment. Whether working the materials of the external world or those of an unconscious more thoroughly theorized in recent times than any other, the ascension of context as *sine qua non* of much art-historical work has failed largely to take into account the notion that context itself might be unconscious, that it isn't at all times something that can be made transparent if only the right concatenation of materials is brought to bear on the work of interpretation, of description, of narrative.

Increasing skepticism of the more purely formal histories of art actively pursued through the 1960s, while correct in their critique of a "methodology" that might seem increasingly bankrupt in terms of accounting for forces of history determining meaning from the standpoint of economics, class, gender, race, etc., along the way did little to recognize the extent to which formalisms might still tell some kind of truth about the historical as well as the presentist. The baby that went out the window with the bathwater of formalism's inability to consider the aforementioned factors in the construction of history was formalism's consideration of the historical as a larger entity, something Michel Foucault would call "total" as opposed to "general" history.[2] This is not to say that a formalist art history recognized its achievement. Otherwise, it might have theorized its hermeneutic assumptions in ways that might better resemble the Bakhtinian rather than the (Horst) Jansonist or the Berensonian. What should have been at stake for the formal history of art, and its concomitant formations as contemporary criticism in the middle of the twentieth century—what should have conditioned a generation's ideologies about how the history of art might be surveyed—was a sense of continuity that was the result of recognizing history as a large, perhaps immeasurable, at times constant, even traumatic, as well as a small, dispersed, ruptured, locatable formation.

I want to be careful here however not to imply that my mission is to reinstate an appreciation of a history of art that follows merely formal inventions, innovations, and regurgitations from one period to another, having abstract painting as the ultimate culmination *and* withering away of something begun roughly five centuries earlier. The force of Freedberg's writing is rather to persuade, if read carefully, that we are seeing already, *c.* 1490–1520, a painting, in Rome and Florence, that has as a part of its aim to do something not entirely different from what we take mid twentieth-century abstract painting to be about. That, as much as any lessons passed down by Bernard Berenson or Heinrich Wölfflin, is the engine that drives the vehicle of Freedberg's art history, and what must ultimately have appealed to Greenberg.

* * *

Freedberg's formalism, his connoisseurship of Italian High Renaissance painting, is rooted in the author's present precisely because that present is only present to the extent that it *is* also past. Thus, how uncanny it can seem, when reading certain passages of a book such as *Painting of the High Renaissance in Rome and Florence*, first published in 1961, but written largely in the 1950s, to come upon passage after passage describing painting as if it is already an exercise in abstraction, in the moving, stretching, sizing, measuring, handling of pigment until it coheres as much as shape, geometry, abstraction, design, even instability, as it does an angel's wing or virgin's halo. In the end one senses that at the same time as form and content are coming together as fully, as illusionistically as ever, they are also pulling apart, the former constantly threatening to render illusion, material, volume, a chimera. Of course, this is one of the tropes of Mannerism, that it begins for a time to leave behind the massed solidity, weight and three dimensionality of High Renaissance painting. But in fact the key to reading this in Freedberg's discourse is the extent to which this distinction comes to seem meaningless. The same modes of description appropriate to early and High Renaissance painting in the end come to make up the Mannerist as well.

And thus, the last lines of the book:

> It was in the very way in which Giulio may have felt it [that the classical style to which he had just put an end is not yet dead,] a kind of truth: though the life of creation of the classical style was ended it had shaped the nature, *even in its antithesis*, of this succeeding style. In a still wider sense it was a whole truth: for centuries to come men would feel the accomplishment of High Renaissance classicism, as they had come to feel that of Ancient classicism, as living presence: as an inextinguishable illumination, but also as *a defeating burden*, for the later world of art.[3]

While these words seem to say simply that little has matched the ultimate achievements of 1508, and 1512, in fact what they argue is that historical conditions holding the history of painting as a practice in Western society between 1521, the chronological endpoint of Freedberg's book, and 1950 make a case as much for the continual repetition of those ultimate achievements in historical moments that emerged seemingly from other contexts. But, because of the repetition of fundamentally similar materials and a shared sense of constraints subtending the most direct conditions of production, history virtually allowed for, even demanded, a formal history of art that contained a grain of truth greater than even it knew.

The key phrase, I think, is "even in its antithesis . . ." a sign that Freedberg's formalism not only takes into account, but counts upon, history's being built out of contradiction. History then is not so much about change, but rather the maintenance of the same within a structuring body of possible human relations and practices that hold that maintenance by dint of a dialectical force that moves and changes while time retains the semblance of stasis, at least formally. Styles *may* change, form does not. While for a moment this may then seem to set up the Renaissance classical as a point of origin, Freedberg is careful to invoke the Ancient's classicism—the classic—less as another potential site of generation than as a marker in the infinite and impossible march of origins back into the past and well into the future. That is, in the end, the "defeating burden for the later world of art": that its originality might be less than ever supposed, while its achievement remains significant in the perpetuation of the antithesis that seems now virtually natural in its law-like status. If Freedberg's art history is a formalism, if it is built of connoisseurial blocks, it is one that makes a place for a complexity of contextual embodiment that is as large as history in its entirety. Freedberg's history, in other words, is at least nineteenth-century in its scale, a heuristic worthy of Friedrich Hegel, Edward Gibbon, Jules Michelet, Jacob Burckhardt, Karl Marx even. It is then, political.

As a result, Freedberg leaves the reader with a defining articulation: the "defeating burden" to which he refers is in some ways the whole of history, rather than simply the legacy of the High Renaissance. In turn, that very epigone, the High Renaissance, comes crumbling down by the very shaping idea that simultaneously asserts the moment's authority; is a victim of the same burden that will defeat successive moments at the very same time it is momentarily propped up as apex. This is held by the phrase ". . . as they had come to feel that of Ancient classicism, as living presence . . ." If Freedberg gets to Harold Bloom's *Anxiety of Influence avant la lettre*, it is only to reproduce something of a genealogical account of the place of the past in the present and future.

The most extraordinary building block for Freedberg, however, is that which might almost be missed. All of the aforementioned is intuited as a result of recognizing, or arguing for, "the very way in which Giulio may have felt it . . ." This is surely a projection, but it would be wrong to assume it is merely, as such, reflexive of Freedberg's preoccupations. What he sees of the historical formation of the High Renaissance is in fact what allows him to "feel" what is then imputed to Giulio as a virtually sentient embodiment or manifestation of the historical, as if history is virtually in or of the body. Like the movement of planets around the sun, bodies move through history, giving voice over and over to the entwining of thesis and antithesis, one becoming the other and vice versa in instance after instance, as if the fulfillment of some biological necessity.

By feeling, then, Freedberg means—Giulio inhabits—more than mere sentiment or a notion born of happenstance. Rather, the felt here, the hinge that turns the crank of history, is something carried forth almost physiologically, made up of truth and its disrobing, its repudiation, at one and the same time.[4] Feeling is simultaneously physical and metaphysical, sentient and cognitive. How appropriate for a language, Freedberg's, that itself is virtually athletic in its prose, its style, its syntax *and* semantics, always seeking to clear some hurdle, or win some contest against the possibility of failure to capture in words what is seen to be physically, materially, formally true.

And thus, the access to a language of formal description for High Renaissance painting that might be likened to that also most appropriate to the historical moment in which painting achieves a putative apex in the materials of its own making, the moment of high modernist practice. For what Freedberg argues ultimately is that the material components of painting are always the same, no matter the moment, and to take their description for a particular historical moment as one's project is to necessarily employ a language that will seem most appropriate in other moments of painting's description as well, whatever painting looks like. This is not so much to argue for the eternal or the timeless, but rather the essential, the totalizing as unavoidable characteristics of history.[5]

As an aside, though, let us consider for a moment the possibility that hidden in Freedberg's discourse is some kind of suspicion of the reality of time. Rather than waxing nostalgic for another time in his seeming privileging of High Renaissance painting, how possible might it be that the author doesn't really believe that the moment in which he writes *is* a different one from that which produced what he writes *about*? To what extent is the movement of thesis, antithesis, etc. one that takes place outside of time, or at least conventional theories of such? How might contradiction occur no less if it were to be so within time? For relations to work in such a way must they not be situated in the same moment? And if history is no more or less than such movements and changes, isn't all time then one time and thus no time? The making of history is then precisely the argument for our existence in the same moment as the Neanderthals, but one whose elasticity is such that an infinite number of changes have occurred in that moment, begging the question as to whether evolution itself is temporal. As time might be the end of history, so history is the end of time; we endure in the aftermath of the Big Bang. It is the jetstream of frictions and abrasions in the wake of that moment that *is* history, that seeds the conditions of the illusion of time. Time is a fiction that history needs as a framing device, but the temporal is no less historiographical than any other discursive device constructed to hold history as such.

This is the defeat Freedberg comes to speak of, the notion that there can ever be any time *after*. In Freedberg's deconstructive thinking *after* is always already over in the present. How else might a "High" Renaissance be possible, despite its semantic promise of a before and after that are neither high. The "High" can only be understood in and of itself. Any notion of succession then will be defeated, rendered impossible. By extension, the language of "after" will be the language of the present, the language of a defeat, a loss always already suffered.

If the denial of time is necessary to the production of history, this is not to deny the possibility of the new, and by extension some kind of concept of difference, an essential and real embodiment of the fiction that is time, though not necessarily the same thing; descriptive, moreover, of something quite atemporal.

Freedberg opens the whole of his text with an assertion of history's very elision of time. Describing the place of a head by Leonardo in a painting executed largely by Verocchio, the author puts it this way:

> This is not an image of transition between two styles except in a literally surface sense: in it an Early Renaissance preciosity of drawing and of finish coexist with

> its novelty of underlying form. To that novelty, however, there is no avenue of transition: there is no bridge between the style of this head by Leonardo and that of Verocchio's portions of the painting. No near-contemporary experiment prepares Leonardo's image, nor is there any evolution toward it we can document in prior work of the young Leonardo himself. Its appearance is more sudden, and less resolvable into the context of art around it, than had been the emergence of the style of Masaccio fifty years before. As in Masaccio, the new identity of Leonardo's image results not merely from the novelty of form that we perceive but from the fact that this form is the manifest projection of a new idea; and this idea depends upon a new conception of the nature of art, and of the role of art in the interpretation of nature and of man.[6]

No transition, no bridge, nothing near contemporaneous, no evolution. Appearance, phenomenon are sudden, without resolution in context; the idea, as such, to be idea, is—has to be—new. As does the whole conception of art and its nature from which the idea follows and into which it flows.

Moreover, here is the antithesis that will later prove the chimera of time when describing the contours of the classical's defeated legacy. Leonardo's head repudiates, antithesizes precisely because it is not connected temporally to Masaccio or Verocchio's truth or reality. Instead of a change in time, Leonardo's achievement is framed by its newness, the lack of its occurrence as sheer phenomenological truth in relation to other moments in time. The new in turn replaces whatever else is present; it does not address itself to a past or future, but simply asserts its newness in relation to what surrounds it as it appears. Here is perhaps the most pointed proof of the nonexistence of the temporal for Freedberg's history—rather than a matter of successive moments, it describes an accumulation of simultaneous instances, one only possible as new alongside, rather than before or after, what it is seen not to be.

Whatever stands as classical then for Freedberg is always a framework for what is possible in, about, a present. The present is a formal structure, a spatial encompasser much more than a temporal narrative story. Thus the primacy of formalism here; form is what rises to the surface in the impossibility of narrative, in the acknowledgment of the latter's status as cipher through which form comes to life, can claim newness. Or, if story has a place, it is a story of the inherent contradictions of form.

Consider Freedberg's description of a passage in a painting by Pontormo:

> An order of arrangement, both of the figures and of space, may be perceived within this panel, but it is imperfectly defined; and *what is defined of it seems less important to the meaning of the whole than are effects that are not comprehensible, in any classical sense, as order*. The meaning of design is less in its discernable

> relations of balance of shape or counterpoise of direction than in its complex, unlogical sequences of angular movemented rhythm, which pervade the surface of the picture and dominate the relics in it of geometry; and the effects of this complex excitement of design are intensified by color. Neither does the handling of space intend logic or stability: in the foreground, figures—of diminished substance—are as busily related in their space as they are in superficial patter; behind them is a gap of middle distance, unarticulated save for one disturbing figure, and high in a farther distance is a populated architecture seen from an unnormal perspective point of view. Interval is not clearly measurable in this space, nor is it, as interval aesthetically sensible. The character of space has been determined not as it is classically, clearly circumscribed and apprehensible, but oppositely, in an unstable and uncertain shape and content. Like the pattern of design on the picture's surface the space too, is illogically active. The relation between depth and foreground has become ambiguous or, perhaps still more positively even in this picture, ambivalent; and it is at once an agency of tension and cohesion between depth and picture surface that the pattern made by forms in space is so evidently knit into the pattern of the foreground.[7]

The key phrase comes early: "what is defined of it seems less important to the meaning of the whole than are effects that are not comprehensible, in any classical sense, as order." Freedberg speaks here of a turn from High Renaissance standards, but in doing so he delivers himself of a set of constraints that still very much determine such standards—the entwining of story and form to the extent that each make sense of themselves so much that what the author calls "classical" order prevails.

But order is no longer of concern when reading the Pontormo, and here already, long before the unfolding present/future that will be defeated by the burden of the classical, painting stands as such, and as such shows how very close even the classical might be to such disorder, might even hold the seeds of its unraveling. What Freedberg describes then is again, as in the case of Leonardo's head of an angel in Verocchio's painting, the new. And in acknowledging it as such, all save for the internal justification of painting as painting seems to recede from the picture plane as claim to reality or truth. In fact, the new is only evident as disorder. And this must have been the case for Leonardo as well; his new could only have brought disorder of some kind to Verocchio's model. Here then is Freedberg's closing argument, the way in which antithesis is held in thesis and vice versa, and thus the stoppage of time as causal engine of change, contradiction, etc. In time's place, the manifestation of idea, always at least immanent, seems the excavator of history, the progenitor of the new.

Measure, aesthetic sensibility, articulation, interval, the very conditions of stability, shape, and even content, are all set on edge as the language of painting's description seems only appropriately historical to the extent that it is self-explanatory, that it struggles toward sense on its own terms, terms that seem voided of sense at the same moment they come to the fore as autonomous. In some ways the formal as historical is what we witness struggling to be born here, what Freedberg invested such eloquence in getting right.

Freedberg's motivation, however, is not as much to do with painting's falling off course as it derails the classical *c*. 1521. Letting slip the bonds of the classical, while seeming to sacrifice all sorts of signs of framework, order, stricture, and constraint, rather gets the painter to a place where painting itself seems the result of a turning in on itself wherein momentarily left to its own devices the receding of importance of familiar anchors and buoys produces the illusion of instability, of incompre-hensibility. But the latter is denied at the same time by the very force of Freedberg's language. In this attempt to turn out something of a formal rationale for diminution of the classical, perhaps unwittingly, the author finds himself left to a syntax and semantics that seek the very properties of discourse that might embody painting itself as a practice of the present, of presentness. As painting is seen to historically become itself, so the language necessary to the explication of such is mobilized. In turn, ambiguity and ambivalence take on positive qualities, as embodiments of content themselves. "Like the pattern of design on the picture's surface the space too, is illogically active."

Painting's doubt of its ability to refer is, first, a sign of denigration. For Freedberg, on the surface, this is what naturally occurs in the wake of an historical apex such as the High Renaissance, such as Leonardo's new. But almost simultaneously, the alacrity with which the author arrives at a solution in formal language for the character of the antithesis speaks in some ways to the shame emergent in the recognition of the fit between verbal and visual language. It is almost as if this fit must be denied, and denied forever, lest it unravel the apex as it describes the decline that comes in its aftermath. As Freedberg describes a traumatic set of historical conditions so he enacts something of the trauma, feels something of it, as Giulio himself is said to have by Freedberg, both figures, the painter and the historian, coming *after* the High Renaissance, both carrying its defeating burden. Yet, as Freedberg also writes from a site of normativity, so he must describe something of redemption in defeat, lest there be no conditions in which history might occur. In order then to get at any notion of truth, to strip away, unconsciously, those partitions that differentiate beyond recovery historical moments as seemingly distanced as the 1520s and the 1950s, Freedberg resorts to, finds in the painting of 1520, a language that seeks essence as a result of *difference*, and along the way produces *the same*, or sees something not dissimilar to that of 1950.

What Freedberg recognizes is that the structure of history, if taken in its long view, will determine something of a shared form in processes struggling in seemingly different historical moments over similar problems. If Freedberg sees Pontormo doing something that *sounds* like what a viewer might experience before an Abstract Expressionist painting in 1955, this is not disingenuous or overly clever, or simply some kind of subconscious grafting of the language of one set of historical conditions onto another, though it is certainly that as well. It is to speak to a limit of questions opened out to painting as a practice, whatever its conditions of production, if also as a result of those conditions. Here begins, as already implied, the long history of antithesis that Freedberg will call the burden of defeat, felt by Giulio and the whole history of painting post-High Renaissance. And thus, reading Freedberg now, or in 1961, one might almost imagine one is standing in front of a Rothko or Pollock, a De Kooning or Diebenkorn, or perhaps reading the criticism of Clement Greenberg.

* * *

In fact, by the early 1960s at least, Clement Greenberg was deeply enamored of Freedberg's art history. In *Arts Magazine* in November of 1964, Greenberg, at the outset of a review of Freedberg's more recent *Andrea Del Sarto*,[8] had this to say about *Painting of the High Renaissance in Rome and Florence*:

> Great writing about art is rarer than great art, and apparently as hard to recognize at first. Otherwise Dr. Freedberg's *Painting of the High Renaissance in Rome and Florence*, which came out over two years ago, would be far better known by now. I know of no book on art that matches it in closeness of perception of writing. I know of no book that digs so tenaciously into the substance of actual works of art. I know of no writing on art that keeps itself more pertinent throughout, with a truer sense of what belongs and does not belong in the discussion of art *as art*, and of what in a given historical context counts and does not count in this connection.[9]

Greenberg's terms should not surprise anyone familiar with his own critical writing about painting. Getting at essence is the lesson, and for Greenberg, Freedberg is a touchstone as an art historian, a contextualist no less, with as close a concern for the vicissitudes of a "given" historical moment as any other qualities to be sussed from the historical record.

But Greenberg goes on to make a distinction between academic art history as he knows it, and what Freedberg is doing, or how the latter gets at his history:

> Dr. Freedberg is an art historian who teaches at Harvard. But he writes as a critic before he writes as an art historian or scholar . . . Dr. Freedberg has a sense—entirely unexpected in an art historian—of the *working* life of art that is confirmed by what I know about how art gets carried on in the present. This

> makes him "professional" in a way unheard of among his colleagues. He is aware of the kind of uncertainty that accompanies ambition, and which has to do with the ineluctable precariousness of quality. He shows the wrestle for that as being always problematic, never settled. And in showing this he also shows how entirely the creation of art is in and of history, and not to be abstracted from it . . . Dr. Freedberg's prose has given some reviewers a pretext for not dealing with what he actually says. I, too, wince at coinages like "movemented," "ponderated," "deliberated," . . . But Dr. Freedberg's prose has the virtues of its faults. I do not see how he could help forcing language in order to report the discriminations of pictorial quality that he makes. And the forcing is well worth it on the whole. Some of his formulations of pictorial experience are among the most telling I have ever come across . . . not because of the difficulty of his prose, but because of the packed superabundance of his matter.[10]

Greenberg identifies Freedberg's history as one inseperable from the practice of the painter, then or now. In doing so, however, the critic does not collapse history into the present, but rather accords the art historian the insight of determining a mode of description that is possible precisely because a sensitivity to context and record have allowed him to find moments of practice that are related and relatable in a larger, broader historical continuum.

The simultaneity of history and criticism are crucial to Greenberg's understanding of Freedberg's writing. At the same time one seems the product of a willful turning away from the other. The question becomes one of the proper material of history, the proper way in which history is made material, the way in which antithesis might even seem the product of congruence. Most importantly, in no way does Greenberg advocate a collapse of historical distinctions in order to champion Freedberg's work; nor does the modernist critic find the same in the latter's writing itself. Greenberg goes so far as to imply that the bridge between historical moments virtually demands the invention of a critical language suitable to getting at what can't be expressed with the normal means of the contemporary critic or historian.

Crucially, for Greenberg, writing as a critic *is* writing as an historian. Though he allows that Freedberg might seem to relinquish some of the props of the academic art historian in the service of criticism, this is merely a momentary acknowledgment of others' criticisms. Not for a moment does Greenberg believe that history is ever discarded in Freedberg's work. The push of words into the historical while being asked to do critical work is what is made to seem the genesis of their perversion by normative standards. Movement becomes "movemented," deliberate "deliberated," and ponder becomes "ponderated" as the present is found in the past and vice versa. The discovery is only made verbal, though, through some kind of traumatic birthing of a language beyond normal experience, beyond that surface skein of phenomenon that manufactures reality as present in order to keep history out of the everyday, something Greenberg had been fighting, resisting, to greater and lesser degrees of success, as far back as "Avant-Garde and Kitsch."[11]

The reader might then be forgiven for a moment of hesitancy over who wrote the following, the art historian or the critic:

> Design now is essentially the making of relations among the kinetic virtues that reside in forms, rather than the disposition in an eventually stable order of their substances . . . There is a pseudo-logic of geometry in the relations among forms: near-balances, repetitions, and near fluent rhythmical connections exist in this design . . . Each shape contains a disequilibrium within it, and as one shape is related, with clear deliberation to another it is simultaneously affirmed that their relation, too, is not in equilibrium. This simultaneity of affirmative and negative relation, of near-accord and dissonance in pattern, puts each shape in a state of tension in respect to others; the kinetic nature of design is both of the separate forms and their relation. However, in the whole picture structure this complex kinesis is finally manipulated into a difficult, restless, and precariously suspended equilibrium, so that the picture as a whole conveys the sense that it contains a complete aesthetic order, and is, in form, an integer.[12]

Freedberg seems to find modern painting *in* that of the period just succeeding the High Renaissance, to find the modern in the moment when painting pulls away from its putative apex. It is not that the author grafts the language of contemporary criticism as it might be practiced by Greenberg onto an earlier moment, but that he is convinced that what comes to fruition in 1950 begins to appear already in 1521. And yet, if we pay close attention to language, distinctions might yet be made between period descriptions. To find "the making of relations among the kinetic virtues that reside in forms," for instance, taking the place of the disposition of the substances of form is not to describe classic Abstract Expressionist painting, but it is perhaps to get at something of a received, perhaps conservative idea as to what happens to painting as its realism fades away over the first half of the twentieth century.[13]

And yet, if the seeds of painting's decline are held in its modernist apex, then perhaps something of the substance of forms *is* sacrificed, in aspects of modernist painting, in favor of kineticism, or perhaps an even less stable metaphor.[14] Would this, then, be the very virtue of Abstract Expressionism as it begins to lay to rest a particular historical model for painting's practice, and why for Freedberg the language of one mode pulling away from apex and movement into the burden of defeat rather than more closely resembling or even matching the achievement of another seemed necessarily the same as the very manifestation of such inherent in Abstract Expressionism? Not as an example of history repeating itself, but rather of the temporal nature of history being at least as short, or non-existent, as the moment that might include 1521 and 1950 as on some level the same. In other words, what may have started in 1521, might only have ended, started again, or simply found continuance/been the same, between 1945 and 1964.

* * *

As a result, history for Freedberg is a palimpsest, and thus a form before it is anything else, a receptacle, but one dense with matter, layered, entangled, knotted, and clotted. And this is always so, in triumph or defeat, each ultimately the same to the extent that they both emerge from and return to that palimpsest. It is from this palimpsest that he seeks to extract the language of his art history, and why (or how) that language comes at times to seem already deformed from residing in such a space.

Greenberg recognizes this too, and is not always in utter agreement with Freedberg as a result. Taking exception to an argument in the Del Sarto book, Greenberg says:

> Dr. Freedberg refers several times to the "ethical content" of the art he scrutinizes. This, like "moral seriousness," belongs to the cant of recent literary criticism. References to the real experienced content of any work of art cannot be made that conceptually precise. If they could be, art would cease being art . . . In the actual experience of art "content" can never put "form" into the shade. That happens only in reflection upon experience, and by an error of reflection that hypostatizes "form" and "content," but which further reflection can correct. Andrea's mastery of form could not be ultimate without having the ultimate in content to master.[15]

Even in disagreement, however, Greenberg advocates a recognition of form/history as ultimate generator of meaning, as master of content/time. As palimpsest, history/form squashes time, suffocating, as does Freedberg's writing at times, and exalting, as it also does, with equal frequency. At the same time, not much more is identified than an idiom, appropriate to the description of a practice that seems to carry traits identifiable in more than one moment of its history. To understand art history and its institutions, however, we must understand how the idiomatic is or becomes historical form, in time, perhaps, but surely as essence too.

## Notes

1 Emerging as a professional art historian at the same time, Freedberg practiced as a critic in the late 1940s and early 1950s, publishing reviews on various aspects of contemporary art for journals such as *Art News* and the short-lived *Perspectives USA*. See "Hyman Bloom, The Career to Date of a Major Modern Painter," *Perspectives USA* No. 6 (Winter 1954)

45–54. The same issue's "Notes on Contributors," 153, puts Freedberg's situation this way: "Though he is perhaps best known in the United States for his criticism of Contemporary American painting, Sydney Freedberg is at the same time a teacher and scholar of art history; in fact, he contends that contemporary art criticism can only be performed by the critic with sound training in historical scholarship . . . Much of his critical writing has appeared in *Art News*, and he was for a time on the editorial staff of that magazine." See Caroline Jones, *Modern Art at Harvard* (New York: Abbeville, 1985) 78–79; 91–95, for a consideration of the intersection of Freedberg's formalism and the emergence of modernist criticism between the 1940s and the 1960s and Caroline Jones, *Eyesight Alone, Clement Greenberg's Modernism and the Bureaucratization of the Senses* (Chicago: University of Chicago Press, 2006) p. 447 note 34 for acknowledgment of Freedberg's adaptation of formalism to the interests of Renaissance art. Jones asserts Freedberg's independence from the modes of critical discourse that would pass from Greenberg to practitioners such as Michael Fried and Rosalind Krauss, but it is my contention that Freedberg's formalism is every bit as moralizing and philosophic, as opposed to purely ekphrastic, as is that of the modernist writers. See also Paul Barolsky, "Sydney J. Freedberg, Historian and Critic: An Appreciation," *Artibus et Historiae*, 1(2) (1980): 135–142, and finally, and most importantly, Henri Zerner, "Mind Your Maniera," *New York Review of Books* 19(3) (August 31, 1972): 25–28. Zerner recognizes full well the root in criticism and the valuation of abstraction that undergirds Friedberg's discourse.

2 See Michel Foucault, *The Archaeology of Knowledge* (New York: Pantheon, 1972) pp. 9–10. Foucault distinguishes between a "total" history and "general" histories: "A total description draws all phenomena around a single centre—a principle, a meaning, a spirit, a world-view, and overall shape; a general history, on the contrary, would deploy the space of a dispersion." Freedberg seems in fact somewhere in between the two possibilities as limned by Foucault.

3 S.J. Freedberg, *Painting of the High Renaissance in Rome and Florence* (New York: Harper and Row, 1961) p. 575.

4 By "hinge" I mean here something not entirely dissimilar to Derrida's usage of the term *charniere*, in *Resistances of Psychoanalysis* (Stanford, CA: Stanford University Press, 1998) p. 78. "This word can be taken in the technical or anatomical sense of a central or cardinal articulation, a hinge pin or pivot. A *charniere* or hinge is an axial device that enables the circuit, the trope, or the movement of rotation. But . . . also . . . the place where the hunter attracts the bird by laying out flesh as a lure . . . a place between opening and closing, that is assured by the workings of a hinge . . . the *fort/da* of a pendulum . . ."

5 I am reminded here of T.J. Clark's words in the "Preface to the Revised Edition" of *The Painting of Modern Life* (Princeton: Princeton University Press, 1999) p. xix. Clark does not speak here necessarily of the timeless or eternal qualities of painting, but does seem to say something about the essence of the practice that is historical by dint of its very largeness, its consistency of applicability through and across time, the way in which it *takes* time, in practice, and by that very deliberation, that very attempt to stop time, does its work.

6 Freedberg, *Painting of the High Renaissance*, p. 3.

7 Freedberg, *Painting of the High Renaissance*, p. 511.

8 S.J. Freedberg, *Andrea Del Sarto* (Cambridge, MA: Harvard University Press, 1963).

9 Clement Greenberg, "Review of Andrea Del Sarto by S.J. Freedberg," in John O'Brian, ed., *Clement Greenberg, The Collected Essays and Criticism* (Chicago, IL: University of Chicago Press, 1986–1993) volume 4, pp. 197–198.

10 Greenberg, "Andrea Del Sarto," in O'Brian, ed., *The Collected Essays and Criticism*, volume 4, pp. 198–199.

11 For the sense of history that follows Greenberg through his writing, either as salutary or dilatory effect, see the debate between T.J. Clark and Michael Fried over "Avant-Garde and Kitsch" and "Toward a Newer Laocoön" collected along with Greenberg's original essays in Francis Frascina, ed., *Pollock and After, The Critical Debate*, 2nd edn. (London: Routledge, 2000) pp. 48–112.

12 Freedberg, *Painting of the High Renaissance*, p. 519.

13 See Iriving Sandler, *The Triumph of American Painting* (New York: Praeger, 1970) for the classic statement of Abstract Expressionism as apogee, whether also the harbinger of decline or not. See also T.J. Cark, "In Defense of Abstract Expressionism," in his *Farewell to an Idea, Episodes From A History of Modernism* (New Haven: Yale University Press, 1999) pp. 371–405, for a corrective to Sandler's notion of Abstract Expressionism's history.

14 This would seem to be an argument for a Harold Rosenberg oriented account of Abstract Expressionism, wherein a term such as "action painting" and all it implied is to be recovered positively, as opposed to a Greenberg/Michael Fried-like narrative devoted more to the materiality and opticality of this mode of avant-garde practice. I want to be clear that I am not championing such a return. In this case, I merely want to point out a similarity or resemblance, but one that is not in fact substantive.

15 Greenberg, "Andrea Del Sarto," 201, in O'Brian, ed., *The Collected Essays and Criticism*, volume 4.

Chapter 7

# Unmaking art history

*Donald Preziosi*

> [A] divine teleology secures the political economy of the Fine-Arts . . .
> Jacques Derrida, "Economimesis," trans. R. Klein, *Diacritics* II.2 (1981): 5

It has been customary for some time to believe that what is commonly called "art" has a "history," and that an adequate understanding of this phenomenon is as a manifestation or reflection of the mentality, spirit, or character of persons or peoples. Such a belief rests, moreover, upon the hypothesis that this phenomenon is essentially pan-human: that (on an analogy with language and social mores) each people has forms of art specific to it at given times and places. It is believed that changes in artistic form over time are symptomatic of changes in a person or people's mentality, values, or social, political, philosophical, or even religious attitudes. Disciplinary history is commonly staged as the developmental evolution of one social symptomatology, professionally and institutionally linked to the development and refinement of other symptomatologies said to account for multiple facets of human endeavor.

Art history has never been isolated or entirely distinct from the institutions that are imagined to frame, contain, reflect, enable, or distort its theories, practices, and protocols, and any such autonomy is an artifact of the metaphorical topologies inherent in disciplinary knowledge as such. The protracted debates constituting disciplinary historiography have demonstrated acutely in recent years that to speak of art history as if it were (or ever had been) a conceptually coherent singular practice, let alone the performance of a consistent method or theory arising out of and applicable to a domain of objects constituting its "data," masks not only its plurality and diversity but also art history's internal ambivalences and contradictions. Despite its modern academic reifications and professional commodifications, art history has also always been a *deponent* practice, one of a series of allomorphic fields that arose historically both in tandem and *seriatim* in connection with attempts to deal with early modern social, ethical, cultural, political, and epistemological problems. Its allomorphs include museology, art criticism, the heritage industry, tourism, the fashion industry, history-writing, psychoanalysis, archaeology, theatre, anthropology, aesthetic philosophy, and art making. It has indeed taken a certain quite rigorously enforced "discipline" to reify and separate out these facets of the modern practice of the self as distinct professions or institutions. What links these deponent practices together is a common yet diversified investment in the romantic and solipsistic dramaturgy of the modern self, realized anamorphically in each institution, profession, and field.

Are there viable alternatives to the enduring matrix of instrumentalist ideologies of art history as a "human science" for defining and demonstrating political and ethical hypotheses about individuals, nations, genders, religions, classes, and peoples by linking together persons, peoples, and mentalities with their artifactual "representations"? If art history is to be understood as an *occasion* for the practice of irreconcilable and conflicting perspectives on the nature of relationships between objects and subjects, what then could it mean to understand art history as the fielding of an impasse? What would our understanding of art history be were we to *begin* (rather than end) with these complexities, pluralities, ambivalences, and contradictions, rather than with the phantasm of distinct and autonomous disciplines that naturalize thought about "disciplines and their institutions"?

There is a certain unease today in reflecting interminably about the state and prospects of an academic discipline calling itself "art history," which like a boomerang perpetually returns to its point of origin, only to go forth again on the same trajectories, the same reviewing of what has been looked at before but hardly ever seen: the paradox of conceptualizing a discipline built to stage and frame an epistemological domain and analytic field whose "objects" are at base radically unconceptualizable. The conundrums of this situation, which derive from the very origins of the modern discourse of art history, remain no less striking today, as art history reanimates and perpetually circumnavigates its foundational dilemmas. But then art history may be no less a taxonomic fiction than other academic disciplines one might name, and its mythomorphic career of configuring and constituting as if they were pre-existent *data* what are in fact *capta* in the service of (one or another) ideological demonstration may also be hardly remarkable.

It may be useful to begin by recalling an essay which was a classic of contemporary criticism four decades ago, namely Jacques Derrida's "Structure, Sign, and Play in the Discourse of the Human Sciences," which distinguished between two interpretations of interpretation:

> The one seeks to decipher, dreams of deciphering a truth or an origin that transcends play and the order of the sign, and for it the necessity of interpretation is lived as a kind of exile. The other, no longer oriented toward origin, affirms play and strives to pass beyond man and humanism, man being the name of that being which, throughout the history of metaphysics or of onto-theology

> . . . has dreamed of the plenitude of presence, of reassuring foundations, of origin and the end of play.[1]

These two interpretations of interpretation, Derrida wrote in 1966, are "*absolutely irreconcilable, even if we live them simultaneously and reconcile them in an obscure economy.*" What is less clearly remembered of Derrida's famous essay was his insistence that this is not a question of choice, of embracing one over the other; rather that what is at stake is the need to reflect on the common ground (*sol commun*) of the two absolutely irreconcilable modes of interpretation, of what in fact keeps in play these two perpetually oscillating perspectives. The principle of affordance, of any unresolvable oscillation.

One name for the "obscure economy" of that *lived simultaneity of irreconcilability*, as I argued recently in my Slade Lectures at Oxford,[2] is "art history," which appears destined to be permanently in thrall to its foundational conundrums and contradictions. Indeed, it might be said that this is expressed most acutely precisely in the ongoing "stock-taking of the various types of historical reflection" on art history of the last thirty years, of which the present volume is yet another instance.

Like a colloidal dispersion in chemistry, this keeping in play in the same epistemological frame of (in one of its key allomorphs) historicism and ahistoricism constitutes what we might call *the* concept of art history as a modern institution and profession. Two modes of knowing may be seen to be embodied in the work of art history; two kinds of propositional or interrogative frameworks: one which relies on a metonymic encoding of phenomena, and one deeply imbued with a metaphoric orientation on the things of this world, grounded in analogical reasoning. With the former, facticity and evidence are formatted syntactically, metonymically, differentially, the very chronological order of the system projecting and legitimizing questions that might be "put" to "data" that unsurprisingly turn out to be astonishingly sympathetic. With the latter, however, form and content are construed as being deeply and essentially congruent, the *form* of the work being the *figure* of its truth. (This double epistemological framework may appear at first to correspond to the contrastive domains of knowledge articulated a generation ago by Michel Foucault wherein art history might be seen to preserve an older analogic order of the same within a newer play of difference and change. But Foucault's distinction, articulated within a scenario of epistemic transformations, may more cogently be represented in art history as ongoing and simultaneous rather than simply marking a transition from one episteme to a more modern one.) And once again, it's not a question of choosing; we need to both foreground these oppositions and find ways to highlight what the poles in these oppositions share in common; what animates them *as* oppositions in the first place, as Derrida rightly insists.

It is here that we may perhaps begin to understand the foundational dilemma that would have confronted the formation of a discipline such as art history: how to fabricate a "science" of objects (and of their visualities) simultaneously construed as unique and irreducible *and* as *specimens* of a class of like phenomena. The "solution" to this dilemma has been the modern discourse on visual artifice, wherein a series of intersecting and deponent institutions—academic art history, art criticism, visual culture, museology, the art market, connoisseurship, tourism, fashion, the heritage industry (the list is long but it is finite)—a field that maintains in play contrasting systems of evidence and proof, demonstration and explication, analysis and contemplation, with respect to objects *both* semantically complete *and* differential (or deponent) in signification. The dilemma is itself an artifact and effect of contested concepts of representational "truth" and of criteria of representational adequacy in the early modern period; contestations which may echo the radical power of *artifice* as such to simultaneously fabricate and problematize the world in which we live.

It might have been refreshing to re-engage with earlier debates on knowledge-production in Europe and America wherein distinctions between "theory" and "practice" came to play a role in political efforts at social reform that relied on the need to keep at arm's length "history" and "fiction," with "history" (like "science," taking the systemic place of religion in modernity) supposedly on the side of "truth," fiction (and in modernity, "religion") its opposition or distortion. Perhaps it may be time to begin attending to precisely that very conundrum.

## I

At the heart of that two-century-old practice of the modern self we call art, the "science" of which we would have liked to have called art history (or perhaps museology, art history's chief allomorph, or even "visual culture," that now largely discredited disciplinary orphan of the 1980s), and the "theory" of which we may still wish to call aesthetics, or even philosophy, (at the heart of all this) lies a series of knots and conundrums, the denial of which constitutes the very relationship between "subjects and objects" naturalized in circular fashion and kept in perpetual play by the "disciplinary" machinery; the epistemological technology, of art history.

It is precisely this *denial* that has grounded, legitimized, and institutionalized that shadow discourse of aesthetic philosophy or "theory" which the art-historical imagination, in varying ways over these two centuries, has continued to project as a "transcendence" of its own (simultaneously co-constructed) "disciplinary" abjection. We need not be surprised that a discipline can be grounded in denial, since disciplinarity as such is founded upon the occlusion of difference and heterogeneity; on explicit channelings of vision.

In his 1996 book *Mass Mediauras,* Samuel Weber observed:

> If the institutionalization of the subject/object relation—the matrix of representational thinking—is the result of the emplacement that goes on in and as modern technology, then those same goings-on undermine the objectivity

> upon which the matrix depends. By determining reality as standing stock, representational thinking treats objects as calculable "data," as "information" to be taken into account or accounted for. Thus, whether in economic practice or in modern art, objects are de-objectified by becoming increasingly subject to the calculations of a subjective will struggling to realize its representations and thereby to place itself in security.
>
> But . . . there are no secure places. Emplacement itself remains tributary to that movement of unsecuring that it ostensibly seeks to escape or to ignore. [3]

The ontological question as to whether or not there really are "secure places," I might add, may, however, obscure the co-determinacy of both.

The academic discipline of art history, the most rigorous and encyclopedic "institutionalization of the subject/object relation" as such, to borrow Weber's words, has evolved historically by living in a virtual future, in a curious space–time of the future perfect tense—*as if* (as an institution) *it shall have been* the "practice" of a philosophy (or a concept or theory which some may continue to call aesthetics), and in so doing, in approaching (whilst never quite reaching) its asymptotic point or horizon of completion, it perpetually reconstitutes and reiterates the problematic of its unresolvable foundational dilemma. This is precisely its *ambivalence* about the constitution of the self in its relation to and entailment with objects; with its object-world; its *Umwelt*. This repetition–compulsion is played out as attempts to keep in play contrary theories of that relationship, as I've just noted, much like the endless and irresolvable oscillations of an optical illusion (the form of your stuff either *is* the figure of your truth, and/or it is *not* . . . ).

It is consequently no mean task to conceive of articulating a critically adroit historiography of a discipline built around such doubly compounded phantasms. And it has certainly been not a little problematic to articulate the evolutionary development of the academic field as if it were some singular evolution of concepts or "theories" of art. That is, the simulacrum of the idea that "art" itself was historically the evolution of a certain *residue in all things*—once you subtract the instrumental and utilitarian (and for some the social-historical) meanings of things, as so clearly articulated in connection with the founding of the Louvre as in part a repository for Napoleon's spoils. That is, a "residue" linked together (as a "history" one might say) to serve ethical and political functions in the present in the practice of critical and museological apologists and ideologues of the new modern nation-state. It would behoove us to step back and try and reconstruct the conditions that led to the invention and naturalization of this remarkable practice of the modern subject; of the modern "citizen" we call art.

If what we call today "art history" is to be framed as an *answer*, what then were the original *questions* to which this quite remarkable profession purported to address? And what was "art" itself an answer to? What circumstances, problems, or dilemmas did "art" and art's "history" (and theory, and criticism, and production, and marketing) purport to address? Of what were they the demonstration? What purpose was served by art history's massive and simultaneous metonymizing and metaphorizing or fetishizing of the built environment; its accumulating and reformatting the relics of the past into episodic chains of objects, wherein the significance or meaning of a thing came to be staged *either* as a function of its position relative to others that come before or after, whether temporally, stylistically, or thematically, *or* as a function of its uniqueness and irreproducibility? And where access into this wickerwork of object-time could be made to seem free for all as material for use in articulating the solipsistic dramaturgy of the mournfully adrift and ever more lonely modern self?

In trying to imagine, then, what exactly it might mean to "conceptualize" art history, the following observations might not be out of place:

(First) To speak of "art" as if it *is* an "it" (rather than, say, a *when*, or, as the ancient Greeks and Romans had it, a *how*) that not only pre-exists early modernity or exists outside Europe and its extensions is to perform an ideological demonstration of using a module or measure to delineate and account for the unity and diversity of human groups over space and time. "Art" in this sense was (and academically remains) an instrument; a "practical science" for defining and demonstrating a wide variety of political and ethical hypotheses about individuals, nations, races, genders, religions, economies, classes, and peoples. Art as a measure of humanness. As *the* measure of the human . . .

(Second) The "order" that art history as a human science seeks *in* the vast variety of artifacts constituting the human object-world constitutes as much a meditation on classification and affinity as it is about its ostensible objects of study themselves. It will have always been necessary to ask what ethical and political ends were served by a belief in a temporal continuity among humanly made objects. A belief grounded in an imputed fundamental analogy between ourselves as temporally continuous organisms and the object-permanence (and continuity) of objects. What functions have the belief in a "structure" in art's history, or a "shape" in (art-historical) time, served? What benefits have accrued, and for whom, with such beliefs? (The short answer is that they have almost invariably been nasty.) The "orders" of art history and the "shapes" of the time of the art of art history constitute as much ideological or philosophical demonstrations of implicit or explicit transcendent truths as they are fabrications or constructions of such truths. It has been noticed that histories, museologies, or philosophies "of" art appear more and more inconceivable apart from the ideologies of *representation* and of race and character which have underlain and motivated such practices for two centuries in every modern nation-state. Are the racist essentialisms (or the specious cultural relativisms they bring in tow) that have molded the foundation blocks of art history (and aesthetic theory) from Johann Joachim Winckelmann to Alois Riegl to Aby Warburg (or from Johann Gottfried Herder to Friedrich Hegel to Hippolyte Taine) "removable" without taking apart the whole house? The short answer, once again, is no. Most of our attempts to engage with this rarely evince an awareness of just how profoundly entailed art-historical theories and practices are with social, political, and religious ideas of racial and ethnic identity.

(Third) It is necessary in this connection to foreground the embeddedness of the aesthetic in all facets of modern social life since the Enlightenment; the fact that, to speak about art in modern Europe was perforce to speak of freedom, spontaneity, self-determination, autonomy, particularity, and universality; those matters that were at the heart of the middle class's struggle for political hegemony. "Art," as the founders of the Louvre argued, being that "liberating" residue in all things that provided the ethical justification for the "liberation" of objects held in "captivity" by unacceptable classes, religious orders, and inferior (usually non-European) peoples. Which is perfectly matched by a recent joint declaration by the directors if eighteen major museums in Europe and America of their "right" not to return indigenous cultural patrimony because of their status as world museums bearing what can only be called a postmodern white man's burden of "showing the world to the world."[4] The reified construction of "art," then, as the romance of the soul of the bourgeoisie, was inseparable from the construction not only of the dominant ideological forms of modern class-society but also from metamorphoses of human subjectivity appropriate to that social order, many of which constituted inversions or sublimations of earlier religious beliefs. From a strictly instrumentalist perspective, these were some of the things that this "thing" called art, art as *a kind of thing*, was to be *for* in the new modern state. Yet the question remains, what did the invention of "art" replace or cover over? (what did the invention of the discipline of art history serve to erase?)

The impulses for substantive historiographic excavation and reassessment that may have motivated this volume are unquestionably sound and sincere: the reality is that "art history"—and any of its repackagings, including, and especially, "globally-sensitive" "visual culture"—studies is rudderless (however much it may be that this is not entirely of its own making). Yet effectively rereading and rethinking our predecessors in what might be called a Benjaminian manner by radically reinventing them as in fact they customarily did to their own predecessors (contrary to what one reads even today in art history's hagiographic bibles of begatting) might very well afford the possibility of bringing back to light what the Enlightenment (re)invention of "art" has *hidden* for so long: that is, what the growth of modern aesthetic philosophy has caused to be *forgotten*—namely, and to give that multiplylayered package a single name, the ancient Aristotelian notions of *artifice* and *decorum*. Our historiographies have yet to contend effectively with the art of art history (and the history of art history's art) as *amnesiac phenomena*. Art history (or visual culture studies) as modes of re-membering the past and of simultaneously acting against any past which does not conform to an image of that from which we would wish to be descended.

I said at the beginning that my remarks aimed to address the paradoxical notion of conceptualizing a discipline built to stage and frame a domain of objects of analysis that were at base radically unconceptualizable. Such a situation is in fact not unusual, and indeed is not unlike that faced, for example, by Ferdinand de Saussure, in whose *Cours de linguistique générale* we may now more clearly see what he himself had asserted at the time but which came to be marginalized by the professional project of modern linguistics—namely the future anterior of a discipline that in its essentials represented an impasse rather than a resolution or a beginning, as Giorgio Agamben quite clearly articulated not so long ago, when de Saussure's complete oeuvre had finally been published.[5] The idea, in short, as I argued in the book *Rethinking Art History* a decade or so ago, of the sign as ambiguously referential and Eucharistic.[6] I'd like now to look at this a bit more closely, for it constitutes the key problem facing all of our endeavors here today, as well as being the fundamental conundrum that not only faces "art history," but constitutes it in its essence. First, a query: What is it about practicing "art history" that allows practitioners to come into contact with their deepest fears and desires without their entering their consciousness? Without entering into the discourse of reason? Without being able to say exactly (for example) why it is one "collects," a point made so poignantly a decade ago by Mieke Bal?[7]

## 2

> Art is troublesome not because it is not delightful, but because it is not more delightful: we accustom ourselves to the failure of gardens to make our lives as paradis[ic]al as their prospects.[8]

This observation by Robert Harbison poignantly articulated not only one of the main expectations for *art* in modern times, but also one of the main aspirations of *museums*—that they would somehow both ground and transform our lives: that they would, in short, *make us better*. By "liberating" the aesthetic potential in all made things, we afford the possibility of what we are induced to believe is our own "spritual" liberation. The placement of such an expectation on art is one of the keystones in an overarching system of quasi-secular beliefs that distinguishes our post-Enlightenment age from earlier times, resting upon certain assumptions about the nature of meaningful relationships between subjects and objects;

between individuals or peoples and the worlds they weave about themselves and which in turn weave them into place. Assumptions, in short, about the adequacy of *representation*.

Art history, museology, and aesthetic philosophy as we know them today owe their existence to the *hypothesis*—and the willed belief—that artifacts offer *significant insights* (and works of "fine art" finer and even *more* significant insights) into the mind and character of their makers as well as their users. The notion that the *character* of individuals or peoples is homologous with their products and possessions is an allomorph of the lingering theological desire that there *should* exist a concordance between them, as between all things under a heaven imagined to have fashioned them in the first place; the world as artifact of a divine artificer. (Art history as a product of a certain monotheism . . .) Individuals are thereby taken as inextricably linked to the forms, materials, and affordances of their object-worlds. The problem of the origins and evolution of this *transformative* thesis about art and about museums as an art of demonstrating and delineating identities; as an art of framing and staging memory and history; and as an art of weaving together and superimposing ethics and aesthetics, is entailed at every point with ongoing and dynamically changing projections of its possible futures or fates.

That the enterprises of art history, museology, and aesthetic philosophy, not to speak of art-making itself, are themselves artifacts and amplifications of these hypotheses should be perfectly evident. Art, in the modern sense this word acquired in the eighteenth century but not earlier, was the correlative and indispensable *means* by which the modern Euro-American subject and its consequent notions of agency have fabricated, sustained, and transformed the rest of the world in its image. The art of art history was crafted in this sense as what might be called the "Latin" of modernity: a universal language, measure, and module by which to compare and contrast, and with which to speak "scientifically" about, all peoples, including one's own.

The "failure of gardens" or houses, cities, artworks, clothing, cars, transitional objects, etc, "to make our lives as paradis[ic]al as their prospects," in Harbison's telling words, is less the occasion in modern life for doubt than for inciting the desire for more of the same. His claim that we really do "accustom ourselves to the failure of gardens" (or art) is of course an ironic one; we simultaneously learn never to be quite accustomed to such failures. Taken together with the presumed entailment of ourselves with our object-worlds, it will be clear that we live in a world in which the work of art is as autonomous and self-determining as the paradigm of the bourgeois subject, and that, indeed, they are not merely "reflective" of each other but co-determinative. The operative word here is "as": an "as" that masks and renders mute and invisible an "as-if," to echo Judith Butler's famous observations about the masquerades and phantasmatic identifications constituting gender in modernity.[9]

One could modify this disciplined and continually cultivated desire for an isomorphic correspondence between style and value, ethics and aesthetics, by saying (as art historians and merchandizers of all kinds do) that not knowing what we're looking at is, equally, the equivalent of not knowing *when* and *where* we are (relative to others who always seem either in advance or behind the here and now). We live in a world defined by corporate entities committed above all to prescribing disciplined and predictable linkages between individuals and their object-worlds. In our world, in short, you are made to be desirous of being convinced that you are your stuff, so that you will become even more desirous of becoming that which even "better" stuff can *say* even more clearly to others and to yourselves about your continually evolving truth—that is, *what you shall have been for what you are in the process of becoming*. To sin in modernity is to be untrue to your "style" (however prefabricated), as every teenager on the planet knows perfectly well, without having to read Proust. Artworks and other commodities ostensify and shape into harmonious unity (for those willing to submit to their logic) the turbulent content of the subject's appetites and inclinations.[10]

This linkage of psychology, physiognomy, genealogy, and teleology is no mere by-product or contingent accident of modernity; it is modernity's topological core. The modern academic discipline of art history is one among several instrumental articulations of the Enlightenment dream of *commensurability* which sustained a desire (itself the performance of what I'll call a *secular theologism*[11]) for articulating *congruities* between subjects in respect to their object-worlds and among objects with respect to their subjects. This is precisely the core concept; the phantasm of art history. Once again, the problem; the dilemma, if you will, of representational "adequacy" versus representational "truth."

This dream, a key ideological desideratum of the modern nation-state, has for two centuries oscillated in art-historical practice between coeval contextualist and formalist modalities of interpretation and explanation; between Flatlandish "social" histories of art or of "visual culture" and equally fundamentalist "returns to the object" (code words for the antipathy to "theory" or, to put it more plainly, to questioning of authority) and to the veneration of what one West Coast American art writer a few years ago called the "intelligence" of art.[12] These poles are not always (as they happen to be at the moment) politically aligned, respectively, with left and right.

## 3

I'd like to repeat the phrase I used at the beginning of the first section of this essay:

> At the heart of that two-century-old practice of the modern self we call art, the "science" of which we would have liked to have called art history, and the

> "theory" of which we may still wish to call aesthetics, or even philosophy, at the heart of all this lies a series of knots and conundrums, *the denial of which* constitutes the very relationship between "subjects and objects" naturalized in circular fashion and kept in perpetual play by the "disciplinary" machinery; the epistemological technology, of art history.
>
> It is precisely this *denial* that has grounded, legitimized, and institutionalized that shadow discourse of aesthetic philosophy or "theory" which the art-historical imagination, in varying ways over these two centuries, has continued to project as a "transcendence" of its own (simultaneously co-constructed) "disciplinary" abjection. (We need not be surprised that a discipline can be grounded in denial, since disciplinarity as such is founded upon the occlusion of difference and heterogeneity; on explicit channelings of vision.)

The issue, of course, is the problem of *representation* (which, not so coincidentally, is an allomorph of the problem of political representation), and specifically of representational "adequacy." In what way and to what degree may an artifact be said to "re-present" truth; the truth of an individual, community, class, gender, "race," nation, place, or period? As I've tried to articulate above, all modern discourses of the visual are grounded upon positions taken implicitly or explicitly with respect to the concept of representation, including (in the parochial case of art history) their frequent historical amnesia about the history of the concept and its relation to "truth"; the fact that not a little contemporary discourse within the discipline with regard to representation is more often than not surrounded by the waters of historical forgetfulness.

The key term here is the *relational* one of adequacy—from *adaequatio* or "adequation," which means "fitting" or "adjustment"; it contrasts with the term *aequatio* and its adjective *aequalis*, with the root meaning of "equal" or "identical." The truth—the *veritas*—in words or things is always one of *adaequatio* or approximation or a tending-toward; an "as-if": (*veritas est adaequatio verbi et rei*) *Aequatio* admits only of true or false; by contrast *adaequatio* is not a formal or quantifiable identity, but an imputed or virtual likeness between two non-identities; a going toward (in Greek, *pros to(n) ison*). In a pathbreaking study published in 1990, Mary Carruthers observed that *adaequatio* has "more in common with a metaphor or heuristic uses of modeling than with an equal sign."[13] This recalls the critique by Roman Jakobson (see note 14) in the 1960s of modernist paradigms of signification in which he foregrounded the remarkable aporia in contemporary notions of representation, the occlusion of a "missing" modality of signification which he named "artifice," harking back to the Aristotelian, scholastic, and early humanist mode of significative relationships marked by the term "adequation." Or, in a word, the "*presentation*" root covered by the concept and term of *re*-presentation. It was the rich and subtle notion of artifice that was historically covered over, displaced, and flattened by the paradigm of "representation" central to modern art-historical conceptions of "art."[14] By what Sam Weber (drawing upon Derrida) termed the "matrix of representation." And what Mieke Bal in a study of the psychology of collecting and fetishism a decade ago had also begun to articulate (see note 7). I am drawn to this concept of "artifice" in no small measure because it allows us to deal with the extraordinary complexities—the fluid and open-ended relativities—of visual meaning in a clear yet non-reductive manner.

* * *

As professional institutions, art history, theory, and criticism have been grounded in *the repression of the impossibility of representation*. The dilemma of *representation* (as *aequatio*) is consequently the fundamental conundrum of art history and museology, which perforce admits of no resolution except, I would suggest, by *historicizing its deponency*; its dependency upon an adequation which is its occluded substrate. We need to step off the historiographic carousel that continues to return our "rethinkings" back to the same starting points. But can we unhinge our profession from its Hegelian binarisms without bringing down the whole art-historical edifice?

The short answer, once again, is no: not without radically re-engaging what it was that art history *replaced*. Not without a deeper recognition of the epistemological *impasse* that not simply has somehow befallen art history but which in fact constituted it in its disciplinarity in the first place; that in its institutionalization has constituted an impasse and barrier between us and a past it renders unthinkable, invisible, and mute.

*Art history as an impasse of conceptualization*: modern art history and museology were themselves inconceivable apart from the contexts and subtexts of that secular theologism which was the co-implicative obverse of the theological aestheticism that imputed authorship to the *world taken as* (not "*as if*" but indeed, one might say, quite eucharistically, *as*) *an artifact*. (We may glimpse here the precise semiological sleights-of-hand that afford and make possible in the first place any "belief" in divinities.) In practice, theological aestheticism and secular theologism relate to each other like the two poles of an oscillating optical illusion. Leaving behind this disciplinary double bind and thinking otherwise would indeed entail proactively refashioning our connections with older traditions of aesthetics, philosophy, and rhetoric buried and occluded, at least to art history as an academic discipline, as one of our modernity's key service industries, by developments essential to the establishment, legitimization, and maintenance of the soulful civilities of the modern nation-state. If we wish our practices to have a viable future, it may well depend on our rediscovery of what the discipline's invention (imagined as a facet of aesthetic philosophy) *occluded*—rather than with our discovering ever more sophistic accommodations to ever more sophisticated forms of identity politics.

Art history and its allomorphs were absolutely essential to the success of the social revolutions of the eighteenth and nineteenth centuries in Europe and the Americas; indeed, they were co-determinative. And while it should be self-evident that they remain no less essential to the forces of globalization and neo-imperialism, they may also, if one follows the logic of the discipline's dyadic phantasms, be enlisted as powerful weapons in our struggles against such hegemonic forces.

In the end, the *point* in understanding how and why all this came to be the case is of course to *change* it. Anything less would be an abrogation of our ethical responsibilities in the current epoch of contemporary neofeudalism or transnational corporate gangsterism called globalization. Of course we may wish to go on pretending that art history is an innocent historical science; a method of historical inquiry, about whose framings we can dispassionately reflect and fine-tune *ad infinitum,* our eyes set and mesmerized by the desire for a horizon of resolution that unsurprisingly never does stop receding.

And we should be prepared to own up to the theologisms grounding and governing such phantasms, and open up the question underlying all our historiographic and ideological endeavors: the power of *artifice* as such to simultaneously fabricate and problematize the forms and institutions of hegemonic power. *Art always has been art history's unmaking and its unmasking.*[15] Only when the discourses on visual artifice begin to engage more explicitly with the radically destabilizing *and* enthralling powers of "art" will they be worthy of further attention.

## Notes

1 Jacques Derrida, *L'écriture et la différence* (Paris: Seuil, 1967) p. 427.
2 Donald Preziosi, *Brain of the Earth's Body: Art, Museums, and the Phantasms of Modernity* (Minneapolis and London: University of Minnesota Press, 2003).
3 Samuel Weber, *Mass Mediauras. Form. Technics. Media* (Stanford: Stanford University Press, 1996) p. 73f.
4 Editor's note: museum professionals' reaction to this statement, which was issued in 2002, can be found in Jane Morris, "Museums Anti-Restitution Stand Provokes Backlash," *Museums Journal* 103 (January 2003): 8 and Tom Flynn, "Artefact Traffic," *Museums Journal* 103 (February 2003): 16–17.
5 See Giorgio Agamben's account of this in *Stanzas: Word and Phantasm in Western Culture*, trans. Ronald L. Martinez (Minneapolis and London: University of Minnesota Press, 1993) pp. 141–151. On his critique of aesthetics, see his *The Man Without Content*, trans. Georgia Albert (Stanford: Stanford University Press, 1999) esp. pp. 68–93.
6 Donald Preziosi, *Rethinking Art History: Meditations on a Coy Science* (New Haven, CT and London: Yale University Press, 1989).
7 Among those in recent years to have begun to address this question is Mieke Bal in her essay on collecting and fetishisms: M. Bal, "Telling Objects: A Narrative Perspective on Collecting," in John Elsner and Roger Cardinal, eds, *The Cultures of Collecting* (Cambridge, MA: Harvard University Press, 1994) pp. 97–115.
8 Robert Harbison, *Eccentric Spaces* (New York: Knopf, 1977) Ch. 1.

9 See especially Judith Butler's *Bodies that Matter. On the Discursive Limits of 'Sex'* (London: Routledge, 1993) pp. 93–120.
10 To paraphrase Terry Eagleton, *The Ideology of the Aesthetic* (Oxford: Blackwell Publishers, 1990) p. 23.
11 Discussed at length in Part III of D. Preziosi, *Brain of the Earth's Body*, pp. 29–43.
12 Thomas Crow, *The Intelligence of Art* (Chapel Hill, NC: University of North Carolina Press, 1999).
13 Mary J. Carruthers, *The Book of Memory: A Study of Memory in Mediaeval Culture* (Cambridge: Cambridge University Press, 1990) p. 24f.
14 This is the opposition between "artifice," in Jakobson's sense, and "icon." An iconic sign-relationship (and we need to be very clear that all of these terms, all these signs, refer to *relationships between things*, not *kinds* of things) is primarily one of factual or literal similarity; an artific(i)al sign is one of imputed similarity; of adequation rather than equality. Of course once again these terms are all "relative," and in practice objects and things necessarily differ from each other in respect to what kinds of sign-relationships are dominant and which are subordinate. All of that can reach a degree of complexity which is beyond the scope of these remarks to more than simply hint at. It is possible that one of the proximate sources for Jakobson's ideas about artifice was the remarkable Czech art and architectural historian Jan Mukarovsky, a fellow member of the Prague group in the 1930s, who at the time was developing a "multi-horizon" model of visual signification (not published until the late 1950s) which aimed at portraying the dynamically variable complexities of artistic meaning-construction and construal. See further in Donald Preziosi, *Rethinking Art History: Meditations on a Coy Science* (New Haven and London: Yale University Press, 1989) Chapter 4, "The Coy Science," pp. 80–121, and "The Art of Art History," in D. Preziosi, ed., *The Art of Art History: A Critical Anthology* (Oxford: Oxford University Press, 1998) pp. 507–525.
15 An earlier version of this essay was given as a lecture entitled "Conceptualizing the Discipline," at an international conference sponsored by the European Science Foundation in Edinburgh, March 2003, on the status of art history as a discipline, held at the Edinburgh College of Art. It also draws upon issues addressed in more detail in the books cited above in notes 2 and 13; see also Donald Preziosi, *In the Aftermath of Art: Ethics, Aesthetics, Politics* with a Critical Commentary by Johanne Lamoureux (London: Routledge, 2006).

Chapter 8

# Rhetoric and motive in writing art history

## A shapeshifter's perspective

*Christopher Bucklow*

The personal observations set out in this essay arise from two sources: from the experience of my having once been an art historian, and also from the fact that since I changed careers and began to make art, much of my subject matter has come out of meditations about the nature of that transformation. I ask: What was the condition of my being when I was a curator? How does my condition today relate to that beginning? And what was driving the need to change? Traffic of this sort, if it is traveling at all, is usually traveling in the opposite direction.

My own transition came after ten years' experience as a curator in a national museum in London. My higher education had been solely in art history—I had not studied studio or fine art, and the academic life had suited me. For those ten years I was completely absorbed in my work—curating exhibitions, writing essays, and delivering lectures and papers: all the while exploring the figures and themes from the history of art that vitally interested me. So far as I was aware, there was no hidden ambition or suppressed need to make art. Writing and curating were creatively satisfying in themselves. So why then the change?

Perhaps there is a clue in the word "vitally," for I would now say, with the benefit of hindsight, that the themes and artists I studied were deeply related to issues I needed to explore concerning my own nature and the nature of my relation to the world of society and the wider universe. What I am suggesting is that my choice of subjects had an existential dimension that was intensely personal. However, those choices were made unconsciously, and indeed the whole personal project was one I was deeply unconscious of. Looking back now over the range of topics I treated in my writing, what I sense is that I was using the study and the practice of writing to search for answers to a set of questions that I did not know I was asking and that these questions were vital to my psychological, philosophical, and perhaps almost religious needs.

As I now see it, the cause of the change in vocation had something to do with the fact that answers to some of these "unasked" questions began to register in my consciousness. This process was in itself protracted and it took many years and many repeated "attempts" for it to break into my conscious area—but by what force this was achieved, I do not know.[1] Because at this stage it was still largely an unconscious process, as they emerged, these answers seemed, at first, to be located "out" in society and seemed to have an "evangelizing" force inherent within them: I felt the need to communicate the "good news"—society needed to change in certain ways that I had identified. Such proselytizing seemed much more appropriately part of an artistic rather than an art-historical mission. So I quit.

If this essay is going to mean anything beyond a list of abstract generalizations, I feel that I will have to give a detailed personal example of what I have called the "existential" dimension to my need to write. I will also have to confess my own situation before I try to make an extrapolation and suggest some tentative conclusions, conclusions that will beg the question: How general is this phenomenon for the writers of art history? I hope this detailed account will not seem too tedious to the reader, for I am aware that we all carry an evolved aversion to speaking about ourselves excessively. I therefore beg the reader's indulgence in advance.

If I analyze my early art-historical writings today, one of the crucial, but I must re-emphasize, unconscious, themes explored beneath the apparent surface of the text concerns the proper place of will in the world. This could also be put as an interest concerning the place of consciousness and human intervention or design in nature. The deeper—and to all intents, invisible—questions being addressed underneath the surface of my texts were about the legitimacy of mind as an agent of transformation in "nature." The topics in which I vicariously explored these personal ends were philosophically flavored essays about the rise of landscape as a genre, or the changing practice of landscape painting in the late eighteenth and early nineteenth century. I also wrote essays which used individual artists from the school known as British Romantic Naturalism—figures such as William Turner of Oxford or Cornelius Varley—to explore the same personal ends. Varley was the inventor of various optical drawing aids and also telescope and microscope lenses. Inevitably, given an interest in this area, I became interested too in the invention of photography and the existence of various indexical printmaking techniques, known today as "nature printing."[2]

All these writings, although ostensibly about a certain interesting phenomenon in history, I am certain now were actually being used to examine questions vitally related to the present day, to my own present, and to my nature as it was at that point, in the first few years of the 1980s. For all of these figures and phenomena exhibit an inherent loss of confidence in the place of conscious will or intention in the world: photography as "the pencil of nature" allowed the world to inscribe itself on the sensitized paper; landscape itself as a genre appears to me now to be part of a general turning away from the human; and, moreover, the ideals of the British landscape school I was interested in were those that gave rise to cults of spontaneity, to a cult of the sketch, and to the promotion of the medium of watercolor as the technique in which immediacy and these consciousness-circumventing methods could be most perfectly displayed.

I felt at the time that these topics were related to the contemporary 1980s fascination with mediation. This gave rise to much talk about contemporary "Mediation Art," where artists such as David Salle and Sherrie Levine were presented by their critical apologists as coming out of profound Skeptical thought with the result that they saw originality and authenticity as impossible. Though when I interviewed Salle in 1986 I was surprised to learn that he was much more involved with Freud than with Baudrillard and felt that the whole mediation discourse was a personal interest of the critics rather than the artists.[3]

Landscape's rise up the genre hierarchy was interesting to me for what that meant in terms of a general shift in consciousness, though it now appears that this was motivated by a sense of what I could make that "history" symbolize in terms of my own internal system or state. This sounds like a kind of unconscious autobiographical metonymy: let this theory of events about the rise of landscape *stand for* myself and my own theory of my internal state. There is a process of identification going on here and a need to feel at home in the world, so that the world is converted into the mirror of the self: either as if one wore mirror-coated spectacles where the mirror is on the inside surface, or that one were in a pre-Copernican vision of the dome of the heavens, where from an anthropocentric centre, the concave inner surface was again reflective.

I wrote about British Romantic Naturalism, indeed I championed it, as having divested landscape of an unnatural imposition—the use of allegory and emblem—and replaced them with the more organic Association of Ideas: "the symbolic premise as a whole came to be seen as an artificial intellectual overlay; as not organically and vitally related to the image, but as an external rational graft imposed upon that image." And I set up the terms to be contended in my "history" in order to refute:

> [the] Christian contention that only by the exercise of reason does man possess a destiny independent of the flow of forces and events operating in the phenomenal world. Dependence on the senses in this scheme, inevitably was seen as casting oneself to the mercy of the compulsions, necessities and determinations of fluctuating material circumstances in which free will was impossible.[4]

Clearly the need is to develop a text in which it is possible to work on the desire to throw off an "alien graft." In actuality, the "graft" can be identified as the laws of society installed within my mind by early contact with parents or with whosoever fulfilled the role of communicator of cultural information. I should note here that this was no rape—as it is often figured in Romanticism—but an influence the infant psyche reaches out for and imbibes in order to source the necessary restraining forces required to exist as a team player in a human social group. The location is firmly here and now rather than there and then, neither back in the eighteenth century nor out there in the society of the 1980s, but in here within the flow of forces in my own psychological economy.

This view of will, or reason, as in some way alien is not as odd as it might first seem. It has deep roots in the mind since the end of the eighteenth century. It is implicit in certain Romantic philosophies, in science and in much modern art. No less a commentator on the Western psyche under the influence of the scientific paradigm as Alfred North Whitehead can be found saying that "scientific reasoning is completely dominated by the presupposition that mental functionings are not part of nature."[5] Such ideas are implicit within our cult of wilderness and overt in the philosophy of deep ecology movements. Artwork by Richard Long seems also to closely follow the Sierra club motto "take nothing but a photograph, leave nothing but a footprint"; and that of Andy Goldsworthy appears to involve a fantasy that somehow the work might almost have made itself.

I now see the discussion of these things in my writing as a self-portrait in many respects. The choice of these topics mirrored exactly internal conditions in my psyche in which the legitimacy of self-will was called into question by the dictates of some restraining force—a force that the Freudians might call the superego and the Jungians a force of collective morality that one has internalized. For me, it would appear, there were indeed "no accidents"; and these internal dynamics were being explored through the substitutive activity of writing history.

The question arises as to how much this situation distorts the subjects that are being treated in the apparent history. This is a difficult question. Of course the meaning of the text is dual. It is clearly still about the events or objects it purports to be about—that does not disappear entirely—but then again, it is highly charged with personal meaning, deeply psychological meaning for the writer. I imagine the situation where the personal meaning hitches a ride on the ostensible subject under discussion as an inquiline-type relationship; not quite symbiotic therefore—for I cannot see how the clarity of the history benefits in such a pair—so perhaps it is more a case of a benign parasite. Clearly a totally parasitic relationship can also be conceived of, where the data of the history weaken, almost to extinction. But in the period I chose to write on, as I have said above, there is a nexus of ideas that all share a certain distrust of the activities of the higher mind: Romantic naturalism in painting, the cult of sketching, cults of the child, the mad, and of drug use, all arise around this time, as did the indexical methods of image making such as photography and nature printing; so there was definitely something happening at that time which much later turned out to be capable of carrying my need to explore similar states within my own mind. Indeed, there is, perhaps, more than just affinity here. Rather the situation is perhaps that of an individual in the late twentieth century, myself, jettisoning ideas, still powerfully active in contemporary society, but which had their origins in the late eighteenth century

If my early essays appear to me now as expressions or symptoms of the nature of my being—my intellectual and emotional orientation of mind at that time—this now stands in high relief, because the process of change initiated in my art-historical investigations caused a revolution in my deepest and most fundamental assumptions. It is hard to get the right emphasis here, for the change was on a structural level, extremely fundamental. But if these early essays have the quality of symptoms of my state of being, the seeds of change were already present: despite the fact that they exhibit signs of internal fission and mental conflict they also contain passages that evidence a striving for fusion and an inclusive internal unity of acceptance. Concentration on landscape painting has aspects of both symptom and cure. For attraction to landscape is a need for inclusion in a category of the world called by us "nature." Nature here is only a symbol of inclusivity and that inclusiveness is really an inner psychological one. Before the rise of landscape the inclusive symbolic set was the religious over-set "creation"—and again I must emphasize that we are not dealing with externals here; this is only a sign of an inner situation, in this case a very ancient one, for the concept "creation" obviously goes back a very long way. The actual demise of that over-set itself—sometime before 1800—must be a sign of a division within the psyche, and the substitution of another over-set called "Nature" around that time merely carries the need on, but in a slightly different container. Again, these units of the division are actually aspects of the self. Is this evidence then of the war of language and instinct, a war of the neocortex and the lower brain: a war of "recently" acquired linguistically installed behavioral processes, ones necessary for group life, but now warring with genetically carried, ancient programs that embody innate instinctual desires? Are we then to be seen as unhappy symbionts—"nature" playing host, with difficulty, to "culture"—genes playing host to a guest called language?[6] Given the very recent discovery that the neocortex language centers are built entirely with commands inherited with the strand of DNA inherited from one's mother, and that the deeper emotional centers of the lower brain stem are built on commands proceeding from the DNA strand inherited from one's father—with the resulting fact that competitive natural selection extends down to the molecular DNA level—this is not as far-fetched as it may sound at first.[7] Be that as it may: the closing of some such division was my unconscious desire. It is no accident that with this aim in mind I became heavily involved in the technicalities of the theories of a movement known in England as The Picturesque. Indeed, I pored over the volumes of eighteenth-century theoreticians such as Uvedale Price, Richard Payne Knight, and Abraham Tucker, whose works seemed to offer a convenient symbolic structure in which the "human" and the "natural" (never forget that in me these are only signs of inner psychological energies) were combined in the harmonious English landscape garden or park.

So it seems that a process had been initiated in the psyche at the very beginning of my art-historical career, that was somehow aimed, perhaps teleologically, at an end point or result that my conscious mind could not have guessed at. This is not ground that Freudian-based psychology is comfortable with, for no such prospective intelligence is proposed; rather it is in the outlook expressed in Jungian writings that one finds concepts that might fit the story better. There one finds hypothesized the existence of some sort of a homeostatic mechanism, a mechanism that self-corrects a psyche that is off balance in one way or another.

This is the point where my art making begins—and the point that I must break off this narrative—for with the art making I step over the horizon of the events that strictly pertain to my topic here. One thing I will say is that the break in occupation, the change in career activity, did not strictly mark a watershed in general self-awareness. For although I began making sculpture which directly dealt with the issues present in the essay quoted from above, I was not yet properly conscious of what it meant, or more importantly *where* the contending issues were located. What I mean by this is that while I was broadly aware that in the artwork I was continuing a dialog first explored in my art-historical writing, I continued to locate the debate outside of myself—in society. This is important if one wants to understand the strange inward–outwardness of the way, if I am not mistaken, my mind and many minds constitutionally operate. An example of what I mean here is this: my text about British Romantic Naturalism speaks of removing an "alien graft" formed of a literary, textual overlay that classical landscape art casts over the scene (something I would now dispute anyway) but the point is that five years after writing my essay I was making my first artworks by creating sculptures by grafting living plant material. Highly human-modified cultivars such as the pear (*Pyrus communis*) were grafted onto the species known in England as the wild "hawthorn" (*Crataegus oxyacantha*). But I saw these sculptures as dealing with issues that were important in the external world: issues that I thought should be thought through in society, questions about the role of human design in the world, questions set in the nervous debate about genetic engineering where the role of will is thrown into sharp focus. But this externalization is also a form of projection, making psychic contents appear external. It was to be a further five years before I became fully aware of the true location of this debate—in my own psychical apparatus.

In general terms what I have been describing is my projection into or onto a subject in order to make a text that one can work with in the psyche. Of course, it goes without saying, I was doing this unconsciously. It is as if the demands of the psyche to debate or decide between competing forces within its structure calls for "objects," symbolic units that it can "handle," can wield, in the hammering out of a compromise between the warring inner factions. I am reminded of the symbolic process in evidence during dreaming, where people, objects, situations are pressed into service as such symbolic "objects" or units that can be used to contend an issue that needs work on it. I am also reminded of the epic poetry of William Blake, with its personifications of the psychic elements within him and their manipulation in a grand working through of an inner cosmic comedy. With Blake many writers are unsure how consciously he put this all together, though I would be astonished if he did not *become* conscious of his process to a very large extent, through its practice. As far as I am aware that would make him the first person in history to do so, predating the efforts of Freud and Jung by more than half a century.

But another general use of projection involves a quest for stability, a stability that mimics instinct. In addition to the phenomenon causing the need for projection as described above, projection might also be thought of more simply as a way of seeing the world according to one's own needs for it to appear in such a way. In such a case it would be being used for purposes of stability: converting other into self. I would explain this in the following way: I emphasize the psychological need for stability from the perspective of my understanding that the human psychological system is uniquely *unstable*. This is through our having evolved to occupy the evolutionary niche of a specialist in unspecialization. That is, we have become a creature whose hard-wired instinctual systems have atrophied in favor of a large mental space capable of loading-up with behavioral systems stored in an external "organ" that we ourselves call "culture." And all the evolutionary advantages accruing from this move are around us as I write, not least this amazing tool that I am writing on. But to return to the point: converting the environment of society or the general world into a mirror of the self confirms and calms shifting identity (a point that will not be lost on the vigilant is that this view mirrors my own being, in the sense that I have shifted identity). Such projection brings the illusion of inevitability into the loop, and the illusion of inevitability is the addiction of a creature whose instincts have been allowed to die.[8]

These then are details of just one example of the complex interlocking web of external data and internal motive that are collapsed, as I now see it, within a text. With this kind of knowledge in mind one is always aware of the pitfalls of projection, and yet life would be dull without conjecture and I feel I must conclude with some speculation that goes beyond my own personal story.

With this in mind, an area I find interesting is the sense in which the chosen subject of an art-historical piece of writing is liable to be used as a self-symbol. By this I mean an external object or system of meanings that one identifies with. I visualize a kind of cat's cradle of psychological strands crossing to and fro between the perceiver and the chosen symbolic object, so much so that the whole thing becomes a knot in which it is difficult to make a distinction between internal and external. Projection is obviously involved but that is not the main point. Projection of the self onto the world seeks to provide an illusion that is useful to inhabit. But self-symbolization of the kind I am interested in might also be useful in *actually* converting the world to a version of the self. My suspicion is that a chosen artist or topic is a self-symbol for the chooser, be that chooser a writer of an article about an artist or art-historical theme, or a museum curator putting on an exhibition. Apart from the results of my own introspection on this point, I note that choosers are often very touchy about criticism of "their" artist or topic and I believe it is justifiable to suspect that this denotes a real link of self-identification going on. If so, then it makes for an interesting cascade of hypotheses in thinking out from this starting point.

It parallels, in the world of the chooser, the nature of the world of the chosen—the artist. The basis of this theory of events is that an artwork is a self-symbol of the maker. The mechanism I see going on is this: I consider that the rectangle of the canvas (or increasingly the video screen) to be an ideal arena in which the ideals of the self are set out—more than set out, in fact, urged might be a better word. The process is that the artist invents or selects ground rules that are then used in a personal art-making "game." The rules of the game, the rules of engagement with the materials—that is the behavior and procedures adopted within this symbolic arena—*stand for* the ideal moral self of the maker, perhaps even the actual moral self of the maker, its nature, and its rules of conduct in society. All the actions and choices made within that rectangle are paradigmatic of the self. Thus criticism of that work is often seen as a stab in the heart. This whole state then gets extended beyond the ideal human mental form of the maker to the ideal mental form in which all individuals in society should ideally be cast. Thus all the artists in society are battling for the acceptance of their ideal selves as they strive to gain success and prominence—acceptance, that is, coupled with a case for the wider adoption of that form of self within society. This may be interesting, but if the situation regarding the psychic motives of the choosers as described above is true, then the real battle of the ideal self is waged between a small handful of writers and curators whose choices fill the pages and walls of our most prominent magazines and museums; it is *their* selves that are symbolized in their adoption and patronage of certain artists and not others. The artist and the artwork and all its paradigms then become signs of the writer or curator's self as that self contends for prominence or even ascendance in the great pool of the contended self which is the Western cultural debate going on in philosophy, in the political sciences, in history, sociology, anthropology, psychology, and many others—including art history.

Indeed art history has taken its place among all these disciplines and is now a space in which they are all permissible evidence or tools used in the study of art, or the contest of the ideal self. How different this is from the connoisseurial stage of art history with its emphasis on aesthetics, though during that first stage I have no doubt that ideals of the self were also being contended unconsciously. But there is a large difference between the activities of those debating within philosophy and those debating within art history. For the ideal self is contested in these other disciplines—philosophy and the rest—in a relatively overt way (even if personal motives for taking a position may be obscure to the exponent of the argument). In writing history it is much more likely that the overt argument is lost, displaced into the ostensible subject under discussion where it becomes covert. There are obviously going to be different degrees of self-awareness on this point. The hybrid artist–theoretician–historians Victor Burgin and Allan Sekula clearly argue a personal case, but how different is that case from Michael Baxandall and Svetlana Alpers? And how conscious are any of these exponents of their deepest personal motivations? We none of us can tell without an open discussion of these issues. As I see it, despite all the nods to post-structural theory, the very use of the word "history" plays to a fantasy of reportage, of explication and interpretation. And this is the precise environment in which covert self-symbolization prefers to flourish.

For some years I was in reaction to my former role and I would wonder at the strange workings of a society that licensed these personal investigations by proxy in a subject called art history. But I have shifted position as some inner need to differentiate my present self from my former self has receded, or indeed the fantasy versions of those two selves. I have come to a position that recognizes the creative side of both professions. What I marvel at today is that society is so arranged—so divided up conceptually—as to corral what it sees as legitimate creativity (and I mean "creativity" here in the large sense that I have been discussing, one that includes psychological projection) into an area walled-off as the province of individuals labeled as "artists." What I suspect is really going on in this is that it is an effort to conceal the true extent to which we are all creators in this larger psychological sense. I would understand that effort to conceal creativity as a part of a conspiracy by the unconscious centers on self-need to cover up or put out disinformation about our true motives, in other words, our self-centered desires. These are radically creative, and worse still if admitted to, they are all there is. And for a social creature addicted to finding a substitute for instinct—to alleviate the pain of choice—they must be concealed at any cost. One of the heaviest costs is the barrier to self-knowledge erected between the unconscious and the conscious systems, a barrier that largely prevents knowledge of the true motives for our behavior.

## Notes

1 I use the word "area" here without accepting the topographical model of the psyche that it implies. Jung would call it the homeostatic force.

2 Among these essays were: "Der englische romantische Naturalismus—der Kreis um Cornelius Varley," in exhibition catalog *The Poetry of Earth—Englische Aquarelle der Romantik* (Berlin: Staatliche Museen zu Berlin Nationalgalerie, 1990) pp. 21–24; "William Turner of Oxford and British Romantic Naturalism," in *The Old Water-colour Society's Club Annual Volume* (1984) pp. 23–52; "The British Historical Context," in exhibition catalog *Land Matters* (Lincoln: Blackfriars Arts Centre, 1986) pp. 11–21; "The Legible Tree," in exhibition catalog *The Tree* (Lincoln: Usher Art Gallery, 1987)

pp. 6–15; "Landscape and the Fall," *Aperture Magazine* (Winter 1988): 10–19; "Horatio Ross: Photography and the Picturesque," in exhibition catalog *Horatio Ross* (New Haven, CT: Yale Center for British Art, 1993) pp. 4–16; *The Pencil of Nature—Watercolour and the Invention of Photography*, handlist to exhibition at the Victoria and Albert Museum, London (1995; in the files of the Photography Section); "John Dillwyn Llewelyn: Instantaneity and Transience," in Mike Weaver, ed., *British Photography in the Nineteenth Century: The Fine Art Tradition* (Cambridge: Cambridge University Press, 1989) pp. 65–78 (originally published in the V&A Album, 1986). All of these essays were published, using my stepfather's surname, as by Christopher Titterington.

3 David Salle in conversation, New York City, May 4, 1987. This interview was never published but is posted on my website: www.chrisbucklow.com.

4 In Bucklow, "William Turner of Oxford," op. cit.

5 Alfred North Whitehead, *Science and the Modern World* (Cambridge: Cambridge University Press, 1926).

6 For a longer discussion of these ideas see Christopher Bucklow talking with Adam Phillips in *Christopher Bucklow—If This Be Not I* (London: The British Museum and the Wordsworth Trust, 2004) pp. 39–101. (Available at enquiries@wordsworth.org.uk.)

7 See Chapter 6, "Growth, Development and Conflict", in Christopher Badcock, *Evolutionary Psychology: A Critical Introduction* (Cambridge: Polity Press, 2000).

8 Further discussion of this in *Christopher Bucklow—If This Be Not I*, op. cit. This radical instability also must account for the resistance I encountered in changing career—for there is considerable social value placed on the idea of having a stable identity.

# Part III

# Instituting art history

## The academy

### Introduction

The university convenes a collection of scholarly disciplines, each with its own data and analytical habits. Those fields and modes of inquiry that have found protection under the umbrella of the academy enjoy public patronage and intellectual legitimacy. No measure goes so far in according disciplinary status to an intellectual endeavor as does university sanction. Art history made its academic debut in the nineteenth century, though then mainly as a series of guest-starring roles whereby a few scholars attained positions in departments of philosophy or history. Only in the early twentieth century would art history become a bona fide academic discipline with discrete departments supporting undergraduate as well as graduate degree programs. Art historians working in the early phases of professionalization recognized the importance of university affiliation as well as the need for art history to appear to be a coherent, cohesive discipline in order to secure this alliance. Writing in 1913, for instance, the first president of the nascent College Art Association of America acknowledges as much:

> The number of institutions giving instruction in the history of art [in the US] is approximately one-fourth of the total of those in which the liberal arts are taught for a period of four years. . . . That there are not more institutions which give such instruction is, doubtless, due partly to the fact that there is no commonly-accepted view even among art teachers as to *what*, *how*, and *when* art shall be taught in undergraduate and graduate courses. College authorities naturally hesitate to extend their already widely-spread resources over new fields whose boundaries and nature are still undetermined.[1]

Smith here announces what will become one of the College Art Association's primary activities: standardizing the field. This effort aimed not only to regularize the various curricula pursued under the heading of "art history" in the United States, but also to endow the discipline with recognizably academic features. In other words, Smith and other proponents of professionalization sought to give art history the disciplinary character of established academic fields: well-defined disciplinary boundaries, pedagogical standards, research guidelines, and peer review prior to publication or professional advancement. Casting art history into the academic mold took place not only in the United States, of course. A similar process occured wherever the study of art history could lead to a university degree.[2] But as much as art history may have strived to seem like other academic fields, the essays in this section reveal that it remains a discipline apart, with distinct scholarly as well as ethical concerns.

Art history, according to Stephen Melville, serves a crucial role in the academy. Among its distinctive disciplinary features is its continual self-critique. Art history's bounds are inherently unstable, Melville explains in "On the Institution of Limits," because the category of "art" itself is unfixable. Any definition of art involves some subjective criteria, and few art historians agree—even temporarily—on a common conception of their disciplinary purview. Thus, the practice of art history, whether in the classroom or at a scholarly symposium or before the computer keyboard, requires participants to accede to a continually shifting data set. As Melville sees it, each invocation of "art" or, hence, of "art history" demands a psychic effort, a summoning of the abstract field over which the discipline asserts itself. In this sense, the discipline of art history disappears and reappears with each encounter, each new transaction between student and teacher, professor and administrator, and even department colleagues. With this inherent reflexivity, Melville argues, art history makes apparent the willful coming-into-being that the comprehensive university itself likewise undertook when it asserted the value of the collective academic enterprise. Art history, then, serves as the memory and, perhaps, even the conscience of the academy.

The notion of art history as the conscience of the university is pursued by Claire Farago in "Remaking Art History." Farago poses the question, "how are we as ethical practitioners of what has come to be called the human 'sciences' to deal with academic practices based on a flawed assumption?" Of particular concern to Farago is the myth of human history as "culminating in the achievements of European civilization." Among other things, this myth justifies the university's historic complicity in Western imperialism as well as its contemporary abetment in the commercialization of higher education, which reduces students to consumers and knowledge to a commodity. Art history, Farago argues, is not only uniquely implicated in promulgating this myth but also uniquely positioned to expose and interrupt its perpetuation. This can be done through appeal to "wonder." Art historians work with data—works of visual culture—that often have the capacity to inspire immediate emotional and highly subjective responses. Managing wonder has become the task of the art historian, as it was historically the role of the colonizer. Instead of ignoring (or worse, tamping out) wonder as merely an emotional byproduct of history, Farago enjoins art historians to see history as a consequence of wonder. Wonder, because it is ultimately unclassifiable and ungovernable, always preserves something of its past: "The work of art yields insights into the realities which ideology hides from view." Failing to seek—and to teach—these insights renders academic art historians "wittingly or not, facets of the . . . infotainment and edutainment industries."

David Carrier likewise discerns the role of wonder in provoking scholarly responses to Islamic art. In particular, highly personal, emotional, even ecstatic experiences to some objects seem to motivate the proliferation of what Carrier describes as "eccentric" art-historical analyses. By eccentric, he refers to a category of art writing that does not participate in the norms of academic discourse. In other words, eccentric accounts of Islamic art rarely deploy stylistic analysis, show no interest in artistic intention, appeal to universal rather than historically specific observations and often arrive at universalizing conclusions after considering only a single artwork. Academic art history, on the other hand, adheres to disciplinary standards for form of argument and sufficiency of evidence. What is more, academic art history relies on other professional norms such as peer review and scholarly consensus, which rarely concern the eccentric author. Where this poses a problem for the academic art historian is in the popular imagination. Because eccentric accounts deliver satisfying conclusions without presuming that readers possess either the art historian's specialized vocabulary or knowledge of the field, these versions of Islamic art history find a popular audience that academic art history generally fails to engage. With their bold, or even fantastical, conclusions, these works are entertaining in a way that academic art history is not. "Unless academics also explain our concerns to the general public in accessible prose, eccentric art writing will continue to attract readers." Pleasure is what eccentric accounts often deliver. But should pleasure be the domain of eccentric art history only? Carrier concludes that this need not be the case for Islamic or any other field of art history. Through the writing of Oleg Grabar, Carrier finds an instance of academic art history that accords great value to the pleasure of looking at art and, hence, the pleasure of reading art history. Like Farago's valorization of wonder, Carrier's focus on pleasure aims to restore the relevance of academic art history for contemporary Western society beyond the walls of academe.

Academic walls, or divisions, lead Robert O. Bork to take a fresh look at the relationship between science and the humanities in the academy. The modern university has instituted barriers between academic endeavors, with "scientific" and "humanistic" disciplines often segregated into different schools or colleges. The physical separation of disciplines has only exacerbated perceptions on all sides that scientists and humanists have little in common as scholars. On the contrary, Bork argues in "Art, Science, and Evolution," art historians have much to gain—and have already gained much—from the sciences. Historically, art history has been enriched through contact with the discoveries and methods of science. The influence of science has rarely been received sanguinely, however. Art historians whose work shows obvious affinities to, for instance, the ideas of Charles Darwin disclaimed such borrowings. Widespread anxiety over art history's possible contamination by scientific thinking seems to have gained ground at the turn of the twentieth century, just as the discipline became concerned with shoring up its disciplinary boundaries. Whatever the cause of art history's wariness of scientific discourse, Bork finds that it persists to this day as does a general lack of understanding of basic scientific principles. It seems that wariness has prompted a willful ignorance. Those scholars who put aside their prejudices and make the effort to breach the barriers their universities maintain between humanistic and scientific study will, according to Bork, be amply rewarded. For one thing, given the recent shift in higher education funding away from disinterested humanistic research toward applied scientific research, Bork argues, it would be only practical to elucidate a kinship between art history and science. More important, though, are the advantages scientific modes of analysis might offer to art history. Art history has more in common with fields such as geology and cosmology than most art historians realize. To refuse to learn from our colleagues in the sciences isn't just closed minded, it's a capitulation to precisely the production-model of intellectual labor that Farago condemns in her essay. Like Farago, Bork argues on behalf of an ethics of teaching and scholarship: "While some might worry that exploration of the analogies between the arts and the sciences would lead to the colonization of one discourse by the other, it seems far more probable that such dialog would underline the autonomy and dignity of each. Since the academy in the early twenty-first century often seems both divided against itself and marginalized by increasingly business-driven social paradigms, the potential benefits of cross-disciplinary communication are simply too great to ignore." Like the other contributors to this section, Bork attributes to art history the capacity to bridge disciplinary as well as ideological rifts, making urgent the need to understand the field's relationship to the academy.

## Notes

1 Holmes Smith, "Problems of the College Art Association," *Bulletin of the College Art Association* I (1913): 7.

2 Art history became a field for undergraduate and graduate study in Europe, Australia, and North America in the first half of the twentieth century; in Asia, Africa, and Latin America art history took root in the academy shortly thereafter.

## Chapter 9

# On the institution of limits

*Stephen Melville*

*Institute*: [f. L. *institut*-, ppl. stem of *instituere* to set up, establish, found, appoint, ordain, begin, arrange, order, teach. f. *in*- (In-2)+ *statuere* to set up, establish: see Statute.]

## Tuning up

Given the invitation to reflect on art history and its institutions, we tend, I think, to find ourselves more or less immediately thinking in terms of an intellectual practice in its exposure to, or embeddedness in, a variety of social facts more or less imaginable as buildings ordered to particular practices—the museum, say, or the university, or—less clearly a "building" but of the same order of social fact—the market. (This sense might be thought of as floating loosely between the *Oxford English Dictionary* (OED)'s senses, 7a ("An establishment, organization, or association, instituted for the promotion of some object, esp. one of public or general utility") and 7b ("Often occurring, like institute, in the designations of societies or associations for the advancement of literature, science, or art, of technical knowledge, or of special education.") Cast in these terms, a major focus of this essay will be art history in its relation to the university.

But the essay will also worry a fair amount at this way of hearing the word "institution" and so of even beginning to think about the possible relations between "art history" and "institution." In particular, it's going to ask that we hear as fully as possible the processual dimension of the word "institution"—"the action of instituting or establishing; setting on foot or in operation; foundation; ordainment; the act of being instituted" (OED). And it will take it that as we become attuned to hearing the word this way such phrases as "the institutions of art history" or "art history and its institutions" will themselves also begin to sound differently—that, in particular, the play in them between objective and subjective, agent and effect, will become more fully audible. An important consequence of this expanded sense of "institution" will be a clearer hearing for the ways in which "art history" belongs essentially to the field of "institutions" rather than simply having relations to institutions more or less external to it or imposed upon it (that is, we'll start catching more clearly the sense of institution that the OED glosses as "a. Elements of instruction; first principles of a science or art. b. A book of first principles, an elementary treatise," the sense, then, in which Heinrich Wölfflin might equally have entitled his book "The Institution—or perhaps The Institutes—of Art History," a title whose proper English hearing evidently calls for a sixteenth- or seventeenth-century ear).

Opening a question of institutions this way—out of a certain play of sense—is these days intellectually "French," although—like the appeal to etymology—the deeper ground of that Frenchness is explicitly Heideggerean, and it presumably emerges in some uneasy tension with another tradition one might less easily qualify as "German" although it's most often more specifically referred to as Frankfurt. And this is just to say that the opening of the question already implies a certain orientation to—and more importantly in—what is now quite broadly called "theory," which is widely taken to play some significant role in relation to contemporary changes in the institutions of art history. Questions of institution raised in this "French" way can be expected to link up with deconstructive remarks on the institution of the trace or of writing, or with Derrida's marked interest in questions of explicit political constitution as they might be continuous with questions he raises elsewhere about the world as "linguistically constituted"—a phrase that one would presumably want to hear in some reasonably sharp distinction from its translation as "linguistically constructed" (as if, simply as bits of language, the one opens toward, say, the kinds of entwining of bodily and political and written sense that nerve a text such as Edmund Burke's *Reflections on the Revolution in France* where the other more easily gives rise to images of the prison-house of language: we think we know how the politics of this contrast fall out, but we may be wrong in that).

It may well be interesting that in even laying out the field this way we find ourselves repeatedly appealing, through the OED, to an order of sense more or less eclipsed by the emergence of the fully explicit modernity we take to be our own. One might note, for example, the tendency of certain of Jean-Luc Nancy's key terms to find their most adequate English translation in words now evidently lapsed in the English—for example, "compearance" in its rendering of "*comparution*"—and in words often enough lapsed because the verb has lost out to its noun (as, for example, "compart," rendering Nancy's "*partager*" and evidently historically lost to the "compartment" that was its effect and now appears to stand well enough alone).[1]

We are then already in the midst of both theory and history, oriented in thought.

## An instance and a preliminary exploration

"Canon" is a word we take easily to belong to a general question of art history and its institutions, and I'd hazard that when we hear the word "institution" in its primarily nominative and substantial sense, we're prone to see "the canon" as something like a warehouse into and out of which things are periodically ferried by more or less recognizable agents whose motives, conscious or unconscious, we might then examine. Should we be convinced that those motives are arbitrary or pernicious, we may be led to propose either some better way of managing the traffic in and out or perhaps the closing down of the warehouse altogether.

Nothing of this picture will make much sense to anyone who takes the fact of canon to be a consequence or concomitant of the institution of art—that is, it will not make sense to anyone who takes it that "art" is essentially exposed to judgment, picked out by such judgment and having no existence apart from it; art falls, appearances to the contrary notwithstanding, under no concept, and so is only ever the object, as Kant says, of critique, of which canon would be one expression. The picture of agents—persons, social forces, or whatever, ferrying things in and out is somehow deeply wrong, mistaking how things might get there—in the canon—for what it is that they are there. "Mary Garrard" may be an answer to how Gentileschi has come to her place in the canon, but it is not an answer to the question of why she is there. The short answer to that question is, "Because she belongs there," and the longer version of that answer will be a sustained gloss on "belonging" and "there" cast as an account of Gentileschi's work (that is, what counts in the end is not Garrard's will that Gentileschi be in the canon, but her work [Garrard's, Gentileschi's]). Transformation of the canon is not up to us; we participate in its ongoing fact.

The art historian who takes the fact of canon to an essential dimension of the discipline's claim to an object has a coherent and defensible picture of the canon. It's also one contemporary art historians, on the evidence, find themselves increasingly uncomfortable with, for fairly good reasons: it doesn't track particularly well with the understandings of research, method, and objectivity that inform current practice. Indeed, those understandings seem to depend on explicitly setting questions of value off to the outside of the discipline (this would be why we tend to be more comfortable with Panofsky, who is clear about these things, than with Wölfflin who seems to repeatedly muddle them up). Visual culture—certainly the largest fact of institutional transformation within the ambit of art history and the university—holds, in at least some of its forms, an equally clear and defensible picture, one in which there is no canon because there is no art in any consequential sense ("art" is, as it were, a term of no more than anthropological interest). The "willful canon," the thing imagined as something on which we might or should vote, the product of our choosings, is by contrast with both of these incoherent and unsustainable. And yet it is the one on which most arguments about "the canon" continue to turn.

They do so at least in part for perfectly good and ordinary enough reasons: we can point to the warehouse—Janson, for example—and we can watch things being ferried in and out from edition to edition. And every year, teaching it, and now frequently defending or attacking our teaching of it, we imagine ourselves to be "teaching the canon." That's of course why it's important to be clear that we are not in fact teaching the canon; we're just giving tours of the warehouse. The interesting question would then be about how we've come to be so confused about our own activity (and so also, often enough, confused about what kinds of challenges to art history visual culture in one or another of its forms may or may not be raising).

Heidegger raises the question of this confusion early on and in particular, complex intimacy with Panofsky's consolidation of that confusion. It's there in the tension in "The Origin of the Work of Art" between art in its origination and in its preservation, more broadly present in the tension across his writings between his extraordinarily high valuation of art—poetry in particular—and his scathing refusal to assimilate that value to what he calls "an inherited and very questionably arranged cultural treasure" (questionable, presumably, because cultural).[2] And although art itself appears to drop out of the picture (except for Heidegger's crucial, difficult insistence on, precisely, "picture"), it's above all there in his writings on technology, and it appears there most interestingly as a question about the university.[3]

What Heidegger particularly proposes is that we, in effect, recognize the warehoused and willful canon as the canon insofar as it necessarily appears (like anything else) within the economy of the "*Gestell*" and its reframing of the world as "standing reserve" or "stock." These particular terms are internal to his more general argument that for technological or instrumental modernity the world—for Heidegger always a finite structure, worked in multiple ways by the shadow that at once marks its horizontal limits, the inevitable cost or consequence of anything that comes to light within it, and the invisible inner lining of its very lucidity—is reduced to a picture (a "world view") that cannot be acknowledged as such. In one notable formulation of this he writes that within modernity:

> to represent means to bring what is present at hand before oneself as something standing over against, to relate it to oneself, to the one representing it, and to force it back into this relationship to oneself as the normative realm. Wherever this happens, man 'gets into the picture' in precedence over whatever is. But in that man puts himself into the picture in this way, he puts himself into the scene. . . . Therewith man sets himself up as the setting in which whatever is must henceforth set itself forth, must present itself . . . i.e. be picture. Man becomes the representative of that which is, in the sense of that which has the character of object.[4]

It may be useful to simply underline how far the linking in this passage of particular senses of object and objectivity with a certain sense of normativity goes toward providing the starting point for Foucault's analyses in *The Order of Things* and after. It's tempting to notice as well how far Lacan's much cited remarks on vision—and particularly the little story of his day out with the fisherman Petit Jean—occasioned as they may be by his reading of Merleau-Ponty—suddenly appear to unfold also within an all but explicit reference to Heidegger.

Elsewhere in the same essay Heidegger asserts:

> under these conditions, human activity [including, most especially art] is conceived and consummated as culture. Thus culture is the realization of the highest values, through the nurture and cultivation of the highest goods of man. It lies in the essence of culture, as such nurturing, to nurture itself in its turn and thus become the politics of culture.[5]

A final useful bit we can take from Heidegger's meditation on these things is his implicit statement that such a politics of culture is continuous with and integral to the emergence of the research institution—or, as we might say, trying out some of the further resonances the word—continuous with the institution of research.

## Some commentary: division and institution

Among those who have written on the question of the university and its disciplines in Heidegger's broadly deconstructive wake, one might mention in particular Christopher Fynsk, Gerard Granel, Peggy Kamuf, and Bill Readings, whose description of what he calls "the university of excellence" seems to me to become ever more compelling as the modern university daily "rages" (in a Heideggerean phrase) "toward fulfillment of its essence."[6] The particular issues I want to explore in relation to the history of art are perhaps most directly approached through Kamuf's reflections on the place of literature in the university.

Her starting point is straightforward and seems as appropriate to art and its study as to literature:

> By convention, or rather by a large set of conventions, we may speak of literature as the instituted name of a set of traditions, practice, conventions, and evaluations, which set, however, is of indeterminable dimensions. This indeterminability of what is (or is not) literature, of what properly belongs to the set called literature is not a contingent condition but a necessary one of continuing to call "literature" by that name.[7]

We can take the bearing of such a remark to be first of all historical—there is some large set of, let's say, works not bound in their moment of initial accumulation by any clear set of rules or any presiding name or concept, and which comes to assume such a name as a condition for its entry into the university (at least). And this means that it is true for the study of art and literature in ways it does not seem to be true for the physical sciences and their objects, that we will repeatedly find ourselves hesitating over whether in one circumstance or another it is better to write simply *art* or *literature* or whether we ought more properly to write *"art"* or *"literature."* This of course also means that there are moods in which we would like, one way or another, to be spared this particular decision, to have some permanent settlement of it (with art we are, I think, most often tempted by the thought that we can settle it through a permanent adoption of quotation marks, whereas the study of literature has been less often tempted this way: no one, evidently, has written "literature" as compellingly as Duchamp made "art," so where "literature" does find its way into permanent quotation marks it does so mostly on the grounds of a general skepticism rather than some particular internal transformation or questioning of its practice).

The simple solution here is, of course, to simply cut the knot—to say that "art" is the fact of a particular "cultural whole"—the term is Arthur Danto's—to be located among other cultural wholes differently dominated (thus, for example, Danto's interest in Belting's reformulation of a significant swath of art history's traditional terrain as that of "the image before the era of art").[8] I have no particular desire here to argue against this solution, at least not directly. It is enough to note that adopting it simply puts an end to any interesting historical or theoretical questions about the institution of art history, which evidently lives in significant part precisely out of problematic but necessary exchanges between *art* and *"art."* And of course my further thought must be that staying with these questions will turn out to make some real difference in how we think about the institution in which we mostly live and work.

Kamuf puts her version of this question this way: "What if the institution of literature, which sets it up through a decision within writing in general, which divides the latter and sets aside a reserve, were a gesture that must itself be repeatedly performed?"[9] If there is within the university no getting over the moment of art or literature's institution—if, one might say, these objects do not enter the university without carrying their history and the history of their becoming an object of study as a question—they evidently inhabit the university on a significantly different basis than those fields that are able to routinely discard their pasts (sometimes, of course, those discarded pasts find themselves taken up into fields such as "literature"—Galileo's *Dialogue on the Two Chief World Systems* may have ceased to be science but may still be or have become "literature"). Kamuf writes:

> In order to spell out the syntax of the subjective genitive, in other words, it would seem we have to anticipate the predicated outcome: an instituted

> literature. Putting subject and predicate together, we end up with an almost perfectly circular or pleonastic sentence: "literature" institutes literature. This is almost, but not altogether, a pleonasm because the quotation marks around the subject of the sentence would be the marks of a suspended nomination, the sign that a familiar, that is *instituted* name has been "borrowed" to designate that which has no ready proper name. Without its quotation marks, literature is a catachresis.[10]

Put it this way: where we are tempted to imagine the university as, at least in principle, ordered to an articulated totality of knowledge without remainder, such objects as "art" and "literature" are scandalous just insofar as they propose and enact a division both oblique to and arbitrary with respect to that order of articulation. Over and against the ordered differences that plausibly let physics lie here and chemistry here and biology there, "art" and "literature" seem to depend both on elusive differences within an evidently more ordinary and natural field (for art, we might call this more ordinary field "visual culture") and a maverick disregard for the more or less well-founded differences among those ordinary fields. If we picture the university as a nicely cut-up pie chart, then art and literature seem to come to it from the outside, taking bites where they wish and refusing to settle into the places most evidently prescribed for them. One way to put this would be to say that whatever the truth of the pie chart—and whatever the truths advanced by those working within it—art and literature know about that chart that it also *appears* (that nothing literal goes apart from the rhetorical, that the letter insists, that art like literature is a catachresis we cannot do without).

What Kamuf underlines is the special role this assigns literature in relation to the articulation of the university:

> [L]iterature is installed there, not merely as one division among others but as divisionality; from the moment, in other words, that the university includes departments of literature among its divisions, it attempts in effect to comprehend its own *founding* within its borders . . . [11]

As she phrases it, this is both a moment of impossible dream or desire and a fact of the actual condition of the university. The institution of literature is the university (it's there that literature exists) and the institution of literature is the institution of the university (the university in its capacity to think its own divisions is a consequence of literature's institution[12]). The question of the department of literature or of art history—the division, as one might say, of the humanities—is less a matter of something included in the university (as if it were an institution whole and secure apart from its contents) than of the university's institution or constitution and so its capacity to think its limits. And it follows from this that a university unable to sustain its departments of literature or art history will find itself deprived of the resources that let it imagine itself as a university, thus no longer able to address its own articulation in terms other than those that belong to it as the purely empirical precipitate of reigning social and economic forces. Unable to imagine the terms of its own disciplinarity, it dreams of an interdisciplinary salvation; unable to figure its objects, it stakes everything on research; closed against its actual forms of objectivity, it breeds stupefaction and cynicism.

What matters in Kamuf's argument is the direct connection she draws between a certain institution of art or of literature—an institution of autonomy just insofar as one will have to speak of literature instituting literature or art instituting art but an institution also never completed, always exposed to the quotation marks that re-mark a division internal to it and so demand its institution not cease—and the institution of the university. As the contemporary university remakes itself on the grounds of a purely sociological and economic self-understanding, it is departments of literature and art history above all that both can and must raise the question of the university just because their own objects are at stake in that question.

To ask now, from within the yawning void of the university of excellence, after a changing discipline and its institutions is to be called upon to resist that institution's essentially sociological and normative construal of its own institutional condition and field. And that means taking on art history's institutions in their full historical and conceptual complexity. If "theory" has come to be a widely shared shorthand for what is changing in the discipline, then it will matter both to unfold the problematic of institution in the various forms theory gives it, and to connect our stakes in theory up with the various ways art history has been and continues to be instituted in, for example, Hegel or Wölfflin or Warburg or Panofsky. To do this is to try to understand fully how the surge of theory in the discipline has gone hand in uneasy hand with a resurgence of historiographical interest as represented by the work of, among others, Michael Podro, Michael Ann Holly, Margaret Iversen, and Georges Didi-Huberman.[13] It will matter too that we be able to see these things within the larger optic of the institution of art, as for example Joseph Koerner has tried to do in his recent studies of Dürer and of the consequences of Protestant iconoclasm.[14]

## A suggestion

If I earlier used the question of the canon in art history as a way into some of the tensions internal to the notion of institution and more particularly the institution of research that is the university, it might be as well to end by pointing to curriculum as the most consequential of art history's institutions, at once the terms of its actual and effective internal articulation and the feature through which it claims its place in the larger architecture that defines the university as such and in its distinction from any other institution. It is not clear to me that we have, by and large, any capacity now to actually discuss curriculum in terms other than those dictated by the needs of administration.

The word "curriculum" means, as we now often say, "literally"—which is to say etymologically—running track or course. The OED still gives as its first definition of "curricular," "Of or pertaining to driving or to carriages"—an example, from 1881 reads, "The four-in-hand is, as it were, the curricular unit. If a man can manage a Coach and four, he can do anything in the way of driving." The terms "track" and "course" have an interesting further carry of their own—toward the things we call "courses" on the one hand, and on things we call "cursive," that is "running" and running in particular relation to writing, on the other. "Track," with less etymological comfort, figures in the system of "trace" and "trait" and so the various ways we have come to imagine or reimagine writing.

If we want truly to think our way through a changing discipline and the terms of its institution we perhaps do well to hang on to these senses in curriculum of movement and of writing in the name of the dual demand that art history not give up on or give over the institution of the university, and that art history not give up on or give over the singularity—say, the dividedness—of its object and the terms of its objectivity.

## Consequences

I don't know any more than you what this might mean (neither do I know any less). I have, as I suppose you do too, my fancies ("Is it really too late for there to be 'schools' of art history?") and sallies ("What if the survey were the seminar and the art of the 1960s the required introduction to the major?"). And I have places I look to—Essex, Leeds, Rochester . . .—where things have appeared, sustainedly or for a time, possible, as well as places, such as the Clark or the Getty, that I look to at the many moments when I am convinced that the university is no longer able to support any form of self-reflection independent of the procedures through which it evacuates itself of sense.

In bringing the word "curriculum" to the fore I mean to be asking whether that term might still name something more particular and more debatable than a simple list of educational consumables on offer—might be more nearly the preliminary articulation of an object in need of proving. I take this phrase—"proving the object"—from Hegel, and I take the deconstructive account advanced by Kamuf to be a radicalization of that formulation.[15] A curriculum taken in this sense functions as a standard: it is a sort of proposal about what a department or program's teaching collectively might amount to. It opens up the thought that what one might expect of, say, graduating seniors is that they be able to make sense of the courses they've taken, give an account of an object and its complexities, and it invites imagining things such as hiring not in terms of coverage but more nearly as an exercise in discovering those hinges in the articulation of a more or less shared object that permit its further unfolding and transformation. Given three departments of the same size and with the same structure in terms of "coverage," when might it make sense for one to hire someone in film, another to hire a medievalist, and a third to seek out a sociologist? "Making sense" here evidently means something like being productive of sense, both in terms of departmental work and in terms of its grasp of its object. If you don't search for a medievalist, even though you clearly have a gap there, have you ceased to be a department of art history or have you merely taken a step toward becoming something specific? Which of these should matter to you more? Which will, under the circumstances, count as giving up on or giving over the singularity of your object?

Some of the language I've evoked here has Lacanian overtones, suggesting that one shape objectivity might assume would be broadly psychoanalytic, built out of some play of desire and limitation, intimate with what we might understand of the structure of persons. Can we imagine—is it worth imagining—a curriculum ordered to the proper names of its faculty? I'm sure in my bones that this—especially in an age when something you might call "myreading" has become an entirely fungible professional commodity, all the freer in its circulation because no one, including the one advancing it, has to believe in it—is going too far. But I don't know that I understand why it would be too far to go. It could well be thought to more accurately map the curriculum students, especially graduate students, who actually pass through than the set of course titles and distribution requirements that we sometimes appear to merely pretend matter to us. It's striking that for all the departmental apparatus in place, graduate students more often than not pursue a largely private itinerary (whereas, by contrast, undergraduates moving through a collegiate structure of the Oxbridge sort operate with little sense of "department" until they are finally asked to take a fully public examination that does not resolve itself into the particular terms of a particular tutor). Lacan's own school asked a candidate coming out of the radical idiosyncrasy of a training analysis to communicate the outcomes of that analysis to a second party in such a way that they could be further communicated to a third . . .

At my university, courses must now routinely include grading, student evaluation, outcome assessment, and, less regularly but with increasing frequency, peer review. Do we understand what any of these things actually are, either individually or in their various relations? Do we have any actual, that is, consequential, idea of what it might be to evaluate a course apart from its instructor? Do we give our students any means of doing so? Are we sure that the ability to evaluate a course should not form a part of its gradable content? Is outcome assessment anything other than the rewriting of grades for customers paying to have knowledge administered to them?

These are the everyday questions of life in the university of excellence and they can be multiplied almost endlessly. "Curriculum" is one ground on which they might be addressed, reordered or rerouted, and it is a ground that matters just insofar as it jointly stakes the institution of department and of university. Where curricular discussion is not possible there is good reason to say that one can no longer speak of the university; given that the university is now well advanced in proofing itself against such discussion, the question is where within it acts of institution—inventions of the university from within its increasingly disparate parts—may yet be possible. If it matters that there be a university, some continuation of its question—and of course it may in fact not matter: perhaps it is enough that we have careers and a place in which to manage them—then we may well want to find ways to insist that art history remains in need of achievement, as if we were not, and could not be, done with its institution—as if our profession (another word to practice hearing otherwise) were still in question.

## Notes

1 I explore this further in a forthcoming essay on the work of Eva Hesse.
2 Martin Heidegger, *Basic Concepts*, trans. Gary E. Aylesworth (Bloomington, IN: Indiana University Press, 1993) p. 7.
3 See Martin Heidegger, "The Origin of the Work of Art," in *Poetry, Language, Thought*, trans. Albert Hofstadter (New York: Harper and Row, 1971) and *The Question Concerning Technology, and Other Essays*, trans. William Lovitt (New York: Harper and Row, 1977).
4 Heidegger, *Question*, pp. 131–132.
5 Ibid., p. 116.
6 Ibid., p. 135. See also Christopher Fynsk, *The Claim of Language: A Case for the Humanities* (Minneapolis, MN: University of Minnesota Press, 2004); Gérard Granel, "Liminaire," in *Traditionis Traditio* (Paris: Gallimard, 1972) as well as further works cited in Fynsk; Bill Readings, *The University in Ruins* (Cambridge, MA: Harvard University Press, 1996).
7 Peggy Kamuf, *The Division of Literature, or the University in Deconstruction* (Chicago, IL: University of Chicago Press, 1997) p. 6.
8 See Arthur Danto, *After the End of Art: Contemporary Art and the Pale of History* (Princeton, NJ: Princeton University Press, 1997) especially Chapter 4, "Modernism and the End of Pure Art: The Historical Vision of Clement Greenberg."
9 Kamuf, p. 8.
10 Ibid., p. 10.
11 Ibid., p. 8.
12 See also Philippe Lacoue-Labarthe and Jean-Luc Nancy, *The Literary Absolute: The Theory of Literature in German Romanticism*, trans. Philip Barnard and Cheryl Lester (Albany: State University of New York Press, 1988).
13 Michael Podro, *The Critical Historians of Art* (London: Yale University Press, 1982); Michael Ann Holly, *Panofsky and the Foundations of Art History* (Ithaca, NY: Cornell University Press, 1985) and *Past Looking: Historical Imagination and the Rhetoric of the Image* (Ithaca, NY: Cornell University Press, 1996); Margaret Iversen, *Alois Riegl: Art History and Theory* (Cambridge, MA: The MIT Press, 1993); Georges Didi-Huberman, *Devant*

*l'image: question posée aux fins d'une histoire de l'art* (Paris: Minuit, 1990) and *L'image survivante* (Paris: Minuit, 2002).

14 See Joseph Leo Koerner, *The Moment of Self-Portraiture in German Renaissance Art* (Chicago, IL: University of Chicago Press, 1993) and *The Reformation of the Image* (Chicago, IL: University of Chicago Press, 2004).

15 "Philosophy has to consider an object in its necessity, not merely according to subjective necessity or external ordering, classification, etc.; it has to unfold and prove the object, according to the necessity of its own inner nature. It is only this unfolding which constitutes the scientific element in the treatment of a subject." G.W.F. Hegel, *Aesthetics: Lectures on Fine Art*, trans. T.M. Knox (Oxford: Oxford University Press, 1975) p. 11.

Chapter 10

# Remaking art history

## Working wonder in the university's ruins

*Claire Farago*

The appeal to a generalized notion of excellence, Bill Readings argued in his influential book of 1996, *The University in Ruins*, marks the fact that there is no longer any idea of the University, or rather that the idea has now lost all content.[1] The modern university is no longer primarily an ideological arm of the nation-state, as it was in its formative era in the nineteenth century. Unlike Humboldt's university founded on the principle of reason, today's university, Readings observed more than a decade ago, functions like any other autonomous bureaucratic corporation. For the humanities, traditionally organized on the model of national culture, the decline of the university's role in educating its citizens to serve the nation-state brings a grim financial prognosis. Sam Weber speculates on the university's diminishing role in the present era of transnational corporate capitalism that much will depend on the ways in which the established humanistic disciplines define their future practices.[2] Disciplines that continue to conceive of their activity in terms of self-contained and sovereign "fields" will find themselves faced with increasing difficulties, both in terms of their attractiveness to outside donors, and in terms of finding an internal constituency among incoming students.

Today, these grim forecasts are matter-of-fact actualities. A current (2006) industry survey of how US colleges are providing job-related training shows universities falling behind. The matter of what a university education should provide no longer seems to merit discussion—those universities that are not working with industry are simply "failing to take advantage of a $13 billion market for job-related training" because they are "slow and unwilling to adapt to necessary changes."[3]

Faced with the circumstances that Readings, Weber, and others describe as the fate of the humanities in higher education, one financially viable form of market expansion has been the development of interdisciplinary programs, which often appear as the point around which administrators and faculty can make common cause in university reform, partly because interdisciplinarity appears to have no inherent political orientation.[4] The *intellectual* attractiveness of interdisciplinary programs stems in part from their attempts to address Eurocentric practices and to institute a more pluralistic historical vision. The openness of interdisciplinary programs should not blind us, however, to the institutional stakes involved. As the language of ethics collapses into that of economics in terms such as accountability, responsibility, transparency, value, and excellence, the modern university continues to reward experimentation on an Enlightenment model of scientific truth that assimilates the unknown to the known.[5] This model of truth is deeply problematic for the humanistic disciplines. Briefly stated, the concern is this: how are we as ethical practitioners of what has come to be called the human "sciences" to deal with academic practices based on the flawed assumption that "internal factors peculiar to each society are decisive for their comparative evolution" culminating in the achievements of European civilization?[6]

Fundamental to the re-conceptualization of all the humanistic disciplines as intellectual pursuits is the question of what constitutes their ethical practice today in the professional setting of academia. Against an Enlightenment notion of truth as the instrument of mastery exercised by the knower over the unknown to bring it within the fold of the same, is the concept of situated knowledge which, in the words of anthropologist Clifford Geertz, surrenders its global pretensions, its reach being limited to its places and conditions of emergence.[7] This is the epistemological relativism that drives Bill Readings's arguments when he advises against the rebirth of the university: better to think within its ruins "as the sedimentation of historical differences . . . [for] change comes neither from within nor from without, but from the difficult space—neither inside nor outside—where one is."[8] Adequate solutions to cultural and ethnic misrepresentation, Weber emphasizes, can no longer justifiably consist of "equalizing" the quantity or quality of "content" among peoples and cultures in museums and history books. We must substantively rethink the polity of practice as such. The problem, in other words, is no longer simply one of "adequate" representation, but of "representation" itself imagined as being unproblematic.[9]

What would an adequate solution look like for the discipline of art history (or visual studies more generally)? The following essay addresses this question by means of a strategic case study. The category of wondrous objects classified as "idols" provides a concrete case for examining what is at stake intellectually and ethically in revising the traditional configuration of the humanistic disciplines on the model of national culture. Wonder is an over-determined category associated with liminal experience, mapped internally on the psyche and also projected into the external world. Wonder is also a problematic once deeply enmeshed in the colonial economy and now at work in the network of globalized capitalism.

A critical inquiry into the history of the wondrous has the potential to integrate the arts and humanities around significant questions involving the formation of modern individual and collective identities. It will be argued here that wonder is a topic of major historical and theoretical consequence that bears on significant contemporary preoccupations with the criteria for what it means to be human and what it means to be excluded—the problematic of what it has meant, historically, not to be human, or not to be fully human is necessarily part of the discourse, often functioning silently, insidiously.[10] Ultimately, this case study allows us to suggest how a critical analysis of wonder in an intercultural framework may find a useful place in the corporatized university—may even justify the retention of fields such as art history, shaped in the crucible of modern nation-state formation—without selling out to the info- and edutainment industries. Studies of cultural interaction lead to questions of whether and how the historical complexities of collective identity formation and dissolution might reorganize research protocols at the institutional level. Critical understanding of the institutional history of material culture, both textual and visual, calls for integrated attempts to define the issues that produced the exclusive narratives of our current disciplinary formations in the first place. Bill Readings proposes a form of interdisciplinarity that retains as part of its structure "the question of the disciplinary form that can be given to knowledges." Disciplinary structures would then be forced to imagine what kinds of thinking they make possible, and also what kinds of thinking they exclude.[11] Readings advises against creating amorphous interdisciplinary spaces in the humanities such as cultural studies, because the question of disciplinarity itself should be a permanent question that might enable the university to "function as a place where a community of thinkers dwell . . . [who] make the destruction of existing cultural forms by the encroachment of the open market into an opportunity for Thought rather than an occasion for denunciation or mourning."[12]

## A brief history of wonder

Wonders of nature and wondrous works of art are traditionally believed to embody forms of symbolic power that the knowledgeable utilize to work marvels. To situate the problematic of wonder within the university as an institution of higher education, it will be useful first to review the historical concept of wonder. One of the earliest disciplinary claims for wonder unfolds in Plato's dialog *Theaetetus*. When Theaetetus complains that he is confused, Socrates redescribes his state as the sensation that arises in the moment of knowing that one does not know. The sensation of wonder (*to thaumalein*), Socrates explains, "is the mark of the philosopher. Philosophy indeed has no other origin." (155D). There is a second *locus classicus* for the Western discussion of wonder, which occurs at the beginning of Aristotle's *Metaphysics*. The context of discussion is similar—wonder again signals the origin of philosophical inquiry in ignorance:

> For it is owing to their wonder that men both now begin and at first began to philosophize . . . since they philosophized in order to escape from ignorance,

> evidently they were pursuing science in order to know, and not for any utilitarian end.
>
> (982b12–20)

Wonder according to the principal ancient authorities is induced by direct observation, leading from the acknowledgement of ignorance to the pursuit of knowledge without "any utilitarian end." According to Lorraine Daston and Katharine Park, co-authors of an ambitious attempt to write a "history of wonder" in relation to natural philosophy, the vocabulary of wonder in Latin and the Romance languages had a well-developed profile by the twelfth or thirteenth century.[13] Wonder in this literature was capable of arousing a wide spectrum of emotional shadings including fear, reverence, pleasure, approbation, bewilderment, admiration, and astonishment. John of Damascus, writing in the eighth century, served as an important source for the typology of contradictory emotions associated with wonder. Following John of Damascus, in the thirteenth century Albertus Magnus and Roger Bacon both discussed wonder and its relation to ignorance, just as the ancient sources had. Borrowing from other parts of the Aristotelian corpus, Scholastic commentaries on Aristotle's *Metaphysics* also helped to establish a new sub-theme for wonder, one with great historical consequences, dealing with the borderline conditions of humanness, or lack of humanness. Typical of the terms of these arguments is the one made by Roger Bacon in the 1240s, that the ignorant man who wonders is only slightly superior to the constitutional ignorance of animals and children.[14]

The most enduring characteristic of wonder is that it defies stable classification. On one hand, wonder is a subjective response to the beauty of nature and art that elicits pleasure; but on the other hand, monstrous and grotesque wonders may elicit horror. For Albertus Magnus, who described the state of wonder as shocked surprise (*agoniam*) or stupefaction (*stupore*) similar to "fear," wonder is a liminal state insofar as the sensations associated with wonder exceed the proper functioning of the senses as Aristotle understood them to function best, that is, as a mean between extremes. Temporary speechlessness, incomprehension, astonishment, delight, agony, fear: bodily states that exceed the moderation of the senses or push sensation into extreme states, were associated with wonder since the medieval period not only in the philosophical literature, but also in travel literature, topographical writings, catalogs of rare and marvelous places, buildings and things, as well as in collections of the rare, the beautiful, and the strange. In this literature, and the material culture associated with it, the condition of wonder is transposed from the observing subject to the things observed. The emphasis in thirteenth- and fourteenth-century travel literature was on the role of the eyewitness and the exotic circumstances that induced wonder. The Far East was typically filled with wonders, or marvels, but in the succeeding centuries, the kinds of experiences that John Mandeville and Marco Polo described were also transposed to the margins of the so-called New World.

## Wondrous idols: whose ignorance?

What sixteenth-century European missionaries called "idols," regarded in terms of their grotesque appearance, were signs of the moral corruption and demonological possession of their potential converts. However, it was also possible at that time to regard the same "idols," still in terms of their appearance, as signs of the subtle creative power of the human imagination—that is, it was possible for the very same grotesque imagery to testify in opposite ways, either as evidence of moral corruption or as evidence of the artist's unlimited ability to invent things out of his imagination.[15] Upon entry into the early modern *Wunderkammer*, what European collectors as well as missionaries called "idols" continued to both attract and repel, but only as phantasms of their former selves: in the context of collecting, idols were experienced in the comfort and safety of the studiolo or the drawing room as exotic curiosities (Figure 10.1).[16] In this manner, artifacts of non-European origin became part of a larger European category of objects to have interesting conversations about.

Relevant to our contemporary understanding of sixteenth-century discussions of idolatry is the intervening history of the term "fetish."[17] Modern scholars usually credit the broader sense that the term fetish gradually acquired to Charles de Brosses's *Cult of Fetish Gods, or a Comparison of the Ancient Religion of Egypt with the Actual Religion of Negritude*, 1760.[18] De Brosses argued that the primordial religion was "fetishism," which he defined, in line with longstanding definitions of idolatry, as the direct worship of earthly material objects for their endowment of divine powers "capable of gratifying mundane desires."[19] De Brosses drew on existing discussions of "idols" as false images, such as Francis Bacon's *New Organon* (1620); and his study of non-Christian material culture as religious superstition complemented other Enlightenment contributions to an emerging field of ethnography and anthropology, such as Giambattista Vico's explanation of the origins of culture in *La Scienza nuova* (1725).[20] Vico subordinated irrationality to rationality, distinguishing the rational from the irrational understanding of the world in terms that discussions of primitive religion at the end of the nineteenth century left unchanged:

> when man understands he extends his mind and takes in the things, but when he does not understand, *he makes the things out of himself and becomes them by transforming himself into them*."[21] (emphasis added).

Writing approximately a century after De Brosses, Karl Marx drew his dialectical image of the commodity-fetish from such Enlightenment critiques of religious superstition cast as a distinction between the moral sphere of society enabled by rational intentionality, on the one hand, and those unable to separate their desires from what Marx would call the "sensuous materiality" of things.[22] In 1790, Kant had offered basically the same distinction in developing the concept of aesthetic judgment: lack of aesthetic discrimination is proof of the individual's

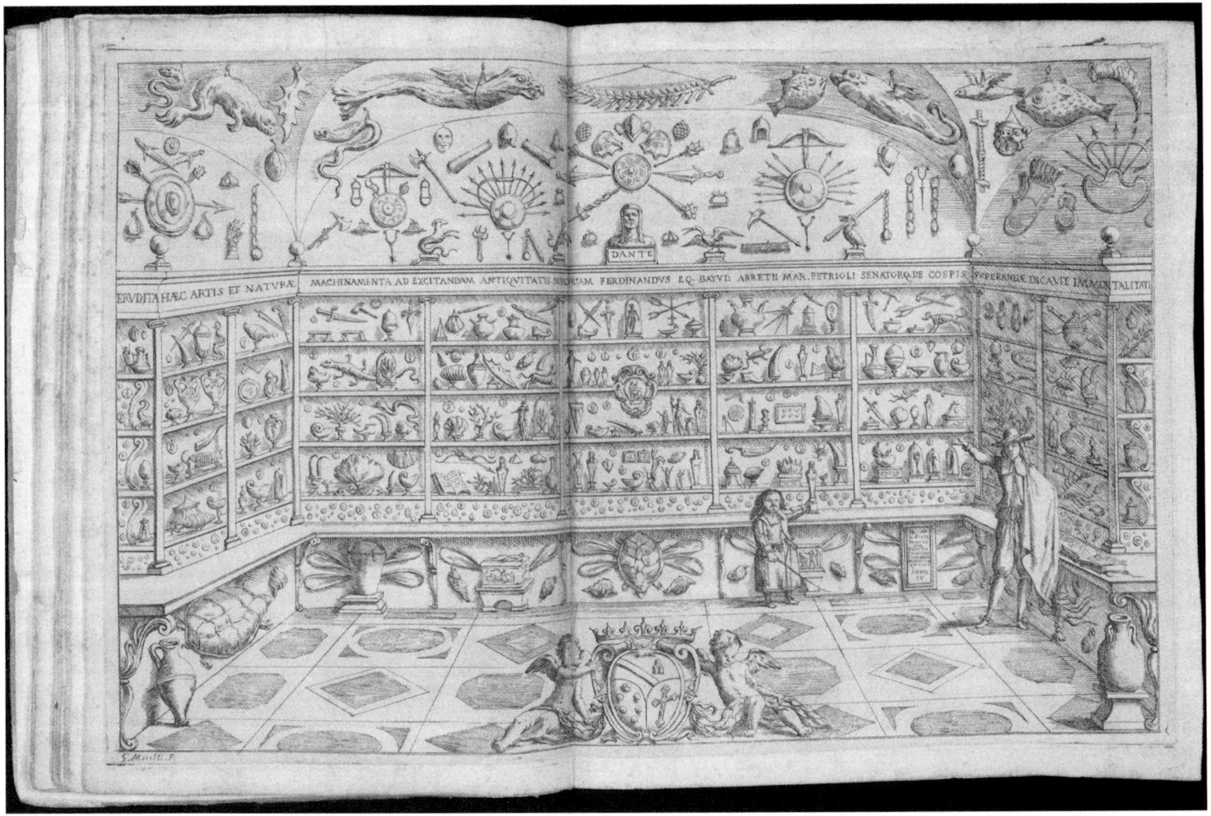


*Figure 10.1* Lorenzo Legati, *Museo caspiano annesso a quello del famoso Ulisse Aldrovandi e donato alla sua Patria*, Bologna: Giacomo Munti, 1677. Engraving by Giuseppe Maria Mitelli. View of the collection of the Ferdinando Cospi.

incapacity for moral autonomy and true freedom.[23] Kant himself gazed at "the starry heavens above" to find "the moral law within."[24]

Although not generally recognized as such, precedents to these modern arguments are found in sixteenth-century Protestant Reformation writing such as Karl Karlstadt and Ulrich Zwingli's theological arguments on the dangers of idolatry.[25] Like Marx, they feared and protested the accumulation of material things as an issue of social justice. The most significant theological contribution to the sixteenth-century discussion of idolatry was Zwingli's analysis of the psychological roots of false worship couched, like Francis Bacon's discussion a century later, in terms of "inner" and "outer" idols.[26] Zwingli defined the idol as a "portrait of a strange god" that is established in man's heart before it is expressed externally in a work of art.[27] Zwingli's argument is a historical precedent to Marx, for whom the commodity hides its true nature under a twofold veil, the outer one a mask of naturalness and familiarity, and the inner one an explicit fantasy, full of grotesque and perverted imagery (*Capital*, I, 72). According to Zwingli, the inner idol, or "Abgott," is anything that displaces God, be it money, glory, or another deity: because of the human need to comprehend reality through material means, what the mind of man grasps is always made into an image; externalization of the inner goods inevitably finds expression in a physical idol.[28]

What is at stake in these theological arguments is the ontological distinction between a lifeless commodity and the living, divine presence in human form. Idols are works made by art. While they may delight or inspire fear, because idols are semblances they disguise their true ontological status. In studying the historical discourse on art and idolatry, it is important to bear in mind that the same neo-Aristotelian theory of human cognition that justified the use of artistic images also justified their condemnation. Zwingli and others identified the *Abgott* in the patron's soul as the source of idolatry that finds its external, monstrous expression in/as works of art. Zwingli's condemnation of idolatry as an inner monstrosity leading to outward manifestations is one extreme position in a broad critical spectrum. Other, mostly Italian, writers discussed the artist's inventive powers in positive terms using the same metaphors connoting the difference between the rational intellect and the sub-rational powers of the imagination. For example, Gian Paolo Lomazzo, writing in the 1580s, considered *grotteschi* synonymous with invention and the highest test of the painter's powers."[29]

Most of Lomazzo's contemporaries were more cautious in their assessment of the artist's productive imagination following the Council of Trent's 1563 decree on images, but they invoked the same contrast between reasoned imagination and the capricious fantasy. Cardinal Gabriele Paleotti, author of an influential treatise on painting (1582; Latin edition of 1594), introduced extensive new qualifications drawn from the standard authorities. The central point in Paleotti's considerations of *grotteschi* is the distinction between the delusions of a dissolute person and the true visions of a prophet.[30] This distinction is the pivotal point in a wide variety of sixteenth-century discussions of art and idolatry by Protestants and by Catholic missionaries. Thomas Aquinas provided the terms of discussion when he differentiated the eternal substance of an object from its accidental, external appearance: the mutation in appearance was external to the visionary's eyes, but the imagination of the dissolute person who could not separate himself from his senses to render a judgment caused him to mistake the image for the thing itself, thus he was captivated by demonic illusions (*Summa theologica* 3.76.8).[31]

At the beginning of the *Metaphysics*, Aristotle distinguishes between the "mechanic" or man of experience and the artist or "master-builder" who is admired not only for his useful inventions but also for his wisdom about causes and first principles. The difference between the philosopher and the expert in one field of applied knowledge is like the difference between the mechanic and the master crasftsman who alone is able to teach the principles of his art because he has both experience, that is, knowledge of individuals, and theory (*scientia*), knowledge of causes (981a15–981b35). The artist and master-builder are admired not only for their artistic productions but also for their wisdom about causes and first principles.

Writing in 1582, with the burgeoning travel literature reporting on wondrous spectacles in the New World and other distant lands evidently in mind, Paleotti condemned the representation of monstrous races, of infernal rites and demonic gods, idol worship and human sacrifice as evidence of the imagination of a dissolute person, that is, one who is not able to understand the relation between artistic productions, and their underlying causes. This frame of reference for discussing the relationship of the work of art to its maker opened up new possibilities for the role of art in New Spain as it did in Europe. By 1537, when Pope Paul III decreed that "Indians and all other people who may later be discovered by Christians" to be endowed with the "nature and faculties" necessary to receive the Christian faith solely by "preaching of the word of God and by the example of good and holy living," the terms on which the Indians' mental capacities were judged were part of an international, transcultural discourse. Bartolomé de Las Casas, the most famous European apologist for the Americans in the sixteenth century, was acutely aware of the problem of classifying his converts and potential converts as lacking in the higher faculties of the human soul. Although he believed that Amerindians possessed the full potential for civility—Las Casas wrote that the Indians possessed skill in the mechanical arts which were a function of the rational soul ("habitus est intellectus operativus")[32]—he also helped to construct an inferior collective identity for the indigenous cultures of the "New World" when he argued that the Indians were only capable of assimilating European culture under European guidance.[33] Similar reports that make extravagant claims about the technical skills of indigenous artists while considering them unable to think abstractly and incapable of creativity and imagination, are part of the historical record of missionaries in Mughal India, China, throughout Latin America, and elsewhere.[34]

The mental capacity to recollect—that is, to draw a series of inferences, as Aristotle and his commentators defined the distinction between the human faculty of memory and the retentive memory of animals—was both directly cited and indirectly implied throughout sixteenth-century discussions of the Native Americans' mental capacities.[35] Although the famous debates on this issue held in Valladolid, Spain, in 1550–1551, left the legal status of Amerindians unresolved, discussions of the humanity of the indigenous peoples of the Americas established the conceptual framework for modern pseudo-scientific theories of "race" two centuries later.[36] At the same time, some jurists today consider Pope Paul III's unprecedented position on human rights to be the true foundation of international law.[37]

This history of classification of peoples also played out more or less directly in European collecting practices. Objects that were initially central sources of sensual and intellectual delight for European audiences now occupy a marginal position in the history of the visual arts. Nearly all the Mexican artifacts known today are located in European collections, where they were originally valued as trophies, gifts, souvenirs—as exotic items sought by European collectors, they are directly associated with the discourse on wonder. The subsequent history of culturally hybrid compilations such as the Mexican painted manuscripts that derived partly from the pre-contact genre of sacred calendars and partly from the European genre of encyclopedic literature documents, the operations by which "idolatrous" content unacceptable to Christian compilers was gradually isolated from content admired by European collectors. As the same material was collected and copied over the centuries, the indigenous material was successively recast. In the earliest records, "idolatry" identified a complex of indigenous practices and cultural artifacts. What was identified and objectified by the missionaries as "idolatrous" was gradually eliminated entirely from the reader's consciousness. Likewise, the early association of these objects with collecting practices that elicited wondrous reactions from viewers was forgotten. Objects that had delighted their initial European owners for their wondrous properties were reclassified as objects of art-historical and anthropological study, while the ostrich eggs and unicorn horns collected alongside them in the sixteenth century were relegated to storerooms in ethnographical museums or simply de-accessioned.

The study of what art was once considered idolatrous, and why, and to whom it pertained, highlights the arbitrary and transitory nature of our established disciplinary and sub-disciplinary formations. While Protestant Reformation theologians denounced lavish religious displays and material aids as idolatrous, their ecclesiastic counterparts in New Spain levied charges of idolatry against their newly colonized subjects.[38] The relationships of power that materialized in such complex exchanges simultaneously taking place at close range and over long distances are ignored as long as historians maintain models of scholarly specialization based on modern nation-state identities that—in fact—only fully materialized some three centuries later.[39] Left with a magnificent but inert treasury of inherited objects, historians who do not stray from their inherited categories are consequently unlikely to articulate complex questions of self–other relationships that produced these storehouses in the first place. Nor are they likely to develop an interest in the marginal position of the culturally dispossessed and the politically disempowered who leave no provenances of ownership or even their names in the historical record.

To return to the general terms of discussion, the *wund* in *Wunderkammer* silently testifies to barbaric practices under erasure: the adventurers who brought idols and many other types of exotica from far off lands to European collectors divested these objects of their original context of use. In the same gesture, philosophers of the Enlightenment developed a discourse of cultural origins that distinguishes primordial religions from secular contemplation of the beautiful in terms of their beholders' engagement with the world. At the same time, the historical category of the Sublime entered this discourse of cultural origins to offer "civilized" humanity an encompassing, total engagement with the world analogous to that of the "primitive." The Sublime in this distorting mirror is the unacknowledged, inverted twin of the primitive subject's passionate engagement with the world. Both are manifestations of the sense-exceeding experience of "wonder," yet only the European subject is given the option of gaining a rational understanding of the world.

How should we remember the historical powers of wonder in our disciplinary and subdisciplinary practices today? As it stands now, connections between the discourse of wonder and the objects designated by these textual practices of thinking with objects are occluded in the archive, trapped in the interstices that divide disciplinary and subdisciplinary practices. More distant still, are the acts of violence such as the eradication of native religious practices, the confiscation of native artifacts, and the colonization of the native peoples, that provided the archival material in the first place.

To what extent should we as scholars operating in today's social networks take responsibility for the effects of the knowledge we produce? Unless we comprehensively attend to the epistemological underpinnings of our intellectual heritage, rather than selecting what seems personally most compelling to study, that which is indefensible will continue to haunt contemporary history writing in precisely the sense that Michel de Certeau defined the mnemic trace as "the return of what was forgotten, in other words, an action by a past that is now forced to disguise itself."[40] For Marx and Engels, Trotsky and Lenin, to name some of the most famous political analysts to consider the work of art in a comprehensive sense, the history of art is far richer and more "opaque" than political and economic theory. The work of art yields insight into the realities which ideology hides from view.[41]

This, of course, is the key issue facing art historians today: the need to re-imagine how art simultaneously has the power to fabricate and to problematize hegemonic power and its stagings. The specifics of Marx's arguments, grounded in typological assumptions of the nineteenth century, are less interesting today than the way he framed the question. We understand works of art as objects whose significance transcends the historical circumstances of their making. Precisely—paradoxically—it is the materiality of the object that is at once affected and unaffected by time. The majority of writing on art in the Marxian critical tradition obscures the relations and oppositions between artwork and commodity, however, and pressures to erase these distinctions entirely (thereby maintaining their conflation) persist in all fields, including art history, art criticism, museology, and visual and material culture studies. The critique of art mounted by Protestant Reformation writers noted that inanimate material objects might replace human understanding of the world rather than enhance it. Marx's immediate predecessors and contemporaries invoked the same fear. In the Romanticist reading of fetishism, clearly audible in Marx's arguments, when "the mind ceases to realize that it has itself created the outward images or things to which it subsequently posits itself as in some sort of subservient relation," it lapses into passivity, "seeing a world of dead relations rather than living images."[42] Marx's explanation of value is based on the essential contradiction between "variable capital," that is labor-power, which adds more than it costs in the production process, and "constant capital" which refers to the objective factors (such as the machinery needed to produce more commodities at a faster rate in order to compete successfully in the marketplace). Viewing profit in these terms, writes Teresa Brennan in an analysis of the role of time in Marx's theory of the political economy, ultimately "depends on the difference a living subject makes to a dead object."[43] By definition, art historians are the labor-power (the living subject) in the production process of art history, just as artists are the labor-power in the production of art.

Where do we want to throw in our lot? If we forget that the discipline is our own creation, we not only exploit ourselves, we may inadvertently produce a world of dead relations instead of the living conditions that made our objects of study possible in the first place. The subdisciplinary boundaries that divide the study of Italian Renaissance art from English Renaissance art from Spanish Colonial art from Native American art—the list of compartmentalizations goes on and on—renders the complicities of historians with nation-state ideology invisible to the individual scholars working in the specialized subfields in which academic practice is encouraged and to which it is largely confined. Those who write within the categories circumscribed by the modern nation-state may tend to discount the sorry history of imperialism or make it out to be trivial or disconnected to us by hindsight, but it is certainly not invisible, trivial or a fait accompli on all sides of the social equation.

Unless our museologies and art histories are linked explicitly to the oldest and most fundamental questions of how our societies should be run, of how free societies in particular should be structured, they will remain, wittingly or not, facets of the corporatized aestheticism of identity politics and of the infotainment and edutainment industries. In the current political climate in the United States and elsewhere, the extent of our responsibilities as academics and intellectuals to link museology, history, theory, and criticism to contemporary social conditions is an urgent and painfully obvious question. The issues I have discussed in this short essay in terms of the field of art history are the preoccupation of philosophers and cultural critics across a wide spectrum of interdisciplinary debate to which art historians, as of yet, have made little contribution.[44]

## Notes

1 Bill Readings, *The University in Ruins* (Cambridge, MA and London: Harvard University Press, 1996) especially Chapter 2, "The Idea of Excellence," pp. 21–43.

2 Samuel Weber, *Institution and Interpretation* (1987), expanded edition (Stanford: Stanford University Press, 2001) especially Chapter 2, "The Limits of Professionalism," pp. 18–32; and Chapters 13–15, on the future of the humanities in the university, pp. 207–254; citing pp. 229–230 here.

3 Paul Baksen, "Colleges seen as failing businesses," *Bloomberg News*, reprinted in *The Daily Camera*, Boulder, Colorado, Tuesday, June 13, 2006.

4 Readings, *The University,* p. 39.

5 Weber, *Institution and Interpretation*, p. 232, citing Readings, *The University*, pp. 34–35, whom he takes to task for falling into the trap of situating his own account within a narrative pragmatics. Weber does not see a "community of dissensus" as a possible future for the university, as Readings, modeling himself on Lyotard, does. Weber sees the university's future as a "coordination" of what is "irrevocably heterogeneous," striving to be "open to the unknowable as the enabling limit of what can be known" (p. 235).

6 Citing Samir Amin, *Eurocentrism*, trans. R. Moore (New York: Monthly Review Press, 1989) p. ix.

7 Clifford Geertz, *Local Knowledge: Further Essays in Interpretive Anthropology* (New York: Basic Books, 1983).

8 Readings, *The University,* p. 171.

9 Weber, *Institution and Interpretation*, p. 230.

10 Although the connections of his arguments to the discourse of fetishism have disappeared from view, the same arguments and distinctions form the implicit ground of Heidegger's widely influential discussion of the origin of the world as picture, a text contemporary with Benjamin's urgent questioning of cultural history, both of which constitute responses to an acute crisis in the history of defining what constitutes the humanity of human beings. Another crisis is being forged on the same anvil of race and aesthetics now. Martin Heidegger, "The Origin of the Work of Art," (1935–1936), in *Poetry, Language, and Thought*, trans. and intro. Albert Hofstadter (New York and London: Harper Colophon Books, 1971) pp. 15–88. On the current situation evolving out of prison torture in Abu Graib, Guantánamo Bay, Afghanistan, and elsewhere, see Giorgio Agamben, *The Open: Man and Animal*, trans. Kevin Attell (Stanford: Stanford University Press, 2004) and Judith Butler, *Precarious Life: The Powers of Mourning and Violence* (New York and London: Verso, 2004). A forthcoming study by Claire Farago, *The Promise of Art*, will address these issues with an expanded version of the present argument.

11 Readings, *The University*, pp. 176–179. See further, John Guillory, *Cultural Capital: The Problem of Literary Canon Formation* (Chicago, IL: Chicago University Press, 1993) another influential text, arguing that course syllabi play an important role through their inclusionary and exclusionary tactics in reproducing (or changing) disciplinary formations. Readings, p. 164, disagrees with Guillory's approach insofar as it treats the university as an apparatus of the nation-state rather than "a potentially transnational bureaucratic-capitalist enterprise." Weber, *Institution and Interpretation*, pp. 228–229, disagrees with Readings's assessment regarding the demise of the nation-state in the era of global, transnational corporations, arguing that there will be important functions left for nation-states related to the organization of social tasks and long-range problems. Those sectors of the university that can provide "differentials" in information that help "extract a surplus value" will attract donations and contracts from the corporate sector.

12 Readings, *The University*, pp. 178–179.

13 Lorraine Daston and Katharine Park, *Wonder and the Order of Nature, 1150–1750* (Cambridge, MA: The MIT Press, 1998) p. 16.

14 Daston and Park, *Wonder*, p. 85, citing Roger Bacon, *Commentary on the Metaphysics*, Questionam supra, I, II, v–x, *Opera*, ed. Steale, fasc. 10, pp. 18–19.

15 Albrecht Dürer recorded in his diary entry of August 27, 1520: "For I have seen therein wonders of art and have marveled at the subtle *ingenia* of people in far-off lands. And I know not how to express what I have experienced thereby." As cited in Erwin Panofsky, *The Art and Life of Albrecht Dürer*, 2 vols (Princeton, NJ: Princeton University Press, 1971) I, p. 209.

16 Although they do not deal with the issue of exotic objects, on the history of the studiolo, see Michael Cole and Mary Pardo, eds, *Inventions of the Studio: Renaissance to Romanticism* (Chapel Hill, NC and London: University of North Carolina Press, 2005) especially the editors' introduction.

17 The term "fetish" is recorded by the OED from 1613 onwards, but restricted to describing religious practices in West Africa until the eighteenth century.

18 Charles de Brosses's *Du culte des dieux fétiches, ou Parallèle de l'ancienne Religion de l'Egypte avec la Religion actuelle de Nigritie (On the Cult of Fetish Gods, or a Comparison of the Ancient Religion of Egypt with the Actual Religion of Negritude)*, 1760, presented to the Académie des Inscriptions et Belles-lettres. See David Simpson, *Fetishism and Imagination: Dickens, Melville, Conrad* (Baltimore and London: Johns Hopkins University Press, 1982) p. 127, note 6. See further Frank E. Manuel, *The Eighteenth Century Confronts the Gods* (Cambridge, MA: Harvard University Press, 1959) pp. 184–209; William Pietz, "Fetish," in Robert S. Nelson and Richard Shiff, eds., *Critical Terms for Art History*, 2nd edn, pp. 306–317 (Chicago and London: University of Chicago Press, 2003).

19 De Brosses himself reserved the term fetish for material objects used in the worship of plants, animals, and inanimate objects (De Brosses, *Du culte des dieux fétiches*, p. 172, distinguishing fetishism from "idolatry properly so called."). W.J.T. Mitchell, "The Rhetoric of Iconoclasm: Marxism, Ideology, and Fetishism," *Iconology: Image, Text, Ideology* (Chicago and London: University of Chicago Press, 1986) p. 191, credits F. Max Müller's *Lectures on the Origin and Growth of Religion*, 1878, for drawing a distinction between idolatry and fetishism on semiotic grounds: a fetish regards something supernatural, while an idol "was originally meant as an image only, a similitude or symbol of something else." I have written more extensively on the history of idolatry in "The Grotesque Idol: Imaginary, Symbolic, and Real," co-authored

with Carol Komadina Parenteau, in Michael Cole and Rebecca Zorach, eds, *Idols in the Age of Art* (Aldershot: Ashgate Press, in press).

20 As discussed in the context of the grotesque in art by Frances Connelly, *The Sleep of Reason: Primitivism in Modern European Art and Aesthetics, 1725–1907* (University Park, PA: Pennsylvania State University Press, 1995).

21 Giambattista Vico, *The New Science*, 3rd edn (1744), trans. Thomas Goddard Bergin and Max Harold Fisch (Ithaca and London: Cornell University Press, 1968) pp. 128–130.

22 Mitchell, "The Rhetoric of Iconoclasm," pp. 160–208, makes the argument regarding Marx's sources in greater detail than I can summarize here.

23 Immanuel Kant, *Critique of Judgment*, trans. and intro. Werner S. Pluhar, foreword Mary J. Gregor (Indianapolis: Hackett Publishing Company, 1987).

24 Immanuel Kant, *Critique of Practical Reason*, trans. Beck (Indianapolis: Bobbs-Merill, 1956) pp. 161–162.

25 See Carlos M.N. Eire, *War against the Idols: The Reformation of Worship from Erasmus to Calvin* (Cambridge and Sydney: Cambridge University Press, 1986).

26 Eire, *War against the Idols*, p. 84, citing *Huldreich Zwinglis Sämtliche Werke*, E. Egli, W. Köhler, F. Blanke, *et al.*, eds (Berlin and Zurich, 1905) vol. 4, p. 96. Zwingli's successors developed his twofold discussion of idolatry. Mitchell, "The Rhetoric of Iconoclasm," 164, citing Francis Bacon, *The New Organon*, 1620.

27 Eire, *War against the Idols*, p. 84, citing *Huldreich Zwinglis Sämtliche Werke*, vol. 4, p. 133. The clearest, most detailed exposition appears in Zwingli's *Commentary on True and False Religion*, p. 1525 (Eire, p. 85).

28 Eire, *War against the Idols*, p. 84. Calvin also located the root of idolatry in man himself—in his efforts to domesticate God, man transferred the honor due to God to material objects. Calvin's most popular published work against idolatry, *The Inventory of Relics* (1543), compares idolators to unreasoning beasts and considers idolatry an ever-present danger because men are by nature metaphysically deranged. See further discussion in Eire, pp. 211–220.

29 ". . . because in the invention of *grotteschi* more than in anything else, there runs a certain furor and a natural *bizarria*, and being without it they are unable to make anything, for all their art." G.P. Lomazzo, *Trattato dell'arte de la pittura*, Milan, 1584, p. 424, cited with further discussion in David Summers, *Michelangelo and the Language of Art* (Princeton: Princeton University Press, 1981) p. 62. On *grotteschi* as emblematic of artistic license to invent, see further David Summers, "Michelangelo on Architecture," *Art Bulletin* 54 (1972): 146–157; and "The Archaeology of the Modern Grotesque," in Frances S. Connelly, ed., *Modern Art and the Grotesque* (Cambridge: Cambridge University Press, 2003) pp. 20–46.

30 Paleotti constructed a theory of style that, in effect, favored the scientific embellishments of optical naturalism, yet he retained the artist's right to depict *grotteschi* as long as these vivid representations were not capricious figments of the imagination. In the 1570s, Pirro Ligorio wrote at great length about *grotteschi*, arguing for their allegorical significance, yet he also condemned "errors against nature." See David Coffin, "Pirro Ligorio on the Nobility of the Arts," *Journal of the Warburg and Courtauld Institutes* 27 (1964): 191–210.

31 The same arguments and sources were used in Spanish America; see Sabine MacCormack, "*Calderás La Aurora en Copacabana*: The Conversion of the Incas in Light of Seventeenth-century Spanish Theology, Culture, and Political Theory," *Journal of Theological Studies* 33 (1982): 448–480.

32 Las Casas, *Apologetica historia sumaria* (1551–), ed. Edmundo O'Gorman, Mexico, 1967, chapters 61–65, citing the Italian humanist Paolo Giovio, a personal friend of Vasari's and advisor to Pope Paul III, on the products manufactured by laborers and artisans and comparing the arts of the Old and New Worlds to prove the rationality of Amerindian peoples. By contrast, according to Francisco de Vitoria (*Obras*, ed. Téofilo Urdano, Madrid, 1960, pp. 723–725), Indians possessed no knowledge of the liberal arts, no proper agriculture, and produced no true artisans: cited by Anthony Pagden, *Spanish Imperialism and the Political Imagination: Studies in European and Spanish-American Social and Political Theory 1513–1830* (New Haven, CT and London: Yale University Press, 1990) p. 20.

33 *Argumentum apologiae adversus Genesium Sepulvedam theologum cordubensem*, 1550, facsimile reproduced in Angel Losada, ed., *Apologia* (Madrid, 1975) fol. 24r–25r. See Pagden, *The Fall of Natural Man: The American Indian and the Origins of Comparative Ethnology*, 2nd edn (Cambridge: Cambridge University Press, 1986) p. 136.

34 See Gauvin Bailey, *Art on the Jesuit Missions in Asia and Latin America, 1542–1773* (Toronto and London: University of Toronto Press, 1999) pp. 32–34.

35 Aristotle distinguished between two types of enslavement: through capture and through being born "slaves by nature," constitutionally incapable of fully human powers of reasoning. See Lewis Hanke, "Pope Paul III and the American Indians," *Harvard Theological Review* 30 (1937): 65–102; Robert Schaifer, "Greek Theories of Slavery from Homer to Aristotle," *Harvard Studies in Classical Philology* 47 (1936): 165–204; Pagden, *Spanish Imperialism and the Political Imagination*, pp. 16–33; and *The Fall of Natural Man*, pp. 27–56.

36 The Scottish theologian John Major was one of the principal authors of the neo-Aristotelian theory of the "natural slave," described in Books I and 3 of Aristotle's *Politics* as lacking in the higher faculties of the human soul, and elaborated in the sixteenth century to discuss the Amerindians' mental capacity. A central issue was whether Amerindians had the ability to maintain dominion over their own property. I have discussed this history further in relation to the evaluation of Indian forms of society and artistic products according to European categories in "The Classification of the Visual Arts in the Renaissance," in Donald R. Kelley and Richard H. Popkin, eds, *The Shapes of Knowledge from the Renaissance to the Enlightenment* (Dordrecht and London: Kluwer Academic Publishers, 1991) pp. 23–48.

37 Ibid., p. 74, citing James Brown Scott, *The Spanish Origin of International Law: Francisco de Vitoria and His Law of Nations* (Oxford: Clarendon Press, 1934) p. 281.

38 On the synchronistic Catholic religion of the later colonial period regarded as idolatrous practices in Spanish America, see Carmen Bernard and Serge Gruzinski, *De la idolatrya: Una arqueología de las ciencias religiosas* (Mexico: Fondo de cultura económica, 1992).

39 In the last quarter century, a new generation of scholars has significantly altered the concept of nationalism on which disciplinary paradigm of art history was fashioned. Ernst Gellner, Eric Hobsbawm, Benedict Anderson, and others restrict the modern concept of a nation to the large-scale political units that emerged in the nineteenth century. See my discussion in "'Vision Itself Has Its History': 'Race,' Nation, and Renaissance Art History," in *Reframing the Renaissance: Visual Culture in Europe and Latin America 1450–1650*, ed. and intro. C. Farago (New Haven and London: Yale University Press, 1995) pp. 67–88, especially pp. 70–72, with further references.

40 Michel de Certeau, "Psychoanalysis and its History," *Heterologies: Discourse on the Other*, trans. Brian Massumi (Minneapolis and London: University of Minnesota Press, 1986) p. 3.

41 Terry Eagleton, *Marxism and Literary Criticism* (Berkeley and Los Angeles, CA: University of California Press, 1976) provides an excellent summary of Marx's discussion of the work of art. See also, Tony Bennett, *Formalism and Marxism* (London and New York: Methuen, 1979).

42 Simpson, *Fetishism and Imagination*, p. xiii.

43 Teresa Brennan, "Why the Time Is Out of Joint: Marx's Political Economy without the Subject," in R.L. Rutsky and Bradley J. Macdonald, eds, *Strategies for Theory: From Marx to Madonna* (Albany: State University of New York Press, 2003) pp. 23–38.

44 For example, Giorgio Agamben and Judith Butler insist upon "acknowledging our complicity in the law that we oppose": "there is in effect something that humans are and have to be, but this is not an essence or properly a thing: It is the simple fact of one's own existence as possibility or potentiality." Judith Butler, *Psychic Life of Power: Theories in Subjection* (Stanford: Stanford University Press, 1997) pp. 130–132, citing Giorgio Agamben, *The Coming Community*, trans. Michael Hardt (Minneapolis: University of Minnesota Press, 1993) p. 43.

Chapter 11

# Deep innovation and mere eccentricity in Islamic art history

*David Carrier*

> Carpets resist art history.
> Tapati Guha-Thakurta

All European art history is a footnote to Vasari. His ways of thinking, extended in Winckelmann's account of classical art, then were developed by Panofsky, Riegl, and Wölfflin, and a whole host of more recent writers. In relation to this main-line tradition, John Ruskin and Walter Pater, much admired nineteenth-century writers, are eccentrics. Ruskin's moralizing view of Turner's landscapes and Pater's anachronistic reading of Giorgione are at odds with the dominant concerns of present-day art history. The authority of this tradition is reinforced by academic institutions. Art historians learn methodology in graduate school, write a thesis under supervision and then publish refereed by their peers. Eccentrics have different kinds of careers. Denis Mahon and Adrian Stokes are twentieth-century outsiders much admired by some art historians. Mahon's prose style is personal, but his writings on Guercino and Poussin deal with academic concerns.[1] Stokes is a more special case, for his manner of psychoanalytic interpretation is radically different from that of present-day art historians. His claims remain too eccentric to inspire debate among Renaissance specialists.[2]

We learn about the structure of academic debate by momentarily stepping outside to study eccentric art history. Within European art history, I have argued:

> to be taken seriously and responded to by your colleagues, you must accept the standards of the community to which they belong. Like all professional groups of any size, the academic world contains various communities, each with its own standards. [3]

Now I show what eccentric historians of Islamic art can teach us. Writing biographies mostly about Italian artists, dealing in the later parts of his *Lives* with near contemporaries, Vasari provides much of the basic material used by modern day Renaissance historians who employ formalism, psychoanalysis, and, now, post-structuralism and feminism to interpret this evidence. The story of Islamic art's history is very different. Art history is an exotic import developed by outsiders. Indeed, the very "idea of a tradition of Islamic architecture and art" like that described in modern surveys "is a creation of late-nineteenth- and twentieth-century Western thought, for there is no evidence that any artist or patron . . . ever thought of his art as Islamic."[4] Even identifying Islamic artifacts as works of art may import Western concepts.

In a large museum the objects displayed in the Islamic galleries are visually distinctive. These works of art mostly look different from those found in the rooms containing African, American, Chinese, European, and Oceanic art. Of course these traditions overlap, but an effective working definition of the essence of Islamic art is possible:

> It refers to the monuments and remains of material culture made by or for people who lived under rulers who professed the faith of Islam or in social and cultural entities which, whether themselves Muslim or not, have been strongly influenced by the modes of life and thought characteristic of Islam.[5]

Discussing the origin, development, and aesthetic value of this body of objects, Islamic art historians explain how and why they differ from art made in other cultures. Only in the late nineteenth century did carpets and other artifacts made by Muslims enter public art museums.[6] In that way, Islamic art was like the painting and sculpture from China (and other Non-European cultures). But:

> unlike the study of Chinese art, which Chinese scholars have pursued for centuries, there is no indigenous tradition in any of the Islamic lands of studying Islamic art, with the possible exception of calligraphy . . ..[7]

The recent rise of academic Islamic art history is a response, in large part, to this collecting. Museums need reliable attributions and suggestive interpretations. Renaissance Europeans treasured Islamic carpets, which were often represented in paintings.[8] But they did not try to understand their meaning. Treating carpets as handsome decorations is merely to respond to them aesthetically. Art museums aspire to do more, to explain the significance of the beautiful artifacts they display.

European art historians are Vasari's heirs. Traditionally Western art history assumes that ideally there is an intimate relationship between an artist's way of thinking and the art historian's commentary. We interpret the art of Michelangelo and his predecessors in ways that have a close relationship to how they themselves understood it. Assuming that European art's development is essentially historical, following Vasari and Gombrich we see the paintings of Giotto, Masaccio, and Raphael as defining progress toward illusionism. Neither of these ways of thinking is relevant to most Islamic art. We can only speculate, for example, about how weavers understood their carpet designs. And since there is no equivalent to the visual progress found in Italian Renaissance painting, the history of carpets is not easy to understand.

Islamic art historians cannot be Vasari's heirs. European art history developed along with the art it describes. Historians extended Vasari's basic model to Poussin, Pissarro, and Pollock, developing ways of thinking these artists themselves discuss, placing their paintings in historical narratives. Because there was no Islamic Vasari, the methodology of Islamic art history is borrowed.[9] Here Hegel's *Aesthetics* provided a very useful resource. Hegel had no special knowledge of, and took no real interest in Islam. (India was the society outside Europe of greatest interest to him.[10]) But if you want to interpret art from a culture without an elaborate tradition of art writing, then his *Aesthetics* is very suggestive.

Hegel claims that a culture expresses its worldview in its art. In his account of the Dutch Golden Age, he explains that these bourgeois burghers wish in their painting to enjoy:

> once again in every possible situation the neatness of its cities, houses, and furnishings, as well as its domestic peace, its wealth, the respectable dress of wives and children, the brilliance of its civil and political festivals, the boldness of its seamen, the fame of its commerce and the ships that ride the oceans of the world.[11]

Hegel's evocative prose (he mentions no Dutch painter by name) gives a good characterization of the Dutch rooms of any major museum. And modern scholarship has not left these Hegelian ways of thinking entirely behind. Svetlana Alpers' *The Art of Describing: Dutch Art in the Seventeenth Century* (1983) very self-consciously takes up Hegel's project. Given that "the study of art and its history has been determined by the art of Italy and its study," in what ways, she asks, can the distinctive qualities of Dutch painting be identified?[12]

Hegel's theory of cultural expression can also easily be adapted to non-European art. When Ernest Fenollosa went to Japan in the late nineteenth century and developed a pioneering account of Asian art, he employed an explicitly Hegelian methodology.[13] Ironically Hegel's Eurocentric aesthetic provided a good way of understanding art made outside Europe. If a culture makes art and has a distinctive worldview, then we can understand their art by treating it as an expression of their ways of living and thinking. Just as Hegel's Hollanders love everyday scenes of prosperity because they are Protestant merchants, not Catholic aristocrats, so Arab Muslims made elaborate decorations because they are desert-dwelling iconoclasts whose culture derives from a sacred book. We find such an Hegelian analysis in such coffee table books as Gabriele Crespi's *The Arabs in Europe* and the enormous volume by Alexandre Papadopoulo, *Islam and Muslim Art*.[14] And Hegelian ways of thinking also appear in more sophisticated writings. Richard Ettinghausen, for example, explains the *horror vacui* in Islamic art by reference to the crowded Near Eastern cities, the empty spaces between them, and "the tendency in the Islamic world toward exaggeration and lavishness, not outwardly in the streets, but in personal relations."[15]

Eccentric historians of European art link painting to politics in unfamiliar ways, find hidden images and propose novel methodologies.[16] Such methodologies are inherently problematic because they uncouple interpretation from reference to artists' intentions. My eccentric commentators on Islamic art employ Hegelian ways of thinking. Muslims have a sacred book, which is the basis for everyday life. And so it is tempting to interpret Islamic art by reference to the culture and literature essential to Muslims, as a form of cultural expression. Hegel's way of thinking is intuitively plausible because there are obvious links between art and its culture. The Dutch did produce distinctive paintings, and art made by Muslims does have some relationship with the geography of the countries in which Islam is rooted. But these useful, vague generalizations about the relationship of art to its culture need to be supported by closely detailed interpretations of individual works of art. Barbara Brend speaks in Hegelian terms when she notes that "the sense of order" characteristic of Islamic art "is rooted in the Islamic view that everything that exists is willed by Allah and has its place in the divine scheme of things."[17] But then she supports her generalization with a detailed account of the diverse art made by Muslims. What distinguishes serious from eccentric Hegelians is the ability to marshal substantial supporting evidence.

Some respectable-looking publications devoted to Islamic art provide surprisingly eccentric Hegelian interpretations. Consider, for example, *The Sense of Unity: The Sufi Tradition in Persian Architecture* by Nader Ardalan and Laleh Bakhtiar. Although this book is published by the University of Chicago Press, its claims are very strange. Ardalan and Bakhtiar note that the four colors, red, yellow, green, and blue, "correspond to the four qualities of Universal Nature and to the four elements of matter."[18] When they link the city to the body, Renaissance scholars will recognize familiar concerns. But their claim that the body grows "through seven means: attraction, sustenance, digestion, repulsion, nutrition, growth, and formation," which relate to "the seven visible planets" is bizarre.[19] And when their "Epilogue" speaks of the goal, presenting "concepts that are primordial and eternally valid," academic art historians will feel uneasy.[20] Contrast the two volumes in the Yale University Press survey history of art, *Islamic Art and Architecture 650–1250* and *The Art and Architecture of Islam 1250–1800*.[21] When, for example, they describe "the non-realistic use of realistic shapes and the anti-naturalistic combination of naturalistic forms," they place Islamic buildings in a tradition of earlier Christian and later Muslim architecture.[22] And when they present fifteenth-century carpet production in Anatolia, they place these designs within a focused historical analysis. The carpets produced under Mehmed's patronage:

> show a rhythmic balance of arabesques with small-scale tendrils. . . . the graphic conception and curvilinear design of Ushak medallion carpets . . . differ from the geometric conception of such earlier types as Holbeins or animal carpets, where the weavers could generate the designs directly at the loom.[23]

Here we find plausible empirical interpretations. Keith Critchlow's *Islamic Patterns. An Analytic and Cosmological Approach* is outsider art history. The Foreword by Seyyed Hossein Nasr says that "Islam is the last of the universal revelations of the present humanity and as such a re-affirmation of the primordial truth, of the Truth which has always been and will always be. . . ."[24] Critchlow's number mysticism is not a proper academic concern. The triangle, he explains, as the first polygon expresses "minimal needs of consciousness (i.e. Knower, Known and act of Knowing), as well as the minimal description of the basic biological needs: ingestion, absorption and excretion."[25] When he links Islamic patterns to the creation of the world in six days and the twelve apostles, then no rational argument is offered. Critchlow never shows that the Muslims who made decorations employed such elaborate speculations. By contrast, Eva Baer's *Islamic Ornament* works within an academic framework. Wanting to give "a historical survey of Islamic ornament," she describes her aim as understanding "ornament as a language, as a vehicle by which Islamic artisans and artists expressed contemporary ideas or modified ancient ones to conform to their own concepts."[26]

Titus Burckhardt, the Swiss convert to Islam, a relative of Jacob Burckhardt, had intellectual prestige. He also was an eccentric. Burckhardt says that the Muslim's "soul vibrates through the idea of the unity and immensity of God which are reflected in the cosmic order and also in the artifacts shaped by the hand of man . . ."[27] Islamic art thus "is essentially the projection into the visual order of certain aspects or dimensions of Divine Unity."[28] Burckhardt appeals to an account of Arabic script, which "proceeds horizontally, on the plane of becoming, but starts from the right, which is the field of action, and moves to the left, which is the region of the heart; it therefore describes a progression from the outward to the inward."[29] The history of an artistic tradition can plausibly begin thus with a definition of its essence. Oleg Grabar, for example, opens *The Formation of Islamic Art* by asking: "What is the range of works of art that are presumably endowed with unique features?"[30] But Burckhardt and Grabar offer very different answers to this question. Burckhardt's belief that Arabic determined the style of thinking of Muslim peoples hardly encourages close looking at individual examples. When he says that geometric enlacement "is an extremely direct expression of the idea of the Divine Unity underlying the inexhaustible variety of the world," he hardly distinguishes Islam from many other religions.[31] And when he tells us that "the most perfect carpets represent nothing in particular; they reflect the cosmos on their own level," then his argument is not suggestive.[32]

Grabar's account of Islamic responses to Christian art notes that "initial awe and admiration" could readily lead "to rejection and contempt."[33] He says much about the relationship of these rival traditions of art making. Images, he notes, "became not merely a characteristic of the Christian world, but one of the most important and dangerous weapons it possessed."[34] By contrast, Burckhardt's ecumenical style blurs key issues. Arguing that rival religions hold the same values is irrelevant when for the art historian what matters is strongly felt rivalries. Burckhardt says: "There is no more perfect symbol of the Divine Unity than light."[35] That idea is too general to inspire productive close looking. Similar problems appear also in the discussion of Christian art in his book on Siena. "In the words of St. Catherine of Siena, the city is the image of the soul, the surrounding walls being the frontier between the outward and the inward life."[36] Speaking of decoration, Burckhardt says that "The threads of the warp are like the Divine Qualities underlying all existence . . ."[37] His conclusion is too facile to interest a carpet historian. Islamic textiles often are interpreted in Hegelian terms. One eccentric says:

> The carpet . . . reflects Heaven and enables the traditional Muslim who spends most of his time at home on the carpet to experience the ground upon which he sits as purified and participating in the sacred character of the ground of the mosque upon which he prays.[38]

This analysis might be convincing did it make some distinction between prayer and domestic carpets. But as it stands, it is too vague to be convincing. Kurt Erdmann's *Seven Hundred Years of Oriental Carpets* discusses the representation of these carpets within European paintings, which allows their history to be recovered; surveys some major collections; and discusses the meaning of carpet designs.[39] What separates his account from eccentric art history is, among other things, concern to identify varied styles of Islamic carpets.

Some eccentric accounts of Islamic art involve attempts to understand abstract painting. The exhibition catalog *Ornament and Abstraction. The Dialogue between Non-Western, Modern and Contemporary Art*, for example, compares modernist abstract paintings and Islamic decorations.[40] Annemarie Schimmel argues that "Viewing an artwork . . . leads almost directly to the core of culture . . ."[41] I do not believe that any art transparently expresses a worldview in this fashion. But even if it did, since abstract paintings serve different functions from Muslim decorative works, these comparisons are pseudo-morphisms. As Grabar notes, "There is little evidence that any one of the [Western] painters involved actually studied works of Islamic art or sought to understand something of the culture which had created them . . ."[42] (The American Philip Taaffe, whose art constitutes an exception to this generalization, self-consciously appropriated Islamic designs.[43]) Abstraction is the product of a long Western development, which has little relationship to Islamic decoration.

One of the most challenging eccentric Islamic historians is the Berkeley architect Christopher Alexander. His early *Notes on the Synthesis of Form* is a straightforward study of design, but his more recent publications make truly extravagant claims.[44] *The Timeless Way of Building*, for example, argues that "there is one timeless way of building. It is thousands of years old, and the same today as it has always been."[45] Just as Burckhardt argues that, notwithstanding their obvious differences, at bottom all the great world religions present the same ideals, so Alexander asserts that all great architecture, including such seemingly diverse buildings as the Alhambra, an old New England house, or an ancient Zen temple displays the same aesthetic.[46] Alexander's *A Foreshadowing of 21st Century Art. The Color and Geometry of Very Early Turkish Carpets* develops an argument like *Ornament and Abstraction*, but with much more detail. "A carpet is a picture of God."[47] Showing a pattern through a window, "the idea of a carpet as a picture of God is an Islamic conception . . ." Alexander motivates this analysis with comparisons. "'If you had to choose one of these two carpets, as a picture of your own self, then which one of the two carpets would you choose?'"[48] He claims that the greatest carpets contain the most power centers. As Grabar notes, Muslims were interested in connoisseurship:

> Why did the Muslim world value the art of the object so highly? . . . much earlier than any other society in the Middle Ages, Islamic culture combined egalitarian ideals and urban values. This synthesis led to the extensive development of beautiful objects that could serve formal purposes in the relationships between men as well as the needs of daily life.[49]

But there is no suggestion that they knew the concept of power centers. The goal of carpet makers, Alexander says is "*the creation of profound, even spiritual space, purely from the interplay of forms* . . ."[50] When a carpet has many centers, it "begins to be a picture of the human soul."[51] He offers no argument that Muslims understood their carpets in these terms.[52]

Ernst Gombrich's critique of the catalog for the World of Islam exhibition, London, 1976 points to the essential problems with eccentric Hegelian ways of thinking. Objecting to the attempts to relate decorations to plant forms, to Islamic science, and to ideals of gardens as paradise, he speaks of:

> the refusal to accept the autonomy of decorative design. The visitor must be reassured that there is more to the arabesque than meets the eye. The revelation

> of symbolic meaning resembles an initiation into the deeper mysteries of the tradition.[53]

This search for meanings coalesces, he adds, with the Hegelian ways of thinking he has criticized here and elsewhere, the search:

> for some principle of unity among all manifestations of a culture or period. Being characteristic of Arabic decoration the arabesque must also partake of the essence of "Islamic thought."

Academics say much about the geographical and historical diversity of Islamic art. Outsiders tend to generalize quickly, identifying with great confidence *the* Islamic ways of thinking. Ironically the eccentric champions of Islam describe the culture they admire as monolithic and essentially unchanging, in the now politically incorrect style of orientalism. Serious scholars hesitate to make immediate global connections between the Qur'an (and other writings from Muslim cultures) and visual art. By contrast, outsider art writers tend to invoke unmediated relationships between art and Islamic written sources. "In order to understand a culture," Titus Burckhardt writes:

> it is necessary to love it, and one can only do this on the basis of the universal and timeless values that it carries within it. These values are essentially the same in all true cultures . . .[54]

I do not believe this claim is correct or even plausible, but I understand why it seems attractive. "Modern science," Burckhardt says, "is ugly . . ."[55] Like Alexander (and our other eccentrics), he finds in Islamic art a refuge from spiritually impoverished modernist Western culture.

Lacking the objectivity of academic scholars, outsiders tend to make sweeping statements, identifying '*the* Islamic ways of thinking', and offering facile links between the Qur'an and art. What by contrast defines academic art history is what Grabar calls the movement "toward precise definitions of the characteristics of specific times and places."[56] When, for example, Ettinghausen, Grabar, and Kenkins-Madina note "the difficulty . . . in relating formal changes in the arts . . . to the profound cultural transformations which affected first Iraq and then the whole Muslim world" in the seventh to eleventh centuries, they are scrupulous historians.[57] Grabar and his colleagues identify the variety of Islamic art and describe its development. Writing as an Orientalist, Hegel claims that no real change is to be found in the non-European world. Notwithstanding all of their sympathy with Islam and its arts, our outsiders hold Eurocentric views about Islamic history and the stylistic explanation of Islamic art. Eccentric art historians are annoying to professional

Islamic scholars in the way that astrologers are annoying to professors of astronomy. When it is difficult to attract readers and support for scholarship, they are frustrating. But outsider writings do respond to a legitimate curiosity about unfamiliar cultures. Most scholarly writing is unavoidably esoteric. But unless academics also explain our concerns to the general public in accessible prose, eccentric art writing will continue to attract readers.

Our criticism of these eccentric commentaries certainly shows the limitations of Hegelian histories. But given, then, the limitations of methodologies imported from European art history, what style of interpretation is appropriate to Islamic art? Grabar's *The Mediation of Ornament* offers an extremely imaginative answer to that question. To the extent that one major concern for Islamic art historians is decoration, Islamic art seems exotic indeed. The traditional central focus of historians of European art is on what Grabar calls "the nonornamental, that grand and grandiose recreation of the natural world that forms, at least within a mainstream art-historical tradition, the major achievement of Western painting."[58] Here Grabar adds, "I part company with Gombrich's position." In *The Sense of Order*, Gombrich does say, "my interest in problems of pure design goes back much further in my life than my interest in the psychology of illusion."[59] But decoration (and so also Islamic art) lies literally at margins of his history of art. The great set piece in *The Sense of Order* is the account of Raphael's *Madonna della Sedia* and its frame. Glancing at it reveals, so Gombrich claims, an "effortless transition from representation to decoration . . .[60] Without a frame there can be no centre. The richer the elements of the frame, the more the centre will gain in dignity. We are not meant to examine them individually. . . ."[61] The decorative frame remains marginal to this Raphael, as in Gombrich's survey history *The Story of Art* Islamic art is marginal. Muhammed, he writes "directed the mind of the artist away from the objects of the real world to (a) . . . dream-world of lines and colours."[62] We find here something more than the understandable need for popularization in an introductory survey. Gombrich believes that restless concern with progress in Western representational art is an artistic version of our culture's experimental scientific attitude.[63] Decorative Islamic art, by contrast, invokes an essentially static worldview.

*The Mediation of Ornament* decenters this well entrenched way of thinking about the relationship of decoration and figuration. No one would imagine Grabar an outsider art historian, but the very originality of his well motivated account makes it difficult to evaluate. I focus on one concern relevant to our evaluation of eccentric Islamic art histories, the relation of his account to traditional histories of European art. Grabar ends with a question: "Is it possible to argue . . . that by providing pleasure ornament also gives to the observer the right and the freedom to choose meanings?"[64] How should we answer this question? I associate interpretative freedom not with Islam but with our Western post-Christian secular culture. The pleasures of Muslims traditionally have been patriarchial. And exclusionary, for the decorations of mosques are only selectively accessible to non-believers. When Grabar responds to Islamic decoration as an outsider, not bound by the ways of thinking of Muslim culture, how does he understand his analysis to be an art-historical account?

Grabar's earlier *The Formation of Islamic Art* (1973) helps answer this question by explaining his strategy in ways that he does not, I think, make explicit. In China the development of art is the product of a very long essentially indigenous tradition. The Christians, by contrast, inherited and dramatically reworked the inherited worldview of classical antiquity, eventually making it their own. And Islam, Grabar notes, faced a very different situation:

> During the first century after the conquest the Muslims were brought into immediate contact with the fantastic artistic wealth of the Mediterranean and Iran. They were strongly affected by a world in which images, buildings, and objects were active expressions of social standing, religion, political allegiance, and intellectual or theological positions.[65]

Suddenly able to afford lavish works of art, they needed to compete with the neighboring Christian world. But because there was no elaborate indigenous tradition, they needed to borrow from these other cultures while expressing their own distinctive identity. The story of how Muslims took over very rich artistic traditions and made them their own might remind the art critic of the situation of postmodernism in the 1980s. If your goal is to yourself be original, then inheriting an elaborate visual culture can cause real problems. Where the Muslims needed to detach themselves from the traditions they inherited for religious reasons, the concern of our postmodernists was to break with an exhausted secular tradition.

Grabar's characterization of ornament as "the ultimate mediator, paradoxically questioning the value of meanings by channeling them into pleasure" owes something to Roland Barthes, who is mentioned three pages earlier in *The Mediation of Ornament*.

> Imagine someone . . . who abolishes within himself all barriers, all classes, all exclusions . . . who mixes every language . . . who silently accepts every charge of illogicality . . . this anti-hero exists: he is the reader of the text at the moment he takes his pleasure.[66]

Grabar imagines someone who takes pleasure from decoration in a similar way. Literary critics criticize the frankly ahistorical approach of Barthes's *The Pleasure of the Text*. The same objection can be made to Grabar's account. How does his analysis relate to the traditional art historian's goal, the reconstruction of Islamic art history? Grabar in effect turns away from merely understanding the decorations of Muslims as they really were understood to describing how he sees these exquisitely attractive patterns. Because the documentation does not tell us how to understand it, we are free to interpret Islamic art. Like the eccentrics, Grabar detaches his account from direct concern with artists' intentions. But where these commentators return all too obsessively to now-dated Hegelian ways of thinking, his analysis, supported by very close detailed study of Muslim art forms and culture, draws inspiration from contemporary styles of interpretation.

To properly understand Islamic art, Grabar suggests, we need to look to recent Western literary criticism. At one point the greatest modernist critic makes an analogous claim. In his collected essays on modernist painting and sculpture, Clement Greenberg draws a parallel with Byzantine art:

> The Byzantines dematerialized firsthand reality by invoking a transcendent one. We seem to be doing something similar in our science as well as art, insofar as we invoke the material against itself by insisting on its all-encompassing reality.[67]

Just as Greenberg would understand Abstract Expressionism by looking to this very distant tradition, so Grabar would interpret Islamic decoration by appeal to Barthes's account of the pleasures of reading French literature. When art is very exotic, we need help from wherever we can get it.

Because Vasari supplied so influential a model, it was natural for pioneering scholars dealing with non-European art to model their accounts on histories of European art. But now looking at the varied architecture and artifacts presented in *Islamic Art and Architecture 650–1250* and *The Art and Architecture of Islam 1250–1800* ought to inspire extreme skepticism about that way of thinking. The shape of Islamic art's history is very unlike that of painting and sculpture in Europe. The concluding argument of *The Mediation of Ornament* offers an immensely suggestive response to this situation. What perhaps then seems ironical is that Grabar, like his most distinguished predecessors, turns to European methodologies in his analysis of Islamic art. Greenberg praised modernist painting for its self-consciousness. Grabar, by contrast, values Islamic decoration because of the lack of any compatible self-awareness with its originating culture.

I owe my epigraph to a distinguished historian of Indian art, who was responding spontaneously to my lecture on multicultural art history in New Delhi, November 2004.[68] Her comment poses a deep question—to what extent do some kinds of visual artifacts resist the usual methods of art historians? One reason that Islamic art is challenging to the academic art historian is that it is intrinsically fascinating.[69] Another reason it deserves attention of non-specialists is that art made by Muslims poses fascinating methodological concerns. At this time when historians of European (and American) art seek to rethink our assumptions, do we not deserve all of the challenges which art from other cultures can provoke?

## Acknowledgement

This essay is for Eva Hoffman and Oleg Grabar, in thanks for inviting my participation in their 2005 College Art Association session devoted to Islamic Art. I take up these concerns from a different angle in my review of his collected essays, O. Grabar, *Constructing the Study of Islamic Art*. 4 Vols, *ArtUs* 15 (October–November 2006) 28–31.

## Notes

1 See my "In Praise of Connoisseurship," *Journal of Aesthetics and Art Criticism*, 61(2) (Spring 2003): 159–169.

2 See my "Introduction to *The Quattro Cento*," Introduction to a republication of Adrian Stokes, *Quattro Cento* (University Park: Pennsylvania State Press, 2002) pp. 1–12.

3 "Deep Innovation and Mere Eccentricity: Six Case Studies of Innovation in Art History," *Art History and Its Institutions*, Elizabeth Mansfield, ed. (London: Routledge, 2002) pp. 115–131.

4 Sheila Blair and Jonathan Bloom, *The Art and Architecture of Islam 1250–1800* (New Haven, CT and London: Yale University Press, 1994) p. 303.

5 Richard Ettinghausen, Oleg Grabar, Marilyn Kenkins-Madina, *Islamic Art and Architecture 650–1250* (New Haven, CT and London: Yale University Press, 2001) p. 3. This paragraph is indebted to Oleg Grabar, *The Formation of Islamic Art* (New Haven, CT and London: Yale University Press, 1973) Ch. 1.

6 See *Discovering Islamic Art. Scholars, Collectors and Collections, 1850–1950*, Stephen Vernoit, ed. (London and New York: I.B.Tauris, 2000).

7 Sheila Blair and Jonathan Bloom, "The Mirage of Islamic Art: Reflections on the Study of an Unwieldy Field," *The Art Bulletin* LXXXV, 1 (March 2003): 153.

8 See my "Islamic Carpets in Christian Paintings: An Alternative Theory of the Origin of the Public Art Museum," *Source*, 1 (Fall 2005): 1–5.

9 The claim that the Persian art writer Dust Muhammad *is* the Islamic Vasari is discussed in David J. Roxburgh, *Prefacing the Image: The Writing of Art History in Sixteenth-Century Iran* (Leiden, Boston, Köln: Brill, 2001) pp. 12–14.

10 On Hegel's knowledge of India see Wilhelm Halbfass, *India and Europe: An Essay in Understanding* (Albany: State University of New York Press, 1988) Ch. 6.

11 G.W.F. Hegel, *Aesthetics: Lectures on Fine Art*, trans. T.M. Knox (Oxford: Clarendon Press, 1975) II, p. 886.

12 Svetlana Alpers, *The Art of Describing: Dutch Art in the Seventeenth Century* (Chicago and London: University of Chicago Press, 1983) p. xix. P. 249, note 1 explicitly links her account to Hegel.

13 See my *Museum Skepticism: A History of the Display of Art in Public Galleries* (Durham, NC: University of North Carolina Press, 2006) Ch. 7.

14 Gabriele Crespi, *The Arabs in Europe* (New York: Rizzzoli, 1986) and Alexandre Papadopoulo, *Islam and Muslim Art*, trans. Robert Erich Wolf (New York: Harry H. Abrams, 1979).

15 Richard Ettinghausen, "The *Horror vacui* in Islamic Art," reprinted in his *Islamic Art and Archaeology: Collected Papers*, Kyriam Rosen-Ayalon, ed. (Berlin: Mann Verlag, 1984)

p. 1309. See the commentary in Eva Baer, *Islamic Ornament* (New York: New York University Press, 1998) p. 126.

16 I cite examples discussed in my "Deep Innovation and Mere Eccentricity."

17 Barbara Brend, *Islamic Art* (Cambridge, MA: Harvard University Press, 1991) p. 225.

18 Nader Ardalan and Laleh Bakhtiar, *The Sense of Unity: The Sufi Tradition in Persian Architecture* (Chicago, IL and London: University of Chicago Press, 1973) p. 49.

19 Ardalan and Bakhtiar, *The Sense of Unity*, p. 79.

20 Ibid., p. 151.

21 Richard Ettinghausen, Oleg Grabar, Marilyn Kenkins-Madina, *Islamic Art and Architecture 650–1250* (New Haven, CT and London: Yale University Press, 2001); Sheila Blair and Jonathan Bloom, *The Art and Architecture of Islam 1250–1800* (New Haven, CT and London: Yale University Press, 1994).

22 Ettinghausen, Grabar, Kenkins-Madina, *Islamic Art and Architecture 650–1250*, p. 19.

23 Blair and Bloom, *The Art and Architecture of Islam 1250–1800*, p. 233.

24 Keith Critchlow, *Islamic Patterns. An Analytic and Cosmological Approach* (Rochester, Vermont: Inner Traditions, 1999).

25 Critchlow, *Islamic Patterns*, pp. 18, 57, 58.

26 Baer, *Islamic Ornament*, p. 5.

27 Titus Burckhardt, "Introduction to Islamic Art," *The Arts of Islam*, exhibition catalog (London: Arts Countil of Great Britain, 1976) p. 32.

28 Burckhardt, "Introduction to Islamic Art," p. 46.

29 Ibid., 47.

30 Grabar, *The Formation of Islamic Art*, p. 1.

31 Burckhardt, "Introduction to Islamic Art," p. 63.

32 Ibid., p. 109.

33 Grabar, *The Formation of Islamic Art*, p. 88.

34 Ibid., p. 90.

35 Burckhardt, "Introduction to Islamic Art," p. 77.

36 Titus Burckhardt, *Siena: The City of the Virgin*, trans. Margaret McDonough Brown (London: Oxford University Press, 1960) p. 53.

37 Burckhardt, "Introduction to Islamic Art," p. 112.

38 Seyyed Hossein Nasr, *Islamic Art and Spirituality* (Albany: State University of New York Press, 1987) p. 39.

39 Kurt Erdmann, *Seven Hundred Years of Oriental Carpets*, Hanna Erdmann, ed., trans. May H. Beattie and Hildegard Herzog (Berkeley and Los Angeles, CA: University of California Press, 1970).

40 *Ornament and Abstraction. The Dialogue between Non-Western, Modern and Contemporary Art*, Markus Brüderlin, ed., exhibition catalog (Basel: Fondation Beyeler, 2001).

41 Annemarie Schimmel, "The Arabesque and the Islamic View of the World," *Ornament and Abstraction*, p. 35.

42 Grabar, *Ornament and Abstraction*, p. 72.

43 Oleg Grabar, "Preface," *Philip Taaffe: Recent Paintings* (New York: Gagosian Gallery, 1994).

44 Christopher Alexander, *Notes on the Synthesis of Form* (Cambridge, MA: Harvard University Press, 1964).

45 Christopher Alexander, *The Timeless Way of Building* (New York: Oxford University Press, 1979) p. 7.

46 Alexander, *The Timeless Way of Building*, pp. 8–9.

47 Christopher Alexander, *A Foreshadowing of 21st Century Art. The Color and Geometry of Very Early Turkish Carpets* (New York and Oxford: Oxford University Press, 1993) p. 21.
48 Ibid., p. 28.
49 Oleg Grabar, "Architecture and Art," *The Genius of Arab Civilization: Source of Renaissance* (Oxford: Phaidon Press, 1975) p. 100.
50 Alexander, *A Foreshadowing of 21st Century Art*, p. 88.
51 Ibid., p. 79.
52 This paragraph borrows from Rufus Cohen, "The Limits of Interpretation," *Hali* 119 (December 2001): 74, a skeptical discussion of claims such as Alexander's about Navajo textiles.
53 E.H. Gombrich, *The Sense of Order. A Study in the Psychology of Decorative Art* (Ithaca, NY: Cornell University Press, 1979) p. 225.
54 William Stoddart, ed., *The Essential Titus Burckhardt: Reflections on Sacred Art, Faiths, and Civilizations* (Bloomington, IN: World Wisdom, Inc, 2003) p. 13.
55 Titus Burckhardt, *Mirror of the Intellect: Essays on Traditional Science and Sacred Art*, trans. William Stoddart (Albany: State University of New York Press, 1987) p. 15.
56 Ettinghausen, Grabar, Kenkins-Madina, *Islamic Art and Architecture 650–1250*, p. x.
57 Ibid., p. 79.
58 Grabar, *Mediation of Ornament*, p. 40.
59 E.H. Gombrich, *The Sense of Order. A Study in the Psychology of Decorative Art* (Ithaca, New York: Cornell University Press, 1979) p. vii.
60 Ibid., p. 161.
61 Ibid., p. 156.
62 E.H. Gombrich, *The Story of Art* (London: Phaidon, 1995 (16th edn)) p. 143.
63 See my "Gombrich on Art Historical Explanations," *Leonardo* XVI(2) (1983): 91–96.
64 Grabar, *Mediation*, p. 237.
65 Grabar, *The Formation of Islamic Art*, p. 96.
66 Roland Barthes, *The Pleasure of the Text*, trans. Richard Miller (New York: Hill and Wang, 1975) p. 3.
67 Clement Greenberg, *Art and Culture: Critical Essays* (Boston, MA: Beacon, 1961) p. 69.
68 My response, in return, to her work is my review of T. Guha-Thakurta, *Monuments, Objects, Histories. Institutions of Art in Colonial and Postcolonial India*, caa-on line reviews. caareviews.org.
69 See my review "Palace and Mosque," *ArtUS* 5/6 (January–February 2005): 68–69.

Chapter 12

# Art, science, and evolution

*Robert O. Bork*

The relationship between art history and natural history, a topic that attracted widespread attention in the decades following the 1859 publication of Charles Darwin's *On the Origin of Species*, deserves careful re-examination in the twenty-first century.[1] Such a reassessment, in fact, could potentially play an important role in promoting the health of art-historical institutions, which face significant challenges in the new millennium. In a broad sense, the increasingly business-driven and anti-intellectual character of public life can force universities, museums, and publishers to privilege profitability over intellectual content. Even within the faculties of arts and sciences that form the heart of the academy, moreover, art historians and other humanistic scholars risk marginalization as research funding increasingly shifts toward scientific projects that promise to have fruitful and profitable application. In this context, it is worth emphasizing both the significant connections between art-historical scholarship and the major currents of modern intellectual life, on the one hand, and the irreducibly unique characteristics of art history, on the other. Fresh consideration of the relationship between art-historical and evolutionary thinking can advance both of these projects, thereby fostering the successful adaptation of art-historical institutions to the challenging climate of the new century.

Art history belongs to a broad class of humanistic and scientific disciplines that attempt to explain the past through analysis of its observable products. Art historians and archaeologists have much in common with paleontologists, geologists, and even cosmologists, all of whom are considered scientists, even though they cannot conduct reproducible experiments in the same canonical way that chemists and physicists can. In methodological and epistemological terms, therefore, the distinction between art history and the sciences turns out to be blurrier than one might at first expect. Art historians, like scholars in the historical sciences, generally aspire to move from mere description to the explanation of past events. In all of these fields, the development of explanatory theory in principle involves the same four basic steps: 1) description; 2) the recognition of pattern in the historical record;

3) the creation of mental models or trial narratives to explain those patterns; and, 4) the testing of each model to see how well it really works, and, if it does, to see how broadly it applies. In art history, ancient authors such as Pliny the Elder, Cicero, and Quintilian understood changes in art largely in terms of individual contributions made by famous artists, which would bring art from a "rude" state to one of greater sophistication and naturalism, after which over-refinement and decline might set in.[2] These accounts of artistic development involve description and pattern recognition, but they are straightforward and literal, in the sense that they do not appeal by analogy to any system outside the artistic sphere.

In the sixteenth century, Vasari's pioneering *Lives of the Artists* introduced an important new theme into the literature of art history by comparing artistic to biological development. For Vasari, the biological metaphor in question involved not the origin of species, which would not be carefully studied until the Enlightenment, but rather the life history of an individual organism. He therefore saw early, middle, and late stylistic phases as analogous to youth, maturity, and senescence. The historical trajectory from antiquity through the Middle Ages into the Renaissance, which had been charted by Petrarch and applied to art history by Ghiberti in his *Commentaries*, thus became for Vasari a story of death and rebirth.

Vasari's seductively simple biological metaphor has strongly influenced subsequent art-historical practice. The metaphor is powerful because it seems to explain, rather than just chronicle, stylistic change. The flaws in Vasari's biological metaphor, however, are many and important. To begin with, it provides no real mechanism for change. On this level, it cannot really be called an explanation at all. In addition, it implies that stylistic development follows a single linear trajectory. Vasari, of course, was aware that different artists working at a given time might work in different styles, but such diversity has no place in his simple biological model. Vasari's metaphor, finally, clearly privileges the mature or classic stylistic phase over the periods of growth and decline. This value judgment has crept insidiously into the writings of many subsequent art theorists, making it difficult to appreciate any art categorized as "late." Late Gothic art of the fifteenth century, for example, is often criticized as over-ripe and decadent, belonging as it does to the supposedly "autumnal" cultural moment made famous more than eighty years ago by Johan Huizinga.[3] The construction of the term "Northern Renaissance" may be understood largely as an attempt to rescue Jan van Eyck's brilliant paintings from this historiographical fate. Many other issues of art-historical interpretation and valuation have been similarly influenced by Vasari's widely influential biological metaphor.

In the sixteenth and seventeenth centuries, parallels between art history and natural history would have been apparent not only in the popularization of Vasari's biological metaphor, but also in the institutional structure of princely collections containing both artworks and natural wonders. In such cabinets of curiosities, products of craft and nature would have appeared as specimens largely isolated from their original contexts. To make sense of such a collection, a viewer would have to actively categorize the objects in question. As the intellectual culture of the Renaissance began to give way to that of the Enlightenment, therefore, issues of taxonomy and categorization became increasingly important.

The eighteenth century saw dramatic advances in biological scholarship, many of which would later go on to have resonances in art-historical writing. An important figure in this development was Carolus Linnaeus, whose work in the 1730s established the basic outlines of modern biological taxonomy.[4] Linnaeus's system was based on careful formal analysis, or, as an art historian might say, connoisseurship. Key features of Linnaeus's system included its hierarchical organization and its flexibility. Linnaeus grouped closely related species together into genera, related genera into families, families into orders, and so on all the way up to the largest categories of all, the plant and animal kingdoms. This hierarchical structure effectively represents species as individual twigs on a branching tree of life. Because of its branching complexity, this taxonomic structure could easily be expanded to incorporate newly discovered species. This flexibility has allowed Linnaeus's system to grow and change as the state of biological knowledge has advanced. Linnaeus's eighteenth-century contemporaries tended to rank species from least to most advanced in accord with the concept of a linear "chain of being," but hierarchy in this sense was not an inherent feature of Linnaeus's taxonomic scheme.

A fundamental advance in biological and taxonomic thinking was the recognition that species are not static. In his early work, Linnaeus had seen species as fixed and unchanging, but near the end of his life he admitted that species were "daughters of time." This idea had already been proposed by the Roman philosopher Lucretius, whose poem *De Rerum Natura* contains some eerily proto-Darwinian passages. Lucretius' writings were known in the Renaissance and the Enlightenment, but the strongest argument for the fluidity of species boundaries came from the French biologist Buffon, who explicitly demonstrated the principle by interbreeding a horse and a donkey to produce a mule. By the first years of the nineteenth century, Jean-Baptiste de Lamarck had developed his own detailed theory of organic evolution. Unlike Darwin's later evolutionary theory, which provided a plausible mechanism for change through natural selection, Lamarck's theory depended upon the incorrect postulate that acquired characteristics could be inherited by later generations. Unlike Darwin, moreover, Lamarck framed evolution in teleological terms, believing that organisms sought to work their way up the chain of being through progress toward optimality. Despite these important differences, however, Lamarck's theory certainly helped to establish an intellectual context in which Darwin's breakthroughs would become possible. Lamarck was, for example, one of the first biologists to champion the notion that the earth was far older than the 6,000 years implied by a literal reading of the Bible, old enough for organic evolution to have taken place. Another significant contributor to biological discourse in this period was Georges Cuvier, whose emphasis on the functional relationship between an animal's form and its behavior suggested the importance of adaptation to the environment.

In the decades around 1800, these newly sophisticated but still pre-Darwinian theories of natural history began to intersect with developments in art theory. By 1785, for example, Quatremère de Quincy had already noted that the territorial distribution of primordial architectural types, such as that of plant species, reflected the influence of environmental conditions. Hegel's writings, which describe the progressive development of the Spirit, have a vaguely Lamarckian flavor, and his *Philosophy of Art* discusses art using terms current in recent biological discourse, such as "evolution," "genera," and "species." As Lauren Golden has recently demonstrated, moreover, eighteenth-century advances in the study of natural history exercised decisive influences on theorists of aesthetics from Kant to the Romantics.[5]

Charles Darwin, working in the middle decades of the nineteenth century, developed a comprehensive theory of organic evolution that forms the foundation of modern biology, but his epoch-making intellectual achievements have to date contributed far less than they might to the discourses of art history and related humanistic disciplines. The main obstacle to a more profound appreciation of his work, ironically, may be the very pervasiveness of older and simpler evolutionary models, whose limitations are all too often erroneously attributed to Darwin's theory. To a certain extent, this confusion may reflect the fact that Darwin's ideas themselves evolved fairly smoothly from the work of earlier evolutionist thinkers including Lamarck and his own grandfather, Erasmus Darwin. Over the course of his famous round-the-world voyage with the research vessel *Beagle* between 1831 and 1836, though, Darwin assembled a greater wealth of evidence for evolution than any of his predecessors had. Over the next two decades, he worked out his evolutionary theories in increasing detail, observing the effects of selective breeding on domestic animal populations, and communicating his ideas about natural selection only with a fairly small circle of scientific confidants, including the geologist Charles Lyell and the botanist Joseph Hooker. It was only in 1858, when he received a paper from Alfred Russell Wallace making many of the same arguments that he had developed, that Darwin decided to publish his work, which appeared in the following year as *On the Origin of Species by Means of Natural Selection, or the Preservation of Favored Races in the Struggle for Life*.

Darwin's book was an immediate sensation, selling out its first edition of 1,250 volumes on the day of publication, but some of the points of its argument entered the popular imagination more readily than others. Perhaps the most obvious point about Darwin's evolutionary model was that it conflicted radically with a literal interpretation of Christian scripture. Darwin himself was no raging atheist—indeed, he had trained for the ministry at Cambridge—but his view of evolution was thoroughly rationalist and materialist.[6] Darwin, moreover, progressively undercut the long-cherished distinction between humans and other animals, first with the general evolutionary theory expounded in *On the Origin of Species*, and then with his more narrowly focused books *The Descent of Man* and *The Expression of the Emotions in Man and Animals*, published in 1871 and 1872, respectively. These challenges to religious and humanistic tradition had already been anticipated to some extent in the work of Darwin's Enlightenment-era predecessors, but it was the publication of Darwin's comprehensive and meticulously researched work that brought evolutionary theory to widespread prominence in the public sphere. The success of his ideas in explaining the diversity of life on earth did a great deal to increase the prestige of rigorous scientific research in the late nineteenth and early twentieth centuries.

Perhaps because the main claims of Darwin's evolutionary theory were so spectacular and controversial, many of its nuances were to some extent lost in the shuffle, at least in terms of the broad public discourse that would go on to influence art historians. Darwin's name has therefore become associated with notions of progress, teleology, and value judgment, even though Darwin's own writings clearly explain that evolution reflects the action of environmental selection pressures rather than any inherent tendency toward the development of more "advanced" forms. One of the classic demonstrations of ongoing Darwinian evolution, in fact, involves the phenomenon of "industrial melanism," in which moth populations evolve to have darker colorations in polluted forests, because the more brightly colored moths become easily visible prey when seen against dark, soot-covered tree trunks. Dark moths are not inherently "better" or "worse" than pale ones; they are simply better suited to the particular conditions of a polluted environment.

The old-fashioned idea of a "chain of being" plays no role in Darwinian theory, but evolution continues to be widely associated in the popular imagination with the idea of linear progress. This misconception likely reflects the impact of widely publicized illustrations showing the successive steps in the evolution of familiar species such as horses and humans. The dramatic sequence of hominid forms leading from small ape-like creatures to boldly striding modern humans, in particular, has achieved iconic status. The fundamental patterns of evolutionary development, however, tend to involve the branching structures of increasing diversity rather than simple linear sequences. Most speciation events involve the divergence of distinct populations, such as the various finch groups that Darwin famously observed on the Galapagos Islands, rather than the progressive development of single type. Even in the context of human evolution, branching diversity has been the rule, with other hominid species coexisting with our direct ancestors until surprisingly recently.[7] The spread of modern humans at their expense has trimmed their branches off the "tree of life" through extinction, but the basic processes of evolution remain irreducibly non-linear. This should be obvious in a broad sense, because ancient types such as dragonflies and ferns continue to flourish alongside types of more recent evolutionary origin such as humans and flowering plants. More subtly, Darwin understood that evolution depended upon the existence of variation within individual populations, because the principle of natural selection involves the relatively greater reproductive success of those individuals in the group that succeed best in their environment—like the dark moths in the polluted forests. If all the moths had been initially the same color, they would all have died out together when they suddenly became visible against trees blackened in the Industrial Revolution. As this example suggests, evolution necessarily involves the action of environmental selection pressures—which may be highly non-random—on populations characterized by a certain amount of random variation. Darwin correctly recognized that this byplay of random and non-random factors could explain the evolution of exquisitely complex organisms such as human beings without any appeal to teleology.

Among the most important and least appreciated aspects of Darwin's theory has been its potential to liberate taxonomy from essentialism. By demonstrating that biological diversity results from ongoing process, rather than reflecting the structure of a single God-given master plan, Darwin showed that category boundaries are not absolutes. Evolutionary theory thus marked a dramatic step beyond Aristotle's stubbornly durable idea that categorical essences could be discerned by stripping away the "accidents" peculiar to each member of a given class. It is precisely this liberation of science from essentialism that the noted evolutionary biologist Ernst Mayr recently cited as Darwin's most fundamental contribution to the history of ideas, the one that earned Darwin recognition by *Scientific American* magazine as the most influential scientist of the past 150 years.[8]

Darwin's impact on the intellectual life of the late nineteenth and twentieth centuries was undoubtedly enormous, but the subtleties of his evolutionary model seem to have been largely lost on art historians and other members of the public not actively involved in biological research. Darwin's greatest influence on the discourse of art history was actually quite broad and diffuse, in the sense that his success contributed to elevating the already high status of scientific research in the very decades when art history was becoming established as a modern academic discipline. Positivism and the collection of objective data became established as fashionable ideals in the humanistic academy, and many art historians of the day aspired to create an objective and methodologically rigorous *Kunstwissenschaft* based on the sciences. Despite the growing prominence of biological and evolutionary terminology in art-historical discourse, however, really close engagement with the Darwinian intellectual legacy remained the exception rather than the rule.

One of the most evolutionarily minded art theorists of the nineteenth century was Gottfried Semper, who already in an 1853 lecture cited the influence of Cuvier's biological research on his own thinking about architectural history. Semper certainly read *On the Origin of Species* when it came out six years later, and he saw his own theories as very similar to Darwin's. Even he, however, hedged his bets somewhat, observing that the "free creations of man" followed different developmental laws than species in nature.[9] Unfortunately, his writings do not explain in detail how he would have extended and modified the Darwinian model so that it could apply more adequately to cultural history.

As Lauren Golden has recently noted, Darwinian evolutionary language also occurs in the slightly later writings of Conrad Fiedler on architecture, while Darwin's work on the expression of emotion in man and animals went on to influence the aesthetic theories of Herbert Spencer and Robert Vischer.[10] Darwin's evolutionary ideas also informed Henri Bergson's philosophy of duration and change, which would go on to impact art historians such as Henri Focillon in the twentieth century, but Bergson's writings celebrated mysticism and intuition as the rigorously rational materialist Darwin never had. On the other methodological extreme, Giovanni Morelli's positivistic attention to formal details in art had more in common with Linneaus's classification schemes than it did with Darwin's evolutionary legacy. Neither Bergson nor Morelli, therefore, really internalized the nuances of Darwin's theories.

Several of the most thoughtful and influential art theorists of the decades around 1900 were downright skeptical of Darwinian thinking, at least as they understood it. Alois Riegl, for instance, explicitly criticized Semper's followers for the naïve "Darwinismus" of their materialist approach to art history.[11] Riegl's own theories of art-historical development emerged from a more Hegelian tradition. Like Hegel, Riegl saw cultural history as a continuum, in which each work deserved to be interpreted in relation to the spirit of its own age, rather than measured against some absolute external standard such as classical realism. Riegl's careful attention to the details of formal development helped give his theory of *Kunstwollen* a degree of precision and plausibility that Hegel's more abstract scheme had lacked, but the Hegelian flavor of Riegl's work remains pronounced, especially in his earlier writings such as the *Stilfragen* of 1893. Interestingly, however, Riegl's later writings, such as the fragments of *Historische Grammatik* that were still unpublished when he died in 1905, suggested a more complex picture of cultural and artistic change. Instead of treating art history as a simple linear progression governed by the immanent logic of form, Riegl began to suggest that different formal solutions might compete with one another in an environment defined by external factors such as patronage and ideology. The demise of classical art in Late Antiquity and the contemporaneous turn toward abstraction, for example, could be understood as a consequence of the adoption of Christianity as the official religion in the Roman empire. This more complex view of artistic evolution through cultural selection presents obvious analogies to Darwin's theory of organic evolution through selection in the natural environment.[12] Having earlier criticized Semper's followers for their supposed

"Darwinismus," however, Riegl does not appear to have recognized the resonances between his own mature views and Darwin's.

Henri Focillon, writing a generation later, similarly appears to have misunderstood the true character of Darwin's evolutionary theory. He found much to appreciate in Bergson's evolutionary philosophy, but in *The Life of Forms*, he faulted evolutionary thinking for its "deceptive orderliness" and its "single-minded directness."[13] Darwinian evolution, though, is neither orderly nor goal-directed. Focillon, in this instance, appears to have wrongly associated evolution with the Hegelian idea of progressive development that he so emphatically opposed.

Heinrich Wölfflin, working mostly in the years between Riegl's and Focillon's greatest achievements, proved more willing to engage with the nuances of Darwin's legacy. In his early career, Wölfflin associated evolution with increasing perfection, but by 1915, when he wrote *The Principles of Art History*, he had come to recognize that divergence rather than linear progress was the key to both artistic and biological development. Wölfflin correctly concluded, therefore, that Darwin's model of organic evolution had much more to offer to art history than Hegelian teleology or the Vasarian biological metaphor of birth, maturation, and death. Wölfflin's mature analysis of artistic development thus depends directly on Darwin's work, with some passages echoing *On the Origin of Species* almost verbatim. Wölfflin's ideas about the psychology and perception of art, moreover, rely to a significant extent on Darwin's *The Expression of the Emotions in Man and Animals*.[14]

The kind of direct art-historical engagement with evolutionary theory seen in the work of Semper and Wölfflin has had few sequels, despite the rapid flowering of evolutionary biology in the past century. Over the nearly 150 years since the publication of *On the Origin of Species*, ongoing research has strengthened the already impressive intellectual edifice built by Darwin. The discovery of genes, and later of DNA, helped to explain the mechanisms of inheritance and the origins, through mutation, of genetic variation. Thanks to these breakthroughs, genetic criteria could be used to help sort out evolutionary relationships, which had previously been inferred primarily from phenetics, the study of external form. These developments fostered the growth of evolutionarily based taxonomy, in addition to providing the initial impetus toward the great scientific undertaking of the early twenty-first century, the deciphering of the human genetic code. Studies of population biology and speciation have advanced the modern biological understanding of living ecosystems, while debates about "punctuated equilibria" and the pace of evolutionary change have characterized discussions of the paleontological past. All of these developments have complicated and enriched the picture sketched by Darwin while confirming the accuracy of its basic outlines.[15] Virtually none of this research, however, has had a meaningful impact on art-historical discourse.

The breakdown of the dialog between evolutionary biologists and art historians attests in part to a more general breakdown of communication between humanists and scientists, which has been particularly palpable since the middle of the twentieth century. Erwin Panofsky, in his 1938 essay on "The History of Art as a Humanistic Discipline," could still wax eloquent about the symbiotic relationship between the sciences and the humanities, but by 1959 the physicist C.P. Snow had already begun to lament the divergence of the "Two Cultures."[16] In the five decades since Snow's famous essay appeared, the relationship between art history and the sciences has become even more vexed, despite the increasingly widespread use of scientific and technical tools such as pollen grain sampling in archaeology, infrared reflectography in the study of painting, and structural analysis in the study of architecture. The usefulness of such tools at a practical level has done nothing to allay more abstract theoretical concerns among many humanists about quasi-scientific explanatory structures, master narratives, and overarching organizational schemes of all kinds. The rise of critical theory, in particular, has led many to question the possibility of quasi-scientific objectivity in historical scholarship. Indeed, many cultural critics from 1970 onwards have argued that scientific objectivity was impossible even in the sciences themselves. Such attitudes mark a decisive repudiation of the widespread aspiration to scientific rigor evident in the scholarly world of the late nineteenth and early twentieth centuries. Members of the scientific community have responded to these developments with varying degrees of chagrin, as expressed most infamously in physicist Alan Sokal's deliberately nonsensical hoax submission to the journal *Social Text*.[17] Biologist E.O. Wilson, meanwhile, has proposed an explicitly neo-Enlightenment project of "consilience" between the sciences and the humanities, in which the mechanism of "gene-culture co-evolution" would play a central role.[18] Despite the more constructive tone of Wilson's project, many humanists might worry that Wilson's unified vision undervalues their expertise in the study of human culture. The stakes in these debates are high, since they have the potential to shape the relationship between scientific and humanistic discourse. The tone of these debates can also affect public and governmental perceptions of the academy, with direct and important consequences for research funding and scholarly life generally.

In this context especially, the methodological and conceptual parallels between art history and evolutionary biology deserve more attention than they have recently received. The current state of relative disengagement between these fields emerges clearly in the comments of two well-respected art historians who have discussed the topic. Linda Nochlin, in her introduction to a special 2003 issue of *Nineteenth-Century Art Worldwide* on "The Darwin Effect," writes unashamedly of her two-month "crash course" on the literature of evolutionary theory, starting with her reading *Darwin for Beginners*.[19] Nochlin deserves credit for tackling the topic intelligently, and the contributing authors effectively document the impact of Darwinism on several later nineteenth-century artists, but it is sobering that a leading humanist scholar such as Nochlin must effectively start from scratch when attempting to engage with an intellectual tradition so central to the modern scientific worldview. In a 2001 article, meanwhile, Eric Fernie advances a curious argument for expunging evolutionary language from art-historical discourse. He begins by quite rightly distinguishing between the ways in which biologists and art historians have used evolutionary language, observing that humanists still tend to associate the term "evolution" with progressive linear development, even though Darwin's own model of biological evolution is neither progressive nor linear. Then, arguing that the usefulness of evolutionary language in art history should be judged by how it *has been* applied rather than how it *could be* applied, he concludes that evolutionary metaphors should be dismissed as unhelpful.[20] This, however, is rather like arguing that knives should be dismissed as useless because they don't cut well when held upside-down. Surely it makes sense to experiment with using a tool properly before rejecting it out of hand. From this perspective, it makes sense to suggest that art historians should carefully consider the possible relevance of evolutionary theory, instead of following Fernie's call to reject this powerful framework for the discussion of formal change over time. Fernie may be too quick to discard evolutionary metaphors, but he makes a useful distinction between such metaphors and evolutionary analyses, for which he has a bit more sympathy. An evolutionary metaphor compares general patterns of artistic and biological development, while an evolutionary analysis allows scholars to bring the techniques of biology to bear on the study of art.

Art historians stand to gain from closer intellectual engagement with evolutionary biology on both the analytical and the metaphorical levels, as Ernst Gombrich appears to have recognized decades ago. At the analytical level, Gombrich noted that theories of art, beauty, and visual perception must necessarily take account of human mental structure, which is itself a product of evolutionary history. In the early years of Gombrich's long career, this point would have mattered only on a fairly abstract level. With the increasing sophistication of evolutionary neurobiology in recent decades, though, the emergence of a genuine neurologically based theory of aesthetics has become a concrete possibility, if not yet an accomplished fact. Among the most eloquent advocates for closer engagement between art historians and neurologists, not surprisingly, have been Gombrich's former student John Onians, and his own student Lauren Golden, whose work involves the biological origins of visual imagination.[21]

At the metaphorical level, meanwhile, Gombrich recognized that Darwinian evolution offered a paradigm for change far more flexible and nuanced than the linear models of history proposed by Vasari and Hegel.[22] Gombrich objected particularly to the collectivism and essentialism implicit in Hegel's idea that works of art and culture merely reflect the guiding spirit of their age. Gombrich even explicitly lamented the way that Aristotelian essentialism continued to constrain art-historical discourse long after it had been rejected in the biological sciences.

Gombrich's admiration of scientific discourse doubtless reflects the impact of his long and fruitful dialog with the noted physicist and philosopher Karl Popper.

Interestingly, though, the methodological parallels between evolutionary biology and art history may be even closer than Gombrich and Popper appreciated. Popper's extensive and influential work on the epistemology of the sciences emphasizes the importance of "falsifiability," the notion that a viable scientific theory must make testable predictions. Theories whose predictions fail to match the results of experiment would then be thrown out or modified, leading to a kind of intellectual evolution toward ever more precise theories. Because physics is a discipline devoted to the study of timeless universal principles, Popper could afford to place a premium on prediction and experimentation. Disciplines such as evolutionary biology, geology, and cosmology, however, deal necessarily with the past, and they therefore cannot be based on prediction in the same strict sense as physics. In both epistemological and methodological terms, therefore, these scientific disciplines have much in common with humanistic disciplines such as art history. Ernst Mayr makes this very point when discussing Darwin's intellectual legacy, suggesting optimistically that such parallels between certain scientific and humanistic disciplines should help open up the lines of communication between the "two cultures" that had been identified by C.P. Snow.[23]

At a fundamental level, of course, the mechanisms of cultural development are different from those seen in organic evolution. Self-conscious human agency provides a mechanism for cultural and artistic change that finds no direct parallel in natural history. This does not mean that Darwinian models have to be rejected in the study of the arts, but it does mean that they have to be modified if they are to prove helpful. One of the most important differences between artistic production and biological reproduction is that, while a given organism will necessarily have just two parents, both of whom belong to the immediately preceding generation of the same species, an artist can incorporate an arbitrarily large number of influences in his or her work, some of which may be ancient or largely foreign to the artist's cultural tradition. A thirteenth-century sculptor such as Nicola Pisano, for example, could be directly influenced by Late Antique reliefs made many hundreds of years before, and a modern artist such as Picasso could draw inspiration from African masks. Thus, while natural history can be understood as a continuously branching "tree of life," the topology of cultural history can be far more complex, incorporating tangles, loops, and multiple rather than singular root structures. Tangled webs of this sort may soon become necessary to trace the origins of hybrid organisms produced through gene splicing and other radical forms of genetic engineering, but they have not been necessary to describe the autonomous flow of natural history.

The convoluted topology of cultural process has important implications for art-historical taxonomy. Unlike biologists, who can work toward a single authoritative taxonomy based on the branching structure of evolutionary history, art historians must be willing to simultaneously entertain multiple taxonomies. The technical details of an artwork, for example, may continue to reflect the artist's early training, even in cases where the overall conception of the work has been influenced by new ideas. The molding profiles that have been so assiduously studied by many students of medieval architecture carry mostly the first type of information, which might be termed genetic because it directly reflects the carver's immediate artisanal parentage. The gross morphology of the building, by contrast, might reflect the aspirations of the designers and the patrons to rival a famous monument that stemmed from a very different artisanal tradition. A given building might thus be seen as belonging to two very different "schools" depending on which set of evaluative criteria are considered.[24]

The pitfalls of a purely evolutionary approach to art-historical taxonomy become apparent when cases of convergent evolution in biology are contrasted with those in art history. Biologists recognize that whales came to have fishlike shapes without ever imitating fish or being directly influenced by them. Biologists have therefore been able to largely abandon the use of categories such as "fish-shaped animals." Comparably vague terms based on external characteristics, however, are likely to remain important in art-historical discourse, because artists often do imitate the external features of art from outside their own traditions. The term "classicizing sculpture," for example, proves useful in the case of Nicola Pisano because his work cannot readily be explained without consideration of antique prototypes as well as his own thirteenth-century Italian milieu. Art-historical taxonomy, therefore, can never be reduced to a single definitive evolutionarily based system in the same sense that biological taxonomy, at least in principle, can be.

In general, analogies between art history and the sciences must be recognized as approximate and imperfect, but potentially powerful. Memory, self-consciousness, and intelligent agency, perhaps the most wonderful of human characteristics, are precisely the characteristics that will always prevent art history from attaining epistemological equivalence with the sciences. Nevertheless, art historians have much to gain from the active consideration of scientific analogies, especially those involving biological evolution. Darwinian language provides a broad and flexible framework within which the rich diversity of the world's artistic output can be readily understood without appeal to essentialism or teleology. In these respects the Darwinian model offers significant benefits that the far more influential Hegelian and Vasarian models of artistic development do not. In fact, the languages of evolution can be taken as a powerful model for art-historical discourse, one that would automatically incorporate many of the most profound insights of scholars such as Riegl, Wölfflin, and Gombrich. Art historians attempting to construct coherent theories of diachronic cultural process, therefore, have good reason to engage with the discourses of evolutionary biology and other historical sciences.

The analogies between art history and the sciences deserve to be pursued not only because of their potential to spawn valuable new theories of artistic development, but also because the ensuing conversation could help heal the discursive breach between the sciences and the humanities. Scientists and humanists both have much to be proud of, and active dialog between the two groups would likely foster increased mutual respect as well as mutual understanding. Humanists may be positively surprised by the power, lucidity, and relevance of scientific intellectual models. Scientists, conversely, may be struck by the subtlety and complexity of the problems that humanists confront in their work, which make the substantial achievements of humanistic scholarship all the more impressive. The fact that the topology of artistic influence is far more intricate than that of evolutionary biology, for example, helps to demonstrate why cultural history cannot be treated in precisely the same way as natural history. Thus, while some might worry that exploration of the analogies between the arts and the sciences would lead to the colonization of one discourse by the other, it seems far more probable that such dialog would underline the autonomy and the dignity of each. Since the academy in the early twenty-first century often seems both divided against itself and marginalized by increasingly business-driven social paradigms, the potential benefits of cross-disciplinary communication are simply too great to ignore.

## Notes

1 A number of colleagues have contributed significantly to the evolution of this essay. The first strong impetus leading me to explore its themes came from Marvin Trachtenberg, who invited me to speak in his session on the parallels between art-historical and scientific models of periodization at the College Art Association conference in 2000. The present essay should thus be understood as a sequel to my talk, which was published as "Pros and Cons of Stratigraphic Models in Art History," *RES* 40 (2001): 177–187. I am grateful to Elizabeth Mansfield for expressing interest in some of the related material on Darwinism that I was not able to include in that short article. I owe particular debts also to John Onians and to his former student Lauren Golden, who generously shared with me her richly detailed dissertation "An Enquiry Concerning the Imagination in Philosophy, Art History and Evolutionary Theory" (University of East Anglia, 2001). Last but not least, I am pleased to acknowledge the guidance and support of my paleontologist father, Ken Bork, who first introduced me to the world of evolutionary theory.

2 Because this essay must cover a vast amount of historiographical ground in a small space, detailed citations will be given only for recent art-historical works. The basic positions of ancient and Renaissance theorists are briefly sketched in, for example Eric Fernie, *Art History and its Methods: A Critical Anthology* (London: Phaidon, 1997) pp. 10–11.

3 Johan Huizinga, *Herfsttij der Middeleeuwen* (Haarlem: H.D. Tjeenk Willink, 1919).

4 A good introduction to the history of taxonomy in paleontology is the chapter on "Systematics" in Donald R. Prothero, *Bringing Fossils to Life* (Boston: McGraw-Hill, 1998) pp. 42–61.

5 For Quatremère de Quincy and Hegel, see Golden, "An Enquiry," pp. 139 and 126–135, respectively. For Kant and the Romantics, see ibid., pp. 99–119 and 130–138.
6 Adrian Desmond and James Moore, *Darwin: The Life of a Tormented Evolutionist* (London: Viking, 1991).
7 On the recent discovery of the tiny *Homo flouresiensis*, for example, see Kate Wong, "The Littlest Human," *Scientific American* 292(2) (2005): 56–65.
8 Ernst Mayr,"Darwin's Influence on Modern Thought," *Scientific American* 283(1) (2000): 78–83.
9 Golden, "An Enquiry," pp. 139–144.
10 Ibid., pp. 150–154.
11 Margaret Iversen, *Alois Riegl: Art History and Theory* (Cambridge, MA: Harvard University Press, 1993) p. 27.
12 I am grateful to Jackie Jung for bringing these evolutionary resonances to my attention. For her translation of Riegl's late work, see Alois Riegl, *Historical Grammar of the Visual Arts,* trans. Jacqueline Jung (New York: Zone Books, 2004). See also Golden, "An Enquiry," pp. 155–159.
13 Henri Focillon, *The Life of Forms in Art* (New York: Zone Books, 1989) p. 47. The book was originally published in French in 1934. For Bergson's influence on Focillon, see Walter Cahn's entry on Focillon in Helen Damico, ed., *Medieval Scholarship—Biographical Studies on the Formation of a Discipline* (New York: Garland, 2000) pp. 263–264.
14 Golden, "An Enquiry," pp. 160–165.
15 These more recent developments in evolutionary theory are briefly sketched in Prothero, *Bringing Fossils to Life*, pp. 66–77. Particularly interesting from an art-historical perspective is the fact that modern evolutionary biologists increasingly distinguish between micro-evolution, which governs small changes in largely stable species, and macro-evolution of the kind seen when new species arise, usually in response to powerful new selection pressures. Art historians, similarly, often differentiate between the moments of bold creativity associated with innovative artists, and the more workmanlike development of their ideas by their successors. Focillon's student George Kubler, for example, used a distinction of this kind to develop the idea of artistic "sequences," which would begin with innovative "prime objects" whose influence could be traced in later versions. See Kubler, *The Shape of Time* (New Haven, CT: Yale University Press, 1962) especially pp. 70–79.
16 Erwin Panofsky, "The History of Art as a Humanistic Discipline," cited in Golden, "An Enqiry," pp. 160–165. Snow originally delivered "The Two Cultures" at Cambridge in the Rede Lecture Series. It has subsequently appeared in print in various versions, for example C.P. Snow, *The Two Cultures: and A Second Look* (Cambridge: Cambridge University Press, 1965).
17 Alan D. Sokal, "Transgressing the Boundaries: Toward a Transformative Hermeneutics of Quantum Gravity," *Social Text* 46–47 (1996): 217–252; and Alan D. Sokal, "A Physicist Experiments with Cultural Studies," *Lingua Franca* (May–June 1996): 62–64.
18 E.O. Wilson, *Consilience: The Unity of Knowledge* (New York: Knopf, 1998).
19 Linda Nochlin, "The Darwin Effect," *Nineteenth-Century Art Worldwide* 2(2) (2003) www.19thc-artworldwide.org.
20 Eric Fernie, "Art History and Evolution from Henri Focillon to Stephen Jay Gould," in Lauren Golden, ed., *Raising the Eyebrow: John Onians and World Art Studies* (Oxford: Achaeopress, 2001) pp. 67–78. Fernie had earlier advanced a similar but shorter critique

of evolutionary language in *Art History and its Methods*, pp. 336–337. In the course of his 2001 article, Fernie critiques two articles examining the relationship between architectural history and biological evolution: Stephen Jay Gould and R.C. Lewontin, "The Spandrels of San Marco and the Panglossian Paradigm: A Critique of the Adaptationist Programme," in *Proceedings of the Royal Society of London*, Series B, Biological Sciences 204 no. 1161 (1979): 581–598; and Robert Mark, "Architecture and Evolution," in *American Scientist* 84 (1996): 383–389. Mark himself rightly faults some of Gould's reasoning, which places less stress than it might on the importance of scale in architectural design, but Gould's desire to work art-historical analogies into evolutionary theory suggests the potential power of this cross-disciplinary exchange. Taken together, these two articles suggest that art historians and biologists should engage with each others' work more closely, rather than less.

21 See John Onians, "Architecture and Painting: The Biological Connection" in Karen Koehler, ed., *Architecture and the Pictorial Arts from Antiquity to the Enlightenment* (Aldershot: Ashgate, 2002) pp. 1–14; Golden, "An Enquiry," pp. 169–293. Golden usefully summarizes many of the main points of "An Enquiry" in the shorter and more accessible "Science, Darwin, and Art History," in *Raising the Eyebrow*, pp. 79–90.

22 E.H. Gombrich, "Evolution in the Arts: The Altar Painting, Its Ancestry and Progeny," in Alan Grafen, ed., *Evolution and Its Influence* (Oxford: Clarendon, 1989) pp. 107–125, especially pp. 107–108. See also E.H. Gombrich, *In Search of Cultural History* (Oxford: Clarendon, 1969); Didier Eribon and E.H. Gombrich, *Looking for Answers: Conversations on Art and Science* (New York: Harry N. Abrams, 1993) p. 168 and John Onians, "Gombrich and Biology," in Paula Lizzaraga, ed., *E.H. Gombrich in Memoriam* (Pamplona: Universidad de Navarra, 2003). For Gombrich's thoughts on classification and essentialism, see E.H. Gombrich, "Norm and Form," in *Norm and Form: Studies in the Art of the Renaissance* (London: Phaidon, 1978) pp. 82–88.

23 Mayr, "Darwin's Influence," p. 80.

24 I first explored these themes in "Holy Toledo: Art-Historical Taxonomy and the Morphology of Toledo Cathedral," *AVISTA Forum Journal* 10(2) / 11(1) (fall 1997/spring 1998): 31–37.

## Part IV

# Old masters, new institutions

## Art history and the museum

### Introduction

Along with the university, the art museum has provided a prominent and influential setting for the professionalization of art history. Pressing distinct institutional needs, the museum helped to identify art history with cultural heritage and the public role of the visual arts. Likewise, methods of art-historical enquiry developed largely in the academy have in turn influenced museum practices. Feminist art history, psychoanalytic approaches to art collecting, methods of institutional critique, and, of course, the field of museology are among the academic modes of investigation continuing to affect the relationship between art history and the museum.

All art historians—whether allied with the academy, the museum, or other institutions—engage to some extent in ordering or arranging artworks into a meaningful narrative. Usually this is done verbally through books or articles or catalogs, but museums and other exhibition spaces are able to construct a narrative spatially, marshalling artworks themselves into the service of a particular argument. Museums have never merely exhibited culture. The arrangement of artifacts and supporting materials within the museum—even the design of the building itself—has always worked to convey a particular narrative, a story about the significance of the culture or cultures on display. Sometimes these narratives are triumphant, as Carol Duncan and Alan Wallach revealed in their foundational essay, "The Universal Survey Museum."[1] Western art museums, especially those with collections and exhibition programs that span many cultures and periods, impart ideological lessons. Duncan and Wallach argued that the layout of galleries in such institutions channels visitors along a deliberate course in which the superiority of the host culture is inevitably signaled as is the indomitable progress of Western society. In this way, "survey museums"—and the art historians who study or care for their collections—are engaged as much in a political and economic enterprise as a cultural one.

That museums function as instruments of state and commercial power is now accepted as a commonplace. In fact, in the decades since Duncan and Wallach's essay appeared, scholars along with museum curators, directors, and even architects have taken pains to expose the ideological investments of these institutions. The consequences of this phase of internal critique are not yet well understood. To what extent has the Western art museum been able to divest itself of its triumphalist bearing? How have efforts toward ideological transparency affected the work of art historians? One manifestation of these changes in institutional behavior is the willingness of some art museums to repatriate artifacts that were illicitly acquired, whether knowingly or not.[2] More striking, even, is the pursuit of legal action against curators suspected of complicity in illicit transactions on behalf of their institutions.[3] Such actions are consistent with current codes of ethics for scholars of art history and museum professionals. However, these are fairly new attitudes. For instance, the College Art Association (CAA) in 1936 issued a resolution condemning the Syrian–French Treaty of Alliance—which would have granted independence to Syria, ruled by French mandate since 1920—because the treaty prohibited removal of Syrian cultural artifacts without official permission.[4] Not until 1973 would CAA officially rescind this view, then vowing "to preserve [foreign] cultural property and its documentation and to prevent illicit traffic in such cultural property."[5]

Cultural property rights is, of course, only one of the issues cast into relief during the past quarter century as efforts at institutional critique gained ground. Each of the authors included in this section considers a different consequence of this reconsideration of the museum. Anna C. Chave addresses the effects of feminist critiques of art history and its institutions in "Figuring the Origins of the Modern at the Fin de Siècle: The Trope of the Pathetic Male." Following the argument laid out by Duncan and Wallach, Chave examines the ideological implications of the arrangement of artworks at New York's MoMA. Specifically, she focuses on the hanging of Paul Cézanne's *Bather* at the head of the permanent collection, questioning the significance of this piece for both the curators and visitors. Far from a work that trumpets aesthetic or personal triumph, Chave argues that Cézanne's *Bather* manifests awkwardness and abjection. It is a representation of modernity—and masculinity—redolent with doubt. The placement of this painting as the keynote of MoMA's cultural narrative comes, she claims, in response to critiques of the modern canon, particularly critiques in which questions of race and gender have been brought to bear on long-standing assumptions about artistic quality and historic relevance. The choice of Cézanne's *Bather* is, Chave explains, ultimately a feint, a way of reasserting the traditional loci of power.

Like Chave, Christopher R. Marshall looks to moments of social stress—especially times of warfare—for seeds of national identity and cultural myth. The need to articulate a uniquely Australian identity has, Marshall explains, informed the development of art and history museums in that country. The means of accomplishing this have shifted significantly, though, in response to the past few decades of institutional critique. What Marshall observes in his essay, "Re-imagining Meaning in the Contemporary Museum: From Things That Go Beep in the Case to the Artist Ex Machina," is a move in museum practice away from a focus on *objects* toward delivery of an *experience*. The chief symptom of this change is a return to the notion of the museum as a site of wonder and magic (exemplified by the new Musée Quai Branly in Paris). The "artist ex machina" cited in the title of his essay refers to a technique whereby the political or historical difficulties inevitably embedded in any museum project are seemingly resolved through novel or striking effects. These effects might be created by the museum itself, as in Daniel Libeskind's Imperial War Museum North in the United Kingdom or the National Museum of Australia, where the architecture overwhelms the visitor and prevents the installation of conventional, linear cultural, and historical narratives. Another response to complaints of the museum's authoritarianism is via interactive technologies, whereby visitors gain a sense of control over the experience, choosing, like a *bricoleur*, from "a kaleidoscopic barrage of visual and sensory impressions." Yet, these approaches, though seemingly liberating, have met with strong complaints from visitors and governing boards alike. And Marshall warns that such strategies can serve as much to disguise ideology as to liberate visitors from it.

Maureen Connor takes a different approach to understanding how museums promulgate ideology. A performance and installation artist whose career has addressed the nature of authority—political as well as cultural—Connor's most recent body of work, *Personnel*, seeks to expose the effects of ideology not only in the museum's public galleries but also in its private spaces, in its systems of organization. These two realms, not surprisingly, operate in tandem, so that problems felt behind the scenes by curators or support staff manifest themselves in the galleries just as the aesthetic or cultural personality of an institution marks those who work there. Connor's essay, "(Con)Testing Resources," describes the impetus behind *Personnel*, the project's roots in conceptual art and her attempts to make visible and to confront systems of power. Often seemingly light-hearted—one project involved museum staff dressing for work in formal wear, pajamas, and regular business attire on three succeeding days—Connor's interventions expose, sometimes painfully, an institution's intractable control over even the most mundane aspects of the lives of museum visitors and staff members alike. Without question, arts institutions are under increasing pressure to attain commercial success in order to become financially independent. With decreased public and foundational sponsorship for their non-profit missions, many arts institutions are emulating commercial enterprises. Marketing, merchandizing, downsizing, outsourcing: how do for-profit business models jibe with the mission of a non-profit organization? Connor's inquiry into the ways in which political, economic, and cultural assumptions play themselves out in the museum finds that the staff offices are as likely to display the effects of ideology as the galleries of MoMA or the lobby of the Imperial War Museum North.

## Notes

1 Carol Duncan and Alan Wallach, "The Universal Survey Museum," *Art History* (December 1980): 447–469. Their ideas on the ability of museums to deliver ideology were first published in "The Museum of Modern Art as Late Capitalist Ritual," *Marxist Perspectives* (Winter 1978): 28–51. Since then, a great deal of work has been done on the art museum as a conduit for cultural claims to dominance. Included among the most recent are Andrew McClellan, ed. *Art and Its Publics: Museum Studies at the Millennium* (Malden, MA: Blackwell, 2003); Gillian Perry and Colin Cunningham, eds, *Academies, Museums, and Canons of Art* (New Haven, CT: Yale University Press, 1999); Donald Preziosi, *Brain of the Earth's Body: Art, Museums, and the Phantasms of Modernity* (Minneapolis: University of Minnesota Press, 2003); Donald Preziosi and Claire J. Farago, eds, *Grasping the World: The Idea of the Museum* (Aldershot: Ashgate, 2004); and Daniel J. Sherman and Irit Rogoff, eds, *Museum Culture: Histories, Discourses, Spectacles* (Minneapolis, MN: University of Minnesota Press, 1994).

2 Although international organizations such as the UN and the International Court of Justice have declared illicit trafficking in cultural artifacts to be a violation of international law, museums have been reluctant to relinquish claims to contested works in their collections. This reticence seems to be lifting, however. In just the first half of 2006, for instance, the Metropolitan Museum of Art entered into an agreement with Italy to repatriate several objects in exchange for permission to exhibit other Italian antiquities on long-term loan; the Swedish Ethnological Museum returned a Haisla totem pole to British Columbia; and two long-standing petitions for the return of artworks looted by the Nazis to their rightful owners were resolved (these cases challenged ownership claims by the Austrian National Gallery and the Dutch Government).

3 The most widely reported case is that of Marion True, former curator of antiquities at the J. Paul Getty Museum, who has been charged with conspiracy to export Italian artifacts without permission. At the time of writing, True's trial enters its twelfth month in Rome, Italy.

4 "College Art Association Board Meeting Minutes," April 9, 1936, *Archives of the College Art Association*, New York.

5 College Art Association Guidelines: Resolution Concerning the Acquisition of Cultural Properties Originating in Foreign Countries, http://www.collegeart.org/guidelines/cultpropres.html [accessed June 28, 2006].

Chapter 13

# Figuring the origins of the modern at the fin de siècle

## The trope of the pathetic male

*Anna C. Chave*

> In the linkage between the male subject, the male image, and the social hierarchy, one of the key components of the political order of patriarchy may, perhaps, be found.
>
> Norman Bryson[1]

Premiere among exhibition sites in the world's modern art museums is the inaugural wall of the painting and sculpture galleries at New York's MoMA. With final preparations underway for the 2004 re-opening of MoMA, the *New York Times* investigated whether the work appointed to command that wall in the Yoshio Taniguchi building would remain as before: "For as long as anyone can remember, MoMA has opened the permanent collection of painting and sculpture with its most famous work by Cézanne, 'The Bather,' on a freestanding panel wall opposite the doorway," noted Arthur Lubow (who delivered the scoop that a Signac might take the key spot instead, however temporarily) (Figure 13.1). As head of the Modern's department of painting and sculpture, Kirk Varnedoe oversaw the installation that Lubow referred to only in the mid 1990s, however. Formerly, multiple paintings normally shared the inaugural wall, sometimes but not always including *The Bather*. Varnedoe's predecessor, William Rubin, who installed the 1984 Cesar Pelli renovation to the building, recalled *The Bather* as having been his own choice of inaugural painting (documentary evidence is scant and ambiguous); and Lubow called that choice a reaffirmation of the decision of the museum's legendary founding director, Alfred Barr.[2] But Barr's collection installation (mounted in 1964) opened instead with Rousseau. Varnedoe's decision to give Cézanne's *Bather* unprecedented prominence—such that it became practically a "poster boy" for the museum—followed in part from an architectural change: In response to criticism that the 1984 installation forced visitors on an unduly rigid route through the permanent collection, Varnedoe had an opening carved through the inaugural wall to allow the public another option, and the "freestanding panel," which accommodated only a single painting, made its debut.[3]

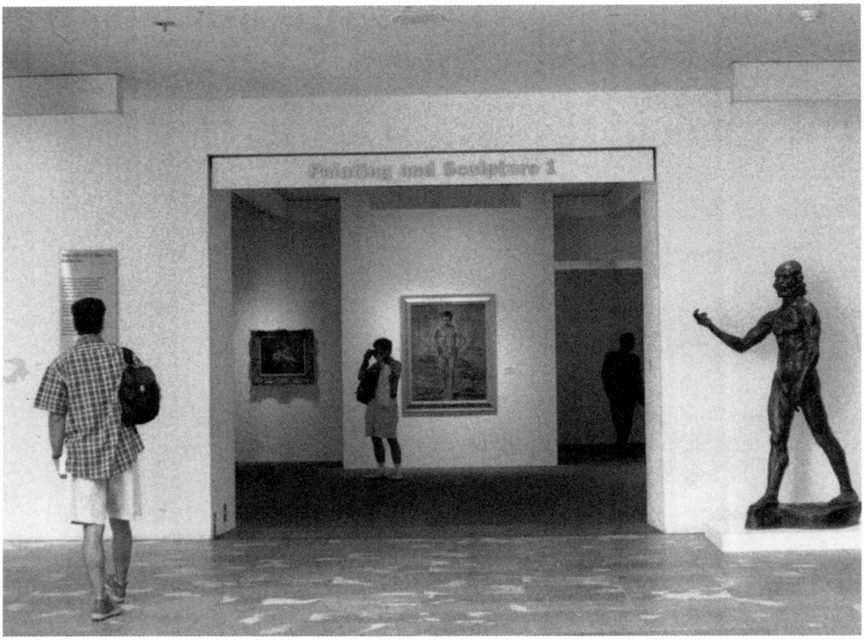

*Figure 13.1* View of entry to permanent collection galleries in the Museum of Modern Art, New York. Photograph courtesy of Mary Anne Staniszewski.

The *New York Times* noted in 1999 the nearly "biblical authority" inscribed in the path of a visit to the Modern, whereby "you turned left at Cézanne's *Bather*"—Cézanne being a kind of "Old Testament" figure, among the "prophets of the coming Light"—and proceeded apace to Picasso's *Demoiselles d'Avignon*, "from which all else descended as from Adam's rib."[4] Just outside the portal to the inaugural gallery stood Rodin's *John the Baptist*, his raised hand gesturing toward the Way, the Truth—and toward Cézanne's *Bather*. According Cézanne this preeminent institutional site of origin for the modernist canon did make a received art-historical sense, of course. In 1951 Clement Greenberg declared Cézanne "the most copious source of what we know as modern art," just as Clive Bell had called him in 1914 "the Christopher Columbus of a new continent of form."[5]

Though granting the logic supporting Cézanne's inaugural status, many museum visitors may not immediately have recognized the 1885 *Bather as* a Cézanne. Large-scaled (50 × 38 1/8″), individual nudes are quite uncommon in Cézanne's production, and his Bather pictures generally depart from his deep commitment to art grounded in the observation of nature. "Only in . . . the long series of nude studies known collectively as Bathers, did he habitually work without having an actual model before him." Often awkwardly drawn, the Bathers have been called "the least 'realized' "[6] as well as the "least 'natural' " of Cézanne's subjects.[7] Though MoMA's indeed difficult *Bather* is a foundational work of its collection (a 1931 bequest from one of the museum's founders, Lillie Bliss), Cézanne's Bather pictures were, as a rule, "added to museum collections only hesitantly and in most cases very late." Critical and scholarly attention newly shifted to the Bathers in the late 1980s and 1990s, moreover (belatedly following the affinity of numerous artists for these works).[8] I will argue that MoMA's emphatic positioning of *The Bather* toward the close of the century was as much a timely as a time-honored choice then, and that the painting served in some ways as an object of specifically contemporary interest.

The same Cézanne who believed fervently in working from nature loathed nude models, so he based the MoMA *Bather* on a stock photograph of a male model, while substituting a head reminiscent of his then thirteen-year-old son, and adapting from another of his own paintings the illogical, disproportionate, oddly generalized landscape. Cézanne contrived *The Bather* by recycling his own and other images, blending firsthand and cribbed experience into a fresh image without troubling to render the synthesis seamless. He contrived an overt pastiche, in short, a category that would happen to have special appeal to postmodern sensibilities . *The Bather*'s 'seams' emerge in its peculiar disjunctions. Barr pointed to the "fumbl[ing]" of "naturalistic scale," for one, which makes The Bather seem to rise "like a colossus who has just bestrode mountains and rivers"[9]—though the outsized figure who dominates both picture plane and landscape is, contradictorily, almost boyish in his internal proportions, and pathetic or defenseless-looking in posture and mien.

Considered in terms of exhibition design, *The Bather*'s suitability for its conspicuous location seems apparent: just as Rodin's pointing, striding, life-sized *John the Baptist* looked the part of a greeter poised at the threshold of the collection galleries, so could Cézanne's frontal *Bather* serve as a potential figure of identification for the arriving spectator. If the prospect of a fellow body is potentially orienting to visitors, however, there could also have been an instant of disorientation, for the inaugural figure museum-goers might have expected to encounter—the paradigmatic "display nude" of the late nineteenth and twentieth centuries—was not male, but female. The consigning of women to object status—whereas the central or authorizing subject of modernist practice has been, from the outset, a specifically or tacitly masculine subject—has served in recent decades as a topic for feminist analysis. In 1989, in a mischievous reading of MoMA's collection installation, Carol Duncan discerned a misogynist subtext in the placement of some notorious female icons, such as *Les Demoiselles d'Avignon* and de Kooning's *Woman I*.[10]

As feminist discourses evolved over the course of the 1970s and 1980s, increasing attention was paid to how men and women are differently socialized with regard to how they look, the dominant paradigm being that men may gaze at will whereas women are habituated to being looked at (and so to being enjoined to look appealing). A libidinal economy long accepted as so natural to modern visual culture as to be beneath comment—one in which the viewed figurative objects would be mostly female, the intended viewers, or voyeurs, heterosexual males (only females have "figures," after all)—was gradually denaturalized by activist critics. Once the privileged position of the voyeur became a target of critical inquiry, once the scrutinizer was vulnerable to scrutiny, his prerogatives were thereby undermined. In some feminist sectors, moreover, the call went out for an embargo against the depicted female body, and in some circles a strategy of turn-about as fair play emerged, as with Sylvia Sleigh's male odalisque paintings of the 1970s.

The decision to foreground a male nude as the first word in the late-century version of the Modern's master narrative bears examination, I think, against this expanding critical field. Varnedoe's showcasing of *The Bather* might possibly be construed, in part, as a sop to activist sensitivities about chronic exploitation of the female nude and the scarcity of comparable male objects—except that Cézanne hardly calculated his forlorn protagonist with a view to the erotic imagination of a female viewership. The morose-looking figure (his genitals sheltered by soft, pale briefs) was less fit as a compensatory object of desire for a late-twentieth-century feminist constituency than as a figure of identification for a pained or beset masculine one—beset in part by said feminists' interrogation of once-gratifying habits of looking, an interrogation linked to demands for gender parity, and so for ever greater social change.

Among the beset, early in his association with MoMA, was Varnedoe himself. A scion of privilege who became a very model of the efficacy of the storied "old boy's network," Varnedoe enjoyed a meteoric career, thanks to a series of powerful mentors—or would have been able to enjoy it freely had it not occurred at a moment when such cronyism was liable to feminist attack. Charges of paternalism were levied at (and within) the museum following Rubin's peremptory designation of the relatively inexperienced Varnedoe as his successor. The 1984 "'Primitivism'" show that Varnedoe worked on under Rubin's authority, and his first major show as department head, the 1990 "High and Low: Modern Art and Popular Culture" exhibition, both met with unusually scathing, and unusually high caliber, criticism. Unusual too, however, was the level of press attention to Varnedoe's person, to his "broodingly handsome" physique. In objectifying treatment more typically accorded attractive women, glamorizing photographs of the curator soon became routine in art world coverage. But a full-page celebrity ad of him modeling an expensive suit for Barneys' department store in 1988, just when MoMA announced his appointment, caused voluble consternation ("And the heavens opened," Varnedoe recalled) (Figure 13.2). On occasion, he was framed as one of a hyper-masculine pair with motorcycle buff Thomas Krens, a fellow Williams College alumnus who was anointed (in his case as Guggenheim Museum director) around

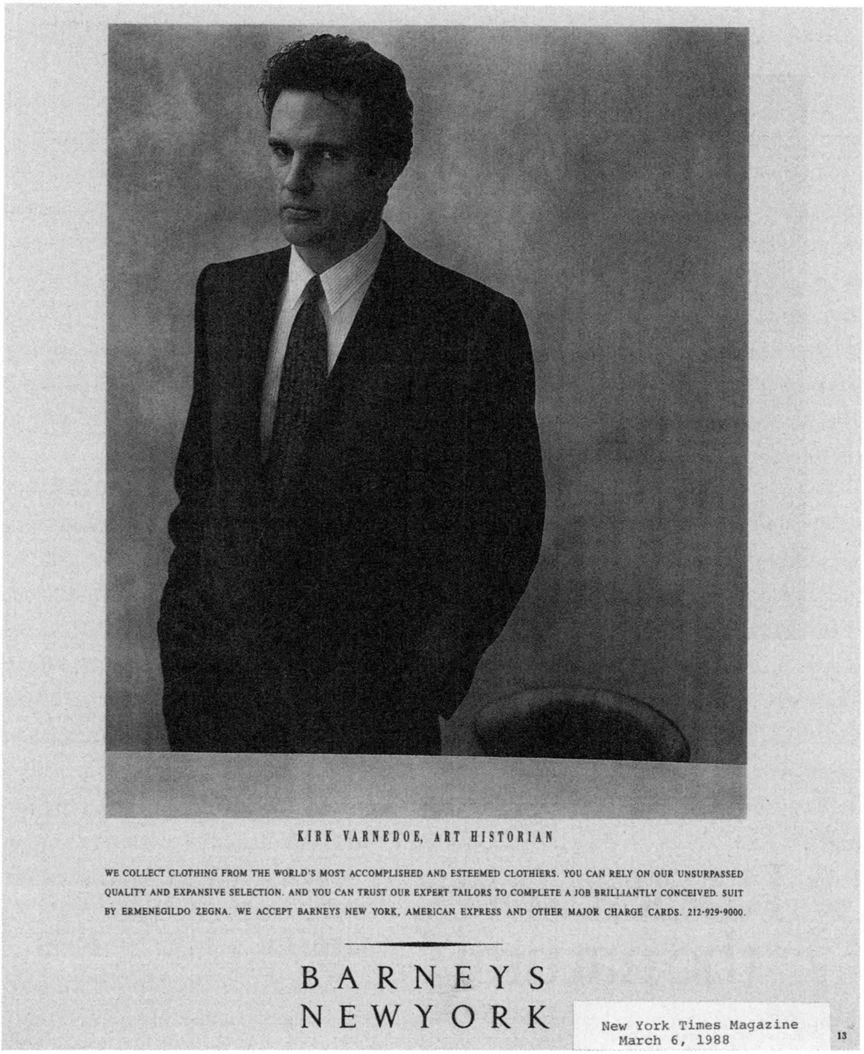


*Figure 13.2* Ad for Barneys New York, 1988. Courtesy of Barneys New York.

the same time as Varnedoe. Yet the *Times* dubbing Varnedoe "MoMA's Boy" might imply some latent doubts on this score; and indeed there was the bias against the art world as an effeminate (read: homosexual) province to overcome. Calvin Tomkins related how displays of athleticism by Varnedoe's college professors had helped to "take the curse of effeminacy off art history" for the young jock.[11] The mature Varnedoe's résumé would reportedly make it "difficult to know where art begins and football leaves off," listing a monograph he published on modern art, titled with a phrase drawn from rugby history ("A Fine Disregard"), alongside his rugby club memberships.[12]

The ideal of the male body in France during the late (nineteenth) century period when Cézanne produced the MoMA *Bather* was "ultra-virile," as a nation consumed by anxiety about emasculation, following defeat in the Franco–Prussian War, mustered a compensatory emphasis on physical exercise and masculine camaraderie.[13] An arms-akimbo posture conventionally signifies authority, defensiveness, or brashness, by bracing and broadening the span of the torso. Yet Cézanne's lonesome, glum figure seems nearly inert and almost torn; though his upper body is braced, his lower body seems to be in motion, and a slight torsion caused by the lag on his right side tugs against his (otherwise) full frontality and centered-ness. *The Bather* "stares tensely down at his feet, like a tightrope walker unsure where the next step will take him," Holland Cotter aptly observed.[14]

Kaja Silverman has pointed to war as one among other forces that may act to annihilate "the positivities of the masculine 'self'." By her (psychoanalytic) reasoning, delusion is a very condition of masculine existence: the delusion of the identity of the penis and the phallus, a delusion of mastery.[15] Maintaining that delusion necessitates the veiling of the phallus, whose very power derives from its being "imagined with symbolic proportions."[16] (*The Bather*'s genitals were of course hidden in conformity with the era's prohibition of full frontal male nudity, a ban that lifted significantly only under pressure from feminist and gay constituencies in the final decades of the twentieth century—a moment when men, such as Varnedoe, became subject to new kinds of public objectification.) The exigencies of wartime may serve to inflict on male consciousness a reality familiar as a matter of course to female consciousness, Silverman suggested: the reality of a lack of mastery, of castration in the Lacanian sense.

Cézanne was by all accounts a man uneasy in his skin, and even more uneasy with female flesh (which he never depicted on the scale of the MoMA *Bather*). Though he did marry and father a son, the painter's agonies over contact with others were legend: "Nobody will touch me . . . will get me in their clutches. Never! Never!" the aging artist screamed to Émile Bernard.[17] In his younger years, until the early 1870s, Cézanne repeatedly conjured fantastic, sexually violent imagery (which, like the Bathers, came newly to critical attention at the twentieth century's close), "scenes whose abiding themes and actions are structured by barely hidden equivalencies: murder and sex, stabbing and intercourse, the woman killed and the woman fucked."[18] The mature artist's fantasy life assumed other, sublimated guises: "I paint still-lifes," Cézanne told Renoir; "Women models frighten me. The sluts are always watching to catch you off your guard. You've got to be on the defensive all the time and the motif vanishes."[19]

Despite this piteous, visceral terror of human and sexual contact, in the summer of 1885, the year the MoMA *Bather* is believed to have been painted, in a possibly unique episode, Cézanne was overcome by desire for a particular, unidentified woman: "I saw you and you permitted me to embrace you; from that moment on a profound emotion has not ceased tormenting me," went the partial draft of a love letter inscribed on the back of a drawing. "You must excuse the liberty that a friend, tortured by anxiety, takes in writing to you . . . Why, I asked myself, should I suppress the cause of my agony?"[20] Cézanne's horror of women did not completely quell his yearning for them, then; and in that awful dilemma—of being "unable to look or to look away,"[21] of fearing the object of his longing—he might be understood as an embodiment (however extreme) of a contemporary masculine predicament.

Cézanne's late (nineteenth) century bathers and nudes resonated with late (twentieth) century ideological struggles over the sexed body, then. And as the opening word in MoMA's narrative of the modern canon, the *Bather* might be read as an utterance, if oblique, on a state of male dolor and oppression, on a hidden threat of female aggression. (The pairing of the Cézanne with the Rodin indirectly reinforced this thematic, inasmuch as *John the Baptist* would suffer decapitation for spurning Salome's advances.) In this light, the Modern's first word correlates tellingly with that of another late-century narrative of modernism, the one framed by T.J. Clark, whose "candidate for the beginning of modernism is *25 vendémiaire Year 2* (October 16, 1793, as it came to be known). That was the day a hastily completed painting by Jacques-Louis David, of Marat, the martyred hero of the Revolution . . . was released into the public realm"[22] (Figure 13.3). In rough outline uncannily like MoMA's inaugural image—though drawn from a prior historical juncture—the image Clark designated also depicts a slumped male bather, one whose pathetic state can (more directly than in the Cézanne) be associated with female predatoriness.

Practically speaking, MoMA must appoint specific objects to initiate its modernist narrative, whereas no such onus bears on the historian. By isolating a single object as inaugural of modernism, Clark made a willful, peremptory, and paternal gesture: marking Clark's locus of origin for Clark's modernism. "As a discourse, 'modernism' has, in part, a disciplinary function" and an "authorizing power," feminist historians have noted.[23] Fixed sites of origin were commonplaces of formerly prevalent "totalizing models of periodization," though trenchant critiques of such models had long since been mounted by the time of Clark's writing.[24] Regardless, Clark heralded the *Death of Marat* for its first-ness, on the grounds that it attests to the "impossibility of transcendence" and to the fact that "contingency rules," by bearing witness to "the accident and tendentiousness of politics in its picture of the world." By Clark's account, David's practice is animated by a tension between his "all-or-nothing sense of the real" and his determination to signify, to make of Marat both the symbolic embodiment of the Revolution and a Christlike

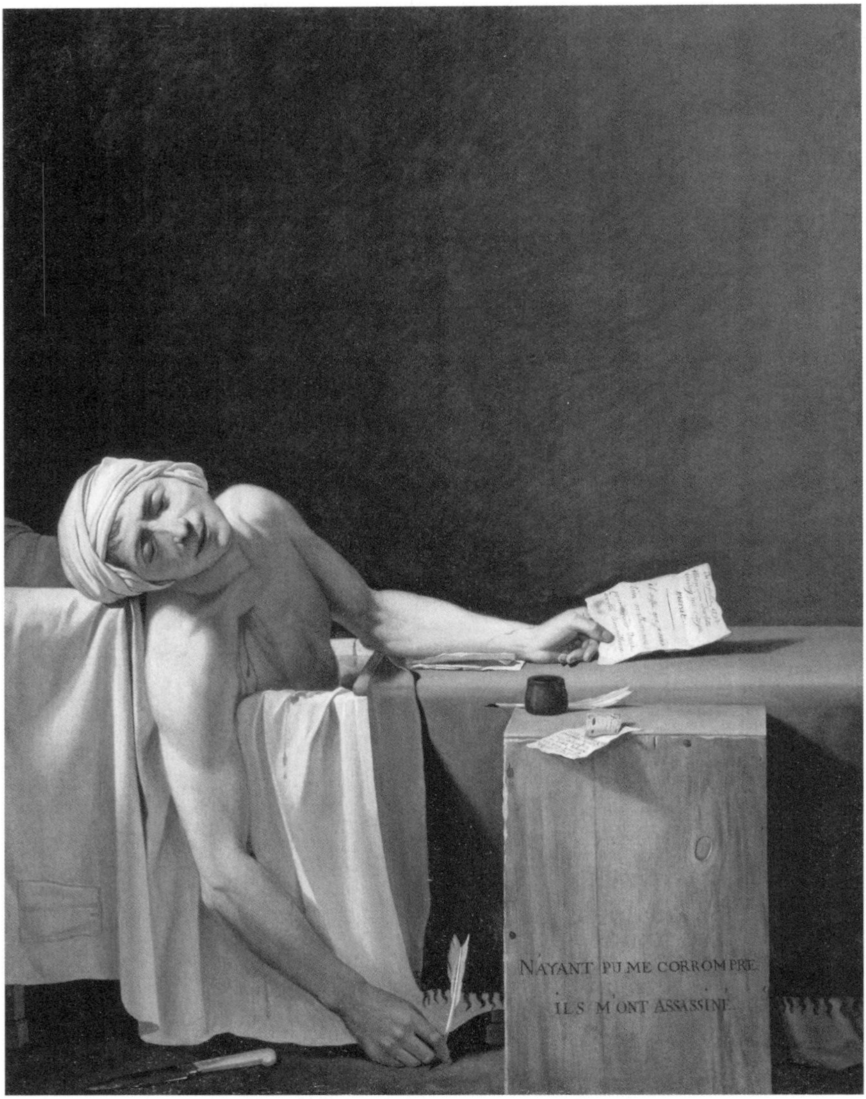


*Figure 13.3* Jacques-Louis David, *Death of Marat*, 1793. Louvre Museum. Photo courtesy of Art Resource.

martyr. Formally, Clark's arguments for the modernity of Marat pivot on its hauntingly vacant top half—the loose rendering of which he finds tantamount to "automatic writing"—and on the subtleties of David's images of writing. Indeed, it is specifically the missive rendered by Marat's hand—a missive that Clark deduces "the picture wants us to believe, is not writing at all—not like Charlotte Corday's patient establishment of every grammatical coordinate"—that Clark pinpoints as the picture's purest kernel of modernism, a locus of origin within the locus of origin.[25] Corday's "letter establishes truth and falsehood as what the picture mainly turns on . . . Corday's words are all true," Clark contends, before adding sinisterly: "It is what is in them, or behind them, that has to be rooted out—what may be hiding in their shadow. If you do not root it out soon enough you die."[26]

Since it is past time for warning Marat against his assassin, to whom does the "you" in Clark's imperative and terrorized sentence refer? In employing the present tense, Clark histrionically impels his (implicitly male?) readers to an act of identification with Marat—impels them to extirpate (feminine) treacheries lurking in the shadows on peril of their very lives. "What matters to the historical imagination, at least in the first instance, is how the actors . . . saw things," Clark believes; and so he would make historic matters vivid in the present day.[27] But the past is ineluctably constructed from a present perspective, in any case. And in the present, a renowned, adulated, at times reviled writer, long self-identified as a radical—that is, Clark—spins his readers a cautionary and sorrowful tale about another adulated and reviled radical writer, Marat, who met a grisly fate at the hands of a dissimulating, presumptuous, exceedingly willful woman. Presumptuous and willful women were of pressing concern in the Paris of 1793—indeed, "The climax of women's political influence was reached during six months of 1793 when women formed a radical group exclusively for women"[28]—but they were positively legion and unstoppable two centuries later, at a time when the women's movement was reaping the fruits of three decades of struggle.

Clark's singling out, as uniquely representative, an image from 1793 of a man outfoxed and undone by a woman might be said to occlude an opposite moment to that year, however, as a date when the French government, decreeing all women's clubs and associations illegal, categorically prohibited women "from active *and* passive participation in the political sphere": a date when men as a class acted to undo women as a class.[29] In the revolutionary credo, "liberty, equality, fraternity," the final term meant "exactly what it says—'brotherhood.' . . . In modern 'fraternal' discourse, like the specifically patriarchal ones that precede it, women are treated as the objects or recipients of policy decisions rather than full participants in them," observe Rosemary Pringle and Sophie Watson. It follows that, "What feminists are confronted with is not a state that represents 'men's interests' as against women's, but government conducted as if men's interests are the only ones that exist."[30] The same year that Corday was executed, 1793, so too was the pioneering feminist Olympe de Gouges. Feminist scholars generally point to a fundamentally conflictive relation between feminism and republicanism, whereby the Republic was effectively "constructed against women, not just without them," in Joan Landes's phrase. She observed:

> Despite the public silencing of women during the Revolution, however, it was then that feminism acquired its modern shape and consciousness, 'as a reply to the refusal of both liberals and republicans to resolve the problem of women's civil and political subordination, and as an effort by women of diverse social backgrounds to participate in and to claim for their own the literary and political institutions of the revolutionary bourgeois public sphere.'[31]

Without reckoning with feminist perspectives on the revolutionary period, or with feminist critiques of extant theories of modernism; without referencing feminist readings of the *Death of Marat*, much less articulating his differences with them, Clark repairs to an endnote to adjudge the "reading[s] of the Marat in terms of Jacobin gender politics . . . I have come across" in peculiarly vituperative terms as "insufferably smug and schematic."[32] Clark effects a blanket erasure of feminist interventions in his topic area then—a gesture in a way parallel to David's erasure of Corday. Clark does mention (in the same protracted endnote) gender politics as entailed in Marat's death, while offhandedly universalizing what might be called a formulaically masculinist response to the case: "It hardly needs saying that the basic facts of Marat's assassination stir up all kinds of oedipal fears and wishes in those trying to represent them," Clark avers, while crediting a passage penned by the Marquis de Sade for "get[ting] that right."[33] "Soft and timid sex," read the pamphlet by "Citizen Sade":

> how can it be that delicate hands like yours have seized the dagger whetted by sedition? . . . Marat's barbarous assassin, like one of those hybrid creatures to whom the very terms male and female are not applicable, vomited from the jaws of hell to the despair of both sexes, belongs directly to neither . . . O too credulous artists—break this monster in pieces, trample her underfoot, disfigure her features . . . [34]

Thus did Sade hyperbolize a plaint heard elsewhere at the time, that in taking the law and the destiny of the state into her own hands, Corday had violated the natural order of the sexes. Herself impenetrable (she was posthumously determined to have been a virgin), she had brutally penetrated a man—one who indeed lacked some unmentionable body parts (owing to the virulent skin disease that would soon have killed him), and one who appears fairly emasculated in David's cosmeticized depiction.[35] Rather than "disfigure" Corday, David figured her strictly through the traces of her visit: the letter that gained her entry, the knife that inflicted the lethal cut, the slotlike stab wound trickling blood. Scholars often remark on David's distinctive act of erasure, but generally without pointing to a viewing subject position it opened up, notably for female viewers: that of Corday's place at the crime scene. What the art-historical patriarch, Clark, anxiously Freudianizes as an

Oedipal scenario holds other valences from a feminist vantage point, for contrary to that scenario, it is not a son, but a daughter who fells a vicious, tyrannical father.

Whereas David's tableau implicitly pits a female monster against a male saint, scholars have lately insisted that Corday's public identity, in her day and since, has seesawed between monster and saint just as has Marat's identity (with far more to recommend the former construction of his role).[36] And Tom Gretton observed that Corday's "premeditated and principled act" of murder conformed with certain of Marat's own "values: the exaltation of political violence, the personalisation of political conflict . . ."[37] The terms in which Corday was reviled in her day, moreover, might render her less alien than familiar, even sympathetic to a contemporary feminist public. An attack circulated by Assembly members charged, for instance, that

> Charlotte Corday was 25 years old, which is, according to our customs, almost an old maid, the more so with her mannish carriage and tomboyish stature . . . she had no fortune and lived a paltry existence with an old aunt; her head was full of books of every sort; . . . she avowed with an affectation which approached the ridiculous, that she had read everything, from *Tacitus* to *Portier de Chartreux*; a worthy *philosophiste*, she was without shame and modesty . . . sentimental love and its soft emotions no longer approach the heart of the woman who has the pretention to knowledge, to wit, to free-thought, to the politics of nations, who has a philosophic mania and who is eager to show it.[38]

If the *Death of Marat* inadvertently opens a position for feminist viewers, the *femme assassin* or *femme fatale* remains, nevertheless, a mixed proposition as a figure of identification for feminists. In an essay on "female sadists" (that examines the nineteenth-century novels of Rachilde), Rita Felski inquired rhetorically: "Given the vehemence of this identification with a principle of masculine power, it may be asked if there is anything liberating in the fantasy image of the cruel woman." Felski responds by pointing to an

> expansion of the symbolic field to acknowledge women's potential status as insurrectionary subjects through a usurpation of a traditionally masculine realm of intense and violent eroticism. As such, [female sadists] challenge one of our most persistent cultural taboos by exploring women's anger, violence, and desire for revenge.[39]

I have linked Clark's late twentieth-century singling out of David's late-eighteenth-century *Death of Marat* with MoMA's contemporaneous singling out of Cézanne's late-nineteenth-century *Bather* on the basis that these choices foregrounded a pathetic or vulnerable male as the very site of origin for modernism at moments when masculine privilege faced some degree of challenge or eclipse. Fins de siècle tend to be characterized as periods of particular social anxiety—all the more so that coinciding with the millennium. Parallels between successive (nineteenth and twentieth) fins de siècle have occurred to others beside myself; and some have pointed explicitly to the late nineteenth century as the locus of a crucial crisis in masculinity.[40] That any one historical moment was significantly more crisis-ridden than others for modern male subjects has rightly been questioned, however, by Abigail Solomon-Godeau: "judging from the range of periods that scholars and theorists have proposed for their particular masculine crises, it would seem that these crises . . . are closer to the rule than to the exception and are, in fact, recurring psychosocial phenomena." By this account, the spectacle of a dephallicized male "need not signal any breach in the actual workings of male power"; rather, as "Tania Modleski has argued, '. . . we need to consider the extent to which male power is actually consolidated through cycles of crisis and resolution, whereby men ultimately deal with the threat of female power by incorporating it.' "[41]

The disconsolate man has been from the first a stock figure of the modern period then. For his part, Clark adopts a disconsolate posture throughout his wistfully titled *Farewell to an Idea* (the 1999 book wherein he republished his 1994 essay on the *Marat*). Clark's goodbyes are directed not only at the best dreams of modernism, but also at those of Marxism, which turned into "a grisly secular messianism in the twentieth century." Nonetheless, "capitalism remains my Satan," the disenchanted Marxist theatrically avows.[42] Satan, hell, Armageddon, holocaust, horror, agony, monsters: this is the hyperbolic vocabulary Clark deploys in introducing his "Episodes from a History of Modernism." While he insists that his modernism is characterized by contingency rather than immanence or transcendence, the biblical, fire and brimstone locutions of Clark's Introduction and the defensively masterful rhetoric of the book as a whole reveal an author haunted by what one reviewer called his "loss of faith in any comprehensive explanatory paradigm,"[43] by the eclipse of master narratives. Clark emerges from his account of modernism as both raging patriarch and suffering son. "[T]he Oedipus complex is a son complex," Klaus Theweleit observed; ". . . And Oedipus is a suffering son (as is Jesus, or Siegfried). Strange how often a suffering son stands at the center of patriarchal religions, myths, art works, or scientific constructs."[44]

Some feminists suggest that pronounced displays of masculine suffering may be the lynchpin of a masculinist strategem; that "the appearance of weakness may be another ruse of power."[45] Barbara Johnson cannily observed that:

> Far from being the opposite of authority, victimhood would seem to be the most effective *model* for authority, particularly literary and cultural authority. It is not that the victim always gets to speak—far from it—but that the most highly valued speaker gets to claim victimhood.

What provokes resistance to feminism, by this account, is that in "substitut[ing] women's speech for women's silence . . . it interferes with the official structures of self-pity that keep patriarchal power in place . . ."[46]

Not to deny the realities of men's sufferings, of course. But white Western men especially—the more so those of affluence, riding high at the top of their professions, as is Clark, and was the late Varnedoe—have as a class enjoyed incredible power and privilege in the modern era (as in those prior). The representation of displays of masculine suffering as holding a pre-eminent truth content where modernism is concerned might be seen as diminishing other truths then—notably those concerning masculine privilege—and as occluding modernist art's countervailing role as an instrument of pleasure, often tailored for a masculine public. (To Matisse, for example, Clark devotes but a few, tortured phrases in an endnote: "I am not saying here that Matisse's paintings do not successfully give pleasure . . .," he hedges before proceeding to ventriloquize Matisse as musing, "'Can't possibly have *pleasure* in the twentieth century, now can we?'")[47] In the end, the disappointed view of modernism limned in the dismal picture of the modern era framed by Clark looks notably distorted to this white Western woman then. Not that I imagine that modernism did deliver on its best promises—promises which were hardly shaped with women's interests centrally in mind, in any case; nor that I am blind to the atrocities of the era. Rather, for women—as for people of color, formerly colonized peoples, and numerous other long secondarized constituencies—the modern era has not been one unending saga of worthy dreams denied, but a period when a modicum of dreams, even some wildly hopeful dreams, met with an increment of fulfillment. Some among us, far from being horribly disenchanted, after Clark's example, persist in a hard-won sense of agency then, and in heartened modes of thinking. Such thinking impelled so much of modernist art practice, after all—if not the woeful images Clark and Varnedoe vaunted as marking modernism's genesis.

## Acknowledgement

My thanks to Judy Sund and Helen Burnham for practical help.

## Notes

1 Norman Bryson, "Géricault and 'Masculinity'," in Bryson, Michael Ann Holly, Keith Moxey,eds., *Visual Culture* (Hanover, N.H.: University Press of New England, 1994) p. 258.
2 Arthur Lubow, "Re-Moderning," *New York Times Magazine* (October 3, 2004): 62, 121.
3 John Elderfield, "Introduction," *Painting and Sculpture at the Museum of Modern Art: 1880 to the Present* (New York: Museum of Modern Art, 2004) pp. 47, 48, 51, 53.
4 Roberta Smith, "Art Every Which Way but Straight Ahead," *New York Times* (November 21, 1999) sect. 2, p. 1. "[A]n air of tension and solemnity, often with suggestions of

the Christian ritual of baptism," is discerned in the Cézanne *Bathers* by Mary Louise Krumrine, *Paul Cézanne: The Bathers* (Museum of Fine Arts [Offentliche Kunstsammlung], Basel/Eidolon, 1989) p. 33.

5 Cited in *Cézanne in Perspective*, ed. Judith Wechsler (Englewood Cliffs, NJ: Prentice-Hall, 1975) pp. 131, 80.

6 Gerstle Mack, *Paul Cézanne* (New York: Alfred A. Knopf, 1936) p. 314.

7 Meyer Schapiro, cited in Wechsler, ed., *Cézanne in Perspective*, p. 136.

8 Krumrine, *Paul Cézanne*, pp. 278, 280.

9 Barr, cited in Sam Hunter *et al.*, *The Museum of Modern Art, New York* (New York: Harry N. Abrams, 1984) p. 46.

10 Carol Duncan, "The MoMA's Hot Mamas," reprinted in *The Aesthetics of Power* (New York: Cambridge University Press, 1993) pp. 189–207.

11 Calvin Tomkins, "The Modernist," *New Yorker*, November 5, 2001, pp. 79, 76, and passim.

12 William Grimes, "MoMA's Boy," *New York Times Magazine*, (March 11, 1990) p. 62.

13 Tamar Garb, "Masculinity, Muscularity and Modernity in Caillebotte's Male Figures," in Terry Smith, ed., *In Visible Touch* (Chicago, IL: University of Chicago Press, 1997) pp. 60, 61, 70.

14 Holland Cotter, "Housewarming Time For Good Old Friends," *New York Times* (November 19, 2004) E36.

15 Kaja Silverman, *Male Subjectivity at the Margins* (New York: Routledge, 1992) pp. 64–65, and Ch. 1 passim.

16 Mary Kelly, in Kelly and Terry Smith, "*Glora Patri*: A Conversation about Power, Sexuality, and War," in Smith, ed., *In Visible Touch*, p. 240.

17 Krumrine, *Paul Cézanne*, p. 257 note 75.

18 Robert Simon, "Cézanne and the Subject of Violence," *Art in America* 79(5) (May 1991): 135.

19 Cited in Meyer Schapiro, *Modern Art: Nineteenth and Twentieth Centuries* (New York: George Braziller, 1978) p. 30.

20 John Rewald, *Cézanne: A Biography* (New York: Harry N. Abrams, 1986) pp. 156–157.

21 Simon, "Cézanne," p. 135.

22 T.J. Clark, "Painting in the Year II," *Representations* 47 (summer 1994): 13.

23 Bridget Elliott and Jo-Ann Wallace, *Women Artists and Writers: Modernist (Im)Positionings* (London: Routledge, 1994) p. 15.

24 Rita Felski, *The Gender of Modernity* (Cambridge, MA: Harvard University Press, 1995) p. 26.

25 Clark, "Painting in the Year II" (a slightly revised version of the 1994 essay, cited above) in *Farewell to an Idea: Episodes from a History of Modernism* (New Haven, CT: Yale University Press, 1999) pp. 22, 18, 38, 34, 45, 43–44. Clark's formal arguments are of such an extreme fineness (as he admits, ibid., p. 46) that they beg to be made in front of the painting; I will not attempt to engage them here.

26 Ibid., p. 40. For contrary, and feminist readings of the painted letters in question, see Helen Weston, "The Corday-Marat Affair: No Place for a Woman," in William Vaughan and Weston, eds, *Jacques-Louis David's "Marat"* (Cambridge: Cambridge University Press, 2000) pp. 138–139, and Erica Rand, "Depoliticizing Women: Female Agency, the French Revolution, and the Art of Boucher and David," in Norma Broude and Mary D. Garrard, eds., *Reclaiming Female Agency: Feminist History After Postmodernism* (Berkeley, CA: University of California Press, 2005) pp. 143–157.

27 Clark, *Farewell*, p. 28.

28 Joan B. Landes, *Women and the Public Sphere in the Age of the French Revolution* (Ithaca, NY: Cornell University Press, 1988) p. 140.
29 Ibid., p. 147. Clark mentions this act of suppression, only to downplay it ("an obligatory trope in histories of the Revolution . . ." ) *Farewell*, p. 410 n. 9.
30 Rosemary Pringle and Sophie Watson (citing Carole Pateman), "Women's Interests and the Post-Structuralist State," in Michèle Barrett and Anne Phillips, eds., *Destabilizing Theory: Contemporary Feminist Debates* (Stanford, CA: Stanford University Press, 1992) pp. 56–57.
31 Landes, *Women*, pp. 94, 171, 169. Further, "the exclusion of women from the bourgeois public was not incidental but central to its incarnation," ibid., p. 7. And, "From the standpoint of women and their interests, enlightenment looks suspiciously like counterenlightenment, and revolution like counterrevolution," ibid., p. 204.
32 Clark, "Painting in the Year Two," p. 57 note 9. (In *Farewell*, Clark curbed his judgment to "smug and schematic," p. 410 note 9.)
33 Ibid.
34 Ibid., p. 18. The "idea of woman-man as monster came to dominate much of the thinking by male revolutionaries about women in the public sphere," observed Lynn Hunt, *The Family Romance of the French Revolution* (Berkeley, CA: University of California Press, 1992) p. 91.
35 Clark proffers an oddly rapturous description of Marat's visage, "Miniaturized, and robbed of the normal signs of masculinity. Fragile as an eggshell, but of course invulnerable. How touching the wisps of hair on the forehead! How heavy the eyelids and delicate the mouth! How accidental your kindest kiss." (Whose kindest kiss?), Clark, *Farewell*, pp. 36–37.
36 William Vaughan and Helen Weston, "Introduction," in *David's "Marat,"* p. 18. As the most fervid spokesman of the Jacobin revolutionary faction, and a friend of Robespierre, Marat was a supporter of the Reign of Terror, endorsing mob violence as a force for social change and espousing liberal use of the death penalty. "Marat could not be made to embody the revolution because no one agreed about what the revolution was, least of all about whether Marat was its Jesus or its Lucifer. David's picture—this is what makes it inaugural of modernism—tries to ingest this disagreement, and make it part of a new cult object," Clark, *Farewell*, p. 38.
37 Tom Gretton, "*Marat, l'Ami du Peuple*, David: Love and Discipline in the Summer of '93," in Vaughan and Weston, eds., *David's "Marat,"* pp. 50–51.
38 Michael Marrinan, "Images and Ideas of Charlotte Corday: Texts and Contexts of an Assassination," *Arts* 54(8) (April 1980): 160–161.
39 Felski, *Gender*, pp. 192–193.
40 See, for example, Elaine Showalter, *Sexual Anarchy: Gender and Culture at the Fin de Siècle* (New York: Viking, 1990).
41 Abigail Solomon-Godeau, *Male Trouble: A Crisis in Representation* (London: Thames and Hudson, 1997) pp. 35, 38.
42 Clark, "Introduction," *Farewell*, pp. 7, 8.
43 David Joselit, "Contingency Plan," *Artforum* 37(9) (May 1999): 31.
44 Klaus Theweleit, *Male Fantasies*, vol. 1, trans. Stephen Conway (Minneapolis, MN: University of Minnesota Press, 1987) p. 299.
45 Solomon-Godeau, *Male Trouble*, p. 135.
46 Barbara Johnson, *The Feminist Difference* (Cambridge, MA: Harvard University Press, 1998) p. 153 (emphasis in original).
47 Clark, *Farewell*, p. 413 note 70 (emphasis in original).

Chapter 14

# Re-imagining meaning in the contemporary museum

## From things that go beep in the case to the artist ex machina

*Christopher R. Marshall*

### From the instructive cabinet to the enchanted environment

In late 1997 the director of one of Australia's oldest and largest state museums was perfectly happy to enter into the public record his intense dissatisfaction with most museums on the grounds that:

> I'm often bored out of my mind. I can't find where you eat, and when you do the food's lousy, it's never what I wanted. The shops are full of the same junk you find in shops everywhere else . . . You see things tucked behind glass which are communicated in a patronizing way in far too many words. Here I am, highly educated, with a great passion for life, and I'm bored. And so I walk out feeling guilty.

This director was just then putting the finishing touches to a grand alternative vision of the museum that was soon to be unveiled following a long period of redevelopment and relocation. When opened, this museum would above all else

> communicate the message that this is a different kind of museum, this museum is relevant. It's not a stuffy, smelly place with shutters where I bless myself and have to speak in a hushed voice. We are instead going to use soundscapes to create stories using this theatre. We can talk about early Aboriginal life if we want to or the early pioneers. We can talk about forest use issues or pollution issues. We can talk about anything we want to.[1]

In prompting these comments, over the course of a long interview for a background piece on the institution in question, I remember empathizing with this director's evident commitment to improving access and the visitor experience more generally. At the same time, though, I can also recall my misgivings about the seemingly iconoclastic aspects of his boldly new museological policy. It seemed, after all, to challenge so many of the foundational tenets of museums, particularly those emphasizing the primacy of long-term curatorial research into often specialized collections that were at one time understood as constituting the central point around which all museums should operate. As I write this though, following the opening of the museum, together with countless other institutions all inaugurated or substantially redeveloped in time for the millennium or shortly thereafter, I am struck by how commonplace these sentiments now sound. The sense of dissatisfaction with conventional displays, and a corresponding emphasis on supplementing or even replacing object-based exhibits with soundscapes or some other form of often interactive communications technology, for example, has become so standard as to feel almost normalized within museums. Comparable strategies can be seen effectively deployed in such diverse recent exhibition spaces as Swansea's National Waterfront Museum (where they enliven a complex narrative on the impact of the Industrial Revolution), or Singapore's Asian Civilisations Museum (where interactives and AV projections help to highlight the lived continuities informing the cultural artifacts kept for the most part behind cabinets) or even Alicante's Museo Arqueologico Provincial de Alicante (Marq) (where audiovisuals and soundtracks help to animate extensive archeological displays).[2]

It's worthwhile, then, reminding ourselves at the outset of this discussion of just how rapid and yet how simultaneously widespread, even ubiquitous, the process of global museological change has been over the past ten years, particularly as a result of the millennial period just passed. In the pages that follow I shall explore some of the implications created by the pleasurable, yet also precarious, ways that we are now being encouraged to experience museums as a result. Clearly, nothing can ever be certain in a world where "Museums never 'are.' They are always 'becoming,'" as one commentator has recently put it.[3] And nowhere is this constantly shifting field of ambiguities as well as possibilities more evident than in the field of multimedia and information communications technologies (ICT) in museums.

One clear trend that can be discerned from among the often frenetic recent developments along these lines is the increasing move away from the use of multimedia technologies as ends in themselves—as things that go beep, if you will—toward a more supple and subtle emphasis on using ICT and multimedia as one element only of a broader palette aimed at making the visitor experience more open-ended, creatively oriented, and even poetically artistic. This is currently emerging as a third phase in a long and rich history of multimedia and ICT usage in museums. To remind ourselves of the first stage, we might nominate the positivist belief in the sheer didactic power involved in the mere act of turning a crank or some other mechanistic process aimed at explicating an otherwise abstract or complex scientific or technological principle. This was followed by the more recent emphasis on sugaring the educational experience by making it less blandly didactic and more lively and entertaining instead—the interactive as edutainment experience, in other words, which has been such a strong feature of science and natural history museums throughout the 1980s and into the 1990s. The third phase, though, and one that has only really become clearly detectable over the past few years, is a trend toward replacing the notion of a more or less straightforward edutainment experience in favor of a more poetic or even mysteriously immersive museum environment.

This, it needs further to be recognized, grows out of a wider trend, in turn, toward moving beyond the rationalist, Enlightenment legacy of the traditional museum in favour of a return to an earlier model of the museum as a site of artistic evocation and even magic. This new approach is evident at all levels of current museological practice. It can be seen, for example, in the recent decision of the Museo Poldi Pezzoli in Milan to commission a contemporary sculptor, Arnaldo Pomodoro, to transform their Sala D'Armi of sixteenth-century European armor into an evocative site-specific environment fittingly described as "tra scultura e museo" in a recent publication.[4] It is also evident in the British Museum's 2003 exhibition, *The Museum of the Mind*, which broke with the conventional structure of a culture- or period-specific study in favour of a more far-reaching analysis of the complex processes of memory itself. It is equally detectable across the Atlantic in the interest in exploring the pre-history and afterlife of "magical" display technologies in the Getty's 2001 *Devices of Wonder* exhibition.[5] And it is also to the fore in yet more strictly academic studies, such as a recent anthology on *Science, Magic and Religion: The Ritual Processes of Museum Magic* jointly edited by Mary Bouquet and Nuno Porto from the universities of Utrecht and Coimbra respectively.[6] In all of these varied activities we can see what Stephen Bann has recently identified as a "return to curiosity" in museums.[7] Perhaps, though, we need to find an even stronger word to define this process of museums seeking to reconnect with their original power to induce reverie and even enchantment in the mind of the visitor. Within this new paradigm, the idea of the free spirit of the artist holds particular sway, as we shall see.

A vivid example of just what this new kind of museum might look like in practice comes in Daniel Libeskind's Imperial War Museum North (IWMN) at Salford Quays, Manchester (Figure 14.1). Opened in July 2002, the IWMN constitutes a radical departure from the standard "great battles and heavy weaponry" model of the traditional war museum (a departure that is made all the more apparent by its continuing contrast with the London branch of the Imperial War Museum which preserves, for the most part, a more traditional emphasis on object displays of artillery, aircraft, and the like).[8] Instead, the IWMN places a prime focus on the human consequences of war with a correspondingly greater emphasis on the internalization of conflict in the experiences of civilians and other non combatants: on women, children, as well as on personal narratives and explorations of the legacies of war. A standard chronology of warfare in the twentieth century has been

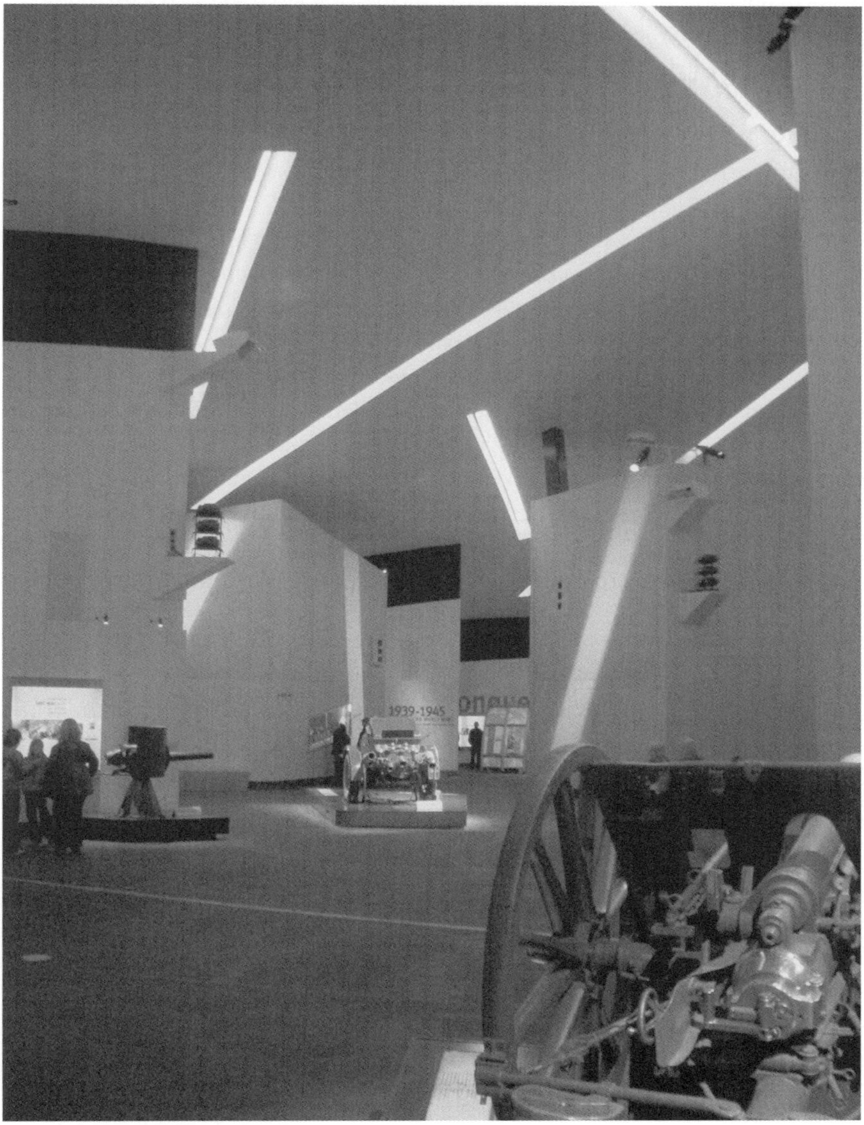


*Figure 14.1* Imperial War Museum North, view into main exhibition hall. Source: Author photo.

given a token prominence via a "timeline" of key periods that runs the length of the gallery perimeter. In practice, however, the experience of visiting the IWMN completely undermines this linear narrative as the traditional museological mainstays of chronology and static object displays are actively dissolved in favor of a much more free flowing and evocative, media-rich and immersive environment. This is particularly evident in a series of six large thematic displays scattered throughout the exhibition in semi-enclosed spaces called silos. Projecting onto the walls of these silos and onto the gallery spaces around them are a further three audiovisual presentations which periodically fill the entire exhibition space with a powerful sound and light show based for the most part on images held in the IWMN's extensive photographic archives.

Presiding over all of this is the persona of the architect who is presented at all times as the institution's creative muse and guiding spirit. The primacy of Libeskind's authorial voice in this respect is even spelt out by the IWMN's positioning of one of his quotations explaining his philosophy in the museum's entrance lobby. Even before reaching this point, though, the visitor has already been asked to pay tribute to the primacy of Libeskind's architectonic-iconographic program. The lobby is preceded by a towering neo-expressionist "air shard" which the visitor is encouraged to climb (much like climbing a cathedral tower, in fact) in order to first admire the building while also pondering Libeskind's central metaphor of the architecture as three interlinked shards symbolizing the globe broken into fragments representing war on land, in the air and on water (Figure 14.2). The architecture itself, then, is just as strong a component of the museum's programmatic narrative as the exhibits themselves—in fact, it is arguably even greater because it dominates the experience and provides a unity to the narrative that is often lacking elsewhere.

So it is that in this particularly insistent example of a widespread trend, the previously noted progression of the soberly didactic curator, as followed thereafter by the entertainment-savvy media provider, has now been replaced with the new paradigm of the artist ex machina—the fabulously creative individual who, in contrast to the more institutionally constrained curators themselves, is at liberty to offer up a much more personalized, creative outsider's perspective alongside that of an institutional one. This has the effect of freeing the museum from the shackles of either a bland objectivity or an overloaded institutional over-bearingness. In this instance it has offered Libeskind a chance to create, as he has put it elsewhere, "a building that was not only intelligently programmed for the events which were to take place in it, but one that moved the soul of the visitor toward a sometimes unexpected realization."[9]

So are we, then, "moved" by Libeskind's creative vision? Any visit to the IWMN will certainly be successful in prompting strong emotions in the visitor and even moments of freely associative poetic reverie. Yet in the race toward adopting such new strategies of display it should also not be forgotten that the model of the artist ex machina is not without its own difficulties, and this is true of the IWMN as well. In the first place, there is an evident ambivalence, or at least uncertainty, regarding the relationship of this new direction with the more traditional one represented by

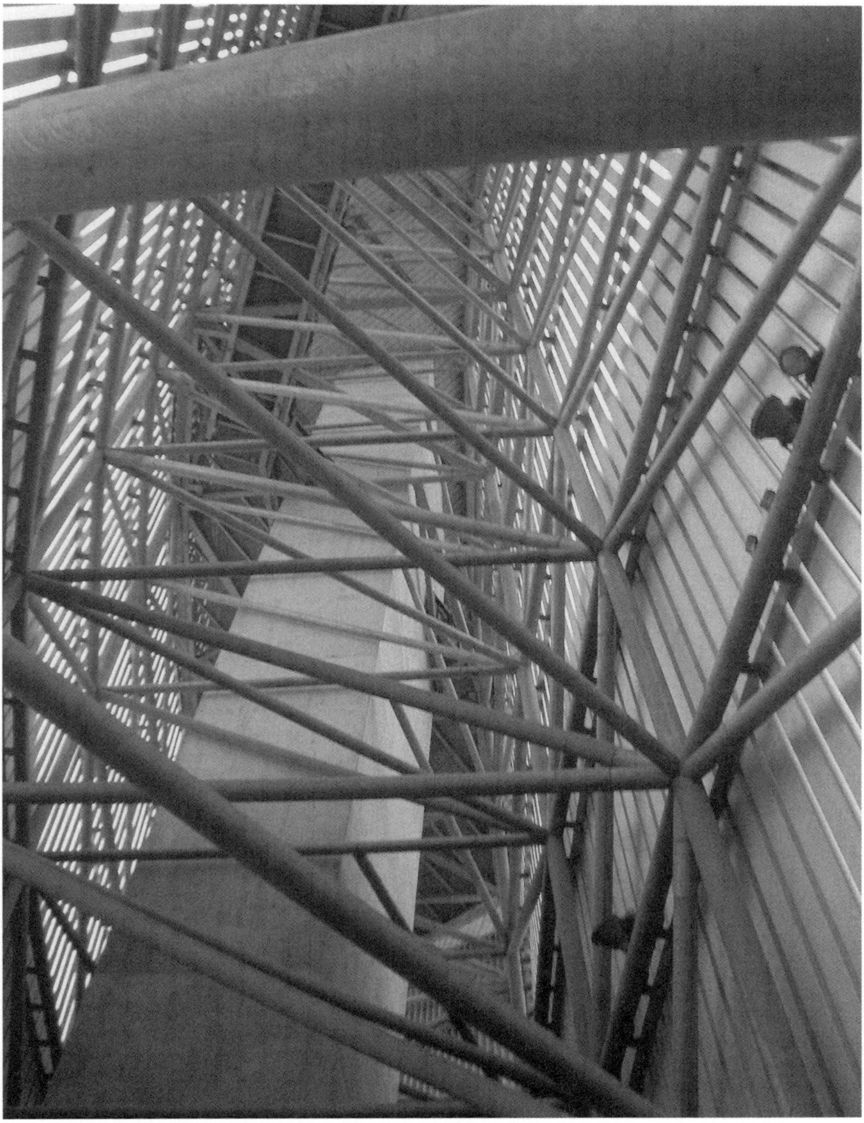

*Figure 14.2* Imperial War Museum North, entrance view toward air shard. Source: Author photo.

a handful of large "canonical" objects that have been allowed to appear in the IWMN's exhibition space.[10] In truth, these token examples of a tank, cannon, jump-jet and even a Trabant car, seem rather like afterthoughts. They are not meaningfully related either to themselves within the space as a whole or to the thematic displays around them. They accordingly appear more like theatrical props standing in the wings of the main event, as it were, rather than as key narrative components in their own right. Similarly, when it comes to the number of actual exhibits on display, there is not that much to see at the IWMN it has to be said, relative to a more traditional collections-based museum such as the Imperial War Museum London. A couple of hours spent wandering around the silos will probably be all that most visitors will require, which accordingly detracts from the museological imperative of stimulating in visitors a desire to return and then to return again in order to explore further that which could not be taken in during an initial visit.

The process of experiencing the IWMN is also in certain respects disappointing in that, for all its much-vaunted innovations, the result is an often curiously non-interactive experience. This is particularly true of the periodic audiovisual shows that literally overwrite the entire exhibition space for large portions of every hour. These presentations appear, in the first instance, rather old-fashioned, especially to an art historian, since they are essentially made up of massed banks of slide projectors bracketed high on the walls. And like any particularly overbearing after dinner slide show, they require visitors immediately to stop what that they were doing in order to sit down and take in the presentation. The result is a strangely passive experience—even one that induces a certain ennui in the midst of the architect's overwhelming spectacle of space, sound, and light.

Yet more fundamental, though, is the issue of the relationship of Libeskind's dominant authorial voice to what is—or perhaps what should have been—the equally clear communications message of the IWMN itself. It has been suggested that the emphasis on an individualistic artistic perspective might not have been appropriate to a space of this kind since it creates the risk of overwhelming or even sensationalizing such a sensitive subject matter. One commentator has even denounced the museum's emphasis on "an art gallery of the destruction-aesthetic."[11] It seems, then, that we have here a further instance of what I have discussed elsewhere as the potential for confusion that arises when visitors are presented with an innovative museum that acts, in effect, more like an individual artist in a contemporary art gallery than how a museum is (or perhaps we should now say was) supposed to act.[12] An obvious response to this would be to suggest that the confusion might derive, rather, from the conceptual limitations of those visitors themselves who are not able to countenance new roles for museums. Yet who is to say that it is the visitor, rather than the museum, that is mistaken in maintaining such expectations, particularly when we are in many ways still programmed in other contexts to expect museums to continue to provide authoritative institutional narratives based around significant artifacts?

All of which is intended to serve not so much as a critique of the IWMN in particular as rather a means of highlighting some of the more evident tensions that are involved in the model of the artist ex machina as it is so commonly evoked in museums today. Having identified these, then, I wish to turn, in the second part of the chapter, to an analysis of the different ways in which these tensions are currently being played out in three directly comparable national museums that are all located in the same capital city. This analysis might further help us to appreciate not only the real time complications created by these developments for visitors and curators alike, but also aid in sharpening our awareness of how different categories of museums are in themselves pre-programmed by their differing mandates to treat these issues in very different ways.

## Media, art and the search for "true identity" in an unreal city

Canberra, which serves as the political, administrative, and ceremonial capital of Australia, presents an especially apposite topic for such an analysis because there is something arguably museal about it to begin with. Like Brasilia or Washington, DC it stands as a classic instance of a planned capital that was chosen as a site for primarily symbolic and political purposes rather than for any previously established factors of commerce or settlement. It was selected at the beginning of the twentieth century—by a process of secret ballot—from a choice of locations that needed to be undeveloped and at least 250 kilometers away (or 150 miles) from the site of the first European settlement at Sydney. As a result it is still both much smaller in population (only 325,000, as compared with the 3.4 million of Melbourne or the nearly 4 million inhabitants of Sydney) and yet at the same time also more formally planned in an abstract ideal city sense than both its larger and older nearby state capitals. It accordingly stands somewhat apart from the rest of the Australian consciousness as an "unreal city," to use a phrase borrowed from T.S. Eliot and that has been adopted, in turn, to describe the city in a recent artists' journal.[13] This effect of unreality is enhanced by the contrast between the wide boulevards and giant axial links connecting different urban components with the city's surrounding pastures and rolling bush land, as well as by the grand ceremonial institutions proclaiming Canberra's "national" consciousness to the rest of Australia and the world.

Here in the north-east quadrant of a large triangular expanse that has been designated the "parliamentary zone" is the National Gallery of Australia (NGA). This is, in fact, one of the world's youngest national galleries, since it was only finally inaugurated, after many years of planning, as recently as 1982 (Figure 14.3).[14] In terms of its treatment of the issues we have been here describing, though, the NGA is of least interest for our purposes. This is in itself significant since, even though it is an art gallery, the NGA shares with other institutions of its type an inherently traditional approach to display that would make it profoundly mistrustful of the initiatives here discussed. The architecture sets the agenda for this in serving

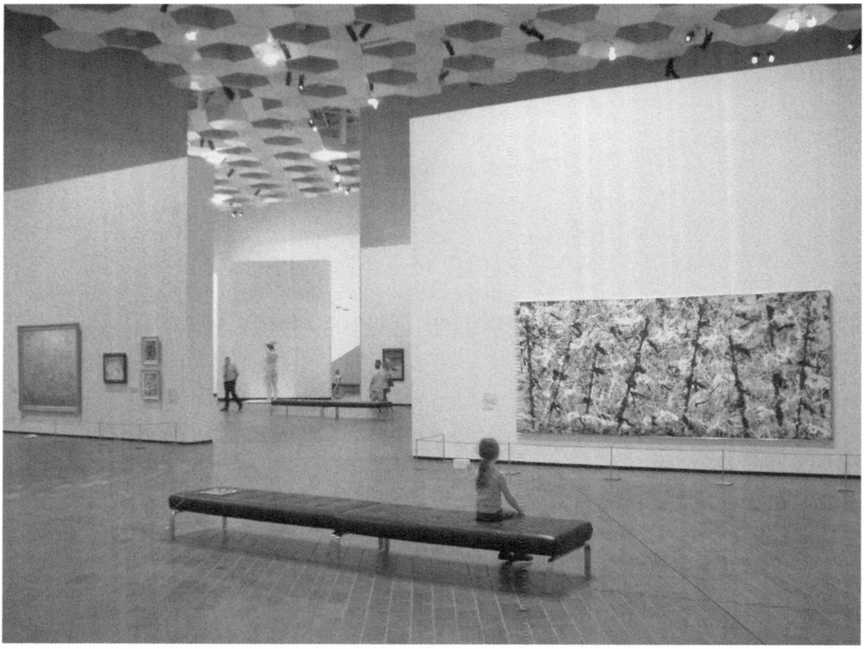

*Figure 14.3* National Gallery of Australia, view into ground floor European and American art galleries. Source: Author photo.

up a rigorously controlled suite of enfilade galleries whose right-angled purity contrasts utterly with the freedom and chaos of Libeskind's sloping floors, walls and diagonals. Even here, though, the architect, Colin Madigan's, slight digression from his template in adopting unusually lofty dimensions and high cathedral ceilings for the ground floor galleries has proven problematic for subsequent curators. Dissatisfaction with these spaces has resulted at various stages in the addition of coves at the top of the partition walls and in a decision to clad the lower sections of the main walls with white plaster in order to reassert a greater sense of a humanly proportioned, conventionally box-like, gallery interior, which now runs like a band along the lower portion of the galleries.[15]

The display of the permanent collection further reflects this in adopting a classically formalist, MoMA-like exhibition scheme that follows the standard divisions of region, period, and chronology. In like manner, information communications technologies are kept to a minimum, quarantined away from the galleries in the entrance lobby, and there are, of course, no interactives to be seen.[16] In these respects, though, the NGA is doing no more than reflecting the standard practices of nearly every other national gallery one could care to mention (and here I refer particularly to the mainstream model of the national gallery, rather than the more divergent display options that are often more available to dedicated contemporary art galleries, such as artist-run spaces, contemporary art centres and the like). The National Galleries of both London and Washington, DC, for example, have similarly placed their visitor computer centres in separate zones situated away from the artworks at either the beginning or the end of the visitor's circulation path. Similarly, although the NGA plays host to various artist-in-residence programs, and commissions site-specific work for temporary exhibitions from time to time, it has hardly ever commissioned artists to engage more critically and creatively with their spaces in ways comparable to those outlined above. An exception is a recent commission for a permanent environmental and sculptural installation by Fiona Hall, but it is surely significant to note here that the project began far less ambitiously, from the gallery's point of view, as a commission for a piece to be added to the gallery's sculpture garden. It was only following the artist's suggestion that the project was changed to incorporate instead "a discrete garden, more like landscape architecture than art" to be sited in a courtyard not otherwise reserved for artistic interventions.[17]

We should not, of course, be surprised by this. The NGA has, to put it bluntly, more than enough art to deal with, and its brief, in relative terms, is to offer up a more neutral frame around its precious aesthetic holdings than a history museum that is charged with interpreting ideas more forthrightly to the public via whatever objects or displays work most effectively for the topic at hand. Yet this obvious distinction also carries with it two fundamental implications that bear repeating in this context. In the first instance it creates the situation whereby public art galleries are, ironically, performing the least artistic role when it comes to the use of artistic effects to create new modes of curatorial interpretation and display. It also means that the NGA—and again this is true of almost all public galleries by definition—remains much more constrained when it comes to the imperative of communicating a sense of meaning and belonging to its visitors via an engagement with contemporary ideas and issues. It remains restricted, in other words, to retaining its traditional role of being a collecting institution with a primary role of being *about* what it collects, rather than a museum that seeks to use its collections as the basis for formalizing and articulating a deeper sense of meaning and identity *for* a particular community.[18]

This more complex role has been relegated, instead, to the national social and natural history museum that is situated on the Acton Peninsula some half a kilometre (or a quarter of a mile)'s distance from Canberra's central nodal point of Parliament House. The National Museum of Australia (NMA) is even younger than the NGA, having been planned formally only since 1980, approved for building in 1997, and opened to the public in March 2001.[19] Like Libeskind's IWMN (on whose work it is partly based, as we shall see) it thus stands as a particularly recent, aggressively contemporary version of a new museological institution in action. In keeping with recent trends, its architecture accordingly spurns the late 1970s Brutalist clarity of the NGA across the way. Drawing heavily on the new modeling possibilities created by recently developed architectural programs, it creates instead a determinedly eccentric series of angled, twisted, cut into, and burrowing forms that express the central metaphor of "tangled destinies" or, as put more theoretically by the principal architect, Howard Raggatt, that evoke an intersecting Boolean knot whose random and unpredictable junctures are intended to evoke the idea of the unpredictable flux of Australian union, intersection, and difference.[20]

This ambitious architectural program has been more than matched by the NMA's foundational aspirations. A vivid sense of these can be gained from comments made by its first Director, shortly prior to its opening:

> The rapid advances in media technologies during the last couple of decades allow museums to address their audiences in ways that dispel the notion of the audience as passive receivers of information. In developing the stories and programs for the museum it would be a serious mistake not to take advantage of the[se] opportunities . . . to find new ways to make messages relevant, engaging and fresh, and to use creatively developing virtual and multimedia technologies.
>
> In 2001, Australians will celebrate 100 years as a federated nation, and we will look to our past as a guide to lead us to a cooperative future. The National Museum of Australia will have a conspicuous role to play in illuminating these messages from the past, and we would be failing in our duty if we shied away from controversy and disagreement in pursuing this role. Active social and political debate about its past and future is vital to any healthy society, and the museum hopes to become a forum for such debate.[21]

The statements stress the importance of two interrelated issues for the NMA: first, the prominent role given to emerging multimedia and ICT technologies as a means of reinvigorating the exhibition experience and, second, the institution's willingness to embrace a complex and even contradictorily unresolved narrative concerning the contested nature of contemporary national identity. In terms of the first emphasis, then, it is certainly true to say that the completed galleries of the NMA have achieved an impressive level of media integration. Conventional object displays and graphics have been freely interspersed with a broad range of projected images, archival video, soundscapes, object theaters, interactives, and the like (Figure 14.4).[22] To enter the NMA is accordingly to feel very much plugged into an evolving form of media museum. No longer is the visitor asked to move through a more or less linear circuit of galleries articulating a progressively developing narrative of relatively fixed meaning, as they still are at the NGA, for example. Instead, we are offered a

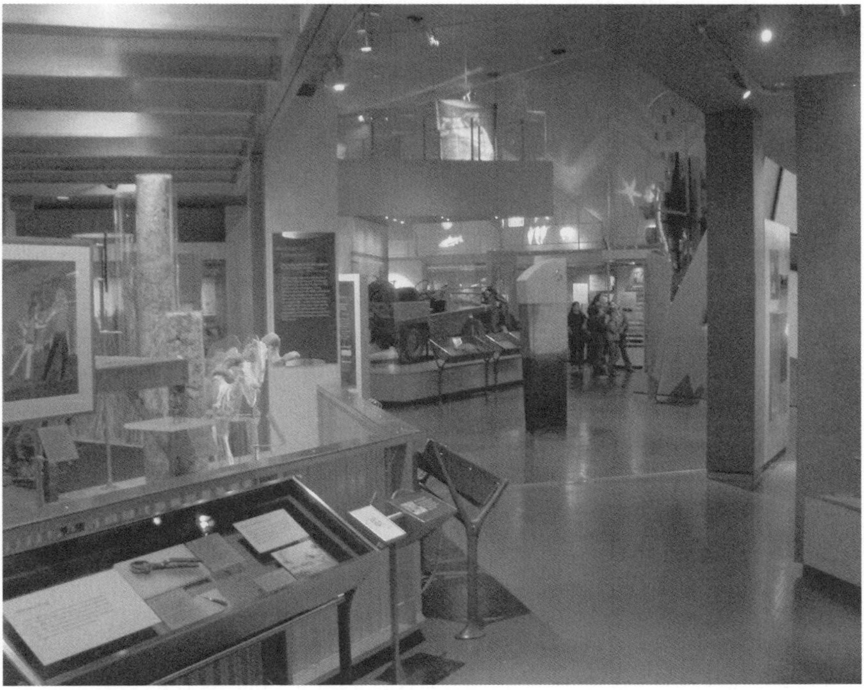

*Figure 14.4* National Museum of Australia, view into galleries. Source: Author photo.

kaleidoscopic barrage of visual and sensory impressions that move us toward a new type of visitor experience altogether. The visitor has, in effect, been cast into the role of late-night internet surfer moving through a darkened and seemingly randomly planned environment where the traditional hierarchies of space, distinction, and authorial distance no longer apply. In their place is an interwoven forest of thematically grouped text and imagery that has been cut and pasted together into a densely packed bricollage display that makes it often very difficult to choose on which element to focus. It is not difficult to see this process as being analogous, in turn, to the experience of clicking on the results of a particularly extensive google search or between multiply-tiled windows on a computer screen.

All of which succeeds in opening out the museum to new interpretive possibilities in a manner that is also becoming increasingly evident elsewhere around the globe (the galleries of Washington's recently instituted National Museum of the American Indian constitute another case in point). But it remains to be seen to what extent such a whole-hearted embrace of a non-linear, post-Enlightenment museum might actually match current visitor expectations. The National Museum of the American Indian is a further example since it has already been critiqued for its thematic emphasis and lack of a clear emphasis on historical chronology.[23] So too has the NMA sought to offset potential criticism along these same lines by inserting into its upper mezzanine a line of cabinets presenting a standard chronological timeline of Australian history. Since it remains unintegrated with the rest of the museum, however, this rather forlorn display can only manage, in the end, to underscore its own variance from the rest of the institution.

## High anxiety in the new museum

The opening of the NMA coincided with the centenary of Australian Federation in 2001. It thus found its messages being appraised against the often harsh glare of a wider reassessment of the national consciousness that occurred during this time. The poetically allusive symbolism of the building's architecture proved a particular focus for the ensuing controversy. A series of large braille words written onto the exterior walls were rumoured (without justification, it transpires) to contain coded references to the government's need to enact a formal treaty of reconciliation with present-day Aboriginal Australians.[24] This would have represented a highly contentious statement in light of the political context of a long-term conservative government who at that stage refused to recognize the need for such a process and who was accordingly adopting a much less conciliatory policy toward Aboriginal relations as a result. Yet more contentious still was the discovery, just prior to the museum's completion, that the floor plan of the Gallery of Aboriginal and Torres Straight Islander Peoples contained a partial quotation of the architectural footprint of Libeskind's Jewish Museum in Berlin. The architecture thus appeared to be drawing a direct analogy between the attempted genocide of the Jewish people during the Holocaust and historic relations between white and black Australia.[25] This ran even more counter to government policy since the Prime Minister was at that very moment refusing to acknowledge what he called the "black armband" view of Australian history and strenuously denying that anything like genocide had ever occurred. Clearly, then, these coded political statements can only have acted as a goad to a government that sat in parliament, it needs to be recalled, less than a mile's distance from the museum.

All of which soon led to charges of an elitist political bias at the NMA that led, in turn, to a call for a governmental review. Although the ensuing report did not thankfully return a finding of political bias against the institution, it did contribute to an overall turn of events against the NMA's founding philosophies. The contract of the inaugural director was not renewed in 2003 and the subsequent directorship has favored the adoption of a lower profile and less politically contentious path. This instance of the politicization of a museum is comparable in the American context to the controversy surrounding the *Enola Gay* exhibit at the Smithsonian, although arguably it was even more traumatic here since it involved an entire institution rather than a single exhibition.[26] An ongoing debate about these events will need to be undertaken before they can be seen to have been in any way constructively resolved.[27] For the present, though, it should be sufficient to note that they clearly underscore just how problematic the counter-institutional perspective can appear when it is embraced by both the institution as well as by the architect as artist who plays such a key role in defining the institution's message and overall orientation. An instructive contrast with all of this can be seen, if we turn now to our last point of comparison, in the context of a Canberra museum that has reflected, by contrast, a close and sustained parity between its own sense of identity and that of the wider political will that has sustained it.

The Australian War Memorial (AWM) has long maintained a privileged position in both the city's urban planning as well as in the deeper symbolic and political landscape that this planning so often evokes (Figure 14.5).[28] In this it stands well ahead of the relatively belated and marginalized NGA and NMA. It precedes them, in the first place, by a good half century (having been planned from the time of the First World War and eventually opened in 1941). It also enjoys a central position in the city's ceremonial orientation since it is situated as the culminating element of a vast perspectival axis running some four and a half kilometers, or nearly three miles, all the way from the AWM to the sites of both old and new Parliament Houses which are understood as forming, in turn, the city's symbolic and administrative dead centre. This axial linkage with the city's chief institutions is further underscored by the AWM's location in between the city's civic center, on one side, and the Royal Military College and Defence Academy, on the other. This last proximity particularly increases the charged nature of visiting the museum since it brings the visitor into contact with numerous military personnel all in uniform and all respectfully taking their hats off before entering the galleries or ceremonial spaces. One could hardly imagine, therefore, an institution as deeply embedded within the mainstream national political and ideological psyche as the AWM so clearly is.

The reason for this is that the AWM has come over the decades to encapsulate the quintessential foundation story of the traditional Australian national consciousness.[29] The modern Australian nation was born, so this narrative goes, fourteen years after Federation during the First World War when the Australian and New Zealand Expeditionary Force (nicknamed the ANZACs) fought for the first time for this newly won democratic consciousness over the course of a long and ultimately unsuccessful engagement with the Turkish forces at Gallipoli. Australia thus discovered its modern identity in the crucible of battle and sacrifice that came thereafter to symbolize the essential lineaments of the nation's character—resourcefulness, bravery tempered with stoicism, and above all else a central concern to look after your fellows—mateship—as it is known.[30] Both later and earlier wars were subsequently grafted onto this narrative in order to create

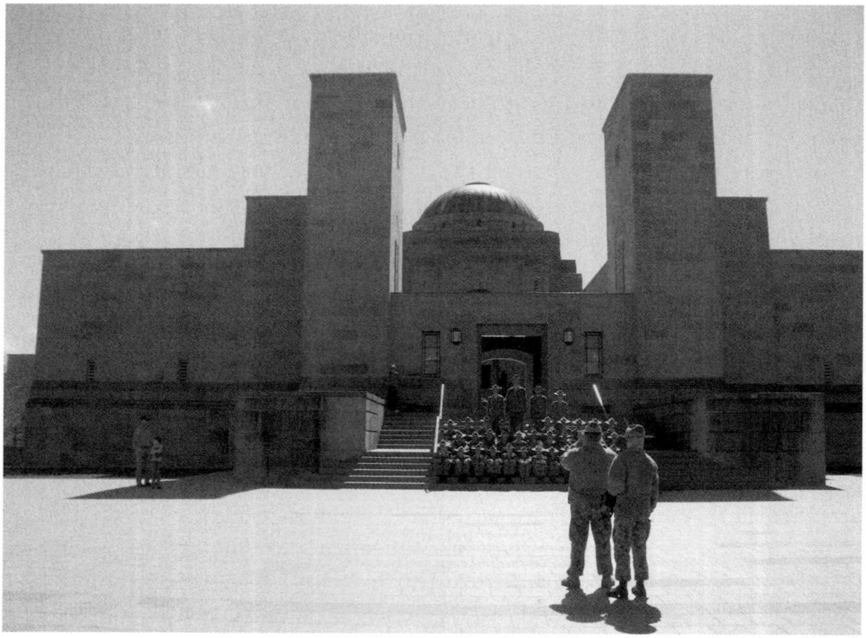

*Figure 14.5* The Australian War Memorial. Source: Author photo.

in the AWM a vast combined shrine, archive, and museum dedicated to the struggles of Australian service men and women during all periods of conflict.

Clearly, then, the AWM represents much more than a "mere" museum. As such, it has always drawn heavily on the symbolic power of art to advance its message. In this it acts as a significant precursor to the interest in harnessing the creative possibilities of more artistic modes of address that we have been discussing here. What makes it so unusual, though, perhaps even unique relative to more recent examples, is the extraordinary degree of convergence that it has been able to achieve between its own expressions of meaning and identity and those of the artists it has employed. The two have become virtually synonymous, in fact, because the vast majority of art works made for the AWM was produced by individuals who served on active duty in the wars in question—either as official war artists or as former military personnel subsequently active as artists following the wars in question. This gave them a uniquely qualified perspective to follow and a complete commitment to their task and it resulted in an extraordinarily meticulous and prominent series of commissions for documentary artworks illustrating the wars.

Perhaps most distinctive in this respect is an extensive series of very large dioramas which were commissioned—in many instances decades before the AWM

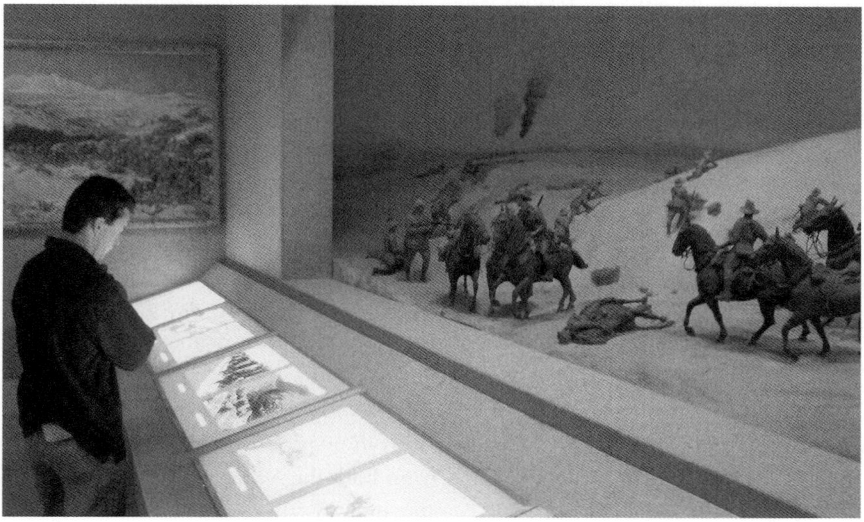

*Figure 14.6* The Romani diorama at the Australian War Memorial. Source: Author photo.

was opened—as three dimensional presentations of the main engagements in the principal theaters of war (Figure 14.6). These were based on extensive field studies of the sites and utilized the skills of many artists, who were all further identified as authors of the work in their early exhibitions. What is arguably most extraordinary is not so much that they were made in the first instance (although they are virtually without precedent in this respect). The idea of vividly reconstructing the events and terrain of far distant battles was, after all, especially important prior to the advent of color photography and during a period in which it was taken for granted that most Australians would not be able to travel to the sites themselves in order to gain an understanding and sense of connection with the places where, in so many instances, their own loved ones had fought or even died. What is yet more striking, rather, is that the dioramas have subsequently become so powerfully embedded within the AWM's own identity as significant artifactual items in their own right. They have accordingly attained an almost venerated status among visitors so that the vast majority is still to be seen prominently on display. This stands completely at odds, of course, with the wholehearted adoption of interactives and multimedia that has encouraged, in turn, the systematic removal of so many other equally painstakingly produced habitat dioramas in ethnographic and natural history museums throughout the world. One especially complex sequence of smaller window dioramas at the AWM, for example, each illustrating a different stage in the transport of supplies from the docks to the front-line, still preserves not only the eighty-year-old dioramas themselves but also their original frames and the very labels detailing in allusive, old-fashioned prose the significance of these activities for the wider war effort.

Within this setting, then, any attempt to modernize the displays would always need to be undertaken with care. This has been well understood by the architects, Denton Corker Marshall, in the most recent extension to the AWM, ANZAC Hall, which also opened in 2001 to coincide with the centenary of Federation (Figure 14.7). Rather than compete with the dioramas, ANZAC Hall supplements them by setting up its own space at the back of the main galleries. In 1941 the idea of augmenting traditional painting and sculpture galleries with a series of immense three dimensional landscapes populated by over-scale model figures set in animated poses must have also created a powerfully innovative and theatrical, immersive effect in the mind of the visitor. Here in a vast longitudinal hall Denton Corker Marshall and the AWM have updated this program by deploying new media in a darkened interior that has been enlivened throughout by dramatic sound and lighting effects. ANZAC Hall nonetheless differs greatly from both the NMA and the IWMN in its treatment of these elements. It is, in the first instance, much more formally structured and even sparing in its articulation of space than the at times chaotically cramped and over stimulatory semi-darkened environment of the NMA. It also

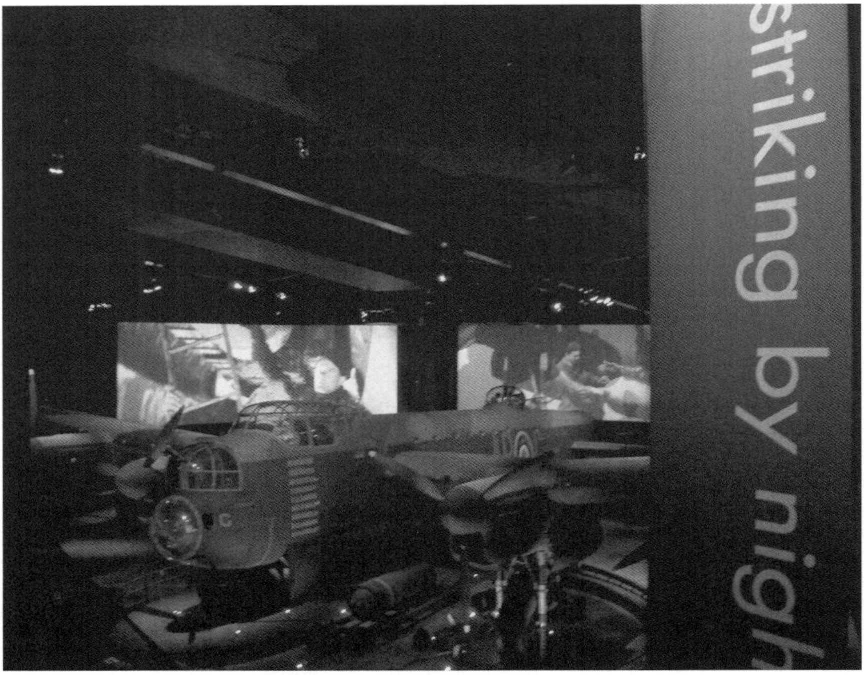


*Figure 14.7* The Australian War Memorial, ANZAC Hall. Source: Author photo.

contrasts with the sound and light overload of Libeskind's IWMN where, as was previously noted, a token scattering of objects are made to appear as rather half-hearted afterthoughts to the main media event. Here, instead, media remains at all times subordinate to the principal objective of animating the stories behind some of the AWM's major artifacts: a reconstructed Japanese midget submarine, for example, or a huge Lancaster bomber used on the night bombing raids on Germany during the closing stages of the Second World War. In the ANZAC Hall, then, the old galleries' immersive environments have been successfully updated with reference to new technologies which remain nonetheless very much in accord with the institution's original intentions and display technologies—one tank even has a painted backdrop that is reminiscent of the painted backgrounds to the dioramas themselves.

The previous account will have underscored the extent to which the AWM remains an inherently traditionalist and politically mainstream institution. This is particularly so if we recall the more contemporary emphases of the IWMN and NMA. There seems little space in the AWM's permanent galleries, for example, for the responses of women and children, let alone the more problematic political ramifications of war or even the alternative perspectives of enemy countries, all of which are approached rather more forthrightly at the IWMN. Yet our task in these pages has been not so much to judge the ideological directions of the institutions under examination as rather to consider the ways in which different categories of museum are themselves pre-programmed in terms of the degrees of what can and cannot be represented within them.

In this sense, then, we have found national history museums to be infinitely more experimental than national art galleries in their readiness to embrace new media and more artistic modes of address. At the same time, though, we have also found these institutions to be simultaneously less flexible when it comes to their ability to accommodate the more lateral implications raised by such initiatives. A significant contributing factor to this is the previously formed expectations that museum visitors will themselves bring to the task of engaging with the institutions in question. These will create often very specific viewing parameters leading to the acceptance—or otherwise—of initiatives along these lines. Visitors will no doubt take Fiona Hall's previously mentioned "discreet garden, more like landscape architecture than art," for example, completely in their stride, when viewing it in the context of its current location in the NGA. Hall's sculptural foray into the traditionally distinct field of landscape architecture certainly poses no particular problems and confounds no fundamental viewing expectations when placed in the courtyard of an art gallery. But will we, by contrast, prove equally as adept in accommodating the idea of landscape architecture crossing over into the realm of art when it is placed in a history museum? This is precisely what we have been asked to consider in the *Garden of Australian Dreams* that serves as the courtyard and centerpiece of the NMA. Here an extraordinarily innovative eruption of landscape architecture doubling as art has been created by the landscape architects, Room 4.1.3 (Figure 14.8). The result is a densely allusive and often very funny scale model of a symbolic landscape (a giant diorama, in fact) which comments on Indigenous and European traditions of mapping and, at least for the Europeans, of possessing the land.[31]

Part of what makes this piece so arresting is the way that it challenges our previously established categories of museum function and display. Just what is it exactly? A courtyard? A contemporary art installation? An adventure playground? An interactive exhibit? Or something else again? Of course it's all of this, and more. But this richness has only added to the perplexity with which it has been received by influential sections of the viewing public. The 2003 Report into the NMA, for example, rejected the *Garden*'s underlying artistic premise altogether. Instead, it recommended the addition of more clearly didactic exhibits—such as geological specimens and even, rather problematically, replicas of Aboriginal rock art. It also asked that the space revert to the more conventional role of a standard courtyard wherein "visitors can reflect quietly. More vegetation and shaded seating would make this space welcoming—a real garden."[32] But if some visitors have had difficulty relating to it, then it seems that even the institution itself has also experienced problems in accommodating some of its more challenging aspects. Thus signs have

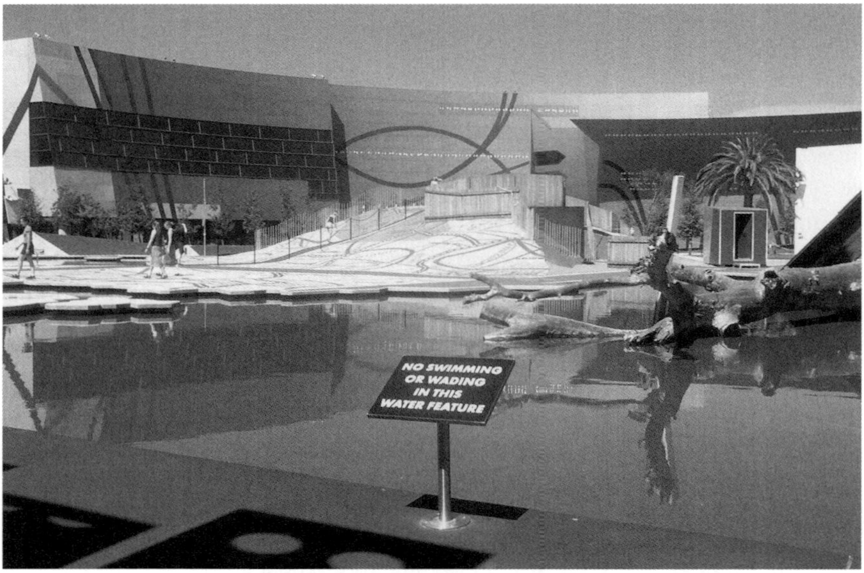


*Figure 14.8* The National Museum of Australia, *Garden of Australian Dreams*. Source: Author photo.

been duly installed to remind visitors that, even though this new form of display may appear to encourage an active and creative artistic response on our parts, it is ultimately, just a "water feature," which we are hereby expressly forbidden to wade in or swim in—no matter how blindingly hot the Canberra sun might become.

Perhaps, then, this odd moment of museological tension can serve as a fittingly emblematic note on which to conclude our analysis. What the museum appears to offer with one hand, it clearly in this instance has to snatch back with the other. In this it can be seen to be grappling in a still unresolved sense with all the often competing expectations and requirements that it is routinely expected to reconcile (such as, in this case, artistic expression versus the issues of visitor safety and insurance liability). For all its innate traditionalism, then, the AWM represents an admirable alternative model of an institution that has achieved a far greater integration and synchronicity between its own institutional settings and those of the artists and more recently derived artistic effects that it has deployed. What this might suggest, then, is that we should continue to build on the great potential of artists and the artistic-immersive approach to media usage more generally for what they can offer in the way of a more creatively lateral alternative perspective to the traditional ones still found in so many museums. The results—as are certainly evident at both the IWMN and NMA—can be in many respects stunning. But we should not perhaps overstretch the possibilities created by these new modes. We should not, in other words, expect the artist ex machina model to be able to effect a kind of belated "miracle resolution" of all the complex political and historical narratives inherent to the museum. The phrase, deus ex machina, which forms the basis of the artist ex machina model here discussed, is also instructive in this respect. Its usage carries with it an inbuilt recognition on the audience's part of the inherent improbability and credulity-straining nature of the miraculously descending piece of stagecraft brought in at the third and final act of the play to pluck an improbable resolution of the earlier narrative out of thin air. We should make the same recognition as we carry the concept over to our own setting and extend it to some of the more extreme and utopian projections of the artist ex machina model in contemporary museums. The use of this model, in other words, does not automatically cancel out the continuing tensions and restrictions inherent to the museum, be they functional, ideological, or those issuing from the pre-existing mindsets of museum users themselves. To believe otherwise is arguably to fall into the trap of creating elaborate constructions and projections that may, before too long, become as extinct as the dodo itself—or as extinct, we should perhaps rather say, as the dodo's diorama.

## Notes

1 Graham Morris cit. Christopher R. Marshall, "Dancing with the Dinosaurs: Graham Morris and the Museum of Victoria's Agenda for Change," *Art Monthly Australia*, 108 (April 1998): 5–6.

2 For the National Waterfront Museum see http://www.museumwales.ac.uk/en/swansea/; for the Asian Civilisations Museum see http://www.nhb.gov.sg/ACM; and for the Museo Arqueologico Provincial de Alicante see http://www.marqalicante.com/ (accessed July 1, 2006).

3 Peter H. Welsh, "Re-configuring Museums," *Museum Management and Curatorship*, 20(2) (2005): 106.

4 Vittorio Fagone, "Tra scultura e museo: Arnaldo Pomodoro e il nuovo allestimento della Sala d'Armi del Museo Poldi Pezzoli," in Carlotta Sembenelli, ed., *Arnaldo Pomodoro e il Museo Poldi Pezzoli: La Sala D'Armi* (Milan: Edizioni Olivares, 2004) pp. 32–43.

5 Barbara M. Stafford and Frances Terpak, eds., *Devices of Wonder: From the World in a Box to Images on a Screen*, exhibition catalog (J. Paul Getty Museum, Los Angeles, 2001–2002).

6 John Mack, *The Museum of the Mind: Art and Memory in World Cultures*, exhibition catalog (London: The British Museum Press, 2003); Mary Bouquet and Nuno Porto, eds, *Science, Magic and Religion: The Ritual Processes of Museum Magic* (New York and Oxford: Berghahn Books, 2005).

7 Stephen Bann, "The Return to Curiosity: Shifting Paradigms in Contemporary Museum Display," in Andrew McClellan, ed., *Art and its Publics: Museum Studies at the Millennium* (Oxford: Blackwell Publishing, 2003) pp. 117–130.

8 Although an important exception to this exists in the Permanent Holocaust Exhibition (1996–2000) eloquently designed by Stephen Greenberg and Bob Baxter, who also played a subsequently important role in planning the original exhibition master plan for the IWMN, for which see Stephen Greenberg, "The Vital Museum," in Suzanne MacLeod, ed., *Reshaping Museum Space: Architecture, Design, Exhibitions* (London and New York: Routledge, 2005) pp. 226–237.

9 Daniel Libeskind, "Conflict Resolution," *New Statesman* (June 24, 2002): 36.

10 As pointed out in a review by D. Martin, "Full Metal Jacket," *Museum Practice*, 7(3) (2002): 29.

11 Peter Blundell Jones, "War stories," *The Architectural Review*, 213(1271) (2003): 36–42 which also cites the criticism of Hanno Rauterberg, "Geniessen Sie die Aussicht," *Die Zelt* (February 14, 2002): 40.

12 Christopher R. Marshall, "When Worlds Collide: The Contemporary Museum as Art Gallery," Suzanne MacLeod, ed., *Reshaping Museum Space: Architecture, Design, Exhibitions* (London and New York: Routledge, 2005) pp. 170–184.

13 In a journal of that title published by the Canberra Contemporary Art Space, for which see Sylvia Kleinert, "Unreal Cities: Real Utopias," *Unreal City* 1(3) (1990): i–v.

14 http://www.nga.gov.au/ (accessed July 1, 2006). For historical background see James Mollison and Laura Murray, eds, *Australian National Gallery: An Introduction* (Canberra: Australian National Gallery, 1982); and Pauline Green, ed., *Building the Collection* (Canberra: National Gallery of Australia, 2003).

15 Robert Bell, "Crystal Clear: The Architecture of the National Gallery," in Green, *Building the Collection*, p. 343.

16 Although the NGA did experiment with a thematic hang for a temporary reinstallation of the permanent collection, entitled *Art Metropolis*, timed to coincide with the gallery's twenty-year celebrations.

17 Harijs Piekalns, "Fiona Hall's Fern Garden" in P. Green, ed., *Building the Collection* (Canberra: National Gallery of Australia, 2003) p. 333.

18 Stephen E. Weil, "From Being *About* Something to Being *For* Somebody" in his *Making Museums Matter* (Washington and London: Smithsonian Institution Press, 2002) pp. 28–52; and, for a discussion of the changed roles and responsibilities of national

museums with particular reference to the Australian museums here discussed, see further Graeme Davison, "What Should a National Museum Do? Learning from the World," in Marilyn Lake, ed., *Memory, Monuments and Museums: The Past in the Present* (Melbourne: Melbourne University Press, 2006) pp. 91–109.

19 Thérèse Weber, ed., *Land, Nation, People: Stories from the National Museum of Australia* (Canberra: National Museum of Australia Press, 2004).

20 Howard Raggatt, "Visible and Invisible Space," in Dimity Reed, ed., *Tangled Destinies: National Museum of Australia* (Melbourne: The Images Publishing Group, 2001) pp. 32–49.

21 Dawn Casey, "The National Museum of Australia: Exploring the Past, Illuminating the Present and Imagining the Future," in Darryl McIntyre and Kirsten Wehner, eds, *National Museums: Negotiating History* (Canberra: National Museum of Australia, 2001) pp. 3 and 9.

22 For an account of the design of the NMA's exhibition spaces see Andrew Anway and W. Scott Guerin, "A Complicated Story," in Reed, *Tangled Destinies,* pp. 160–167.

23 Mark G. Hirsh, exhibition script editor, National Museum of the American Indian cit., "Newcomers to the National Mall: The National Museum of the American Indian," *Organization of American Historians Newsletter*, 34/1, 2006, available at http://www.oah.org/pubs/nl/2006feb/hirsch.html. (accessed July 1, 2006).

24 Patrick McDonald and Emma Kibble, "No Apology in Braille Phrases," *The Advertiser*, (March 26, 2001): 20.

25 Piers Ackerman, "Museum Is an Originalimitation," *The Sunday Telegraph* (April 8, 2001): 97.

26 For the *Enola Gay* debate see Ken Arnold, "Balancing Acts: Science, Enola Gay and the History Wars at the Smithsonian," in Sharon Macdonald, ed., *The Politics of Display: Museums, Science, Culture* (London and New York: Routledge, 1998); and Steven C. Dubin, "Battle Royal: The Final Mission of the Enola Gay," in his, *Displays of Power: Memory and Amnesia in the American Museum* (New York: New York University Press, 1999).

27 For an overview of the NMA within the context of the 2001 "history wars" see Stuart Macintyre and Anna Clark, *The History Wars* (Melbourne: Melbourne University Press, 2004) particularly pp. 191–215. For an account of the controversy from the point of view of the foundation director, see Dawn Casey, "Reflections of a National Museum Director," in Marilyn Lake, ed., *Memory, Monuments and Museums: The Past in the Present* (Melbourne: Melbourne University Press, 2006) pp. 110–123.

28 For the symbolic and ceremonial roles of Canberra see David Headon, *The Symbolic Role of the National Capital: From Colonial Argument to 21st Century Ideals* (Canberra: National Capital Authority, 2003); and National Capital Authority, *The Griffin Legacy: Canberra, the Nation's Capital in the 21st Century* (Canberra: National Capital Authority, 2004).

29 Michael McKernan, *Here is Their Spirit: A History of the Australian War Memorial, 1917–1990* (St. Lucia: University of Queensland Press in association with the Australian War Memorial, 1991); no author, *The Australian War Memorial: A Place to Remember* (Mascot: Bartel Publications, 2002).

30 For a recent official explanation of the ANZAC story see Jo Pillinger and Amy Hibberson, *ANZAC: A Day to Remember* (Canberra: Australian War Memorial, 1998). For the development of the ANZAC Day movement more generally see K.S. (Kenneth Stanley) Inglis, *Sacred Places: War Memorials in the Australian Landscape* (Melbourne: Melbourne University Press, 1999).

31 Richard Weller, ed., *Room 4. 1. 3.: Innovations in Landscape Architecture* (Philadelphia, PA: University of Pennsylvania Press, 2005) pp. 204–242.

32 John Carroll, Philip Jones, Richard Longes, and Patricia Vickers-Rich, *Review of the National Museum of Australia, Its Exhibitions and Public Programs: A Report to the Council of the National Museum of Australia* (Canberra: Department of Communications, Information Technology and the Arts, 2003) p. 38.

Chapter 15

# (Con)Testing resources

*Maureen Connor*

How is art history made? For an artist the question is complex—it records and reflects the legitimation process as it affects their contemporaries and themselves. In Andrea Fraser's *A Speech on Documenta* she describes art making as "a profession of social fantasy" in which "(t)he representative function of art as a class culture, and its ideological function as public culture is partly based on the enormity of the aspirations fostered by its producers . . ."[1] And making art history, which for an artist should perhaps be rephrased as making it into the official history of art (which could then be reduced simply to "making it") is part of this "enormity of aspirations." Traditionally, artists make the work and art historians, curators, and critics inscribe it into the canon—first through reviews in newspapers and art magazines, then in catalogs and books. Who decides what gets included in the accounts of each decade or movement as time passes? Or will such an approach even continue to be the way art history is documented? As one of the few artists whose writings are included in this anthology I follow a sequential and movement-based methodology in this essay even as I try to expand and disrupt such a model. Despite these goals perhaps I am still too dependent on existing forms of art history. After all I'm neither an art historian nor a theorist of critical or visual studies so what qualifies me to enter the discourse in this context? When an artist's legitimation traditionally depends upon the disinterested judgment of respected members of the field how does my description and contextualization of my own projects qualify as "making art history"?

Certainly since the early twentieth century artists have challenged the framework and structures used by the dominant class to define art. Although it has been well established that institutions that present art (museums, galleries, books, art journals, and magazines, etc.) contribute significantly to the meaning and value of the work they support there are many aspects of these contexts that remain unexamined. In the research presented in this essay I have restricted my field of inquiry to institutions whose primary function is to exhibit art, observing how the mechanisms of art function at the level of the mundane. Narrowing the field still further, I have focused on the attitudes and behavior of the staff of museums and similar exhibition spaces—an area of study which, up to now, has been largely overlooked in favor of examining other aspects of institutional relations.[2]

I begin with the premise that each such institution represents its particular version of art discourse and, based upon this assumption, infer that the same philosophy that determines exhibition policies is also reflected in hiring practices and workplace politics. Taking this perspective one step further I speculate that everyday staff relations and office politics have a greater impact on the presentation of art than has been considered. In this essay I will describe projects that investigate some of these dynamics as they exist within specific institutions. In addition, I will propose a somewhat expanded historical context through which these projects might be understood.

The research that has resulted in this essay began about eight years ago when I mistakenly received a catalog in my faculty mailbox. It is not unusual to get misdirected mail at any university but rarely is this lack of order and organization so serendipitous. The catalog, from a company called CRM Learning, offered "business and management training through award winning . . . training media to optimize workplace productivity." The cover featured a still from a video titled "The Attitude Virus: Curing Negativity in the Workplace" showing two men in maximum protection hazmat suits presumably decontaminating an "AV" infested office. Beneath the image the promotional blurb stated that "poor work attitudes are often more harmful than poor work skills. If there's gossip, misdirected anger or a lack of commitment, there's a good chance the virus has hit. [This video] provides the tools for vaccinating your organization . . ."[3]

I was both intrigued and repelled. Mostly I was surprised that such so-called learning materials even existed not to mention that people might take them seriously. From the looks of the video stills and the promotional language I imagined I might have stumbled upon an interesting new form of ready-made performance art. I thought about ordering one of the tapes but was deterred by the cost— $845 for purchase and $195 for rental—for a twenty-minute video!

Then, in the summer of 2000, as the opening date for a long-scheduled survey show of my work approached, the originating venue was in the depths of a crisis among its employees that made further planning and preparation almost impossible. When I heard from several staff members that the director had brought in a management-training consultant to help resolve the situation I began to consider making my own kind of intervention into the museum's workplace.

Although the consultant they had hired was entirely reputable by existing standards, it was obvious that he had produced negligible results and even some ridicule among the staff. And, while I hadn't yet watched CRM's videos, I had become aware of a variety of other references to workplace training—enough to make me suspect that a new and perhaps somewhat questionable profession was taking shape.[4]

My approach to the project was twofold: I wanted to see if I could find another way to work with the demoralized and uncooperative staff so as to avoid having to cancel the show and, in the process, raise some questions about the methods (and perhaps the ethics) of workplace training.

So I began an experiment: I decided to reserve a large portion of my allotted exhibition space for the use of the museum's staff and began discussing this possibility with each of the institution's fifty-two employees. I explained that I wanted to offer them gallery space and asked each of them if there was any way this might help solve their work related problems. I knew I was unable to offer them what they really needed: higher salaries, more autonomy, better benefits, but I could supply them with working conditions in which their needs were considered and, in some cases, even met, if only temporarily. In fact my focus on space and physical comfort was partly a ruse. My real interests lay in the social dynamics so I hoped discussions about physical space would also reveal interpersonal issues. And sometimes they did, occasionally to an overwhelming degree.

My response to the interviews was to create an installation, which I titled "Personnel", that offered an alternative to what a majority of the staff felt was a lack of privacy and personal space. The piece was designed as a simulacrum of a vacation retreat, with cabins, actually specially ordered garden sheds, placed in the galleries. Meant to be used by staff for meetings, breaks, and even naps, each cabin had furniture, borrowed from various young designers, that specified its possible uses: comfortable chairs (for reading), a cot (for napping), a desk (for doing work that required more concentration than the offices provided), etc. Projected onto the wall behind the sheds was a panoramic video image of a forest.

To provide a critical frame for these seemingly Utopian spaces I focused on the techniques and processes of workplace training. (In addition to the staff interviews my research for *Personnel* included viewing training videos as well as other materials from a variety of businesses and organizations offering workplace-oriented instruction.[5]) Using these and other sources I designed a video installation for one of the sheds that was a simulation of a museum surveillance station. A group of monitors played three-minute video loops made from museum surveillance footage that was interwoven with clips from the training films with topics ranging from conflict resolution to museum practices. Also included were short excerpts from Hollywood 'workplace' classics such as *Nine To Five*, *Working Girl*, and *His Gal Friday*.

I'm not sure how much my project contributed to the well-being of the staff in the end. In some ways it probably made their situation more difficult because it brought many previously hidden problems out in the open. The installation was never really used by most of the staff because the director imposed an implicit interdiction. And, although the individual spaces were private, the surrounding spaces were surveillable from the staff offices and hallways which overlooked the gallery—something I had egregiously failed to consider when designing the installation.

There were other unsuccessful aspects: I had hoped that staff would use the simulated "outdoor" spaces (as opposed to the interior of the cabins) for lunch or coffee. (I had included picnic tables and chaises longues.) In fact the lack of a comfortable place to gather had been another problem expressed by many staff members. But in addition to the disapproval conveyed to all staff who ventured into the installation, there was another prohibition— no eating or drinking allowed in the museum. When I pointed out that my work filled most of the museum and that I had no objection to having food in my installations, in fact I wanted to encourage it, the maintenance staff expressed concern about who would be responsible for keeping the spaces clean. I could say that these problems were symptoms of directorial and curatorial inflexibility as well as learned attitudes about appropriate behavior which museum professionals are trained to enforce. But in retrospect I view these difficulties as challenges not just to the professional practices of the museum staff but to my own behavior as well— challenges I had taken on as part of my role as workplace problem solver. Once my installation was complete I began, mostly unconsciously, to play the role of "artist," expecting the full support of the staff in whatever I considered necessary. (Before, I had been careful to take nothing for granted and to negotiate almost everything I needed.) Since I was no longer their advocate, the staff, also unconsciously, felt betrayed by my changed behavior. None of us realized that I had become complicit with the standard conventions of artist–curator interactions.

---

Clearly *Personnel* makes reference to and builds upon the work of many artists and theorists who have examined the institutions of art. The official story of institutional critique, at least as it has been constructed up to now, is well known— one might even say it is solidly institutionalized, even canonized by such influential art critics as Benjamin Buchloh and Douglas Crimp with a pantheon of equally institutionalized artists.[6] Since this history is so established it seems more useful to recount some of my own activities as they were informed and in some ways determined by other culturally significant concurrent events. In doing so I also hope to encourage a greater awareness of the broad range of experiences that exist in and also influence culture. I believe this approach might productively expand the parameters of an art discourse still mired in expectations and values that reinforce only a private, contemplative, aesthetic experience. Unfortunately it is too often the personal, repressed, or even unspeakable experiences that are considered the most instrumental to an artist's development while attention is rarely paid to their encounters with broader cultural conditions. Or if such information is allowed into the understanding of an artist's work it remains specifically biographical and seldom has an impact on the usually narrow range of events believed to define an art-historical movement. This is certainly the case with the development of the discourse that surrounds institutional critique.

I was exposed early on to the many challenges posed to the formal, traditionally aesthetic relationships contained within the discrete art object. Although minimalism is usually given credit for the first, post-Duchamp assault on the autonomous work of art, I was drawn to different anti-institutional practices such as Happenings, Fluxus, and other kinds of performance-based work.[7] The possibilities inherent in the idea of site specificity (another aspect of the 1960s paradigm shift also attributed to minimalism[8]) first began to reach me through a number of other encounters. Among these were my exposure to a series of highly immersive installations (then called environments) at the Architectural League,[9] the Joshua Light Shows at the Filmore East, and the participatory theatrics of anti-war demonstrations.

In the canonical version of art history, conceptual art is viewed as the primary manifestation of institutional critique. Although the list of conceptual art's most important practitioners is open to dispute critics mostly agree concerning the requirements for inclusion in what might be considered the 'classic' version.[10] First, the work responded directly to some aspect of minimalism, the particulars of which were often acknowledged by each artist elsewhere, in written form. (In fact many conceptual artists considered writing to be an important part of their practice.[11]) Ultimately, however, these artists rejected and abandoned minimalism's perceptual and architectural components because such work remained dependent upon traditional art venues, art criticism, and related institutions for its validation as art. Instead, the artists most consistent with the developing aesthetics of conceptual art worked to expose as well as oppose the invisible ideological mechanisms that define art. Also, at least nominally, they made an effort to make work that did not depend entirely on the conventions of exhibition but developed forms appropriate to alternative methods of distribution or reception.[12] Hans Haacke's *Gallery-Visitor's Profile* remains one of the most explicit examples of the latter. Using questionnaires to catalog information, which included the visitor's age, gender, religious belief, ethnicity, class, and occupation, he then used statistics to produce a portrait of the average gallery-goer. In this way his audience was instrumental in the production as well as the reception of the work, providing informational material individually, statistical data collectively, and, once the collected information was interpreted, viewing themselves as an ideological construct—the privileged group that constitutes the art audience.[13]

Although this narrative is quite convincing at the level of critique, it fails to account for the fact that it was impossible for such work to find an audience or to be understood in any context other than one that framed it as art.[14] In addition it leaves out any number of artists who were part of what Lucy Lippard termed the "dematerialization of the art object"[15] but do not fit this particular set of criteria. However, rather than question the arbitrary boundaries of such histories it is more productive to consider the legacy of conceptual art. In fact conceptual art's approach to art's institutions has had an impact on almost all subsequent art production, making practitioners conscious of the fact "that all art is dependent upon pre-established discursive structures and institutional conventions."[16]

In the early 1970s when I attended graduate school in Fine Arts at Pratt Institute Preston Heller and Andrew Menard, two founding members of the New York branch of the Art and Language Group, were fellow students. At that time they, together with Michael Corris, had joined Joseph Kosuth, Mel Ramsden, and Ian Burn to continue the development of one of the principal iterations of the aforementioned "classic" forms of conceptual art.[17] While I respected the radical nature of their work, I considered it much too narrow and circumscribed, and not only because it set parameters that excluded the inflatable fabric sculptures I was then making. In fact, work that challenged the formal limits of gender representation as mine did was soon recognized as another aspect of the assault on the established tenets of high modernism. Recalling my interactions with these artists now, it seems that we failed to fully understand the extent to which we were all on the same side in our rejection of the old formalist paradigm as well as in our desire for social transformation.[18]

For these reasons, as well as the fact that both minimalism and language-based conceptual art were quite male dominated, I continued to find other models of art's radical transformations more interesting, particularly performance art of all kinds.[19] As is well known there was a fast growing feminist movement in the art world of the early 1970s and many women artists adapted performance practices to express their sexual politics, especially those that referred to or represented mundane activities—an approach which had evolved from Happenings and Fluxus. (Although both of these movements were also largely male dominated, their ethos produced an atmosphere more open to women and gender disruption.)

At the same time that I became active in the feminist art movement I also sublet a loft space from Fluxus artists Alison Knowles and Dick Higgins.[20] They were both quite generous with information and support, introducing me to a network of artists and offering me many new opportunities. Among their immediate group the most significant figures for me were the artists Jean Dupuy and Olga Adorno[21] who played a major role in 1970s performance, organizing large thematic events that provided showcases for many young artists. The most meaningful of these occurred in 1978 when I was invited to perform at the wedding of Fluxus founder George Machiunas which took place shortly before his death from liver cancer. Interventions into ceremonies such as weddings and other ritualized social events were characteristic of the movement's interest in questioning the value of such traditions, and this event was quintessential Fluxus.[22]

---

Simultaneously high spirited and macabre, it was, perversely, a cross between wedding and funeral. The ceremony itself was performed twice, and although the first was not quite tragedy, the second, after the couple solemnly exchanged clothing, was certainly farce. All performances were meant to be erotic and mine was a kind of parody of a striptease titled *25 less* in which I removed twenty-five pairs of underpants, beginning with nineteenth-century pantaloons and gradually paring down to a final pair of lace bikinis. To counter the usual burlesque bump and grind with its gradually increasing exposure of flesh, I remained covered throughout in a modest, vintage Edwardian dress. Lifting the skirt with my left hand, which also clutched a large bundle of petticoats, I struggled out of the underpants. My right meanwhile, balanced a plate of raw eggs, all to the accompaniment of the surging, staccato, Balinese Gamelan Monkey Chant. Only two minutes long, the music paced my performance, limited its duration and made it seem more like a game show contest than a striptease as I raced to finish my task before the sound ran out, all while steadying the plate of eggs. I describe this piece at length because it represents not just my own version of Fluxus-Feminist performance but also suggests some of the possibilities of performance art, which was often combined with sexual politics to question traditional and cultural as well as art world institutions.

---

Probably the movement that had the most direct impact on the institutions and organizations that exhibit art, beginning in the early 1970s, involved activism rather than aesthetics.[23] If minimalists questioned the internal autonomy of the discrete art object, the Art Workers' Coalition (AWC) took on the "reform of the art institutions that oversaw the circulation, presentation and consumption of artworks."[24] In addition to making demands concerning such issues as artist's contracts and sales agreements with collectors, the AWC was active in determining the role of museum personnel within their institutions, participating in protests with curators and other employees that culminated in the unionization of MoMA's professional staff. As the first museum in the United States to unionize, the curators at MoMA took the lead in redefining their jobs, identifying more with artists and the creative process than with the wealthy and powerful members of their board.[25]

In a few short years this unprecedented union of artists and museum professionals would devolve into the conservative backlash of neo-expressionism and the cynical opportunism of "commodity" sculpture. Although it is beyond the scope of this essay to analyze this transition it is possible to focus on several key moments in which museums gradually shifted their support away from art that questions its institutions. In his book *On the Museum's Ruins* Douglas Crimp explores this issue by citing an interview with William Rubin, then director of MoMA's Department of Painting and Sculpture. Rubin wondered if conceptual art and earthworks could possibly represent the end of modernism because they might "want another environment (or should want it) . . . (or) another public."[26] By 1979, however, Rubin's "question had been withdrawn," replaced by a renewed interest in painting by most art institutions . . ."[27] It is no coincidence that this shift in direction, which demonstrated a move away from conceptual work, also represented the beginning of an unprecedented expansion of art's presentational institutions—museums, galleries, publications—with a concomitant demand for art professionals of all kinds, a demand that has continued to grow ever since.[28]

In the early 1990s, looking back at the previous decade, Andrea Fraser recognizes that there has been another "shift in the status, meaning and function of artistic activity." Theorizing this shift under the heading "Services" she notes that it includes a broad range of practices which had evolved from 1960s and early 1970s work that challenged the autonomous art object—site specificity, scatter art, etc. She goes on to classify such projects within an expanded set of terms that include community-based art, public art, context art, project art, and cultural production.[29] Calling attention to the proliferation of such "services," Fraser's aim is to explore some of the functions they perform in and for art institutions. Making clear that these projects are not similar thematically nor were the artists part of a new generation or movement, Fraser proposed that the call for such efforts was driven by other needs:

> (D)epending on the character of the given situation . . . (t)he demand for community based projects appeared to be related to a need by publicly funded organizations to satisfy the public service requirements of their funding agencies. The demand for institutional interventions . . . related to a need to engage artists in . . . a collaborative effort at public education and institutional reflection. The demand for projects in response to specific curatorial concepts could be related to a need on the part of curators and their organizations to induce the "usual suspects" to produce something special in the context of the exponential expansion of contemporary art venues—and thus exhibitions—in the 1980s, as well as of the corps of curators, swelled by the graduates of at least a half-dozen new curatorial training programs.[30]

If Fraser finds the new forms of "service" required of artists "troubling" and in need of interrogation, the mechanisms of such "project work" seem to overlap in even more disturbing ways with the contemporary corporate workplace. Andrew

Ross was the first of a number of theorists to point out that what were traditionally considered the privileged components of artistic production—creativity, autonomy, flexibility—have been transformed into tools to increase productivity and decrease labor costs. In the "new economy" bosses "routinely barter discount wages for creative satisfaction on the job."[31] Although it may seem obvious to trace this situation back to the development of supply side and trickle-down economics of the Chicago school in the 1970s and the subsequent policies of Reagan and Thatcher in the 1980s, theorist and artist Brian Holmes shows this cross pollination between business and art to be even more insidious. Pointing out that the anti-hierarchical approach to economic organization was a response to the 1960s revolt against "authoritarianism and standardization," he explains how neoliberal social policy experts capitalized on these values to exploit the "immaterial laborer(s)" of newly developing technological industries. By metamorphosing the specific anti-establishment qualities "that made the sixties 'hip'"—"authenticity, individuality, difference, rebellion"—into the perquisites of job description, neoliberals were able to instill "a new form of internalized vocation, a calling to creative self-fulfillment" that shaped and directed employee behavior. "It is a distorted form of the artistic revolt . . . the revolutionary energies which emerged in the Western societies in the 1960s, and which for a time seemed capable of transforming social relations."[32]

Thus, while business is able to extract more work for less pay by convincing workers that they have increased freedom and creativity, art institutions (which have always paid less by offering employees the cultural capital of association with the status of high art) now use the rationale of business models not just to organize fund-raising or to increase attendance but to instrumentalize artists. And artists, desperate for the legitimacy these institutions offer, not only sacrifice some of their autonomy to institutional interests, but do so in the context of projects whose lineage can be traced to conceptual art and, by implication, institutional critique.[33]

Neoliberal economic policies have also been supported by the new approaches to human resources and management consulting that led to *Personnel*. Although when I first began the project in 2000, it was only the first phase of the dot com bust, the firing of massive numbers of workers had already begun and corporate trainers were brought in as consultants to evaluate the effectiveness of the workforce (who should stay and who should go) and to help with the problems this created. This role traditionally belonged to personnel or human resource departments which, themselves, had already been downsized, hence corporate trainers emerged to fill the gap. As outside experts or "specialists" rather than co-workers, their practice carries the aura of a therapist—someone focused on the best interests of those involved—thus masking the fact that they are really there to deploy the demands of management and consider the bottom line.

Not all approaches to corporate training are as easily dismissed as "The Attitude Virus." At best the techniques of corporate trainers reflect the enforced optimism of self-help but sometimes their methodologies are much more manipulative and sinister. For example, Marshall Goldsmith, ranked among the top ten corporate coaches by *The Wall Street Journal*:

> subjects his clients to a brutal regimen: 360 degree feedback—he asks their colleagues . . . for comprehensive assessments of their strengths and defects . . . (then) he confronts them with what everybody really thinks. Then he makes them apologize and ask for help in getting better.[34]

While this approach may sound unnecessarily cruel it is apparently quite effective, especially for the most interpersonally challenged of Goldsmith's clients. Somehow, though, it seems to have given new form to more traditional modes of public humiliation. It might even be compared to the forced confessions of the Middle Ages, denouncements during China's Cultural Revolution, and the confronta-tional methods of the 1960s encounter group. (In fact Goldsmith got his start running encounter groups in Los Angeles.) Now, however, the willingness to submit to such psychological torture is neither for salvation nor social acceptance but rather a higher salary. And for the corporate managers paying Mr Goldsmith's bill the dollar value of behavioral control can be measured in terms of investment *with interest*.

As the *Personnel* project has evolved my relationship to some of these issues has changed as well. With the initial version my goal was primarily instrumental—a performative investigation of the problems of a particular institution with the hope of creating a more cooperative environment in which to produce my show. As my methods became more refined and my understanding of the problems deepened the project became broader. Now my interest is focused on the way value and legitimacy are determined and promoted in and by art institutions. In order to do this I adopt the role of workplace consultant but with contrasting strategies and values, tactics which owe a debt to Fluxus, the anti-war movement, and, yes, conceptual art. By using the tropes and techniques of human resources management but without their usual focus on the bottom line, I hope, by implication, to encourage staff members at art institutions to question the standard art world markers of status and legitimacy.

---

If the first installation of *Personnel* was geared specifically toward a troubled institution and adopted a primarily spatial/architectural and somewhat practical approach to mediating a variety of interpersonal workplace problems, the two subsequent versions which were held at venues with strong, dynamic programs were very different in both direction and form. Both of these were part of a traveling group exhibition titled *Indivisuals*, organized by Barcelona-based independent curator, Jorge Luis Marzo, which analyzed the complex relationships between technology, social space, and the individual. The exhibition premiered at the Mendel Art Gallery in Saskatoon, Saskatchewan, Canada, 2002 and traveled to the Fundació Tàpies in Barcelona, 2003.

The preparation for each version of *Personnel* for *Indivisuals* began with a visit to the exhibition's venue at which time I documented the space and interviewed the entire staff. My discussions with staff members took place in groups as well as individually and were geared toward drawing out as much information about the staff and its relationship to its institutional workplace as possible. I made it clear that staff comments were totally confidential and the only records I made consisted of handwritten notes.

I was much better prepared and organized for these interviews than I had been for the first version of *Personnel*. At this point many of my questions were derived from books on workplace design. Usually I began by asking participants to explain the primary functions of their institution, a question that often revealed information about each person's specific job as well as how they viewed themselves in relation to their workplace. Another important issue was the influence specific exhibitions have on staff attitudes: do some exhibitions affect them more positively or negatively than others? Additional topics for group and individual discussions were feelings about the space and its uses, its best and worst aspects, how each person would like to see it change.

At the Mendel Art Gallery, as with many Canadian museums, its remote location belied the sophistication of its staff and its connection to the international art community while reinforcing its role as a local and regional center of art and culture. Sometimes disagreements about how best to serve these disparate communities arose between staff members as well as among the museum's supporters. In this context it seemed necessary to develop a project that could enlist the entire staff as well as to engage the interest and curiosity of Mendel Art Gallery's public. So I decided to try an approach that differed in every way from the previous installation's focus on offering ostensibly practical if partial and temporary solutions to workplace problems.

I spent three days making a video of the Mendel staff as they went about their work at the museum but with a twist. On the first day everyone dressed up—the women in gowns and party clothes, the men in tuxedos and dress suits, all donated for the day by local clothing stores. On the second day everyone wore pajamas, nightgowns, robes, and slippers. On the third day everyone dressed in his or her normal work clothes. During this period I set up cameras in the offices and workrooms and recorded their activities.

As a group the Mendel staff were used to participating in artists' projects. Some staff members were quite enthusiastic about the process while others viewed it as more of a nuisance or a distraction. Many of those with a skeptical

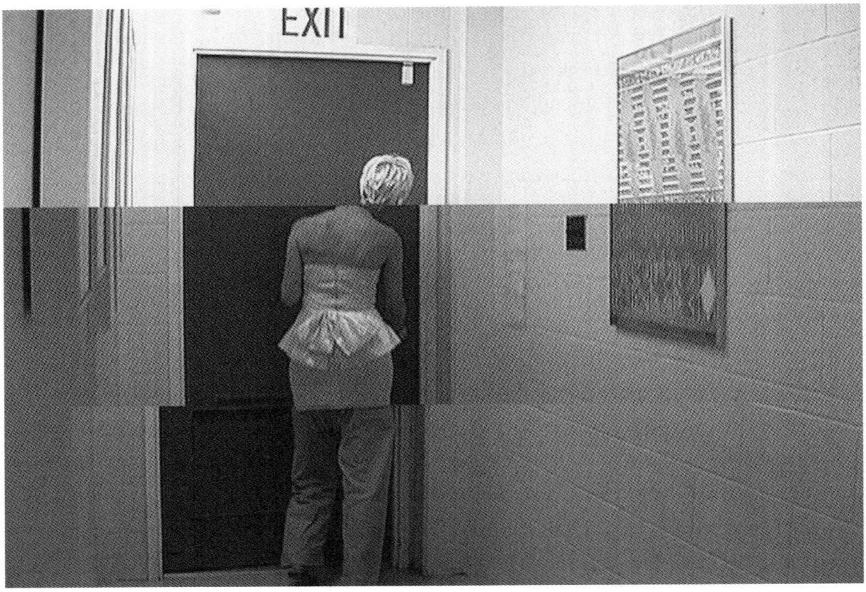


*Figure 15.1* Video still from *Personnel 2*, Mendel Art Gallery, Saskatchewan, Canada, 2002. Courtesy of the author.

or negative attitude had good reason—in past projects they had experienced frustration due to (to put it euphemistically) the lack of established protocol for such situations concerning relations between artists and staff.[35] It was a challenge to convince these reluctant personnel to participate—but, with the help of the curator and supportive staff members, one that I was prepared to accept as part of the process this time around.

On the first day of shooting, once the staff arrived in their evening clothes, most of the resistance disappeared. As is well known, clothing is a form of social control as well as social expression and different clothing elicits different behavior. Since the staff were not used to interacting in the workplace using such unfamiliar behavioral codes—those associated with wearing evening clothes on one hand or with pajamas on the other— they seemed slightly unfamiliar to one another and behaved accordingly.

It was my intention to represent this strangely uncanny mood in the first of two video installations. By dividing each person's video image into three parts I created a version of the surrealists game of exquisite corpse in which the top (head and shoulders) section was taken from dress up day, the middle (torso) from "everyday clothes" day, and the bottom (legs) from pajama/nightgown day (Figure 15.1). With this ever-changing collage of differently clothed moving

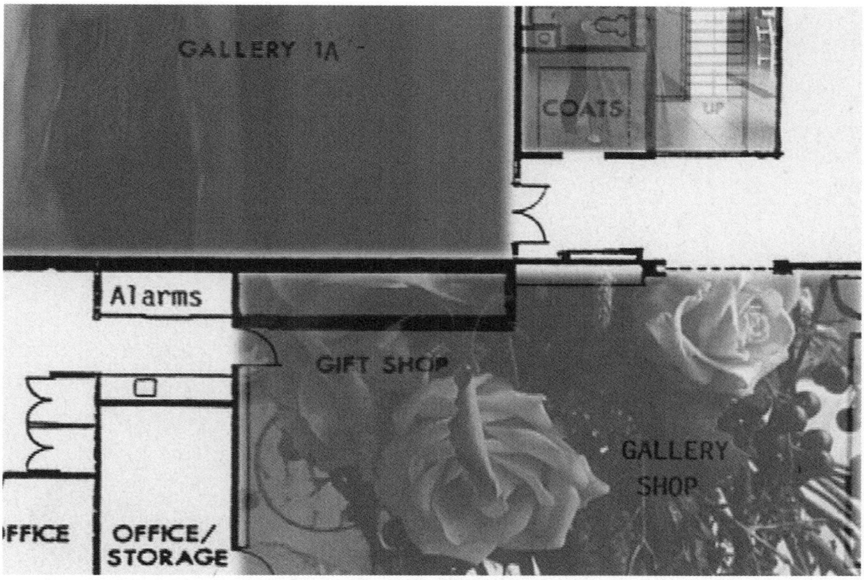


*Figure 15.2* Video still from *Personnel 2*, Mendel Art Gallery, Saskatchewan, Canada, 2002. Courtesy of the author.

body parts I wanted to capture a sense of the unfamiliarity of the staff members to each other.

In addition to creating changes in the character of their interactions, the clothing gave mundane activities a theatrical quality and made a spectacle of even the simplest task. And, while each staff member performed the duties they do regularly to make an exhibition happen, the documentation of these actions would also become part of the exhibition they were preparing. Thus their role in exhibition production, usually hidden and unacknowledged became the central focus as both the subject and object of an artwork.

For the second installation I focused more on the idea of staff members performing themselves. Using floor plans of the Mendel Art Gallery as a framing device and template I created short video narratives of individual staff members. Each video was placed on the floor plan in a different location but played simultaneously to indicate the many activities going on at once in the museum. Because of the multiple cameras I had placed throughout the building I was also able to edit together sequences in which I followed events and activities as they developed and moved through the museum's spaces. For example, a beautiful but strangely decadent bouquet of flowers was delivered to the director, who had recently resigned and was soon to leave the museum.

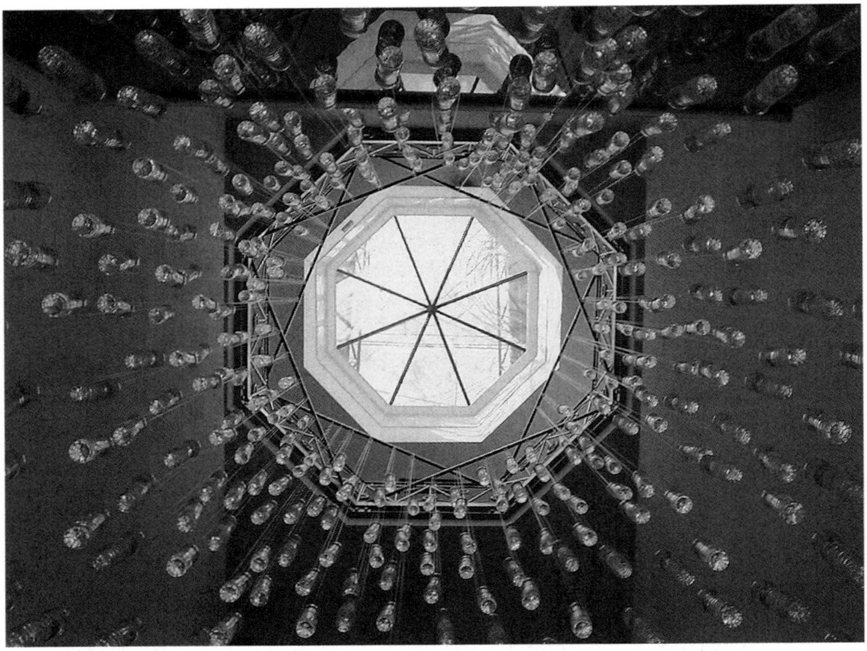

*Figure 15.3* View of *Well* from *Personnel 3*, Fundació Tàpies, Barcelona, Spain, 2003. Courtesy of the author.

I was able to track and edit together the path of this farewell gift from the time it was delivered to the gift shop to the moment the director placed it on the table in his office. When shown in the context of the building plan and surrounded by other short looping videos of the staff performing such tasks as making photocopies or constructing pedestals, this narrative became the focus of the installation. As an acknowledgment of the loss of the director I felt it defined the identity and concerns of the staff at that moment (Figure 15.2).

Located in a city with many museums and cultural institutions most of which are under tremendous pressure to present programs that contribute to the region's cultural economy the Fundació Tàpies plays a unique role. Renowned as the most "cutting edge" museum in Barcelona, Tàpies' international reputation is sometimes at odds with the local reception of its exhibitions, which have on occasion been considered "too conceptual" and "difficult" for the general public. For this, as well as other reasons, each member of the Tàpies staff seems to do the work of two or three people as they labor to counter the perception of intellectual elitism by developing extensive public programs while not compromising their exhibition schedule. Obviously this leaves little time to

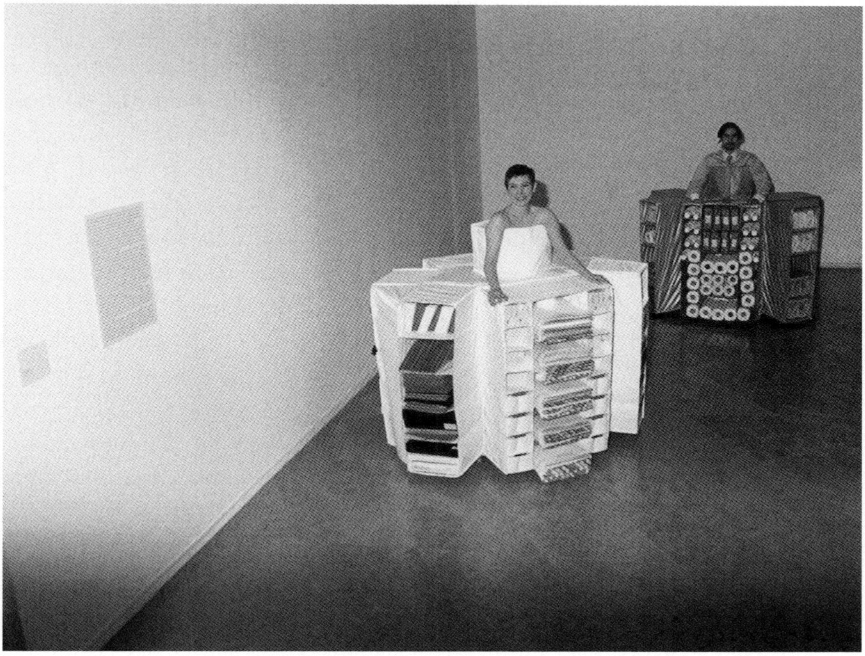

*Figure 15.4* View of *Portable Workplaces* from *Personnel 3*, Fundació Tàpies, Barcelona, Spain, 2003. Courtesy of the author.

deal with the needs and problems of individual staff members. In the version of *Personnel* for Tàpies it seemed important to find a way to do something that could actually make the workplace function better on a practical level, as well as to make the public aware of the excessive pressures placed upon this institution.

Discussions with the staff revealed many practical problems within the workspace but the most obvious and, in some ways, the easiest to solve was a storage problem that was annoying and disruptive. The storage area, which contains such necessities as water and stationery, was only accessible through the office of one of the staff members. This created continuous interruptions for the occupant while giving the rest of the staff the uncomfortable choice of either disturbing him or waiting for him to leave his office to obtain what they need. As a temporary solution I placed many of these items in more accessible locations while making them highly visible to the museum audience to alert them to the problem.

For one installation, *Well*, 360 bottles of water (a one-year supply) were hung under a large, round skylight from an octagonal balcony on the top floor of the museum (also the location of the offices) with each suspended from its own line (Figure 15.3). This way individual bottles could be pulled up easily by staff members as needed. Together they formed a fragmented, cylindrical volume of water lit from above by the skylight and from below by the main museum door. (It was the first thing visitors saw when entering the museum.)

The remaining items, which included coffee, milk, juice, paper towels, toilet paper, and assorted stationery, were arranged within another installation, *Portable Workplaces*, two movable/wearable storage units. Based upon the forms of the dresses in Las Meninas, these structures were fabricated to function as clothing, furniture, and architecture simultaneously. Meant to be worn/inhabited by the office staff they could be used as portable work and storage spaces and, because they were on wheels, could be moved to any location. These pieces were symbolic, however, as well as functional: constructed to overwhelm the wearer, they made movement awkward and the performance of even the simplest of tasks nearly impossible (Figure 15.4). In this way they represented the extensive and multiple jobs of the Tàpies staff and denote some of the problems that arise when each individual carries so much responsibility.

Although more successful in terms of engaging the staff and communicating with the audience than my first installation of *Personnel,* I did have some reservations about the work I produced for both versions of *Indivisuals*. The video installations for the Mendel Art Gallery, while capturing some enigmatic and subtle moments, were too abstract to adequately elucidate the complexity of the transformation that occurred during the three days the staff were videotaped. In retrospect I suspect a longer, single channel video that tracked various staff members through each of the three days would have better conveyed the experience. At Fundació Tàpies the object-oriented installations produced different problems. While the spectacle of the hanging bottles in *Well* was as visually striking as I envisioned, I also hoped staff would use them and thus erode their more traditionally aesthetic impact as well as expose traces of workplace activities. Instead, its visual success produced responses that, as with *Personnel 1*, reinforced the conventions of the inviolate, untouchable art object that the *Personnel* project aims to break down.

*Personnel 4*, 2004, for the Wyspa Art Institute, Gdansk, Poland, located in the historic Gdansk Shipyard, was commissioned for the exhibition *Health and Safety*. The Gdansk Shipyard is now in a transitional period, in which its economic and political history and legacy would coexist with its new identity as an art center. When I began this project the three-person staff had no specific plan for their offices and only the most provisional of furniture, a situation that made this installation unique: rather than analyzing the design and function of an existing workspace in relation to its social dynamics I had the opportunity to develop an original plan. In addition, the working relationship of this three-member staff had only existed for several months so the context in which their interactions would evolve was also left to me.

Just as the "white cube" still functions as the degree zero of art exhibition space there is also a largely unexamined set of codes for the design of a curator's or museum director's office. My focus was to offer an alternative to the stereotypical "well designed" spaces (e.g. MoMA via Knoll and Herman Miller), that pretend to offer comfort and efficiency but actually reinforce hierarchy and status. Some aspects of such codes have a particularly charged (and even sinister) meaning to Eastern Europeans: shoddy copies of furniture by the above-mentioned designers were so ubiquitous as to become permanently linked to a different kind of hierarchy— that of Soviet bureaucracy. This installation sets out to rupture these corporate, bureaucratic, and museological codes (and some of the behavior that goes with them) that have defined the art institution's workplace by combining found objects with elements of modernist design while making reference to the shipyard's history.

My approach is to represent the past by printing curtains with a blown-up version of a found photograph of one of the Wyspa Institute's windows taken during its former identity as a factory. The same size and shape as most of the others in the building, the large window in the photo had a view that framed the hoist towers and loading equipment characteristic of the shipyard. Although somewhat banal, its photogenic quality can be found primarily in the dead potted plants on its shelves, which seem to represent traces of a rushed and perhaps reluctant abandonment. In the resulting curtain, the image of a window, very similar to the real one but from an earlier time, will continue to symbolize the history of the shipyard even as the view outside changes with time.

In addition to the curtains I also assembled mobile furniture and storage containers that is more boudoir than boardroom yet can be adapted to a variety of needs, both present and future. With the help of the organization Artslink I am now in the process of making a couch for the space using multiple casts of a toilet—a Soviet issue porcelain model—scavenged from another abandoned building in the shipyard. Although the toilet has been somewhat transformed it is still quite recognizable as such, and with respect to any remaining Duchamp references I hope it is able to raise questions about how seriously the director, the curator, their assistants, and their visitors can take themselves, each other, and their activities when they are all sitting on the toilet together.

## Acknowledgement

I would like to thank Anna Chave, David Diao, and Mira Schor for their perceptive critiques of this essay as well as their indispensable support. For their encouragement and patience I would also like to thank Andrew Perchuk and Matthew Jesse Jackson who chaired the session "Before and After Institutional Critique" at the 2006 College Art Association Conference in which an earlier version of this paper was presented.

## Notes

1 Andrea Fraser, "A Speech on Documenta" (1992) in Alexander Alberro, ed., *Museum Highlights: The Writings of Andrea Fraser* (Cambridge, MA: The MIT Press, 2005) p. 150.
2 Although I know of no artist with an art institution's personnel as the main focus of her work, some artists have exhibited projects focused on the staff of a gallery or museum: Group Material, Rickrit Tiravanija, Andrea Fraser, Glenn Seator, Rory Francis, Lee Mingwei, and Sophie Calle.
3 CRM Catalog, 2000.
4 Online research into the topic of workplace training and coaching produced an extensive list of companies and practitioners.
5 In addition to training videos my research materials included CD-ROMS, workbooks, tests, and instructors' manuals.
6 For more on this see Andrea Fraser, "From the Critique of Institutions to the Institution of Critique", *Artforum* (September 2005): 278–279.
7 A good introduction to the relationship between these practices (although couched in the concept of the work that artists do to produce art) can be found in Helen Molesworth, "Work Ethic" in Helen Molesworth, ed., *Work Ethic* (University Park, PA: Pennsylvania State University Press, 2003).
8 The original source for this reading of minimalism was actually a negative critique by Michael Fried in "Art and Objecthood" in Gregory Batcock, ed., *Minimal Art: A Critical Anthology* (New York: E.P. Dutton and Co. Inc., 1968) pp. 125–126. There are many critics and theorists who have reinterpreted Fried's experience as a radical phenomenological encounter with the art object. See Benjamin Buchloh, "Conceptual Art 1962–1969" *October* 55 (Winter 1990): 130, Douglas Crimp, "Photographs at the End of Modernism" in *On the Museum's Ruins* (Cambridge, MA: The MIT Press, 1993) pp. 16–17 and Andrea Fraser, "It's Art When I Say It's Art or . . . ," in Alexander Alberro, ed., *Museum Highlights: the Writings of Andrea Fraser* (Cambridge, MA: The MIT Press, 2005) p. 37.
9 Among these were James Lee Byars's *Mile Long Garment*, 1968, and Les Levine's *Slipcover*, 1967. Architectural League website: www.archleague.org.
10 See for example Benjamin Buchloh, "Conceptual Art 1962–1969" *October* 55 (Winter 1990): 108–119. See also Alexander Alberro, "Reconsidering Conceptual Art, 1966–1977" in Alexander Alberro and Blake Stimson, eds, *Conceptual Art: A Critical Anthology* (Cambridge, MA: The MIT Press, 1999) pp. xvii–xxv. For a more inclusive definition of the 'classic version,' see Michael Corris, "Introduction", in Michael Corris, ed., *Conceptual Art: Theory, Myth, Practice* (Cambridge, MA: Cambridge University Press, 2004) pp. 1–18.
11 Buchloh, pp. 108–119.
12 Ibid., pp. 119–124. See also Alberro, *Conceptual Art: A Critical Anthology*, pp. xxii–xiii.

13 Alberro, *Conceptual Art: A Critical Anthology*, pp. xxiv–xxv.
14 The Art and Language group was, however, very conscious of developing a new kind of art audience. For more on this see Corris, p. 8.
15 Lucy Lippard, *Six Years: The Dematerialization of the Art Object, 1966–1972* (New York: Praeger, 1973).
16 Alberro, *Conceptual Art: A Critical Anthology*, p. xxix.
17 For more on this see ibid., pp. xviii–xx.
18 Christopher Gilbert has elaborated on the socio-political intentions of the Art and Language group in Christopher Glibert, "Art and Language, New York, Discusses Its Social Relations in 'The Lumpen Headache,'" in Michael Corris, ed., *Conceptual Art: Theory, Myth, Practice* (Cambridge: Cambridge University Press, 2004).
19 Benjamin Buchloh has acknowledged the sexist tendency in defining the boundaries of conceptual art. Buchloh, *et al.* in "Round Table: The Reception of the Sixties," *October* 69 (Summer 1994): 18.
20 If my recounting of these experiences appears to contradict my wish to explore a broad range of cultural responses I should explain that I'm trying to present myself as an example. By chance I came into close contact with active participants in the conceptual art movement whose radical view of art excluded not just the gender component of my work but also its anti-formalist technological aspects. In this way my experience is an illustration of the perceived differences that separated artists whose work seems, in retrospect, not that far apart.
21 Involved with the Fluxus movement since the early 1960s, both of these artists were also known for working with Experiments in Art and Technology.
22 Judith Rodenbeck, "Fluxus," in Helen Molesworth, ed., *Work Ethic* (University Park, PA: Pennsylvania State University Press, 2003) pp. 178–180.
23 There were many discussions at meetings of the Art Workers' Coalition about whether art could be overtly political. Also minimalists Carl Andre, Sol Lewitt, and others participated in the organization.
24 Fraser, in Alberro, ed., *Museum Highlights: The Writings of Andrea Fraser*, p. 57.
25 Ibid., p. 73.
26 Crimp, p. 85.
27 Ibid., p. 271.
28 Fraser, *Artforum*: 282–283.
29 Fraser, in Alberro, ed., *Museum Highlights: The Writings of Andrea Fraser*, p. 48.
30 Ibid., p. 49.
31 Andrew Ross, "The Mental Labor Problem," *Social Text* 63, 18(2) (Summer 2000): 28.
32 Brian Holmes, *A Rising Tide of Contradiction: Museums in the Age of the Expanding Workfare State*, www.republicart.net (site consulted August 7, 2006).
33 James Meyer, pp. 93–94.
34 Larissa MacFarquhar, "The Better Boss: How Marshall Goldsmith Reforms Executives," *The New Yorker* (April 22, 2002): 84.
35 Andrea Fraser discusses the lack of accepted professional standards for such situations in *Museum Highlights: the Writings of Andrea Fraser*, pp. 154–155.

# Index

*Note:* Pages containing relevant illustrations are indicated in *italic* type.